PRICELESS MOMENTS
LESSONS FROM OUR GRANDCHILDREN

Darlene Welsh

Priceless Moments

Copyright © 2023 by Darlene Welsh
All rights reserved.

Published by Broken Yoke Publishing, LLC.
BrokenYokePublishing.com

This publication is the intellectual property of the author. No part of this publication may be resold, reproduced in any form, stored in a retrieval system, or transmitted by any means, without the prior written permission of the author. Doing such would constitute theft and is illegal.

All Scripture references, unless otherwise noted, are from the World English Bible.

The World English Bible is in the public domain (no copyright). The World English Bible is a trademark. It may only be used to identify faithful copies of the World English Bible as distributed on eBible.org.

ISBN: 978-1-955941-22-8

Contents

January 1

    Happy New Year 2

    The Sleepover 3

    Snowflake Waffles 4

    Rice Krispie Treats 6

    Puzzle Time 7

    Please and Thank You 8

    Who Would You Like to Meet? 10

    Swaddling 11

    LEGO Fun 12

    Not Homework Again 14

    Let's Build a Fort 15

    Can We Make Hot Chocholate? 16

    I Need Hand Lotion 18

    Choosing a DVD 19

    Martin Luther King Jr. Day 20

    The New Tablecloth 22

    Olympics 23

    Hockey 25

    Can We Look at Pictures? 26

Bath Time 27

Matching Tablecloth, Napkins and Paper Plates 29

My Favorite Picture 30

Can I Wash Dishes? 32

Computers 33

Kinetic Sand 34

That's My iPad 36

I Did a Split 37

Time for Church 39

Open Your Bibles, Please, To... 40

Here's Some Money 42

Don't Take My Picture 43

February 45

Basketball 46

Groundhog Day 47

Blueberry French Toast Casserole 48

The Singing Dog 50

Can I Play the Piano? 51

Dress-Up Time 53

What Do You Want To Do Today? 54

The Seahorse 55

My Best Friend 57

My Sweetest Valentine 58

Super Bowl Sunday 59

Lincoln's Birthday 61

Mardi Gras 62

Valentine's Day 64

How Do You Spell LOVE? 65

What's In a Name? 66

Puppy Love 68

That's Hot! 69

President's Day 71

Boy Scouts 72

Girl Scouts 73

Washington's Birthday 75

My Favorite Babysitter 76

Who Were They? 77

Honesty First 79

But They Need To Eat, Too 80

My Favorite Food 81

Maple Syrup Fun 83

Leap Year 84

March 87

    Just Checking In 88

    I Love Animals 89

    The Turkey Parade 90

    Parade of Bucks and Does 92

    Turkey and Deer 93

    What Smells So Good? 94

    Peanut Butter Pie 96

    Can I Make a Wish? 97

    Track 98

    Daylight Savings Time 100

    The Jeweled Pen 101

    BINGO 103

    Can We Share? 104

    My Favorite Lovey 105

    I Really Like Your Hair 107

    The Color-Changing Lights 108

    St. Patrick's Day 110

    See My Fingernails 111

    Spring Cleaning 113

    Spring 114

Spring Break 115

Partridge In a Pear Tree 117

I'm a Star Student 118

Palm Sunday 119

Do You Like My Crown? 121

Marshmallow Bunnies 122

Coloring Eggs 124

Easter Egg Hunt 125

Good Friday 127

The Empty Cross 128

Easter 130

April 133

April Fool's Day 134

Let's Ride a Bus 135

The Calendar 136

My Training Wheel Bike 138

Trampolines 139

Fishing 140

The Corner Office 142

Colors of the Rainbow 143

Catch the Gecko 145

Can We Go To the Library? 146

A Kleenex, Please 148

My Favorite Story... 149

Scrabble... 151

Water Puddle Boots 152

What Is Income Tax... 153

Hi, Grandma, It's Me 155

Battery-Operated Tea Lights.. 156

You Didn't Say Goodnight 157

Military Dog Tags 159

Antique Cars.. 160

Kites.. 162

Baseball 163

Earth Day... 165

Let's Plant a Tree... 166

What's a Secretary?.. 167

The Rainbow-Colored Whisk.. 169

My Sunglasses 170

The Sleeping Bag 172

Do You Have an Umbrella? 173

April Showers… 175

May 177

...Bring May Flowers 178

Fake It Until You Make It 179

Temper Tantrum 181

The Crusty Old Lady 182

Cinco De Mayo 184

Can We Pray? 185

I Didn't Mean To Say That 187

Play-Doh 188

Cookie Cutters 190

Noah's Ark 191

Mom's the Word 193

Mother's Day 194

I'm Student of the Week 196

Can We Go Visit Someone? 197

A Banana Sandwich 198

Police Officers 200

The Jeep 202

Armed Forces Day 203

Papa's Military Picture 205

Can I Help? 206

The Mouse Trap 207

Battleship—Who's Move? 209

The Dancing Bear 210

What? 212

My Dream 213

The Treasure Box 214

Memorial Day 216

The Teddy Bear 217

What's a Tithe? 218

RV Fun 220

The Jesus Revolution 221

June 223

Praise God for the Rain 224

The "Meany" 225

The Telephone Book 226

Bumps, Bruises, Cuts, and Scars 228

Grandma, Hold My Hand 229

Papa Always Knows What To Say 231

Swimming 232

Let's Plant Pumpkins 233

Children's Day 235

S'mores 236

Family Time 238

The Eagle's Nest 239

Stickers 241

Flag Day 242

My Little Chair 243

Father's Day 245

Solar-Dancing Toys 246

The New Dining Room Light 248

Juneteenth 249

Fly, Fly Away 250

Summer 252

The Summer List 254

Time for Vacation 255

Sand Castles 256

Where To Now? 258

Kick, Kick, Kick, Kick 259

Smoothie Time 260

My Favorite Song 262

Peek-A-Boo 263

Family Reunions 264

July ... 267

I'm Thirsty ... 268

It's a Girl ... 269

The Raspberry Factory ... 271

Independence Day ... 272

Fireworks ... 274

Hey, That's My Seat ... 275

Snack Time ... 276

Founding Fathers ... 278

Patriotic Marshmallows ... 279

The Rolling Pin ... 281

Boating Down the River ... 282

Etch-A-Sketch ... 284

Church Bells ... 285

Toying With Your Food ... 286

The Back End Booty Dance ... 288

Daddy's Picture ... 289

Can We Fix This? ... 291

Let's Have Ice Cream ... 292

My Special Cup ... 294

The Tree House ... 295

Tiny Little Fingers 297

Picture Perfect.. 298

Can You Take the Time…? 300

Blowing Bubbles... 301

The Gifts 303

The Washing Machine.. 304

Papa Bear 306

The Spillway 307

Filing Papers 309

For Every Child 310

Details, Please 312

August 315

I'm Not Bad 316

I Do It Myself 317

The Clocks, Bells and Chimes 319

Let's Do Devotions 320

The Hot Tub... 322

Let's Pray for Peace 323

Lighthouses 325

The Cookie Jar 326

What's an Interview? 328

Ants On a Log 329

Hey, Mister, That's Bad For You 331

The Empty Bottle 332

Please, Don't Yell At Me 334

Let's Have Pizza 335

Full Armor Of God 336

Carpenters 338

My Secret Mission 340

The Bouncy House 341

More, Please and Thank You 343

A Stronger Crab 344

Starving Children 346

Gone in 60 Seconds— 30 Seconds—10 Seconds— 0 Seconds 347

A Promise 349

Time For School 350

Do You Think They Liked Me? 351

Bed Time 353

Where Are My Pals? 354

The Touch Lamp 356

I Can Help 357

The Cactus Plant 359

Do I Have To? 360

September 363

    Have a Boyfriend 364

    Labor Day 365

    A Little Bit Of Duck Tape 366

    Football Season 368

    There's a Monster Under My Bed 369

    Will You Tuck Me In? 371

    Talk To Me 372

    A New Life 374

    That's MY Grandma 375

    Grandparent's Day 376

    Patriot Day 378

    I Helped Him Up 379

    Blueberry Muffins 381

    Pass It On 382

    Little People 383

    Never "Neverand" 385

    A Little One's Prayer 386

    My Room 388

    Booster Seats 389

I Lost My Giraffe 391

Bed Time Story 392

Autumn or Fall 393

Can We Pick Apples? 395

Can We Make an Apple Pie? 396

I Already Found Him 398

I Have a Brother, Too 399

Grandma's Closet 401

I Have To Do My Chores 402

The Wrestling Match 403

Fun Fruits 405

October 407

Story Time 408

What's My Surprise? 409

I Carry My Bible 411

The Bobblehead 412

It's Spam Again 413

The Circus 415

Watch Your Attitude 416

What is Wisdom and Knowledge? 418

The Birthday Cake 419

Television 420

The Magic Pen 422

The Quilt 423

Open That Bible 425

Columbus Day 426

Empty Arms 428

Painting Rocks 429

Bone Broth 431

You Dog-Gone Grandma 432

Help, My Tooth Is Loose 433

That Man Smiled At Me 435

My Dad's Like Noah 436

Color Changing Spoons 438

Don't Yell At Me 439

RUN! 441

Is There Really a God? 442

Can We Pray? 444

Shine Your Light 445

I Love Music 447

The Water Wheel 448

Let's Make Cookies 450

Halloween 451

November 453

    Feeding Time 454

    The Raisin Factory 455

    The BOMBSHELL Masterpiece 456

    Photo Albums 458

    Election Day 459

    Rubber Band Necklace 461

    The Rubber Band Necklace Demise 462

    My Fleecy Jacket 463

    Cheese, Crackers and Soup 465

    Sparkles 466

    Veteran's Day 467

    Papa's Hat 469

    I Like My Teacher 470

    The Wrapped Present 472

    Emptying the Dishwasher 473

    My Favorite Movie 474

    Monkey In the Middle 476

    The Matching Snowmen 477

    Chai Tea 479

Oh, No! Not Rules Again 480

The Fruitcake 481

The Broken Snowflake 483

Turtlenecks 484

Snowball Battle 486

My B-I-B-L-E 487

Indians 488

Pilgrims 490

Thanksgiving 491

Yay, It's Snowing 493

Look At That Star 494

December 497

It's Coming, It's Coming 498

What Are WE Doing For Christmas? 499

Picture With Santa Claus 500

The Christmas Program—Part 1 502

The Christmas Program—Part 2 503

Hanukkah 504

Pearl Harbor 506

What Is Chrismas? 507

The Christmas Traditions —Part 1 509

The Christmas Tree—Part 2 510

The Christmas Lights, Candles & Luminaries—Part 3 512

The Christmas Ornaments & Candy Canes—Part4 513

The Christmas Bells, Tree Topper & Gift Giving—Part 5 ... 515

The Christmas Star & Christmas Carols—Part 6 516

The Holly, Ivy, Wreaths, Poinsettias & Dove—Part 7 518

Can We Go See Chrismas Lights? 519

Singing Carol 521

Gingerbread House 522

The Christmas Wreath 524

Winter 525

Making Snow Angels 527

My Favorite Spot For Christmas 528

The People Who Don't Have Anything 529

Jesus' Birthday Cake 531

Bubble Bread 532

Thank You For the Presents 533

When Jesus Was a Boy Like Me 535

My Glow In the Dark Dinosaur Sleeping Bag 536

My Light-Up Shoes 538

New Years Restitutions 539

Happy New Year's Eve 541

Dedication

I dedicate this book to our loving and supportive children, their spouses, and our grandchildren, who were the inspiration and source of material from which to write. They gave me the time needed to work on the project, being my greatest supporters and sources of encouragement.

Also, I dedicate this book to our wonderful group of friends—from childhood, school, college, community, and church family—who have always been our cheerleaders throughout the different seasons of our lives.

In memory of our loving, godly parents, grandparents, Sunday School teachers, and other family members and friends who encouraged, taught, and mentored me throughout my childhood and young adult life, pointing me to the narrow road and strengthening my faith.

Also, to my loving husband, who preceded us to heaven and whose constant support and encouragement still bolster me today to work for our LORD.

But, most importantly, all glory and praise to our faithful LORD and Savior, who literally gave me the words to put on the blank pages to provide us with this devotional.

Introduction

Many of us will have the privilege of loving and observing our precious grandchildren from the moment they enter our lives until we exit theirs, or we have had the privilege to love and care for someone else's grandchildren as those people share their gifts from God with others. When we were raising our own children, we may have been too busy to see the simple yet powerful insights these precious little ones have to share. Throughout this year, I would like to share some unique and valuable lessons our grandchildren have taught me. May we all open our hearts to see the innocence and openness to God in their lives.

DAILY DEVOTIONS

No matter what you're doing,
Nor the hour or the day,
Take time to read your Bible,
Study, meditate, and pray.

God will honor seekers who
Instinctively turn to Him,
Pouring out their hearts and souls
Not just on some needy whim.

They've learned communication
With their Father up above
Meets hurting and happy hearts
Filling them with so much love.

They have no trepidation
To approach God's holy throne,
But justice, comfort, and peace
Being cherished as His own.

So pick up your Bible and
Read the coolest news in the land,
Learn about God's Creation—
Spoken and made with His hand.

Daily devotions will help
Keep your heart and mind on track
To follow God's perfect will
And keep you from slipping back.

Builds a better barrier
'Tween you and the evil one
A more committed Christian
Who follows His Only Son!

If you've not yet met the Savior
And desire a different path
Acknowledge you're a sinner
Then get a "baptismal bath."

Now total dedication
To the LORD has been declared
Telling your awesome journey
Your commitment now is shared.

To join other believers
Seek out Christian fellowship
Praising the name of Jesus
For His awesome leadership.

Stories of the patriarchs
And judges from Israel,
Prophets foretelling Christ's Birth
And Death to save His people.

So arise every morning
And start your day with the LORD,
Thanking, praising, worshiping
To remain in one accord.

He'll honor your diligence
To put Him first in all things
You will marvel and enjoy
Blessings His faithfulness brings.

Keeping God first in your heart
At the center of your life
Brings peace beyond measure
Throughout happiness and strife.

Study to show thyself approved
A workman for the LORD,
Growing in wisdom, knowledge,
Stature—His blessings outpoured.

There are no limitations
To the hearts God will prepare
He'll go on before you to
Direct the "Who," "When," and "Where!"

Trust the Spirit's leading to
Guide wherever He deems fit
To those hungry and lost souls
He knows are ready to submit.

Change how you think and act through
Daily devotions and prayers
And you can change the world
Helping others become God's heirs!

Priceless Moments

January

Only be careful, and keep your soul diligently, lest you forget the things which your eyes saw, and lest they depart from your heart all the days of your life; but make them known to your chidren and your children's children—

Deut. 4:9

Priceless Moments

January 1ˢᵀ

Happy New Year

A new year brings about a fresh start, a clean slate, and a new beginning. If we can stay up and stay awake, we can welcome the new year in many ways: host a party to spend time with family and friends, play games, eat pizza, have a movie marathon, read the Bible from the beginning, or so many other fun things. Sharing those closing moments of the year with loved ones and close friends brings an opportunity to share past memories of their childhood dreams as well as goals for the new year. For the little ones, it's a time to sit at the adults' feet and listen to stories new to them. These revelations to the youngsters bring about many questions as they try to absorb information and understand all the different words used in the grown-up world. These little hearts and minds are influenced by the types of conversations and topics, often mimicking them later in their play. They sound so grown-up, but they don't always have a full grasp of things.

As their grandma, I love listening to them and trying to help them understand, expand their horizons, and learn more about their parents, grandparents, aunts, uncles, cousins, and friends. After celebrating Christmas, they asked, "Tell us more about Jesus' birth and His life." This is a challenging question to answer since they don't have the same experience with Jewish family traditions and celebrations as we do. I gave them enough information to whet their appetite. The topic soon changed, and these conversations were tabled for a later time.

The children stimulate my heart and mind with a desire to know more about Jesus—from creation to eternity—and to share with them when little hearts and minds are hungry for more.

Thank You, LORD, for a child's curiosity. I pray You make my mind a sponge to absorb all I can to share with them in a drop or a downpour as they 'squeeze' the information out of me.

Priceless Moments

Proverbs 1:7*: The fear of Yahweh is the beginning of knowledge; but the foolish despise wisdom and instruction.*

Job 28:28*: Behold, the fear of the Lord, that is wisdom. To depart from evil is understanding.*

2 Peter 3:18*: But grow in the grace and knowledge of our Lord and Savior Jesus Christ. To him be the glory both now and forever. Amen.*

January 2nd

The Sleepover

The weekend after New Year's, before the grandchildren returned to school, they asked, "Grandma, can we have a sleepover at your house?" Of course, I said, "Yes." Sleepovers are always a special time for loving, caring, sharing, and, yes, spoiling. We cook dinner Thursday nights for our children and their families, so I asked the parents, "Can we start the sleepover Thursday night since you will be here anyway? This will give you an opportunity to get some things done and have a little alone time." You know, parents need a break—and give grandparents more time for spoiling. They agreed.

Thursday night, after dinner, the little ones rushed their parents out the door, saying, "Goodbye. Have fun; yes, we know; help Grandma," then shut the door. As promised, they helped clean up the kitchen, immediately got dressed for bed, brushed their teeth, and then begged, "Can we watch a movie?" I said, "If we compromise on a half hour of movie, then off to bed." They knew if they cooperated, there would be a special activity tomorrow, a fun lunch, and a reward for good behavior—the rest of the movie. *Air Bud* was selected. After a few minutes, they didn't want to watch anymore, saying, "It's an adult movie." "Why do you say this?" They responded, "It's just about a dog and grown-ups. Not enough action."

Priceless Moments

I couldn't help but think how often people will misjudge serving God as *not enough action*, or *it's for someone else, not me*. When a little more time is invested, their perspective can totally change—just like the kids in the movie when the *action* started. They had to get invested in the movie to enjoy it. Same with adults: we need to get invested in the kingdom to understand the eternal rewards.

Thank You, LORD, for giving us a life of adventure when we get invested in Your kingdom. I pray You show us how to reward our little ones for good behavior and lead them to a saving knowledge of You.

Psalm 62:12: *Also to you, Lord, belongs loving kindness, for you reward every man according to his work.*

Matthew 13:44: *Again, the Kingdom of Heaven is like treasure hidden in the field, which a man found and hid. In his joy, he goes and sells all that he has and buys that field.*

Philippians 4:19: *My God will supply every need of yours according to his riches in glory in Christ Jesus.*

January 3rd

Snowflake Waffles

"Grandma, can we do something special for breakfast? We were really good last night and did everything you asked" Those little darlings were as good as gold, and I had already planned a special breakfast of snowflake waffles, hash browns, and sausage, so I responded, "Well, absolutely. I have a special snowflake waffle maker…." That's all I could get out as shrieks of "Yes, yes, yes." rang out in the kitchen. We plugged in the waffle iron, got out the ingredients, measured them, and combined them to make the

Priceless Moments

batter. When the iron was hot, we sprayed it and baked the snowflakes one by one.

At our house, the favorite way to eat waffles (or pancakes) is with applesauce and cinnamon, and, of course, whipped cream. As we were eating, our granddaughter commented, "These snowflakes are all alike. Did you know each one God makes is different, but each has six arms? I haven't been able to check out many since they melt before I can get a good look at them." Amazed and surprised at her awareness of snowflakes, I commented, "Well said, honey. Every one of God's creations is perfect and unique, including the beautiful snowflake. As each snowflake falls from heaven, they are blown around and shaped by their journey to earth."

Isn't it amazing that our awesome God made everything in His creation beautiful and unique, molded by our journey throughout life? Each one of us is distinctly different from another. I marvel at the diversity God built into creation, not for the purpose of dividing us but rather to unite us through our own precious contributions with which He has gifted us. Some of those gifts are innate, while others can be developed over time, being shaped like the snowflake on its journey.

Thank You, LORD, for Your gift of life and for molding and shaping us into vessels to serve and honor You. No matter our walk in life, our profession, or home address, we are all valuable and useful in Your sight.

Isaiah 64:8: *But now, Yahweh, you are our Father. We are the clay and you our potter. We all are the work of your hand. "*

Matthew 10:29-31: *Aren't two sparrows sold for an assarion coin? Not one of them falls to the ground apart from your Father's will. But the very hairs of your head are all numbered. Therefore don't be afraid. You are of more value than many sparrows.*

Psalm 147:16: *He gives snow like wool, and scatters frost like ashes.*

Priceless Moments

January 4th

Rice Krispie Treats

Close to snack time, our grandson went exploring in the pantry to check available options. He spotted the holiday colors of Rice Krispies and asked, "Can we make our own snack—Rice Krispie treats?" How could I say no? We always have so much fun doing things together, so I said, "Yes, of course. It sounds like fun." The kids came running, asking, "Can we use the Christmas molds and carry them to the table? We can get the cooking spray for the molds and our hands while you get the bowl, butter, and marshmallows ready." I said, "That sounds good to me."

As per any cooking protocol at our house, hands must be washed first. Before I could remind them, they had already marched off to the bathroom—whoa, they must really want to do this. I got the marshmallows and butter melting, plates for the finished shapes, and cereal measured out. They returned and said, "We washed our hands before you could ask, so we're ready to have our hands sprayed." I replied, "First, choose the molds you want to use so they can be sprayed, too." They chose the stars, trees, bells, and snowman shapes, saying, "We are ready to have our hands sprayed so the marshmallow stuff doesn't stick to us." I sprayed hands and shapes so the cereal would drop out easier. All was ready as the cereal was added to the melted marshmallows and butter, stirring until well blended. They so enjoyed making the different shapes. When the batch was done, they asked, "Can we make more to share with the neighbors and those in need?" I thought it was very kind of them, so we made a second batch.

As we packaged the finished treats for delivery, I was reminded how tender their hearts were for sharing with others and anyone in need. They were turning their enjoyment of making the treats into serving others.

Thank You, LORD, for the Christian heritage we passed on to our children and they to theirs. At any age, I pray we keep our hearts tender and open to noticing those in need or doing something for them to brighten their day.

Romans 12:13: *Share with God's people who are in need. Practice hospitality. NIV*

Proverbs 19:17: *He who has pity on the poor lends to Yahweh; he will reward him.*

Hebrews 13:16: *But don't forget to be doing good and sharing, for with such sacrifices God is well pleased.*

January 5th

Puzzle Time

Puzzles are a fun activity with the grandchildren and take many hours to put together. They enjoy the challenge of finding the right pieces the first time they pick up a puzzle piece but are disappointed if it isn't right. Much trial and error, pieces falling on the floor, and the occasional piece pocketed—to be the one to put the last piece in place—make the activity challenging and rewarding when the end goal is achieved. I heard, "I finally see our finished picture, and it looks like the one on the box." He was amazed that they were one and the same.

It was hard not to laugh out loud. I was struggling to keep the amusement to myself, when big sis blurted out, "Well, what did you expect? We looked at the picture on the box the whole time." A little heart was broken, so I said, "You know, this puzzle is a lot like our lives. It may be hard to realize what we are working on at any given time. We keep thinking, 'If I knew how this would turn out,' 'If I had this one piece of information,' or 'If I took a certain piece from someone else without asking,' all things would fall into place. We don't need certain pieces in our lives because others will fall into place when God is ready for them to do so. He may be holding back a piece, waiting for us to trust Him before He puts it in place.

Through this activity, they learned patience and persistence to reach a desired goal. I also learned patience and persistence to let them find the pieces themselves, especially when they have the correct piece in hand. They try to put it in place three different ways, but don't rotate it the fourth time to see it fall into place. Also, I've learned God holds all the pieces of my life together, putting them together at the right time for His purpose.

Thank You, LORD, for allowing family activities to become a teaching ground for insights into Your plan for our lives. I pray that we trust You to complete us as a beautiful picture for Your glory and purpose.

Romans 8:28: We know that all things work together for good for those who love God, for those who are called according to his purpose.

Philippians 1:6: being confident of this very thing, that he who began a good work in you will complete it until the day of Jesus Christ.

Jeremiah 17:14: "God, pick up the pieces. Put me back together again. You are my praise. NIV

January 6th

Please and Thank You

One of the important things I like to teach the grandchildren is the use of words like please, thank you, you're welcome, and sorry. "Grandma, why should we use these words all the time?" "Using courtesy words allows you to show respect to and for others while showing them you have learned great manners. When you set a good example for others, you can make them feel better about themselves, and hopefully they will pick up on using these words themselves when they talk with other people. It's called a ripple effect."

"What's a ripple effect?" they asked. I said, "A ripple effect is a way of starting something in a small way until it spreads out to bigger and bigger areas." "Grandma, do you mean it's like throwing a pebble in the water and watching the rings expand farther and farther?" I replied, "Yes, just like that. Think of how rewarding it will be to know you have an opportunity to change other people's behavior for the better." Silence fell upon the thinking youngsters until one finally responded, "Jesus would be proud of us for helping others."

YES. He hit the nail on the head. Jesus would be so proud of all of us for exhibiting behaviors to help others see Him through our conduct, reflecting His love and consideration for those around us. As we expand our circle of influence, considerate behaviors and clean, respectful speech will affect how others choose their words.

Thank You, LORD, once we have accepted You into our lives, for changing our vocabulary to express Your love language to others, especially those in our family, sometimes our greatest critics. I pray we are mindful of giving and doing our best for our Master.

Ephesians 5:4*: Let there be no filthiness nor foolish talk nor crude joking, which are out of place, but instead let there be thanksgiving. NIV*

Proverbs 25:15*: By patience a ruler is persuaded. A soft tongue breaks the bone.*

Philippians 4:8-9*: Finally, brothers, whatever things are true, whatever things are honorable, whatever things are just, whatever things are pure, whatever things are lovely, whatever things are of good report: if there is any virtue and if there is any praise, think about these things. The things which you learned, received, heard, and saw in me: do these things, and the God of peace will be with you.*

Priceless Moments

January 7th

Who Would You Like to Meet?

We like to talk about different people in history who have influenced our future as a nation and our individual lives. This particular day I asked the grandchildren, "Who would you like to meet someday?" Different answers included "Mickey Mouse, Barbie, Fiona, Isabella, Prince Eric, Ariel, Captain Hook..." Ah, Disney characters, I thought. So, I asked, "What real person would you like to meet?" "My sister's teacher, our firemen, policemen, missionaries." I responded, "Those are real people, but can you give me some names?"

Total silence and puzzled looks were the result of my last question. Tapping of the chins, rubbing of the foreheads, deep breathing in and out, and fidgeting in their seats did not yield any names. At last, the oldest granddaughter said, "Grandma, I've really thought about your question, and I would like to meet Jesus. I have so many questions I would like Him to answer." I was surprised, but couldn't think of a better choice. "What would some questions be?" I asked. She responded, "Did getting spikes hammered into Your hands and feet hurt? Or the crown of thorns pushed down on Your head? I know You were dead, but did You feel the sword jammed in Your side? Did You know they were going to do all those things to You? I feel bad they didn't realize You were God in the flesh."

Wow. She left me speechless. It made me realize how much information this little girl had absorbed. I wish I could ask Jesus some questions myself, but I'm sure once I get to see Him, those questions will no longer matter. Singing praises and sitting at His feet would jump to the top of my list—forever.

Thank You, LORD, for making a way for us to spend eternity with You, singing praises and worshiping You for eternity. I pray the things of this earth will no longer be our focus to ask about, but we will focus on You.

John 3:16: *For God so loved the world, that he gave his one and only Son, that whoever believes in him should not perish, but have eternal life.*

John 1:14*: The Word became flesh, and lived among us. We saw his glory, such glory as of the one and only Son of the Father, full of grace and truth "*

John 14:2-3*: In my Father's house are many homes. If it weren't so, I would have told you. I am going to prepare a place for you. If I go and prepare a place for you, I will come again, and will receive you to myself; that where I am, you may be there also.*

January 8th

<u>Swaddling</u>

"Grandma, why do you wrap the baby in a blanket, so her hands don't move? She looks like a burrito." I chuckled to myself and responded, "Good question, honey. It's called swaddling when you wrap babies securely in a blanket with only the head sticking out the top. Her arms and legs are wrapped, so she is warm and comfortable but snug inside the blanket, just like a security blanket. It reminds her of being snug and safe inside mommy's belly." They asked, "Were we ever swaddled like that? What is a security blanket? Did we have a security blanket, too?"

I had to smile at their questions. I took a minute to look back on holding all of them, then said, "Yes, as a matter of fact, all of you were swaddled for about the first four months. You slept well and were very comfortable, but once you started to move around, you were no longer swaddled during daytime naps. You had learned to comfort yourself and no longer needed swaddling. Then, the nights were stopped as well. A security blanket provides comfort for you when you go to bed, like the one you took to bed with you when you were younger, but now you take a *lovey* to bed." "OK, but could you swaddle us, so we know how it feels?" "Sounds like fun. Absolutely, who's first?"

The grandchildren got me thinking of how God swaddles new believers in Jesus with other Christians to help us learn about Him and become comfortable in our new role as Christians. As we grow in Him and learn of Him, we are slowly weaned to go out and start discipling others so we can increase the number of believers committed to Him.

Thank You, LORD, for providing us with the fellowship of other Christians to strengthen our faith and enable us to branch out to reach others for You. I pray we will learn, grow, and leave the nest, being dedicated witnesses for our LORD.

Acts 22:15: *For you will be a witness for him to all men of what you have seen and heard.*

Deuteronomy 31:6: *Be strong and courageous. Don't be afraid or scared of them; for Yahweh your God himself is who goes with you. He will not fail you nor forsake you.*

Isaiah 41:10: *Don't you be afraid, for I am with you. Don't be dismayed, for I am your God. I will strengthen you. Yes, I will help you. Yes, I will uphold you with the right hand of my righteousness.*

January 9th

LEGO Fun

A favorite activity of our grandchildren of late is building with LEGOs. We had saved the LEGOs our children played with when they were young. When they purchased their own homes, they were given their LEGOs, which were then put into storage until "someday." "Someday" has arrived, and those sets have been pulled out. They have been a big hit with the little ones. They have

Priceless Moments

learned to follow the picture directions to build the "feature" as well as to create their own model, spending endless hours in their imaginations to create interesting designs at any time, day or night, all year long.

The big requests for Christmas were for LEGOs. Each child received several sets of those little plastic building blocks, enabling them to play and create with them over and over. Initially, creations were torn apart, but now that has changed. "We want to leave our creations together to see what we have. They're so neat to look at to see what all we've done." Pride and joy illuminate their faces as they show off the latest project. While I was walking in the door, they grabbed my hands, saying, "Come quickly. You have to see what we made today. It's really cool." So, off we go to the playroom and the LEGO masterpieces.

The thought of our LORD seeing us tear apart things He has done for us, then try to create our own version out of the pieces, is heartbreaking. When we decide to follow His directions and move forward with His plans, we can look back across our lives and see how far He has brought us along our journey called life.

Thank You, LORD, for Your patience with us when we mess up, helping us pick up the pieces and move on to still make something beautiful out of our lives when we stay in Your will. I pray we never feel too old to be of service for You.

Jeremiah 17:14: *God, pick up the pieces. Put me back together again. You are my praise. NIV*

Matthew 6:33: *But seek first God's Kingdom and his righteousness; and all these things will be given to you as well. "But seek first His kingdom and His righteousness, and all these things will be given to you as well."*

Colossians 2:6-7: *As therefore you received Christ Jesus, the Lord, walk in him, rooted and built up in him, and established in the faith, even as you were taught, abounding in it in thanksgiving.*

Priceless Moments

January 10th
__Not Homework Again__

One of the first things the grandchildren are to do after school is to complete their homework, and then we can play. I hear complaints: "I'm tired; I don't want to do homework now." "I hate homework because we always have to do it." "My friends get to watch TV first." I replied, "I understand you want to watch TV or play on your iPads, so enough is enough. It is time to move beyond this silly stuff." After a brief pause, I asked, "When do you want to do your homework?" They were sitting with arms crossed, heads down in a humph, saying in unison, "NEVER."

It's time to appeal to their desires. I said, "Well, let's make homework fun, like we are playing. After we get done, we can have a snack." Heads whipped up, eyes widening, and they were ready to eat. "Fun homework first," I said. After looking over the homework, we made a game out of it, completing it in record time. To ensure they had learned the lesson, I asked questions, letting them answer to beat the timer. It worked. Learning and fun had taken place, so they were rewarded with a snack and playing a game together.

I realize that, at times, we act like these kids, needing motivation to complete our tasks. Sometimes, the house chores seem endless, the laundry insurmountable, and the dishes beyond what fits in the dishwasher. This may even include reading our Bibles, having a prayer time, and witnessing. We need to realize heaven is our eternal reward, so get moving.

Thank You, LORD, for the promise of eternal life. I pray You give us the grace to complete the household chores in a timely manner so we can do the important homework to "make the grade," learning more about You every day to become more like Jesus.

Luke 2:52: And Jesus increased in wisdom and stature, and in favor with God and men.

Priceless Moments

Ephesians 2:8-10: *for by grace you have been saved through faith, and that not of yourselves; it is the gift of God, not of works, that no one would boast. For we are his workmanship, created in Christ Jesus for good works, which God prepared before that we would walk in them.*

Psalm 145:9-10: *Yahweh is good to all. His tender mercies are over all his works. All your works will give thanks to you, Yahweh. Your saints will extol you.*

January 11th
Let's Build a Fort

Winter is a fun time to be outside, and the weather forecast sounds promising for tomorrow. I awoke to shrieks of "Grandma, Grandma, Grandma. Get up. Get up. It snowed a lot last night. You have to see this." As I shook off the last vestiges of sleep, I looked out the window. Sure enough, God had dropped a new blanket of snow. After breakfast, the deep snowfall sparked the kids to grab boxes for packing snow to make blocks to build something. Repeated stuffing and dumping of the frozen crystals were stacked up over and over again until they were formed into a recognizable shape—a snow fort. The big blocks of snow made a strong barrier against the wind. They played all kinds of games inside the fortress until a great idea surfaced: "Let's add a roof to the fort so we can stay out of the wind and be warmer." That was an interesting idea.

They talked with each other until a plan was made to create a roof. "We can put in a pillar and set the blocks on pieces of the pillars." "We can make the snow blocks half the size of the fort walls." Many attempts were made, but nothing worked when trying to use snow. "Snow gets too heavy for the roof," I said. "We need another idea." Their faces lit up when they spied something sticking out of the recycling container and asked, "Can we go get the big piece of cardboard over there and use it for the roof?" Awesome idea, I thought, saying, "Sure, and I'll help you." We pulled the *roofing* from the container and covered the fort.

I couldn't help but think about how we put our own effort into doing things throughout life until we accept Jesus as our Savior. He helps by guiding us and sending His Holy Spirit to cover our lives.

Thank You, LORD, for covering our "fortress of life" with Your Holy Spirit. I pray we always stay under Your cover for protection and guidance in all areas where You lead us to do Your bidding, keeping us strong in our resolve to follow You in the good as well as the bad times.

Job 37:6a: *For he says to the snow, "Fall on the earth,"*

Psalm 18:2: *Yahweh is my rock, my fortress, and my deliverer; my God, my rock, in whom I take refuge; my shield, and the horn of my salvation, my high tower.*

John 15:4: *Remain in me, and I in you. As the branch can't bear fruit by itself unless it remains in the vine, so neither can you, unless you remain in me.*

January 12th

Can We Make Hot Chocholate?

After hours of playing outside and building a snow fort, the grandchildren were ready to go inside. "Grandma, I'm cold. Can we go inside to warm up?" Halfway inside, another question was asked: "And, can we have hot chocolate with marshmallows? We have some in the cupboard. Mommy always gives us some after being outside." For a treat after playing outside and getting chilled to the bone, hot chocolate sounds good to me, too. Besides having a lot of health benefits, chocolate is a very satisfying liquid for

Priceless Moments

young and old alike. Naturally, I said, "Yes, little ones, hot chocolate—with marshmallows—it is."

Once inside, wet clothes were hung up to dry, hot chocolate was made, and a conversation started regarding the previous activities. "We had so much fun making a snow fort and coming up with a way to make a roof." "I can't believe how fast our time went." "Thank you for taking us out to play and helping build the fort. Can we go out and play in it again someday?" "Of course," I replied. "After all your hard work, I hope we get to enjoy it again before Mr. Sun comes out and melts it away." They giggled at the response, coming up with melted marshmallow mustaches.

In response to the warming liquid flowing throughout my veins, I thought of how God's love warms us as we sense His satisfying presence in our hearts. His feeling of contentment floods our soul and relaxes us as our coldness melts away, restoring a balance of refreshing mental clarity and satisfaction within our soul.

Thank You, LORD, for the warmth of Your love as You flow through our bodies from head to toe and melt our sin away. I pray You remain ever present in our lives, regardless of where we are in our walk with You, providing guidance with each step we take along the way.

1 Thessalonians 3:12: *May the Lord make you to increase and abound in love toward one another, and toward all men, even as we also do toward you,*

Titus 3:5: *not by works of righteousness which we did ourselves, but according to his mercy, he saved us through the washing of regeneration and renewing by the Holy Spirit,*

Isaiah 40:31: *but those who wait for Yahweh will renew their strength. They will mount up with wings like eagles. They will run, and not be weary. They will walk, and not faint.*

January 13th
I Need Hand Lotion

Our granddaughter's hands became very chapped this winter, so her mother put a small bottle of hand lotion in her backpack. "When you experience dry, cracked skin at school, please use the hand lotion in your backpack." She also counseled her, "After washing your hands, you need to be really thorough in rinsing the soap off of them, then drying them completely." As any child would say, "Yes," she added, "Do I have to?" Priceless responses, right?

Weeks passed by, and still the hands remained chapped and painful. She said, "Grandma, what do you do to keep your hands from getting chapped?" I responded, "The same thing your mother told you. So, please show me how you wash your hands." A little soap was used, followed by one quick turn around her hands, followed by a two-second rinse, and finished off with a run of the towel over her hands. "Here, let me show you how I do it." Together, we washed, rinsed, dried, and put lotion on her hands. She said, "OK, now I understand what you want me to do. I'll try to do this each time like you showed me." Weeks later, her hands were completely healed.

I am not sure what made the difference between the talking and the showing, but different people learn in different ways. I realized it's much the same with leading others to Christ. We need to lead by example in thought, word, and deed. Sometimes, talk is cheap, so being hands-on in leading others through discipling and showing them how to disciple others is very beneficial. The old adage *actions speak louder than words* is crucial for those seeking Jesus to see Him in what we say as much as in what we do.

Thank You, LORD, for mentors to teach and lead us through discipling, both through example and hands-on, on-the-job training in witnessing to others together. I pray we demonstrate a Christ-centered walk in every area of our lives.

2 Timothy 2:2: *The things which you have heard from me among many witnesses, commit the same things to faithful men, who will be able to teach others also.*

1 John 3:19: *And by this we know that we are of the truth, and persuade our hearts before him,*

1 Thessalonians 5:11: *Therefore exhort one another, and build each other up, even as you also do.*

January 14th

Choosing a DVD

Years ago, my husband and I became very convicted about any inappropriate actions or words in movies, so we watched every movie, weeding out the ones we felt were unfit for adults or children to watch. We didn't want to be concerned with what someone would pull off our shelf, let alone God. The movies that didn't pass muster found their way into the garbage can. We weren't about to sell or give them away because we didn't want to put inappropriate material in anybody else's hands.

One evening, all the grandchildren begged to watch a movie. We selected a DVD, popped it in the player, and sat down for some family fun. The movie started a little slowly—the kids called it an adult movie. I couldn't help myself because inside I was screaming, "How do they know about those?" Pulling it together, I asked, "Why do you say that?" The reply was, "Because it's slow, there's not enough action for us." Inside, I breathed a huge sigh of relief. I thought, "Here we go again. They said this about the last movie we watched." I said, "Give it a few more minutes, and if you want to change the movie, we can." They agreed. Within less than thirty seconds, they were rolling with laughter. The joke is: they asked for THAT movie for the next movie night. Go figure.

Priceless Moments

How many times do we find ourselves saying, "Come on, God, get to the good part. This is taking too long. I want something else." Yet, when we back off and wait a little longer, God brings something wonderful into our lives at just the right time—rarely early, never late, but always on time. It may be what we've been praying for, or it may be completed differently, but God knows best.

Thank You, LORD, for taking an active role in our lives and selecting what will be best for us at the proper time. I pray we are accepting of Your goodness; although we may not agree with or understand Your answer, we realize You see the entirety of our lives from beginning to end, providing what we should have in Your time.

Ecclesiastes 3:11: *He has made everything beautiful in its time. He has also set eternity in their hearts, yet so that man can't find out the work that God has done from the beginning even to the end.*

2 Peter 3:8-9: *But don't forget this one thing, beloved, that one day is with the Lord as a thousand years, and a thousand years as one day. ⁹ The Lord is not slow concerning his promise, as some count slowness; but he is patient with us, not wishing that anyone should perish, but that all should come to repentance.*

Proverbs 16:9: *A man's heart plans his course, but Yahweh directs his steps.*

January 15th

Martin Luther King Jr. Day

Our grandchildren had the day off from school to celebrate this federal holiday. Of course, curiosity sparked the question, "Who was this man?" I replied, "Reverend King's birthday is celebrated

Priceless Moments

to remember his impact, or legacy, because he gave his life for civil rights and social justice in the area of racial equality. As a Baptist minister, he encouraged people to bring about these changes in a nonviolent manner, aiming to heal our country and bring hope to all mankind, regardless of their skin color, which is only skin deep. We are all the same on the inside. The holiday is sometimes called Civil Rights Day. All this means every person should be treated the same—with kindness and respect, the same way Jesus treated His fellowman."

"This day is for talking to our families about racial equality, why people try to stir up trouble between other people groups, to support our fellowmen, and to educate ourselves on the true history of this great man and the original intent of his actions. Experience has taught us that others who want to destroy our country twist and rewrite the truth." The little minds were absorbing our chat, and one responded, "You mean like how Satan twisted things for Adam and Eve and how he is still trying to do that today?" "Yes, you totally get it."

I am amazed at how well little ones can understand and apply what they have learned from Scripture and relate it to current events. Many times we underestimate all they can understand. I wish more people would be open-minded enough to view current events through the lens of Scripture to ferret out the truth—and apply it.

Thank You, LORD, for men who are willing to give their lives serving You and for little minds grasping Your word and truth. I pray You help us be like little children by absorbing, understanding, and exercising Your truth.

***Ecclesiastes 7:29**: This is all that I have learned: God made us plain and simple, but we have made ourselves very complicated. NIV*

***1 Samuel 12:24**: Only fear Yahweh, and serve him in truth with all your heart; for consider what great things he has done for you.*

Priceless Moments

1 Corinthians 15:58: Therefore, my beloved brothers, be steadfast, immovable, always abounding in the Lord's work, because you know that your labor is not in vain in the Lord.

January 16th
The New Tablecloth

I wanted to go shopping in search of two tablecloths, one to serve through Christmas and the other through winter. "Grandma, can we go with you to help choose your tablecloths?" The grandchildren like to go shopping with me, and I let them help select what we need. Off we went on a "scavenger hunt," so named by one of the granddaughters. We looked through the many "offerings" at different stores. One child liked this one, another liked that one, and yet another liked something altogether different. At the last store, I heard, "Oh, guys, look at this one." Each child looked at her find and called me over to see a white tablecloth with silver and gold snowflakes. Although very pretty, it was not exactly what I had in mind—until a little voice pops up and says, "Oh, Grandma, it's just perfect. God must have had this one saved for you."

Her enthusiasm was startling, pricking my curiosity as to her comment. So, I asked, "OK, honey, why do you feel this one is perfect?" She gave me a rather shocked look and said, "Look at it. See, God created the snowflakes for us all through Christmas and winter, so this is just like you wanted. You only need one tablecloth." The other grandchildren echoed her reasoning, saying, "Grandma, you have to get this one. Everyone will love it." On second thought, I really liked their reasoning. Oh, and yes, it looks great on our table.

I understand that a child can see God's beauty in everything when they are sensitive to His leading. I pray we are looking at things

Priceless Moments

from more of God's perspective than from our own point of view. God's vantage point is so much better than ours, anyway.

Thank You, LORD, for little children being willing to share You with adults. I pray they help us to rethink and change our perspective on important life issues so we can look for and invite You into our decision-making.

Philippians 4:6-7: *In nothing be anxious, but in everything, by prayer and petition with thanksgiving, let your requests be made known to God. And the peace of God, which surpasses all understanding, will guard your hearts and your thoughts in Christ Jesus.*

2 John 1:8: *Watch yourselves, that we don't lose the things which we have accomplished, but that we receive a full reward.*

2 Timothy 3:14: *But you remain in the things which you have learned and have been assured of, knowing from whom you have learned them.*

January 17th

Olympics

"Hey, Grandma, what are the Olympics?" "The Olympics were created in ancient Greece to honor their god Zeus. The first Olympics were held in the summer of 776 B.C., then once every four years. The goal was to build peace and a better world for youth through sports, teaching fair play, unity, and friendship. Interestingly, participants competed in the nude." "What do the winners receive?" "Winners of games like wrestling, long jump, chariot racing, boxing, discus, and javelin throwing received an olive wreath. In A.D. 393, the games were banned, being viewed as a pagan festival. The modern-day Olympics were started in the summer of 1896 in Athens, Greece, with twenty-three countries

Priceless Moments

participating. Unpaid athletes participate for the love of the games. The Winter Games began in 1924. Games were canceled three times due to war, once for World War 1 and two times for World War II."

"What other things go with the Olympics?" "The Olympic flag has five rings to represent the unity and solidarity of the five continents: Africa, the Americas, Asia, Australia, and Europe. More than 200 countries and nations participate in this sports competition. Several countries are banned or not allowed to participate. The Summer Olympics have thirty-two games, and the Winter Olympics have one hundred nine events. The five ring colors of blue, green, yellow, black, and red represent at least one color found on every national flag. The Olympic flame goes from Greece to the host city through relay runners. The game winners receive first, second, and third place medals of gold, silver, and bronze, respectively, which were first used in 1904."

Receiving medals made me think of, once we are saved, running the race to keep our faith until the end of our lives, where we all earn the ultimate medal of eternal life.

Thank You, LORD, that whosoever will can run the race set before us and receive the ultimate goal of this life—eternity with our LORD and Savior.

Deuteronomy 20:4*: For Yahweh your God is he who goes with you, to fight for you against your enemies, to save you.*

2 Timothy 4:7*: I have fought the good fight. I have finished the course. I have kept the faith.*

1 John 5:4*: For whatever is born of God overcomes the world. This is the victory that has overcome the world: your faith.*

Priceless Moments

January 18th

Hockey

"Grandma, what's it called when people wear ice skates and hit a little round thing on the ice with a long wooden stick?" "I believe you're talking about a game called hockey," I responded. "It's a team sport for two teams of six players on each team. They try to hit the little round thing, a puck, with their hockey stick past a goal line on the other team's side past their goaltender, the one protecting the net, into the net to score goals. This fast-paced skating game can sometimes get into physical contact or fights between players. This results in penalties and, many times, injuries to some players."

Silence filled the room as the little minds absorbed the information. "So, Grandma, the whole point of hockey is to make points by scoring goals, right? Is it like other sports where the team with the most points wins?" "Correct," I answered. "When and where was the first hockey game played?" they asked. "The first organized game was played in Canada in 1875, becoming the National Hockey League in 1917. It eventually became an Olympic sport in 1920. The U.S. had won two gold medals, eight silver medals, and one bronze medal at the Olympics."

My mind wanders to the idea of Christianity becoming a team sport. We cheer on God's side against His opponent, Satan. Sometimes the encounters get rough, with Satan having a new play. But God will always have a better plan and beat Satan at his own game. Therefore, being a member of God's team will assure we're on top as the winners.

Thank You, LORD, no matter the sport being played or the encounters we happen to experience, courtesy of Satan, having You as our Team Captain will ensure we are always on the winning side. I pray we fight Satan long and hard to win the race for our heavenly reward.

Priceless Moments

Psalm 108:13: *Through God, we will do valiantly. For it is he who will tread down our enemies*

1 Corinthians 9:24-25: *Don't you know that those who run in a race all run, but one receives the prize? Run like that, that you may win. Every man who strives in the games exercises self-control in all things. Now they do it to receive a corruptible crown, but we an incorruptible.*

2 Timothy 4:7*: I have fought the good fight. I have finished the course. I have kept the faith.*

January 19th
<u>Can We Look at Pictures?</u>

The little ones like to see themselves as infants and watch themselves grow through pictures. I said, "I enjoy looking at you and seeing how much you have changed and how much you have stayed the same. The best part is when you try to guess who is who." Fortunately, I can still remember… Anyway, as the children are getting older, they ask questions like, "Can we see pictures of our parents?" "Of course. We have plenty of them to share." They remark, "Oh, look at them—that's a hoot. What are they doing?" They laugh at their parents' pictures, so I tell them, "Remember how you are laughing at their pictures now because someday your kids will laugh at your pictures." "Oh, now, come on, Grandma, our kids won't laugh at us because we're cool."

For grins and giggles, I found pictures of their parents and them in the same clothes at their respective ages. Sometimes, it is almost impossible to tell them apart. Little mouths drop open, and they are speechless—imagine that. Although they are similar, I start pointing out their differences, at which point they begin to recognize who is who. They like this game. "Can you show us more? We want to be able to tell our parents about these funny pictures." "Sure. They have fun looking at these as well."

Priceless Moments

I thought, isn't it amazing how much we look like the world until we accept Jesus as our Savior? At that point, the similarities change, and the differences begin to emerge. The more we grow in Christ, the more those differences are noticed by our fellow man.

Thank You, LORD; the more we serve You, the more we change from looking like the world to reflecting more of You. I pray that the change toward Your image becomes more evident in us with each passing day.

Genesis 1:26a-27: God said, "Let's make man in our image, after our likeness. Let them have dominion over the fish of the sea, and over the birds of the sky, and over the livestock, and over all the earth, and over every creeping thing that creeps on the earth." God created man in his own image. In God's image he created him; male and female he created them.

Ephesians 5:1, 2: Be therefore imitators of God, as beloved children. Walk in love, even as Christ also loved us and gave himself up for us, an offering and a sacrifice to God for a sweet-smelling fragrance.

2 Corinthians 3:18: But we all, with unveiled face seeing the glory of the Lord as in a mirror, are transformed into the same image from glory to glory, even as from the Lord, the Spirit.

January 20th
<u>Bath Time</u>

A favorite of all children is the fun time to splash and enjoy making waves in the bathtub. This generation has the privilege of bath bombs, colored finger paint soaps, and bath toys to enhance their cleansing process. Of course, we keep a supply of bath-time favorites. "Grandma, may I have the tube of blue finger paint?" or "Do you have any strawberry-scented bath bombs?" They could

Priceless Moments

spend hours getting clean, but once the water gets cold, out they go. But, never fear, they have found a way to delay the process—by adding hot water every so often to the bath water.

When they started to write letters and spell words, I was asked, "Can you turn around for a minute and not look until I tell you it is OK to look?" "Sure," I'll play along. My favorite message was "I love you ♡". Although they were soggy and soapy wet, I gave them each a great big hug and kiss. Those types of messages from their beautiful little hearts just melt my heart. "Thank you, Grandma, for letting us play with the paints. Can we do it again sometime?" The only possible answer was, "Of course."

I thought of how God had given us His "I love you" message in the form of this sinless creation, His Son—birth, death, and resurrection—and a promise of an eternal home because of His great love for us. We don't need to clean up our lives, but to come as we are, letting Him cleanse us, and then go from there to learn more of Him.

Thank You, LORD, for Your message, written in red, to cover, wash away our filth, and cleanse us from all unrighteousness. I pray we strive to pass this message on to those who need to hear it, then show them the way to get clean to live for You.

1 John 1:9: *If we confess our sins, he is faithful and righteous to forgive us the sins, and to cleanse us from all unrighteousness.*

James 4:8: *Draw near to God, and he will draw near to you. Cleanse your hands, you sinners. Purify your hearts, you double-minded.*

Ezekiel 11:19,20: *I will give them one heart, and I will put a new spirit within you. I will take the stony heart out of their flesh, and will give them a heart of flesh; that they may walk in my statutes, and keep my ordinances, and do them. They will be my people, and I will be their God.*

Priceless Moments

January 21st
Matching Tablecloth, Napkins and Paper Plates

"Hey, Grandma, you know that snowflake tablecloth we bought yesterday. I was thinking that we need to look for napkins and plates to match the tablecloth." I had to smile because, you know, with kids, time is fairly irrelevant when they are young, so everything was *yesterday* in their mind. Better yet, I was surprised our grandson wanted all these things to match. So, I asked, "What do you think we should do about it?" Immediately, he responded, "Let's go shopping."

We visited a variety of stores, finding paper plates that matched the tablecloth perfectly but no napkins to even match a little, so we bought a few packages of the paper plates. On the way out of the store, he asked, "Can we look on the internet for napkins?" We came home and checked the internet but didn't find anything both of us liked. "Grandma, why don't we go back to that one store that had silver snowflakes and a skinny blue line on the edge? I really liked those." I thought it was a good compromise. We had to go to the grocery store to get some things for supper, so we stopped and bought a couple packages. He set the table using those napkins, telling our guests the story of how they came to grace our table.

I'm sure God appreciates it when we search His word to find answers to our needs. Also, we have to pray about His will in these matters. Persistence in prayer and searching the Scriptures will bring about the answer, which you can relate in the form of a testimony to others, with as few or as many details as you see fit. The overall goal is to let others know that God STILL answers prayers.

Thank You, LORD, for the answers in Your Word, combined with persistent prayer and supplication, to see Your plan for our lives, pointing us in the direction that brings honor and glory to Your

Name. I pray we exercise our faith through prayer for answers from You.

Psalm 116:2*: Because he has turned his ear to me, therefore I will call on him as long as I live.*

Acts 1:14*: All these with one accord continued steadfastly in prayer and supplication, along with the women, and Mary the mother of Jesus, and with his brothers.*

James 5:19-20*: Brothers, if any among you wanders from the truth, and someone turns him back, let him know that he who turns a sinner from the error of his way will save a soul from death, and will cover a multitude of sins.*

January 22nd
My Favorite Picture

I talked with each grandchild separately to see which picture I had taken of them that they liked best. Amazingly, they all replied with the same response: "My favorite picture of me is the one with all of us kids taken after the baby was born." The baby they all referred to was our youngest granddaughter, their cousin. I found the unanimous response most amazing, so I asked, "Why was that picture so special to you?" It was almost the same type of response: "Because we were all together at one time, getting to play, eat, sleep, and watch movies together. It was a special picture because our being together could only happen this one time because all of us will grow some more before we all get together again."

This was the first time they were all together with the new little one, but not the first time with the four older kids together. Again, I asked, "But what is different this time from other family gatherings?" By the looks on their faces, you would have thought I

Priceless Moments

had grown a third eye. "Come on, Grandma, you know. God gave us another cousin to love and to teach about the love of Jesus. We can teach her to pray at mealtimes, before going to bed, and lots of times in between." Now, that's an answer.

Reflection by the cousins and myself was counted as a blessing since there was a new life among us, so we will have the privilege to love and teach them about Jesus. Each new generation taught to understand and love Jesus has the privilege of helping carry the torch into the future.

Thank You, LORD, for counting another life as another opportunity to share Your love. I pray the beginning of each new day provides us with the chance for each new person we meet and each newborn as a golden opportunity for You to open new doors to reach the world, one person at a time.

Mark 16:15: *He said to them, "Go into all the world, and preach the Good News to the whole creation."*

Romans 10:12-13: *For there is no distinction between Jew and Greek; for the same Lord is Lord of all, and is rich to all who call on him. For, "Whoever will call on the name of the Lord will be saved."*

Psalm 67:1-5: *May God be merciful to us, bless us, and cause his face to shine on us. Selah. That your way may be known on earth, and your salvation among all nations, let the peoples praise you, God. Let all the peoples praise you. Oh let the nations be glad and sing for joy, for you will judge the peoples with equity, and govern the nations on earth. Selah. Let the peoples praise you, God. Let all the peoples praise you.*

January 23rd
Can I Wash Dishes?

The little ones seem to have a knack for wanting to be helpful. One day, while cleaning up after breakfast, both kids asked, "Can I wash dishes?" They looked at each other and said, "But I asked first." I jumped in quickly with a solution: "You can take turns being helpful. One can wash a few dishes while the other one dries, then switch places." They thought this solution sounded fair—but who was going to wash first? "OK, the person who picks a number from one through ten closest to what I'm thinking can go first." This seemed fair to them since we had done it many times before for other things. The proverbial "coin" was tossed, and a "winner" emerged.

With the crisis averted, "I have praise for both of you for being such good sports and "sharing" in the fun." They were so pleased with themselves that they asked. "Who is going to go first at playing a game? Can we do the number game again?" I chuckled and said, "Jesus would be very pleased with you both for being so considerate of each other. How can we get other people, kids and adults, to be so considerate of each other?" I heard, "We need to pray about it for God to touch their hearts and see how He would want them to handle it." Sometimes I'm not sure if I'm talking to children.

They made me think of how some adults are more childish about things than children. They are on the right track to take everything to the LORD in prayer, whether we know them or not, because God knows them and their needs, what they are going through right now, and how to handle their situation.

Thank You, LORD, for little children who have learned how to reach out to You in every situation. As adults, we need to learn from them and follow their lead by taking everything to You in prayer. I pray we come to you with childlike faith, trusting You in all we say and do.

Priceless Moments

James 1:5: *But if any of you lacks wisdom, let him ask of God, who gives to all liberally and without reproach, and it will be given to him.*

Hebrews 13:16: *But don't forget to be doing good and sharing, for with such sacrifices God is well pleased.*

Proverbs 19:8, 11: *He who gets wisdom loves his own soul. He who keeps understanding shall find good.*

January 24th

Computers

"Grandma, can we play on the computer? Our homework's done, and we'd like to play a game together." "Let's play a game," I responded. "If you can name all the parts and tell me what they do, then okay." "We love to play these games with you. First, turn on the electric bar so it will have power to run. Push the power buttons on the monitor to see things on the screen, and the modem to connect the computer to the internet. Next, a game is selected from a drop-down bar or an app, depending on whose computer we are using. I click on the one we want, and we can play our game. If we have to stop before we're done, it will stay right where we stopped so we can start there again next time." "Wow, guys. You're remembering more and more each time we do this. I'm really impressed."

"Did you know the first computer filled an entire city block and could only remember twenty numbers yet cost over $486,000." Wide-eyed, they responded, "Wow, that's a lot of money. Why did they build something so expensive?" "Charles Cabbage, a mathematician, wanted to find a way to work with numbers and eliminate man-made mistakes. His idea created a need for other people to use their ideas and skills to make the other parts of the system to build a computer that was error-free. Over the years, newer ideas and smaller parts were made to let the computer do bigger and better things. Not only do they work with numbers, but you can also look up information, store data and pictures, play video games, talk to others, etc. Today, computers are so small they can be held in your hand."

I am amazed at how much our relationship with God is like a computer. We must turn on the *power bar* of prayer to open the lines of communication. The computer components improve with time and new insights. We can make it better by reading our Bible and exercising our faith, drawing us closer to God.

Thank You, LORD, for giving man a mind to conceive time-saving devices and fun things to improve our lives. I pray our understanding is always credited to You, not to ourselves.

John 1:3: All things were made through him. Without him, nothing was made that has been made.

2 Chronicles 26:15: In Jerusalem, he made devices, invented by skillful men, to be on the towers and on the battlements, with which to shoot arrows and great stones. His name spread far abroad, because he was marvelously helped until he was strong.

Luke 14:28-30: For which of you, desiring to build a tower, doesn't first sit down and count the cost, to see if he has enough to complete it? Or perhaps, when he has laid a foundation, and is not able to finish, everyone who sees begins to mock him, saying, "This man began to build, and wasn't able to finish."

January 25th
Kinetic Sand

"Grandma, a friend of mine gave me a gift for my birthday of something that's some kind of sand. Have you ever heard of it? If

Priceless Moments

so, what is it?" "I think you're talking about kinetic sand, a soft, crumbly, moldable play sand that holds its shape when pressed into your hand, in a mold, or cut into shapes. It's coated beach sand that's hypoallergenic, non-toxic, gluten-free, never dries out, and is easy to clean up, so I know it's a good option for you to play with. The grandchildren loved it, saying, "Wow, Grandma, that's it. Where can you find this?" "Well, kinetic sand can be bought by itself and in play sets. I decided to look for some you would like to play with. There are all kinds of molds and shapes in your closet, so we can see what you can do with those."

"Grandma, we got the shapes and molds from the closet." Kids, filled with anticipation, settled around the table, ready for their project to begin. "Here you go. Different colors of sand are here, so let the fun begin." Hours later, the sand was gathered up. There were more colors afterwards than before since they had a blast "mixing and matching." They all pitched in to wipe up the table and collect the little bit that fell on the floor. Clean-up was a breeze.

My mind wandered as to how moldable we are in the hands of the Potter. Like the sand, are we willing to be shaped, reshaped, and shaped again as our circumstances change so God can make us the best we can be for His service throughout our lives?

Thank You, LORD, for Your kindness to see us as a work in progress, molding, and reshaping throughout our lives so we can represent You as the best option in life. I pray we stay moldable every day as You choose to reshape something about us along our earthly journey.

Job 10:9: *Remember, I beg you, that you have fashioned me as clay. Will you bring me into dust again?*
Hebrews 4:12: *For the word of God is living and active, and sharper than any two-edged sword, piercing even to the dividing of soul and spirit, of both joints and marrow, and is able to discern the thoughts and intentions of the heart.*

Priceless Moments

Jeremiah 18:1-4*: The word which came to Jeremiah from Yahweh, saying, "Arise, and go down to the potter's house, and there I will cause you to hear my words." Then I went down to the potter's house, and behold, he was making something on the wheels. When the vessel that he made of the clay was marred in the hand of the potter, he made it again another vessel, as seemed good to the potter to make it.*

January 26th
That's My iPad

I walked into our son's house one day to hear, "No, that's my iPad. Give it back now or I'll tell mom?" Another little voice replied, "I don't have to, and you can't make me." I was thinking, "Which parent is here—and where are they?" Just then our "granddaughter" came running in and almost knocked me over, wanting to be petted. I gave her a quick pat and went to find the kids. In the living room, I saw raised fists on both of them. I said, "Hello," startling them. "What's going on?" They both froze in place. "Nothing, Grandma" (as fists drop). "What are you doing here?" "I came for a visit. Your parents are going out tonight, and I have the privilege of spending time with two of my favorite people."

I requested, "Let's sit down so we can talk." They did so. I said, "Do you remember the story about Cain and Abel?" They shook their heads and said, "Yes." So, I asked, "Tell me what happened?" One said, "There was yelling. Cain got mad at Abel and killed him." The other one chimed in, "And his blood called out to God from the ground." "That's correct," I said. "Was it OK to kill his brother?" An echo of "No" was heard. "Then why were you two yelling at each other?" SILENCE, followed by "I'm sorry."

I couldn't help but think of how many times we may yell at and raise our fists at God. Usually, we look at or think about things from a slanted point of view, blaming God for any little misunderstanding. Later, after thinking it through and objectively looking back at the situation, we realize our error. Hopefully, we go to God and ask for His forgiveness immediately, and we have learned to look at facts before reacting to feelings.

Thank You, LORD, for Your long-suffering acceptance of our behaviors. You understand the total picture of our problem(s) and patiently guide us through the "tunnel of despair" until we "see the light," which is a different perspective. I pray we remain open and willing to listen to Your voice and to correction and leading as often and for as long as You deem fit.

Psalm 147:3*: He heals the broken in heart, and binds up their wounds.*

Acts 1:8*: But you will receive power when the Holy Spirit has come upon you. You will be witnesses to me in Jerusalem, in all Judea and Samaria, and to the uttermost parts of the earth.*

2 Timothy 3:16*: Every Scripture is God-breathed and profitable for teaching, for reproof, for correction, and for instruction in righteousness,*

January 27th
I Did a Split

Our granddaughter has been taking dance lessons for several months. She practices and does stretching exercises. One day she came into our house and said, "I can do a split," then proceeded to demonstrate her new skill. We all clapped for her and said, "We are so proud of you. You have worked really hard to be able to do it so easily." Actually, I was really jealous because I am not that

Priceless Moments

limber anymore. Anyway, she said, "Grandma, look at this." She proceeded to twirl around and stand on her tippy-toes. Her face was beaming at her success.

She proceeded to do another split, then asked for the rest of the "house" to participate in her "craft." Sadly, but wisely, no one took her up on her generous offer. She said, "All of you are missing out. It feels so good to stretch out like this. Maybe you can try it with me later." All of the observers smiled and thought to themselves, "Yeah, right." She proceeded, "I'm inviting all of you to come to my dance recital, where our class will perform a special dance for a live audience of other parents, grandparents, family, and friends. I'd love to see all of you come to watch me show how much I've learned." Now, that I can handle, so I responded, "Oh, that sounds marvelous. Count us in."

I thought of how God wants us to stretch our witnessing muscles, but many Christians do not see the benefit of doing so. Is it because of a lack of courage or a lack of knowing what to say? Yet, there will be a grand recital at the end of the age. We will either be humbled at how many people are in heaven because of our invitation or embarrassed due to our lack of extending an open invitation for all to come and see…

Thank You, LORD, for the courage and words You give us to say when we exercise our witnessing muscles. I pray we become more comfortable with each witnessing experience.

Acts 1:8: *But you will receive power when the Holy Spirit has come upon you. You will be witnesses to me in Jerusalem, in all Judea and Samaria, and to the uttermost parts of the earth.*

Luke 14:13, 14: *But when you make a feast, ask the poor, the maimed, the lame, or the blind; and you will be blessed, because they don't have the resources to repay you. For you will be repaid in the resurrection of the righteous.*

Priceless Moments

Isaiah 1:18: *"Come now, and let's reason together," says Yahweh: "Though your sins are as scarlet, they shall be as white as snow. Though they are red like crimson, they shall be as wool."*

January 28th
<u>Time for Church</u>

Sunday morning has come around once again, so we are privileged to go to the House of Worship to learn more about our Savior. The grandchildren spent the night, so it's time to awaken them and have breakfast before heading out. "Good morning, little ones. It's time to rise and shine and give God the glory, glory, glory." Realizing I had sung part of a song, they joined in. "Rise and shine and give God the glory, glory, children of the LORD." What an awesome way to start the morning. Now, it's time for breakfast, getting dressed, and brushing their teeth. "Grandma, do we get to go to church every Sunday?" "Yes, we do. God has blessed the country in which we live so our doors are always open to attend worship. We need to pray that God continues to bless us and our country so that we can always be privileged to attend worship services."

They were in a good mood now. Everything went like clockwork, and we left on time. They chatted along the way, saying, "I wonder what we will learn about today? I hope we learn more about David and Goliath. It's my favorite story." "Well, I want to learn more about Esther. She was very brave."

I thought of how they had already absorbed so much of God's Word but were still ready and willing to learn more. As adults, we need to keep that childlike enthusiasm for learning, particularly God's Word, embedded deep within our hearts and minds so that the enemy can never take it away from us.

Thank You, LORD, for these beautiful children, ready to learn more of You. I pray that, as adults, we keep our hearts and minds attentive to continue hiding Your words in our hearts so that we might not sin against You, as well as showing others the importance of going to church to worship with fellow believers.

Psalm 25:8-9: *Good and upright is Yahweh, therefore he will instruct sinners in the way. He will guide the humble in justice. He will teach the humble his way.*

Proverbs 1:7: *The fear of Yahweh is the beginning of knowledge; but the foolish despise wisdom and instruction.*

Hebrews 10:25: *not forsaking our own assembling together, as the custom of some is, but exhorting one another, and so much the more as you see the Day approaching.*

January 29th
Open Your Bibles, Please, To...

"Grandma, have you ever noticed some people carry their Bibles to church and others don't? Of those who do, some never look at it the whole time they're at church. Why is that?" "Wow, you are very observant to notice all of that. Yes, I've noticed the same things. People carry their Bibles for two reasons: one is because it's the right thing to do. The other is to let others know they treasure God's Word and want to let others know they are a believer, a form of testimony. Sometimes people may carry their Bible but not use it since the Scripture is put up on a screen, or they use their iPad or iPhone."

She thought for a minute and asked, "Do you carry your Bible to church, or do you prefer the screen or phone?" "I carry my Bible for several reasons. I like holding this precious book in my hands to read the words as God's personal message to me and not be distracted by looking up at the screen or the messages that could pop up on my device while reading along with the Scripture. I can

Priceless Moments

mark a Scripture when God speaks to me to find it again for future reference, as well as during my personal Bible study." "Should I carry my own Bible to church?" "That is your own personal choice, but that is one of the reasons Papa and I bought you each a Bible and cover so you could read it yourself and take it to Sunday School and church."

Commercials talk about *never leaving home without it*. Our Bible is our sword, the very Word of God, containing answers to all of our needs to protect our hearts and minds from the enemy.

An important part of your story is whether or not you include God in all areas of your life. The story you tell without God could be completely different than the one you tell with God in your life. Unfortunately, as Christians, many of us have gotten out of the habit of carrying our Bibles, our *swords*, with us to mark references to help us be prepared to do battle with Satan in the future, as well as to share with others so they can protect themselves as well.

Thank You, LORD, for giving us a weapon to use to teach, share, and do battle with on a daily basis. I pray we hide those words in our hearts and minds so they can be drawn upon, as needed, at a minute's notice.

Psalm 119:105: *Your word is a lamp to my feet, and a light for my path.*

Luke 12:34: *For where your treasure is, there will your heart be also*

Luke 6:35: *But love your enemies, and do good, and lend, expecting nothing back; and your reward will be great, and you will be children of the Most High; for he is kind toward the unthankful and evil.*

January 30th

Here's Some Money

One day, our grandson came over and asked to talk to me. "Grandma, I have something for you." He reached into his pocket and pulled out a small plastic bag and put it in my hand, saying, "I know you can use this to go shopping for what you need." I looked at the bag as he said, "Open it." He was beaming with pleasure as I opened the little bag. Inside I found fifteen cents. "Grandma, that's all I could get for now, but if you need more, I can work to get it out of my piggy bank." He is a very generous soul, willing to give to others and to share with others as he sees a need.

I just stood there, trying to think of an appropriate way to return the money. I finally said, "Oh, thank you, honey. This is so generous of you, but I can't take your money. Put it back in your piggy bank for when you would like to buy something for yourself. I'm sure you would like to buy some more LEGOs soon." He said, "No, you keep it." I realized how much it meant to him, so I said, "Well, thank you. I will keep it in my purse for a very special occasion." He was still beaming.

How often does God look at us and inspire us to unselfishly give something we have to others, be it time, food, money, or material possessions? If a child feels the need to share, we also need to realize there needs to be a recipient of their generosity. If not, we deny them—and God—of being a cheerful givers.

Thank You, LORD, for a child's generous heart, giving of the little he has. I pray we follow His example and are cheerful givers as You lead us to be. And, if the tables are turned, may we also be cheerful receivers so we do not rob others of the blessing of being cheerful givers.

2 Corinthians 9:7: Let each man give according as he has determined in his heart, not grudgingly or under compulsion, for God loves a cheerful giver.

Priceless Moments

Proverbs 11:25: *The liberal soul shall be made fat. He who waters shall be watered also himself.*

Matthew 6:33: *But seek first God's Kingdom and his righteousness; and all these things will be given to you as well.*

January 31st
<u>Don't Take My Picture</u>

There are times when people don't like to have their picture taken, especially children. They have to be in the proper mood or forget it. On such an occasion, the older grandchildren were playing with the younger ones. They were playing so beautifully together that I wanted to preserve this memory to share with them later. Our granddaughter saw me pull up the camera app on my phone and get ready to take pictures of their interactions. "Don't take my picture," she said. "I hate that." Once she made her comment, they all chimed in about not wanting their picture taken, so I put my phone away.

About a half hour later, the younger ones were playing and said, "Grandma, take our picture. I want to see what we look like." So, I complied. Then they asked to see the pictures. A request was even made to see the pictures from the earlier frivolity. When I said, "I don't have any," they asked, "Why not?" I replied, "Because I didn't want anyone to get upset with me, so I respected your wishes." "But we were having fun and getting along so well, you should have taken some pictures anyway." "I'm sorry, but when someone asks you not to do something, we all need to be respectful of them and honor their wishes, even if it means disappointment later. I realize this is a hard lesson to learn, but I need to set an example for you to follow."

I thought of how adults can get testy when having their picture taken. Sneers, jeers, and smart comments are made to the "photographer" on hand. Later, they, too, want to see their

Priceless Moments

memories, only to realize how bad they looked or that none were taken. We only have these God-given moments as pictures in our minds for these special memories.

Thank You, LORD, for being ready to forgive us for our behaviors towards others. I pray we are not a sore spot but rather a bright spot in their day.

Proverbs 15:30: *The light of the eyes rejoices the heart. Good news gives health to the bones.*

John 16:33: *I have told you these things, that in me you may have peace. In the world you have trouble; but cheer up! I have overcome the world.*

2 Corinthians 9:7: *Let each man give according as he has determined in his heart, not grudgingly or under compulsion, for God loves a cheerful giver.*

February

From the lips of babes and infants
you have established strength,
because of your adversaries,
that you might
silence the enemy and avenger.

Psalm. 8:2

February 1ST
Basketball

Our grandchildren were talking about playing with a bunch of other kids and having fun. Curiosity got the best of me, so I asked, "What game are you playing today?" They replied, "We're not sure yet, but we want to toss around a ball or something." What is it about kids wanting to throw and bounce balls? Ah, an idea just came to mind: "What about the basketball in the toy box outside? I know you've watched other kids play it, and we've even tossed a few into the hoop." Eyes lit up, and they asked, "Can you tell us about basketball? How many kids do we need? How do we play the game?"

I began, "Basketball is considered a two-team sport, usually with five players on each team. The goal is to shoot or throw the ball into the other team's hoop to score points, some worth two or three points. The other team is trying to stop their attempts to score. Things cause fouls—something that violates the game rules, like unsportsmanlike conduct on or off the court or different types of personal contact. These fouls can result in free throws for extra points for the opposing team." We went out to the hoop for "on the court" training to help them understand what the rules were and to play a good game.

I thought of how our spiritual life is like basketball: two teams, captained by Jesus and Satan. Our team, playing for Jesus, is always on the offensive to keep Satan's team from scoring any points, which leads to them turning away from Jesus' team. May we learn our "craft" and know our "rules" so well that we do not "foul out" of the game. We need "on the court" training to teach others how to be disciples and then to disciple others, working from the home court advantage.

Thank You, LORD, for little ones' curiosity about the world around them to help us see more of You. I pray our minds stay curious and our hearts open to the truth You want us to see.

Acts 26:18: *to open their eyes, that they may turn from darkness to light and from the power of Satan to God, that they may receive remission of sins and an inheritance among those who are sanctified by faith in me.*

John 8:32: *You will know the truth, and the truth will make you free.*

Isaiah 40:30-31: *Even the youths faint and get weary, and the young men utterly fall; but those who wait for Yahweh will renew their strength. They will mount up with wings like eagles. They will run, and not be weary. They will walk, and not faint.*

February 2nd

<u>Groundhog Day</u>

"Grandma, why are we talking about a groundhog today?" "Because the history and things done to celebrate this day are very interesting. Since 1887, in a little town in Punxsutawney, Pennsylvania, a groundhog named Phil has resided on Gobbler's Knob to make his official weather forecast. Every morning on February 2, Phil is coaxed out of his burrow, or hole, to predict the arrival of spring. If he sees his shadow due to clear weather, winter will go on for six more weeks. If he does not see his shadow because of cloudiness, spring will arrive early in six weeks. This seems to be a version of the Christian festival of Candlemas in German-speaking areas. They used a badger to do the same type of thing. Thousands of people visit Gobbler's Knob every year to observe the ceremony and get first-hand prognostications, or the predictions of the groundhog." "That sounds silly. Is it really true?"

"Yes, it is. Phil's forecasts each February 2 are recorded in the Congressional Records held in the National Archives at the

Priceless Moments

Library of Congress in our nation's capital. Interestingly, other communities around the world have picked up this tradition: Canada's groundhog Shubenacadie Sam; Colorado's yellow-bellied Stormy Marmot; Oregon's hedgehog Fufu; Florida's burrowing owls Owliver and Owlivia; North Carolina's squirrel Pisgah Penny; New York's chicken Clucksatawney Henrietta; Connecticut's Scramble the duck; Texas' armadillo Bee Cave Bob; Oregon's beaver Stumptown Fil; Louisiana's Claude the crawfish; Lancaster County, PA's whistle pig Octarara Orphie; and many more.

It's amazing how many people try to prognosticate their own futures, but God has given us the best *predictor* ever, His Holy Bible. Between its pages, more answers can be found than one can fathom. Get up early and, like these prognosticators, open your Bible to see what God has in store for you today.

Thank You, LORD, that we can rely on Your promises, which never fail or change but are reliable, dependable, and true. I pray we turn to You every morning to learn all You have planned for our day.

Jeremiah 29:11: For I know the thoughts that I think toward you," says Yahweh, "thoughts of peace, and not of evil, to give you hope and a future.

Romans 8:28: We know that all things work together for good for those who love God, for those who are called according to his purpose.

February 3rd
Blueberry French Toast Casserole

Thursday morning has arrived once again for our family breakfast. As the grandchildren walked in the door, they shouted out the

Priceless Moments

dish—one of their favorite guessing games. I laughed and said, "On the menu: blueberry French toast casserole, a dish comprised of bread, cream cheese, and blueberries held together with whipped eggs, then baked and topped with a blueberry sauce, is awaiting you." They made a mad dash to the table, saying, "It's a family favorite." It sat there, all hot and bubbly. Daddy said, "I'll dish out a piece to each of you to cool, then you can ask the blessing." I chuckled as one ate the blueberry sauce off the top before eating the rest of the dish, while the other did the opposite, saving the sauce for last.

As we ate, they talked excitedly about the planned events for the day—playing at the park, riding bikes, and other kid-oriented activities. While cleaning up the dishes, they asked, "Can we have more of this for lunch?" I said, "Maybe you can take some home for tomorrow so we can have something else for lunch." In unison, I heard, "Then its tuna wraps with cheese, OK. You know how much we love tuna wraps." "Yes, I do. Why do you think I keep extra cans of tuna in the pantry?" They just giggled.

Thoughts trailed off to God's provisions for us. He keeps things ready for us all the time, but we need to open His "pantry" and see what all He has ready for us. Our lives can consist of doing all the things we have planned, or we can follow God's plan for our lives, finding these plans more rewarding. Check His Book for instructions.

Thank You, LORD; Your Scripture is the best road map we can use to keep us growing in the right direction to be at the right place at the right time to fulfill Your will. I pray we stay filled with Your Word and share the good news.

***Jeremiah 15:16**: Your words were found, and I ate them. Your words were to me a joy and the rejoicing of my heart, for I am called by your name, Yahweh, God of Armies.*

Priceless Moments

Ecclesiastes 9:7*: Go your way—eat your bread with joy, and drink your wine with a merry heart; for God has already accepted your works.*

John 6:35*: Jesus said to them, "I am the bread of life. Whoever comes to me will not be hungry, and whoever believes in me will never be thirsty.*

February 4th

<u>The Singing Dog</u>

Papa has a variety of animated musical bears and dogs that he enjoys playing for the grandchildren. Today's visit evoked an interest in the singing dogs. They played all of them over and over again, singing and dancing with them until one particular dog got their attention. It was one that sang *I Feel Good, Like I Should*. The musical dog was played over and over until the batteries died. Unfortunately, we were out of the size needed to bring it back to life. Our grandson said, "Grandma, can you go to the store now and get more batteries? I really want to play it some more. Please, Grandma, please?"

That sweet child with good manners found a soft spot in my heart, but there was no time to head to the store. I thought for a minute to find a solution, and then I had it. I asked Papa, "Could you please take the batteries out of one of the musical bears and replace the dead batteries in the dog?" A smile crossed his face, "Of course I can do that." He turned and said, "Come on, little man. Let's pull a switcheroo from those dead batteries to the good batteries." Those little eyes started dancing as he replied, "Oh, yes, Papa. Let's do that." All was well again.

I thought of how many times we beg God to do something for us, but our dead ideas need to be replaced with fresh ones from God. Once we are infused with His *charge*, all will be well again. The only way to do this is to have our hearts and minds prepared by staying charged with things of the kingdom.

Thank You, LORD, for taking the mess of things we bring to You and filling us with Your Holy Spirit and power to work for You. I pray we keep up with reading Your Word, praying, and exercising our faith to foil the switcheroos Satan tries to sneak in on us.

Psalm 121:1–2*: I will lift up my eyes to the hills. Where does my help come from? My help comes from Yahweh, who made heaven and earth.*

1 Thessalonians 3:12, 13*: May the Lord make you to increase and abound in love toward one another, and toward all men, even as we also do toward you, to the end he may establish your hearts blameless in holiness before our God and Father at the coming of our Lord Jesus with all his saints.*

Romans 15:5, 6*: Now the God of perseverance and of encouragement grant you to be of the same mind with one another according to Christ Jesus, that with one accord you may with one mouth glorify the God and Father of our Lord Jesus Christ.*

February 5th

<u>Can I Play the Piano?</u>

Instead of just helping themselves, I am thrilled each time the grandchildren want to play the piano, they ask for permission. I have endeavored to teach them a few basics to spark an interest in music, and it seems to be paying off. "Grandma, can I play the piano? I will be careful and not bang on it." "Of course, you can," I replied. "Thank you for the good manners of asking first. I appreciate it." Then, one sits down and gently starts picking at the keys until something sounds like a melody. "Hey, Grandma, did you hear that? I think I played… (they name some tune). Did you

Priceless Moments

know that one?" Somehow, my ears did not perceive the same tune, so I replied, "I guess I don't know that one. But keep at it; you are doing a great job."

As one strums along, another soon joins for a duet, at which time things tend to go awry. To prevent yelling and banging of keys, I ask, "Did you ask permission to play, too?" A "No" is usually uttered, and a disappointed child gets up and walks away, often apologizing to the first virtuoso and then to me. "Thank you," I say, "you may have the next turn." Ah, all is well again. Courtesy has triumphed over animosity. The first virtuoso gets up, and immediately another sits down to play. When she returned, she said, "Hey, what are you doing? I was there first." The second responds, "Move your feet; lose your seat." No further comments were made.

I remember how Jesus wants us to be kind to one another, to treat them as we would want to be treated, be they family, friends, or foes. A kind word will protect their ego and allow for the needed changes to occur without giving way to anger. As usually happens, once corrected, they will sing along with the current maestro.

Thank You, LORD, for Your words of wisdom in dealing with others. Our source of joy is in You, not others. I pray we will all be able to sing praises to You, whether or not we are treated with love and respect.

Psalm 95:1: *Oh come, let's sing to Yahweh. Let's shout aloud to the rock of our salvation!*

James 5:13: *Is any among you suffering? Let him pray. Is any cheerful? Let him sing praises. "Is any one of you in trouble? He should pray. Is anyone happy? Let him sing songs of praise.*

Psalm 96:11-13: *Let the heavens be glad, and let the earth rejoice. Let the sea roar, and its fullness! Let the field and all that is in it exult! Then all the trees of the woods shall sing for joy before Yahweh; for he comes, for he comes to judge the earth.*

Priceless Moments

He will judge the world with righteousness, the peoples with his truth.

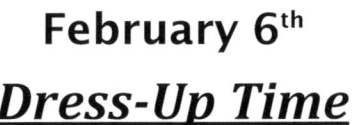

February 6th

<u>Dress-Up Time</u>

When the grandchildren get together, they enjoy playing dress-up. Since four are girls and one is a boy, the girls don the fancy princess dresses while the little macho man becomes their escort throughout the house. Comments like, "Aren't we beautiful." "Do you like my dress?" "Who do I remind you of?" "Can you guess my princess character?" float through the room as the girls parade around us. Their *escort* dresses in the few *manly hero* costumes, saying, "My lady, may I help you?" "Take my hand, and I'll help you up the stairs." "Who is next, Elsa or Pocahontas?" On occasion, he will have a princess on each arm.

As adult observers, we have to smile at the gentility of the "ladies" and the chivalry of the "man." On occasion, a question will be asked: "What character are you dressed as this time?" But eyes just roll as they continue the parade of characters, much like a runway at a fashion show. When they tire of the constant changing of clothing, they return dressed in their "street clothes," requesting a snack because "all that up and down the steps made us hungry."

I thought how God must smile at us as we parade our "finery" in front of Him, be it with pleasure or chagrin at our haughtiness towards Him and others. When we return to our street clothes for business as usual, we return to acting like the individuals God intended us to be.

Thank You, LORD, for the pleasure You have in us and also for being willing to lovingly disciple us as needed. I pray that regardless of where we are or what we are doing, we continue to be good in thought, word, and deed—and dress.

1 Timothy 2:9: *In the same way, that women also adorn themselves in decent clothing, with modesty and propriety, not just with braided hair, gold, pearls, or expensive clothing,*

1 Corinthians 11:1*: Be imitators of me, even as I also am of Christ.*

Philippians 2:3-5: *doing nothing through rivalry or through conceit, but in humility, each counting others better than himself; each of you not just looking to his own things, but each of you also to the things of others. Have this in your mind, which was also in Christ Jesus,*

February 7th
<u>What Do You Want To Do Today?</u>

Often times, I ask myself, let alone the grandchildren, who also desire to be active in doing things, "What do you want to do today?" I try to plan ahead, but they have their own ideas of things to do. When they came, I beat them to the punch and asked, "What would you like to do today?" The different responses were: "Go to the playground." "Ride the bike and tractor (on the back patio)." "Go for a walk." "Watch a movie." "Play with Play-Doh, paint rocks, or blow bubbles." There is certainly a variety to choose from. To keep the masses happy, I suggested, "Let's go for a walk to get to the playground. When we come back, we can take turns with the Play-Doh, painting rocks, blowing bubbles, and riding the bike and tractor on the back patio. Depending on time, we can fit in lunch, watch a movie, and, my favorite, make a smoothie."

Cheers resounded from all the grandchildren. They chatted happily amongst themselves because each person got to see their suggestion be accepted and planned for, so they could enjoy their time together. A successful day came to fruition, filled with fun, laughter, and the opportunity to enjoy each other.

These moments make me realize how important it is to validate each child so they can enjoy everything about the others' ideas and desires. I pray this positive flow of acceptance continues between them, hoping they learn some compromise and rearranging may be needed for good things to happen.

Thank You, LORD, for the wisdom to keep peace and contentment in our lives with family, friends, strangers, foes, and, most of all, with You. I pray we look upward for wisdom to keep peace while validating others, regardless of where they are in their walk with You.

Ephesians 2:4-5: But God, being rich in mercy, for his great love with which he loved us, even when we were dead through our trespasses, made us alive together with Christ—by grace you have been saved—

Micah 6:8: He has shown you, O man, what is good. What does Yahweh require of you, but to act justly, to love mercy, and to walk humbly with your God?

Exodus 34:6-7a: Yahweh passed by before him, and proclaimed, "Yahweh! Yahweh, a merciful and gracious God, slow to anger, and abundant in loving kindness and truth, keeping loving kindness for thousands, forgiving iniquity and disobedience and sin;

February 8th

The Seahorse

When our first grandchild was celebrating her first birthday, her parents elected to take her to one of her favorite places—the aquarium. She was totally mesmerized by watching the animals

Priceless Moments

and their antics. While walking through the aquarium, she was taking in all the statues of animals and checking out each window to find out what animals were there. Totally unlike her, she took off running from one exhibit to her stroller—of course, we were right on her heels—when she picked up her singing seahorse. Unsure of why, we soon understood her behavior. She took her seahorse over and put it on the statue of a seahorse, which none of the four of us had noticed, but she did. Beaming from ear to ear, she held onto the statue with one hand while clutching her seahorse with the other.

It is amazing how observant a one-year-old can be, drawing associations so rapidly, and finding ways to let us adults know what she has discovered. I thought of the innate intelligence God has placed within each of us, just waiting to be unleashed. Sadly, many of us will never discover how fearfully and wonderfully we are made, never tapping into our unlocked God-given potential. Things can be right in front of us, but we will never discover the association God wants us to make. We turn a blind eye to things of God, which ultimately affects our ability to discern things in our secular world.

Thank You, LORD, for the opportunity to see things through a child's eyes. I pray we will realize You have placed an innate ability within all of us. Our task is to discover what is within each of us, then discover just how You want us to use it. I pray we be willing to be taught about Your goodness through our children and grandchildren.

Ephesians 2:10: *For we are his workmanship, created in Christ Jesus for good works, which God prepared before that we would walk in them.*

Philippians 1:6: *being confident of this very thing, that he who began a good work in you will complete it until the day of Jesus Christ.*

Priceless Moments

Psalm 139:13-14: *For you formed my inmost being. You knit me together in my mother's womb. I will give thanks to you, for I am fearfully and wonderfully made. Your works are wonderful. My soul knows that very well.*

February 9th

My Best Friend

It is so interesting to hear the grandchildren talk about their best friend, be it from their community, church, school, or in their own home. "Grandma, do you know who my best friend is?" I ventured a few guesses, but none of those suggestions were correct. "Oh, come on, Grandma, you know. Guess." Since we don't go to all the same places, I truly had no idea of any other prospects to guess. The best friend's description was given in detail, but it did not trigger the names of any prospects. I was informed, "Well, Grandma, for your information, my best friend is, uh, I forgot his name. But he's in my class at school."

I guess I don't feel too bad knowing someone's name when the person trying to get me to guess it can't remember his name either. I did not make a big deal about it but rather changed the subject. "Do you know who my best friend is?" His mouth dropped open, and he just stared at me. I asked, "Don't you think I can have a best friend, too?" It took a few minutes for a response, so I hopped in and said, "As a matter of fact, I have many best friends. One from diaper-days, several from high school, several from college, and many new ones have been made in each area where we have lived. But my very, very best friend is Jesus." He said, "Wow. What an awesome answer."

Naming Jesus my best friend made those listening to our conversation mull over my declaration. Hopefully, all of those listening, of all ages, if they haven't yet made this very important decision, will make Jesus their best friend from this day forward, as well.

Thank You, LORD, for always being available, not only as our Savior but also as our big Brother and best friend. I pray we realize You are someone we can turn to in bad times as well as good, 24 hours a day, 7 days a week, 365 days a year.

Proverbs 17:17: *A friend loves at all times; and a brother is born for adversity.*

1 Thessalonians 5:11: *Therefore exhort one another, and build each other up, even as you also do.*

Colossians 3:13: *Bear with each other and forgive one another if any of you has a grievance against someone. Forgive as the LORD forgave you. NIV*

February 10th

<u>My Sweetest Valentine</u>

Valentine's Day is coming, and the grandchildren are very excited about selecting and writing out Valentines for classmates and a few special friends. Talk of selecting the best Valentine in the package for someone special in class crossed all of their lips. Their moms took them out to choose the package they wanted to buy so they could get started on writing all of them out themselves, getting assistance as needed.

As they were writing their names on the back of each Valentine, they would decide which one suited their friends the best. Some of the "decision" responses were, 'It's so cute, just like 'Johnny.'; "She's mean, and I don't like this one, so I'll give it to her."; "I didn't write my name very well on this one, so I'll give it to So-and-So."; "I kind of like him, so I think this one would be best." On and on, these comments were made, matching each card with what they thought about each potential recipient. I asked them,

Priceless Moments

"Should we look at friends differently than those we do not like?" Silence hung in the air. Finally, a response was heard: "Jesus said to love our enemies."

God reminds us to love one another, regardless of our feelings towards them. We should be the first to show everyone kindness and consideration, even forgiveness if needed, all the while interceding for them in prayer, something that requires us to truly desire good things for them. If we follow God's commands and learn to love our enemies with the goal of helping them become our friends, it is a win-win situation.

Thank You, LORD, for showing us how to interact with others. I pray, regardless of the circumstances, to expand our circle of friends by humbling ourselves and showing them the love of Jesus.

Luke 6:27-28: *"But I tell you who hear: love your enemies, do good to those who hate you, bless those who curse you, and pray for those who mistreat you.*

Romans 5:8: *But God commends his own love toward us, in that while we were yet sinners, Christ died for us.*

1 John 4:9-11: *By this God's love was revealed in us, that God has sent his one and only Son into the world that we might live through him. In this is love, not that we loved God, but that he loved us, and sent his Son as the atoning sacrifice for our sins. Beloved, if God loved us in this way, we also ought to love one another.*

February 11th
<u>Super Bowl Sunday</u>

"Grandma, are you going to watch the Super Ball with us this year? Mom and Dad are talking about all the cool food we're going to have. It sounds like so much fun, and I don't want you to

Priceless Moments

miss it." "Actually, I thought I would skip it this year because none of my favorite teams are playing. But I could come just to be with you guys if it sounds good to you." Enthusiasm seethed from her. "Yes, yes, yes; please do come. Maybe you could tell me why it's called a super ball." I had to smile and say, "This event is called a Super Bowl. Interestingly, the name came from the owner of the team watching his children play with a super ball. The football is called a pigskin because it was once made from pig's skin. Today, they are made from cowhide."

"The Super Bowl is played like a regular football game, with the same rules, positions of players, and scoring. It is a very important game played at the end of the football season between the top two teams in their division, or league, called the AFC and NFC." "How do they decide where to play the game?" I thought out loud, "The city to host, or have the game played there, is chosen for its location, reliable weather, hotels, and restaurants that are close to the stadium. A newer stadium with a covered dome increases their chances of being selected." "Can we go to their field to watch the game?" "Actually, it's better to watch the game from home to see great plays shown over and over again, called an instant replay. Tickets and hotel rooms are sold out, so it would be very expensive to go. At home, you are safe and warm, and it's easy to get food, and you still have your money in your pocket."

I reflected on her begging me to come over and watch the game, about which she became curious to learn before the big day. Our big day, the rapture, is also coming. May we learn our position in the kingdom as one chosen to work diligently to do our part to bring others across the goal line into heaven.

Thank You, LORD, for the pleasures You have given us in this life. I pray we appreciate all You have done for us as well as share our knowledge of Your saving grace with others.

Isaiah 43:1: *But now Yahweh who created you, Jacob, he who formed you, Israel, says: "Don't be afraid, for I have redeemed you. I have called you by your name. You are mine."*

Priceless Moments

John 6:44: *No one can come to me unless the Father who sent me draws him, and I will raise him up in the last day.*

Galatians 1:15–16: *But when it was the good pleasure of God, who separated me from my mother's womb and called me through his grace to reveal his Son in me, that I might preach him among the Gentiles, I didn't immediately confer with flesh and blood,*

February 12th
<u>Lincoln's Birthday</u>

"Hey, guys, do you know who Abraham Lincoln was?" Our granddaughter's eyes lit up: "Our teacher said he was one of our presidents." "That's correct," I replied. "He was born February 12, 1809, in a one-room log cabin in Kentucky. His family moved to a wild area of Indiana when he was eight; and his mother died when he was ten. He grew up working on a farm, putting forth great effort to gain knowledge. He left home at twenty-one, working as a boatman, store clerk, and surveyor before joining the Black Hawk War."

"After the war, he became a lawyer. He was elected to the Illinois Legislature in 1834. Meanwhile, he married and had four sons. In 1846, he was elected to the U.S. House of Representatives. In 1860, he was elected as our 16th president. Soon, he wrote the Emancipation Proclamation to free slaves from the south in 1863, dedicated the Gettysburg military ceremony, and won re-election in 1864. Unfortunately, Lincoln was shot and killed by a man named John Wilkes Booth while attending Ford's Theatre on April 14, 1865." They interrupted and asked, "Why did he shoot him?" "Booth thought he was helping the South, but actually he made it worse."

I couldn't help but think about how Jesus gave His life to set us free from our slavery to sin. Like Booth, Satan thought he was doing himself and the world a favor by inciting a man to turn them away from Jesus. Fortunately, he was wrong, doing the world a favor. Jesus, once again, bridged the gap between heaven and earth, making it possible for us to personally approach the throne of grace.

Thank You, LORD, for Your willingness to give all for mankind, In spite of man killing You, You literally "rose to the occasion" to save all who willingly gave their lives to Your service. I pray we realize Your sacrifice was one to set us free from slavery to sin into freedom in You.

Psalm 119:45*: I will walk in liberty, for I have sought your precepts.*

2 Corinthians 3:17: *Now the Lord is the Spirit and where the Spirit of the Lord is, there is liberty.*

Galatians 5:13-14*: For you, brothers, were called for freedom. Only don't use your freedom for gain to the flesh, but through love be servants to one another. For the whole law is fulfilled in one word, in this: "You shall love your neighbor as yourself."*

February 13th

Mardi Gras

We were shopping one day when our grandson asked, "What are these unusual glasses-type masks for?" I had no idea what he was looking at or referring to with his comment. "Why don't you show me, and we can figure it out together?" "Here. What are they used for?" "I know. They are called Mardi Gras masks; they were created to hide a person's face or identity because most people don't want to be recognized attending some of the things that happen after dark." "When is this?" "It always starts on January 6th, a day called Epiphany, which celebrates the wisemen bringing gifts to the Child Jesus. A King Cake with a plastic baby Jesus baked inside the cake is served. The last day of the celebration is called *Fat Tuesday*, as people will eat large amounts of food before giving up something for Lent to fast and repent of their deeds for forty-seven days until Easter."

"What kind of things happen there?" I knew I had to be selective with this answer. "There are parades with floats where people throw trinkets, like beads, plastic coins, and plastic cups; food, like potatoes and carrots; and marching bands." "How can they tell what the date is for Mardi Gras?" "The answer is kind of involved, but here it goes: since Mardi Gras is always tied to Easter, which falls on the first Sunday after the full moon following the spring equinox, and because the day before Ash Wednesday, which marks the beginning of Lent, was a day of feasting, it came to be known as *Fat Tuesday* or, as the French would say, *Mardi Gras*. The choice of date to end the celebration was so people could be silly and indulge as they wanted before they started to fast."

How often do we try to go before our fellowmen or God pretending to be someone we're not? Sooner or later, we will be discovered and humiliated in the sight of God and man.

Thank You, LORD; we don't need to hide behind a mask to approach You. I pray our guard is always down, as You see the true us anyway, honestly and openly coming to the throne with hearts receptive to Your truth.

Luke 12:2-3: *But there is nothing covered up that will not be revealed, nor hidden that will not be known. Therefore whatever you have said in the darkness will be heard in the light. What you have spoken in the ear in the inner rooms will be proclaimed on the housetops.*

2 Corinthians 11:14: *And no wonder, for even Satan masquerades as an angel of light.*

Matthew 7:15: *"Beware of false prophets, who come to you in sheep's clothing, but inwardly are ravening wolves.*

Priceless Moments

February 14ᵗʰ
Valentine's Day

As per their usual curiosity, "Grandma, how did Valentine's Day get started?" I began, "February has been associated with romance, a month that marks the start of mating season for birds. Two different legends are around to answer your question. One, this holiday has its roots in a three-day feast when men drew names of women to be matched with during the festival. Roman Emperor Claudius II executed two Christian martyrs named Saint Valentine on February 14. As the holiday spread, its name may have gotten confused with another celebration called Galatin's Day. Second, a theologian and teacher named Valentinus was imprisoned and sentenced to death for his Christian beliefs. From prison, he wrote a farewell note to a girl, signing it "From Your Valentine." The next day, February 14, he died."

"Now, both legends merge. As the years passed, it grew into a sweeter, more loving type of holiday where individuals made cards to express their affection for each other. Soon, the holiday and card-making came across the ocean to America. A card company named Hallmark was the first to make Valentine postcards in 1910 and greeting cards in 1912, and they offered valentines as part of their cards every year. Birds get associated with Valentine's Day since couples are called "love birds." They were excited to get busy and finish their cards.

Sharing special cards is an awesome reminder of how God shares His love with us by sending the very best "special" on a given day, but, unlike the valentines, God's gift is a daily reminder of His love.

Thank You, LORD; You are the sweetest Valentine anyone could ever hope to receive. I pray we understand Your sacrifice to show us Your great love for all mankind.

1 John 4:7: *Beloved, let's love one another, for love is of God; and everyone who loves has been born of God, and knows God.*

1 Corinthians 13:4-7: *Love is patient and is kind. Love doesn't envy. Love doesn't brag, is not proud, doesn't behave itself inappropriately, doesn't seek its own way, is not provoked, takes no account of evil; doesn't rejoice in unrighteousness, but rejoices with the truth; bears all things, believes all things, hopes all things, and endures all things.*

Psalms 5:11-12: *But let all those who take refuge in you rejoice. Let them always shout for joy, because you defend them. Let them also who love your name be joyful in you. For you will bless the righteous. Yahweh, you will surround him with favor as with a shield.*

February 15th
How Do You Spell LOVE?

With young grandchildren in elementary school, they are learning to sound out and spell many new words. It is fun to help them study spelling words, to try to understand how they hear the word, and then assist by using this skill to get them right. One granddaughter asked, "Will you help me study so I can remember how to spell the ten words on this week's list?" We managed to get through most of the words, learning to look for smaller words within each vocabulary word. For example, friend: she could hear the f-r but hesitated on the last four letters, being unsure if the "i" or "e" came first. She had already learned to spell "end" at the beginning of the school year, so I showed her the smaller word in it: the ending of "end." The internal lightbulb lit up, and she got excited: "f-r- i-end. I understand now. Oh, thank you, Grandma. You're the best."

Then she asked, "Will you give me clues about all the words so I can remember them easier?" At her request, we began the guessing game. She did very well on guessing the first nine words. When we got to the last word, I said, "The last one is someone you know and like but Who probably is not related to you physically but spiritually." She gave me the funniest look, then smiled, rattling off, "J-e-s-u-s. I know that wasn't the answer you were looking for, but He's the best friend, f-r-i-e-n-d, a person can have." I said, "B-i-n-g-o. You know more than just your spelling words because you have learned the most important lesson of all."

Sometimes, we need a little help along the way to see parts of things more clearly so the whole picture makes sense. When the internal light bulb goes on and understanding takes place, we accept Jesus as our Savior. This is such an awesome reminder of who our best friend should be: J-E-S-U-S, our LORD.

Thank You, LORD; we have been given the opportunity to accept You and to learn more about You along this journey of our Christian walk. I pray we stay aware of Your leading, be it baby steps or giant leaps, in our faith.

Matthew 11:29: *Take my yoke upon you and learn from me, for I am gentle and humble in heart; and you will find rest for your souls.*

Deuteronomy 32:12: *Yahweh alone led him. There was no foreign god with him.*

Psalm 27:11: *Teach me your way, Yahweh. Lead me in a straight path, because of my enemies.*

February 16th

What's In a Name?

An activity at story time became centered on the grandchildren telling the meaning of their names. Nice idea, I thought. Our oldest granddaughter started, "I was named for my great-grandmother, so

Priceless Moments

I will never forget her. It means *goodness* and *generosity*. She always hugs me and says, "I like your name". Another said, "My name means *life* or *voice*. Another said, "My name means *fairest* or *most beautiful*. Our last girl said, "My name means *God will give*. Our grandson said, "My name means *fire*. Grandma, what does your name mean?" Surprised that he wanted to include me in the activity, I said, "Thank you for asking. My name means loved one. I, too, was named for someone special to me, my great aunt."

As I reflected upon the meaning of each one's name, I said to them, "Together, we all honor God with our names. We can say, 'We are fair and beautiful, using our life and voice God will give us to express His goodness and generosity to light a fire in others for Him because we are His dear loved ones.'" They loved it. "Grandma, can you write that saying down so we can share it with our parents?" "Of course, little ones, I'd be happy to." "Grandma, would it be OK to also share this with our teachers and friends?" "Absolutely."

Reflecting on our fun had become serious to me as I realized that we, indeed, have a mission for our LORD: to take who He created us to be, how He inspired our names, and become a witness on fire for Him because He cherishes each and every one of us as His dear loved ones. Jesus' name means *God is Salvation*, *Healer* and *Savior.*, When we realize how much He loves us, it's easy to share this with everyone we meet.

Thank You, LORD; we are chosen by You and bear Your Holy Name upon our lives. I pray we always think about it and strive to reflect You in the light of Your love and goodness to us. Like the children, may we share who we are in You with others, and remember how You lived up to Your name.

Proverbs 22:1: *A good name is more desirable than great riches, and loving favor is better than silver and gold.*

Isaiah 443:6b-7: *Bring my sons from far away, and my daughters from the ends of the earth— everyone who is called by my name,* *and whom I have created for my glory, whom I have formed, yes, whom I have made.*

Proverbs 18:10: *Yahweh's name is a strong tower: the righteous run to him, and are safe.*

February 17th

Puppy Love

Well, Valentine's Day is over, and love is in the air. "Grandma, my boyfriend gave me this special Valentine. Isn't it pretty? No other girl in the class got one like it, so I feel very special. He even included a heart-shaped lollipop. All the other girls' lollipops were just round." She was beaming as she related her story. "That's nice, honey. Have I met him before? What's his name?" Astonishment crossed her little face. "I don't know." I reminded her, "Look on the back of the card to see his name." Relief crossed her face as she read his name, and she said, "I'm glad he signed this, or I would have to ask one of my friends about his name. That would be so embarrassing."

In came another—her little brother was home from school. "Oh, Grandma, I got a special Valentine from my girlfriend. She gave me a matchbox car, too. I felt so good because no other boy in class got a matchbox car." He showed me her card and gift. Here we go again, I thought. "That is so special. You're a lucky boy. What's her name?" He smiled, saying, "Her name is Sweetie. It's not her real name, but that's what she wants me to call her." I looked at the back of his card, and, sure enough, it was signed Sweetie.

Ah, for the days of *puppy love*, when all seemed right with the world. Yet, reality sets in and our hearts are broken time after time until, one day, God brings a truly special someone into our lives. The initial puppy love grows deeper and stronger every day until a point of no return is reached. We've fallen in love. This is like our relationship with Jesus. We hear about Him from family or friends. We like what we hear and see in them and are drawn into a closer relationship until we reach the point of committing our lives to Him.

Thank You, LORD, for providing Christian family, friends, and even strangers who shared the gospel message with us and led us into a saving knowledge and relationship with You. I pray we can introduce others to You who can move beyond the puppy love stage to become fully dedicated to Your leading and will.

John 3:16: *For God so loved the world, that he gave his one and only Son, that whoever believes in him should not perish, but have eternal life.*

1 John 4:8-9: *He who doesn't love doesn't know God, for God is love. By this God's love was revealed in us, that God has sent his one and only Son into the world that we might live through him.*

John 13:35: *By this everyone will know that you are my disciples, if you have love for one another.*

February 18th

That's Hot!

It's amazing how many times a child can be told, "It's hot. Don't touch. I don't want you to get burned." I found myself saying this after heating soup on the stove. Then… Through a river of tears, she said, "I heard you say not to touch it, but it didn't look that hot. I only saw that little red light in the middle of the stove, not under a burner. I'm so sorry I didn't listen to you. Now, what can you do to help me? It really hurts." I am not good with injuries, so my husband usually takes care of this side of life. Well, he wasn't here, so I'm on it. As I picked up her little hand, I prayed for wisdom and strength.

Priceless Moments

I said, "Dear LORD, we ask You to be with us now and take away her pain. She is Your child, and she needs Your help immediately. Thank You, LORD, for hearing our prayer." Her tear-stained face lifted: "Thank you for praying because it always helps." Previous experience with burned fingers showed me I needed to crush ice in a damp washcloth and wrap it around the palm of her hand. Once done, she said, "It still hurts, but not as bad. Will you rock me and sing songs to me, please?" I grabbed her favorite fleece blanket off the couch, wrapped it around her, and then we rocked and sang until the pain subsided.

I realize there are many times when Scripture and the Holy Spirit warn us not to do certain things, but Satan is there tempting, "Give it a try; it won't hurt anything." That deceiver catches us in a moment of weakness, and we end up stepping out of God's will for our lives. Thankfully, God is there to pick us up, wrap us in His arms of love, and bind our wounds until we are feeling better. He tells us, "It's OK, My child. I forgive you."

Thank You, LORD, for Your forgiving nature and for loving us when we have sinned. I pray the scars left from those experiences are reminders of how much we need to follow Your leading and Word.

Luke 11:28: But he said, "On the contrary, blessed are those who hear the word of God, and keep it."

Jeremiah 33:3: Call to me, and I will answer you, and will show you great and difficult things, which you don't know.

James 1:19: So, then, my beloved brothers, let every man be swift to hear, slow to speak, and slow to anger;

Priceless Moments

February 19th

<u>President's Day</u>

"Our teacher told us we are going to talk about President's Day tomorrow. What is that?" They are curious about learning new things, and I love to cultivate this healthy curiosity. "President's Day is a holiday to celebrate individuals who have served as presidents of our country, the United States of America." "Cool. How many presidents have we had?" "Excellent question," I continued. "To date, we have had forty-six presidencies served by forty-five men." "How come those numbers don't match?" "Another excellent question. One man, Grover Cleveland, served two non-consecutive terms. That means he served four years, the time of service per election, was voted out of office, then won the next time around to serve another four years."

After some thought, another question was asked: "What do those guys do before they become president?" "Some served in the military, as a minister, college professors, lawyers, governors, senators, representatives, another president's cabinet member—meaning they worked for him either at the White House or in another country, Vice Presidents, and some had no previous government experience." "Wow, they were busy guys. What did they do after their time was up?" "Super questions. Some went on to serve as representatives or senators, died in office, or were not re-elected. Most returned to their private lives. With this information, hopefully you will better understand what your teacher shares tomorrow."

It's amazing to realize what the presidents did before and after serving in the White House. Such dedication from them inspires the Christian to be equally devoted to serving God and their fellow man, regardless of their past, present, or future occupation. We should strive to be used right where we are.

Thank You, LORD, for our leaders; both governmental and spiritual. I pray we each find our calling in Your kingdom, fulfilling it to the best of our ability.

Priceless Moments

Psalm 78:72: *So he was their shepherd according to the integrity of his heart, and guided them by the skillfulness of his hands.*

Proverbs 11:14: *Where there is no wise guidance, the nation falls, but in the multitude of counselors there is victory.*

Luke 12:48b: *To whomever much is given, of him will much be required; and to whom much was entrusted, of him more will be asked.*

February 20th
Boy Scouts

"Grandma, why is there an eagle statue and an American flag thing up on the cupboard?" "Your dad received those at his Eagle Scout ceremony as a symbol of all he did and the values he learned. They are the highest award a young man can earn in Boy Scouts. The eagle is a symbol for freedom, longevity, and strength. The plaque with the American flag is to remember his accomplishments. Only six-percent of all scouts earn the rank of Eagle Scout."

"How did he become an Eagle Scout?" "Good question," I said. "As he grew up, through camping trips and other outings, he earned merit badges and ranks, holding different leadership positions, helping others with their scouting work, selling popcorn to earn money for their troop, community service, God and Country badges, and doing a special project at the end." "What did scouting help him do?" "Well, he worked on his character, citizenship, physical and mental fitness, developing new types of skills, and learning more about God. All these things helped him to be a better Christian, son, brother, friend, husband, and now your father. He learned the scout law, oath, motto, slogan, sign, salute, and hand clasp." "Wow," eyes wide, "can he teach me those things?" "I'm sure he can. You'll have to ask him."

Isn't that like us with God? We learn so many things, but they become ingrained when we put them into practice. Each thing by itself tends to be a little lackluster, but things change when they are used for a common goal. In our case, we're moving to the best rank in this world—and the next—a child of God.

Thank You, LORD, for helping us grow in our Christian faith by putting into practice the new things we've learned. I pray we continue to strive for a rank that's *out of this world*.

Hebrews 13:14: *For we don't have here an enduring city, but we seek that which is to come.*

John 15:19: *If you were of the world, the world would love its own. But because you are not of the world, since I chose you out of the world, therefore the world hates you.*

1 Peter 2:12: *Live such good lives among the pagans that, though they accuse you of doing wrong, they may see your good deeds and glorify God on the day He visits us. NIV*

February 21st

Girl Scouts

"Is Girl Scouting a lot like Boy Scouts? Do you know anyone who was a Girl Scout?" "To answer you, 'Yes' and 'Yes.' Since 1912, Juliette Gordon Low had started this group for girls to have new adventures of all kinds while learning positive value-based skills. Your dad's sister, your aunt, received the Gold Award, the highest award for girls. It is equivalent to the Eagle Award. The gold is a symbol for finishing first in a competition of some kind. The percentage of eligible girls earning the Gold Award in only five-point four percent. It takes hard work and dedication to complete

Priceless Moments

badges and a project comparable in difficulty to earn and as prestigious as the Eagle Scout Award."

"How did Auntie earn the Gold Award? Did she have to do things like Daddy did?" "Yes. She worked on badges, participated in campouts, helped her brothers with their Eagle Scout projects, earning all the badges possible every year. She learned her own pledges, motto, handshake, and others just like the boys." "That's really cool. Do you think my sister could learn those, too?" "Anyone who wants to join scouting is able to do so as long as they attend meetings, work on badges, and enjoy what they are doing. It's helpful to the troop that they sell magazines, nuts, and cookies, as much of that money helps pay for activities and supplies."

Thinking of all the planning; designing; securing materials; locating, assigning and directing others throughout; and ultimately, the hard work and dedication it took for our daughter to earn her Gold Award, I'm thankful becoming a Christian is different. The Holy Spirit is our Leader, guiding us through the process of joining the family of God. We don't do good works to earn salvation; rather, we do good works as a result of our salvation.

Thank You, LORD, for individuals with a vision to guide young lives, providing them a broader perspective of life. I pray we can step into those precious lives and provide a love and understanding of You, giving them a broader perspective of Christianity as the only way to have fulfillment, peace, and true joy in life.

John 15:12: *This is my commandment, that you love one another, even as I have loved you.*

Matthew 5:16: *Even so, let your light shine before men, that they may see your good works and glorify your Father who is in heaven.*

Romans 12:18: *If it is possible, as much as it is up to you, be at peace with all men.*

Priceless Moments

February 22nd

Washington's Birthday

"Hey, Grandma. I remember hearing something about George Washington on President's Day. Today, our teacher said his name again. Can you tell me more about him?" "He was our very first president. They wanted to make him king, but he didn't think a ruler should be a lifetime position. Instead, he chose the term president, serving for eight crucial years in our history. Some important things to remember about him are these: He added the words *So help me, God* to the presidential oath; he relied on God and counseled his troops and fellow Americans to do the same; he was honest, known for saying "I cannot tell a lie;" he resisted political pressure; he was *first in war* by discouraging the enemy from attack, and *first in peace* by always being ready for war and letting the enemy know it; he believed he must preserve the constitution, the principles by which we are governed; and that our freedom must include responsibility, personally and as a nation.

"Wow, Grandma, he must have had Jesus living in his heart if he would say, "So help me, God." I think he wanted us to be responsible for our own behaviors and things we do and to put God and country first. Is that why you like to wear red, white, and blue?" "That is one reason," I said. "Those colors also represent Jesus: red for His blood shed for us; white for His righteousness or being just and pure; and blue represents heaven, the color of the sky."

It's amazing that a godly president was unashamed to declare his faith at home and around the world. He stated that religion and morality were necessary for good government. How far we have drifted from those tenets. There is a statement by the philosopher John Stewart that "The only thing necessary for the triumph of evil is for good men to do nothing." We need to stand up for our faith in all arenas of life, regardless of backlash or persecution. Remember, Jesus stood up for us."

Thank You, LORD, for Your conviction to save a fallen world. I pray You help us to do the same.

Psalm 33:12: *Blessed is the nation whose God is Yahweh, the people whom he has chosen for his own inheritance.*

Philippians 3:20: *For our citizenship is in heaven, from where we also wait for a Savior, the Lord Jesus Christ,*

Acts 5:29: *But Peter and the apostles answered, "We must obey God rather than men."*

February 23rd
<u>*My Favorite Babysitter*</u>

"Grandma, do you know who our favorite babysitter is?" To me, that seems like a loaded question, so I asked, "Not really. Who is it?" They replied, "You silly Grandma, you know it has to be you. Even though you make us listen, you always let us do fun things together and watch some movies when we show you good behavior. Did you really not know that?" "Let's say," I started, "I was hoping that was the answer. Sometimes you get really upset with me when I tell you it is time to wash your hands for supper, get dressed for bed, pick up your toys, or make your bed."

They got really quiet, thinking of a good comeback: "There are times we ask you to do some things and you don't have time." I asked, "Like what? I need examples." Again, silence filled the room. A retort: "Like when you say you need to make dinner or change the baby's diaper." Ah, two can play this game. "Next time you ask me to play around dinner time, we just won't eat. As for changing the baby's diaper, that is not negotiable. It must be done, but we don't have to eat." A chorus of "You win." rang out. They were helpful in setting the table and making dinner. Before bedtime prayers, the kids wanted to read the book *How to Babysit a Grandma.* I guess they thought I needed some more ideas.

At times, God must look at us as a bunch of children who love Him one minute and question Him the next, seldom satisfied with our lot in life, always wanting something a little different, or questioning His leading. Fortunately for us, He loves us in spite of our behavior and desires fellowship with us.

Thank You, LORD, for calling us to account when we start to get out of hand. I pray we understand Your correction and heed it promptly to avoid further discipline, not looking at You as our babysitter, but as our LORD and Savior.

Psalm 116:2: *Because he has turned his ear to me, therefore I will call on him as long as I live.*

2 Peter 2:20: *For if, after they have escaped the defilement of the world through the knowledge of the Lord and Savior Jesus Christ, they are again entangled in it and overcome, the last state has become worse for them than the first.*

Proverbs 31:26: *She opens her mouth with wisdom. Kind instruction is on her tongue.*

February 24th

Who Were They?

Have you ever talked to some people who acted like they knew you, only to question yourself after they walked away? "Who were they?" The other day, the grandchildren and I were out shopping. A couple stopped us and starting talking about the weather, the kids, and how was school going—all appropriate questions that fit our circumstances perfectly. After they walked on, the kids asked, "Grandma, who was that? How do you know them? They seemed really friendly and knew a lot about us." These comments caught me off guard." I responded, "I thought they were someone you kids knew; therefore, they were polite to me as well. How else would they know so much about all of us?"

As we tried to figure out the connection between all of us, our granddaughter said, "Jesus must have told them who we were and asked them to come over and be polite to us. How else would they be able to talk so nicely to us?" Good response, I thought. I said, "Maybe they have been watching us and saw how well we treated each other with respect and consideration and wanted to meet us."

I thought of how often others observe our interactions within our family or friend groups when we are in public. I know I have observed others and whispered a prayer for God to open their hearts and minds to become aware of their inappropriate behavior towards others in their group or regarding others who have passed by them. Then, I whispered a prayer for myself to show love and kindness to family, friends, and strangers alike.

Thank You, LORD, for acknowledging us as Your own. I pray we stay as faithful as You are and claim You at every opportunity we get, not forsaking You when it would seem better for us to deny You. You have set the standard, and we must rise to the occasion to meet it.

Hebrews 13:16: But don't forget to be doing good and sharing, for with such sacrifices God is well pleased.

1 Thessalonians 5:18: In everything give thanks, for this is the will of God in Christ Jesus toward you.

James 1:12: Blessed is a person who endures temptation, for when he has been approved, he will receive the crown of life, which the Lord promised to those who love him.

February 25th
Honesty First

I remember teaching our children to be honest with themselves, us, others, and God. Years later, this same lesson is being repeated with the grandchildren. During playtime, we observed our one granddaughter hitting her sister. I said, "Excuse me, honey, why did you hit your sister?" She looked me in the eye and said, "I didn't hit her." I questioned, "Then why is your sister sitting there crying? And see the red mark on her arm? How did that get there?" Again, she looked me in the eye and said, "I don't know."

Trying to maintain a loving voice and demeanor, I said, "Would you want her to hit you, then tell me she didn't do it?" Her head dropped, and she threw her arms around her sister, saying, "Sissy, I'm sorry I hit you. I wanted the toy you were playing with. I didn't want to ask because I knew you would say "No." I thought you would drop it if I hit you, but you didn't." I said, "Thank you for telling the truth. I know that is hard to do, but telling a lie is even harder." She asked, "Why?" I responded, "Once you tell a lie, you have to remember what you said in case you have to tell another lie. It soon gets to be hard to keep all the lies straight. That's when you get caught and punished. When your dad was little, we told them to be honest the first time, and the punishment will be less compared to telling several lies and then getting caught. At that point, the punishment will be worse."

I realize how disappointed God is with us when we try to lie to others, since there is no *big*, *little*, or *white* lies. A lie is a lie. It may not be discovered by those it affects, but God knows. We won't be able to sweet-talk our way out of it with Him. It can only be dealt with by asking forgiveness from God and the unsuspecting person we attempted to hurt or protect, whichever is the case.

Thank You, LORD, that there is forgiveness in Your plan for our lives, be it against somebody else or You. I pray our hearts are tender and open to Your voice of correction. The sooner we heed

Your correction, the less long-term damage it can do to our soul and to our witness to others.

Leviticus 19:11*: You shall not steal. You shall not lie. You shall not deceive one another.*

Proverbs 6:16-19*: There are six things which Yahweh hates; yes, seven which are an abomination to him: arrogant eyes, a lying tongue, hands that shed innocent blood, a heart that devises wicked schemes, feet that are swift in running to mischief, a false witness who utters lies, and he who sows discord among brothers.*

1 Corinthians 6:9*: Or don't you know that the unrighteous will not inherit God's Kingdom? Don't be deceived.*

February 26th
But They Need To Eat, Too

When I was cooking dinner one evening, the grandchildren asked, "Can we cook extra food tonight?" I asked, "Why would you like extra food? I am not sure if we have enough extra to add to what we have started." They added, "Well, we could go to the store and get more, if needed." Again, I asked, "Why do you want more food?" They started, "You know those people who don't have anything? We are talking about them and realize they need to eat, too. We haven't taken them anything for a while." I told them, "I'm so proud of you guys for thinking about and being concerned about others. Let's look at what we have here to see if we need to go to the store or not. We can be creative in our choices with some plain, down-home fun." They cheered, "Yes, let's do that now. It should be a lot of fun."

Careful scrutinizing of the pantry and refrigerator enabled us to add crackers and cheese, an extra tossed salad kit, extra green beans, and cornbread to our menu of Cuban chicken and rice. The

Priceless Moments

excited youngsters exclaimed, "We did it. All the extras we needed are here. We will really make a great meal with enough leftovers to take over to the neighbors without having to buy anything. Can I make the cornbread?" "Why don't we do it together?" After supper, we packaged up the extras and gave them to the *needy neighbors*.

I thought about why the kids perceive the neighbors to be a needy couple. No reason was apparent to me. I wondered, "Do others perceive us to be something we are not? Do we play the part of a Christian or really live the part? How do we relate to others?" This led to a season of prayer and soul-searching.

Thank You, LORD, that our perception of You is that You are holy, genuine, loving, kind, and faithful. I pray we do not send out mixed signals to others but display a consistent, authentic relationship with You.

Acts 14:17: Yet he didn't leave himself without witness, in that he did good and gave you rains from the sky and fruitful seasons, filling our hearts with food and gladness.

Ephesians 4:32: And be kind to one another, tender hearted, forgiving each other, just as God also in Christ forgave you.

Proverbs 19:17: He who has pity on the poor lends to Yahweh; he will reward him.

February 27th

My Favorite Food

"Grandma, can we fix our favorite food now? We are really getting hungry and will do what we can to help you." I just had to ask, "What is your favorite food? And I don't know if we would have what we need to make it." "Come on, Grandma. You know we love Papa's kind of pizza, made with ham and lots of

Priceless Moments

pineapple. Do you have any ham and pineapple? And, anyway, why does Papa like those kinds of toppings together?" Funny they would ask. "Of course, there is ham in the refrigerator and pineapple in the pantry. Papa has liked those toppings since his military days in Hawaii, where they grow fresh pineapple. He used to make it with fresh pineapple, saying it gave the pizza an extra special taste."

We gathered the ingredients. "Grandma, can I mix the crust? I love to mix it up and pat it into the pan." Helpers volunteering to help: "Sure you can." "Hey, Grandma, I can chop up the ham and pineapple." I said, "That leaves me to preheat the oven, grease the pizza pan, and sit back to watch you guys work. Every good job needs a supervisor." They laughed, having fun doing their part for our special treat. The pizza was assembled and popped into the oven. As the aroma began to stimulate our sense of smell, I heard, "Can I have the first piece? It smells so good." The other child responded, "But, I want the first piece." I jumped in before the argument went further. "We'll compromise. I'll cut the pizza and give each of you a piece at the same time." They were both happy with that.

Our lives are like a piece of pizza. We get divided into so many portions or different obligations that we become exhausted trying to keep up. We end up picking our favorite and dropping the rest. We must remember to keep God as the top priority portion of our lives, tapping into the *"food to eat that you know nothing about."*

Thank You, LORD, for making mankind a top priority in Your creation plans and on to Your return day. I pray we realize we are the *topping* of Your creation, Your favorite creation, and that we are very good.

Genesis 1:27, 31a: *God created man in his own image. In God's image he created him; male and female he created them. God saw everything that he had made, and, behold, it was very good*

Priceless Moments

Revelation 4:11: *"Worthy are you, our Lord and God, the Holy One to receive the glory, the honor, and the power, for you created all things, and because of your desire they existed, and were created!"*

Ephesians 4:23-24: *and that you be renewed in the spirit of your mind, **and** put on the new man, who in the likeness of God has been created in righteousness and holiness of truth.*

February 28th
Maple Syrup Fun

"Hey, kids, do you know how maple syrup was discovered and how it is used?" A few of the ideas suggested were very interesting. They guessed, "It was found in stores; it's made by bees; and someone decided to make a new recipe, but it didn't work, but they ended up discovering the syrup"—to name a few. "Those are some good ideas," I said. "Actually, God created dry ground, allowing trees to appear when all kinds of trees were formed. There are three legends centered around the Iroquois Indians. One says the Chief saw squirrels drinking maple sap. Another time, the Chief threw his tomahawk into a maple tree in the winter, only to discover later that sap was running out of the tree. Thirdly, they saw sap running out of a broken tree branch. They used the sap to cure their meat.

"Today, trees are tapped between mid-February and mid-March, collecting sap in metal buckets before progressing to using tubing systems to collect the sap. It takes forty gallons of sap cooked, or reduced down, to make one gallon of syrup. Now, three different grades of syrup, which provide vitamins and minerals to support a healthy body, can be used to make pancake syrup, or candy, a natural sweetener for ice cream, a topping for hot cereal, to cook vegetables, as an icing for cinnamon rolls."

Priceless Moments

Such a sweet treat leads to sweet memories of the glorious ways nature continues to feed and treat us. God had such a special plan at creation that even with Adam and Eve's sin, He still found ways to care for us.

Thank You, LORD, for Your every-day provisions dating back to the beginning of time. Your foresight is beyond understanding. I pray we thank You again and again for including sweet treats as part of Your plan.

Genesis 1:9: *God said, "Let the waters under the sky be gathered together to one place, and let the dry land appear;" and it was so.*

Psalm 1:3: *He will be like a tree planted by the streams of water, that produces its fruit in its season, whose leaf also does not wither. Whatever he does shall prosper.*

Revelation 22:14: *Blessed are those who do his commandments, that they may have the right to the tree of life, and may enter in by the gates into the city.*

February 29th

Leap Year

"What is a leap year, why do we have it, and how often do we get one?" "Those are all excellent questions. Let's see if I can answer them for you. Leap year occurs once every four years when the year can be divided by four, adding an extra day to our calendar on February 29th, giving us 366 days instead of the usual 365. Two time measurements are involved. The earth rotates on its axis every 24 hours to make one day. This is done to correct for the actual rotation of the earth around the sun being 365.24 days per year. This almost quarter of a day is added up over the four years, which makes a whole day, causing the extra day in February since it was already the shortest month." "Wow. How long have we been doing this correction thing?" "Scientific advisors to Julius Caesar noticed the years were getting out of sync with the seasons. The Roman Emperor decided to correct this by adding an extra day every four years."

"By 1582, Pope Gregory XIII was told the alignment of seasons and time had continued to drift by ten days. He decided to take ten days out of October, jumping from the 4th to the 15th. In addition, if the end of the century year could be divided by 400, an extra day would be added to make up for the lost 0.1 of a day every year. This became known as the Gregorian calendar, the one we use now." "What happens if your birthday is February 29? Do they still get to celebrate?" "Yes, they do. They celebrate the day after February 28, which is March 1."

I marvel at how much children absorb and the depth of their questions to gain understanding. We need to keep that childlike sense of wonder and curiosity to delve into Your Word, seeking answers about You and eternity.

Thank You, LORD, for giving us minds full of curiosity. I pray we develop a greater curiosity for the things You have documented for us to prepare us to stimulate the curiosity of others to learn of You as well.

Proverbs 27:20: *Just as Death and Destruction are never satisfied, so human desire is never satisfied. NIV*

Ecclesiastes 1:8: *All things are full of weariness beyond uttering. The eye is not satisfied with seeing, nor the ear filled with hearing.*

1 Peter 1:14: *as children of obedience, not conforming yourselves according to your former lusts as in your ignorance,*

Priceless Moments

March

See that you don't despise one of these little ones, for I tell you that in heaven their angels always see the face of my Father who is in heaven.

Matthew. 18:10

Priceless Moments

March 1ˢᵀ
Just Checking In

"Grandma, can we go to the playground or a park? We haven't gone in a long time. It's not very cold out today, so we could go for a while, then come back home… or go out for lunch, if you'd like." "Since you are home from school on the holiday, why not go have some fun?" I checked for a gift card to one of their favorite restaurants—as a surprise, especially since it was hinted at in their question. "Your behavior and cooperation will be the determining factors in what we do." We loaded up and headed off—to the playground. The kids basically had the place to themselves, so they were privileged to play on the equipment of their choice. We weaved our way from one side to the other until my phone rang. I saw it was a call I needed to take.

I told them where I was going to sit and talk, but I wanted them to stay close. After a few minutes, our granddaughter came over and said, "I'm just checking in," then left to play. Still in my sights, I saw her coming again, saying, "I'm just checking in," before leaving again. When my call ended, I walked over to the kids to see how much longer they wanted to stay and play. They said, "We're ready to go eat," so we headed to the car. On the way, I asked our granddaughter, "Why did you check in with me several times?" She responded, "Because I wanted to be sure you were OK." That touched me deeply, so I gave her a big, long hug—and took them out to lunch.

How often do we say to God, "It's me, LORD; I'm just checking in today. I want you to know I need You every second of every minute of every hour of every day for the rest of my life." I'm sure He likes to hear us come to Him to check in, not only in times of need or want, but just to express our appreciation for Who He is.

Thank You, LORD, for always being willing to listen each time we come to You. I pray we continually make a concerted effort to check in with You daily to be sure all is well with our soul.

Priceless Moments

Psalm 33:22: *Let your loving kindness be on us, Yahweh, since we have hoped in you.*

Isaiah 41:10: *Don't you be afraid, for I am with you. Don't be dismayed, for I am your God. I will strengthen you. Yes, I will help you. Yes, I will uphold you with the right hand of my righteousness.*

John 14:27: *Peace I leave with you. My peace I give to you; not as the world gives, I give to you. Don't let your heart be troubled, neither let it be fearful.*

March 2nd
<u>I Love Animals</u>

"Oh, Grandma, we went to the zoo, and we saw all kinds of animals. A lot of them we've seen before, but a lot were new to me." "Nice. Which one was your favorite?" "I really liked the koala bears. They look so cute and cuddly. Truly, I really liked them all. What can you tell me about animals?" "First off, animals are divided into many categories: mammals—meaning they are warm-blooded, mothers nurse their young, they all have hair; fish—they have a backbone, live under water, breathe in oxygen through their gills; birds—they have feathers and wings, lay eggs in a nest; reptiles—they are cold-blooded and have scales; amphibians—they are also cold-blooded, their skin is smooth and moist; invertebrates—they don't have a backbone, including all bugs."

"What does it mean to be cold and warm-blooded? I've never heard that before." "Cold-blooded means the animals have a body temperature that changes with the environment. Warm-blooded animals keep a steady body temperature all year round." "Can you give an example to help me understand what you're saying?"

"Sure. Fish and reptiles live in water, and as water temperatures change throughout the year, so does the body temperature of these types of animals. We are considered warm-blooded animals, so we keep the same body temperature all year long. Our temperature only changes when we're sick." "Cool. I want to look at more animals now and see which category they fit into best."

Reviewing all the information was really fun. I enjoyed seeing their eyes light up as they shared, asked questions, and took away something new.

Thank You, LORD, for the diversity of the animals in Your creation. I pray our eyes light up with excitement when we learn something new about them, since it will also reveal something more about You and Your love for each part of creation.

Genesis 1:24-25: God said, "Let the earth produce living creatures after their kind, livestock, creeping things, and animals of the earth after their kind;" and it was so. God made the animals of the earth after their kind, and the livestock after their kind, and everything that creeps on the ground after its kind. God saw that it was good.

Psalm 50:11: I know all the birds of the mountains. The wild animals of the field are mine.

Proverbs 12:10: A righteous man respects the life of his animal, but the tender mercies of the wicked are cruel,

March 3rd

The Turkey Parade

There is a flock of turkeys that like to hang out in the trees nearby our sons' house as well as parade across their backyard. If you're lucky enough to be looking out the kitchen window when they're visiting, you can see up to four hens and four toms. The males

Priceless Moments

would strut, spreading their tail feathers and dragging their wings, trying to impress the females. One day the grandchildren were eating breakfast at the counter when the turkeys decided to make their appearance. "Hey, Grandma, look at that. Do you see those turkeys out there? The ones that spread their feathers are called toms, and the skinny little ones behind them are called hens." "That's right. Do you know why the toms do that behavior?" "Yeah, they're trying to get a date."

I almost lost it. I didn't dare ask where he got that idea, but he was pretty much on target with his response. "You are correct. It's a form of courtship, letting the females know how healthy and strong they are and that they would be a good choice for a mate." "Gee, they act just like we do. I like a girl in my class, and she likes me. She even invited me to her birthday party." He sat there and puffed out his little chest as he shared that little tidbit of information. I said, "Wow, aren't you the lucky little man, and she is one lucky little girl." He was grinning from ear to ear.

God must chuckle at us as we strut around in front of others, trying to be noticed. We should always have our eyes on the LORD, and He will bring the people and things into our lives that we need. His choices for us are always better than those we make without Him.

Thank You, LORD, for always being there when we call upon You to make our choices. I pray Your answer, either in favor of or against, is heeded because You know what is best for us.

Matthew 6:33: But seek first God's Kingdom and his righteousness; and all these things will be given to you as well.

Exodus 20:3: You shall have no other gods before me.

Proverbs 3:9-10: Honor Yahweh with your substance, with the first fruits of all your increase: so your barns will be filled with plenty, and your vats will overflow with new wine.

March 4th

Parade of Bucks and Does

A beautiful sight in our son's back and front yards is the parade of stags and hinds. At the base of the driveway is a magnificent mulberry tree, the delight of all—human and animal—who pass by. One morning our granddaughter said, "Oh, look. Oh, come quick, Grandma. The deer are crossing in the backyard." We watched as the kids counted six large bucks and four does taking their time to traverse the yard over to the neighbor's apple trees. "Oh, look, Grandma. That one deer is trying to climb the tree to get to the apples. Look, another one is rubbing his antlers on the tree trunk. Can we go outside and watch?" "No, I think you are safer inside and can see quite well from here." We watched them for about thirty minutes before they moved on into the woods.

That evening, a shriek of "Look everyone, now. Don't wait. You have to see this. Hurry." The urgency in her voice commanded everyone to the front windows. "Look. Aren't they beautiful. I've never seen so many bucks in one place." As we looked out the window, there were twelve bucks lined up, looking at the house like they were posing for a picture. Some were standing behind others who were kneeling, antlers all up, straight, eyes forward, all ready for their photo op. "Daddy, please, please, please take a picture before they move." Our son pulled out his phone and documented this spectacular sight with a picture-taking session.

I thought of what an awesome experience it was to view so many of God's magnificent creatures in one spot, all calm and observing us as much as we were observing them. What is even better is to view a full sanctuary each time the church doors are opened, full of people lined up and ready for God to take our picture as we worship Him.

Thank You, LORD, for providing so much beauty in every part of Your creation. I pray we take every opportunity to enjoy nature and fellowship, both precious gifts from Your hand.

Jeremiah 10:6: *There is no one like you, Yahweh. You are great, and your name is great in might.*

Psalm 96:4: *For Yahweh is great, and greatly to be praised! He is to be feared above all gods.*

Ephesians 3:20, 21: *Now to him who is able to do exceedingly abundantly above all that we ask or think, according to the power that works in us, o him be the glory in the assembly and in Christ Jesus to all generations forever and ever. Amen.*

March 5th
<u>Turkey and Deer</u>

One morning as I was doing devotions, the grandchildren arrived on the scene for the day, yelling, "Come quick, Grandma, come quick, come quick! You've got to see this, Grandma. Come quick, come quick!" I wasn't sure what or if anything had happened, so I rose quickly and ran to the door. Across the field, I could see turkey and deer playing back-and-forth with each other, quite a sight to behold., "Grandma, do you see that one deer chasing the turkey, and then the turkey chases the deer? They are having so much fun together. I've never seen anything like this before. Can we watch them a little while before we have to go inside?" After observing such frivolity in nature, I replied, "Absolutely. I'm really enjoying the fun. I've never seen anything like this before either."

We observed them playing back and forth for fifteen minutes before they decided to move on, the deer going one way and the turkey another. As we walked back inside, our granddaughter commented, "Those animals are so different, yet they found a way to get along. I wish some of the kids in my class would realize their differences are given by God so He can help us do more for Him."

Pause. The wisdom of a seven-year-old transcends most of the adults in this world. She should give each of us a reality check. We need to look beyond the outside trappings of our earthly bodies and into the souls of those around us. If we take the time to do so, we'll find out we are more alike than different. Yet, all of us are here to serve our LORD.

Thank You, LORD, for our individual spirits designed to work together for a common purpose. I pray we use this common ground to be more in tune with each other, reach out to the unsaved, and usher them into Your kingdom.

__Proverbs 12:10__: A righteous man respects the life of his animal, but the tender mercies of the wicked are cruel.

__Job 35:11__: Who teaches us more than the animals of the earth, and makes us wiser than the birds of the sky?

__James 3:7__: For every kind of animal, bird, creeping thing, and sea creature, is tamed, and has been tamed by mankind;

March 6th

What Smells So Good?

At any given point throughout the day on Thursdays, family dinner night, you can smell a wonderful aroma coming from something in the oven, crockpot, or instant pot. Last night, I put a roast in the crockpot to flavor and cook. This morning, the aroma filled the whole house. I cut up the roast, added onions, carrots, and potatoes, and replaced the lid. When the kids arrived for breakfast, our granddaughter said, "I thought we came for breakfast, but I don't smell hash browns, sausage, or eggs, like you promised." Her countenance fell as she slowly walked to the table. Then a glimmer of hope appeared as her eyes focused on the table. "Yes, my favorite breakfast. But what smells so good?"

I explained, "I started supper cooking last night and finished it this morning, so we have a full day to play. I wanted all our time together to be fun." "I know what we can do that would be fun. We can make a dessert because I don't see anything on the counter." I inquired, "How do you know there isn't something ready in the refrigerator?" Her eyes twinkled as she replied, "Because I know you. You always save this part for us to do together. I'm right, aren't I?" "You've got me. Indeed, we do have a dessert to make later." She blurted out, "What are we going to make?" True to form, I replied, "I guess you will have to wait and see to be sure you eat all your breakfast." "No problem, Grandma, no problem."

Many times, we think we are to do one thing but end up being led in a different direction. Was it our wishful thinking before clarifying it with God, or were we just not sure of His leading to begin with? Confusion can reign until we seek God's face to know His will, being still long enough to listen to avoid rushing off blindly.

Thank You, LORD, for giving us ears and a heart to listen to Your still, small voice. I pray that the more we wait upon You, the sooner we begin to recognize Your voice and become more productive in Your kingdom.

John 10:27: *My sheep hear my voice, and I know them, and they follow me.*

Isaiah 40:11: *He will feed his flock like a shepherd. He will gather the lambs in his arm, and carry them in his bosom. He will gently lead those who have their young.*

Revelation 3:20: *Behold, I stand at the door and knock. If anyone hears my voice and opens the door, then I will come in to him, and will dine with him, and he with me.*

Priceless Moments

March 7th

Peanut Butter Pie

My granddaughter and I were home alone when she asked, "Is it time for us to make a special treat for supper?" She had done really well with not asking until this point, so I said, "Sure, it's time. What would you like to make?" She thought a minute, then said, "I'm really hungry for peanut butter pie. Do you have everything we need to make that?" I told her, "There's only one way to find out. Let's go check out the refrigerator and the pantry to see if we need to go to the store." Fortunately, we found everything we needed, pulling it out from its current location."

"Grandma, can I measure stuff and put it in the mixer?" What a good practical experience it is to read a recipe and follow it through to completion, so I told her, "Sure. But what am I supposed do while you do all the work?" Her response brought a smile to my face. "You can be my supervisor, making sure I don't do anything wrong." I said, "I can do that for you." She whipped the ingredients together to make a luscious consistency, stirring frequently to be sure the peanut butter was thoroughly mixed in. The project was in capable hands and soon ready to be popped in the refrigerator. She perked up and asked, "Do you know the one thing I like more than making this?" I knew what she would say but didn't want to deny her the pleasure of saying it. "No. What do you like more than making this pie?" Her eyes danced as she responded, "Eating it." I said, "Good answer. Me, too. I can't wait until supper."

I thought it was so nice to do things with her. God must feel pleased to work with us, too, when we follow His *recipe* to complete His given project, with Him as the Supervisor. His guidance results in the fruits of our labor being something all of us can enjoy at a later time.

Thank You, LORD, Your recipe book never changes, but it always remains the same. I pray we can appreciate Your consistency in all You ask us to do.

Hebrews 13:8: *Jesus Christ is the same yesterday, today, and forever.*

Malachi 3:6: *For I, Yahweh, don't change; therefore you, sons of Jacob, are not consumed.*

James 1:17: *Every good gift and every perfect gift is from above, coming down from the Father of lights, with whom can be no variation, nor turning shadow.*

March 8th
Can I Make a Wish?

It was a lovely night outside when, across the expanse of the sky, we saw a shooting star. The grandchildren knew the song *When You Wish Upon a Star* and asked, "Do we get to make a wish upon that shooting star? Jiminy Cricket sang a song about it in the movie *Pinocchio*." "I think it's OK to make a wish as long as you realize shooting stars can't make your wish come true. If you wish for something good, you can use it as a goal to work towards making it a reality. Even Jesus made a wish before going to the cross, asking His Heavenly Father if there were another way to save mankind, but He ended His prayer by saying, *"Father, if You are willing, take this cup from Me; yet not My will, but Yours be done."* (**Luke 22:42**) We need to be sure to follow Jesus' example and always end our requests asking for God's will to be done."

We all made a wish upon the shooting star, only to see another one make a quick trek across the sky. "Can we make another wish?" "Of course, but I think it may be a busy night for making wishes." An inquisitive question: "Why do you say that, Grandma?" I acknowledged, "The reason we are out here tonight is to watch a meteor shower or shooting stars. If we are in the right spot at the right time in a dark location, we can see plenty of them. When you see another shooting star, watch in the same area since they tend to follow a similar path." "Oh, look, there's another, and another. It's a good night to be out, right, Grandma."

I'm always impressed when the kids can tell you where they heard something and from whom they heard it. I found my heart wishing we knew our Bibles as well, so we could quote when and where something was said and by whom and give the application behind each verse.

Thank You, LORD, for giving us unlimited access to Your Word, commentaries, pastors, Christian friends, and You to interpret the parts we do not understand. I pray we avail ourselves of these resources to fully understand the things You want us to know and hide those truths in our hearts and minds for quick retrieval when needed.

John 15:7: *If you remain in me, and my words remain in you, you will ask whatever you desire, and it will be done for you.*

Matthew 7:7: *Ask, and it will be given you. Seek, and you will find. Knock, and it will be opened for you.*

Genesis 12:3: *I will bless those who bless you, and I will curse him who treats you with contempt. All the families of the earth will be blessed through you.*

March 9th

Track

"Do you see them running, Grandma? They are really fast. I know my Daddy and Mommy run faster than they do, but these kids are so much fun to watch." I smiled at him and said, "You're right. Your parents are fast. Daddy ran cross-country and track in high school and many other types of races after he graduated. After your parents met, they did many races together. Papa and I would

Priceless Moments

travel around different places to watch them." His eyes grew wide. "Wow. Did you guys ever run, too?" "As a matter of fact, we ran several races with them as well as with your other Papa. Several years in a row, we all placed in our respective age groups. It was a lot of fun."

He was quiet for a few minutes. "If there are lots of people in our family who are runners, do you think I will be a runner someday? If so, what will I have to do to be a runner?" Oh, he's planning ahead. "A good place to start is to wear a good pair of running shoes before walking each day, working up to thirty minutes. When you feel comfortable with this, mix walking for two minutes and running for one minute, lengthening the running time over walking until you are running for the entire thirty minutes. Gradually increase your time to build up how long you can run, called endurance, before working to build up speed." "Thanks, but how do you know that?" "I used to teach a group of women in a beginning runner's group."

Teaching running reminded me of teaching new Christians to increase their faith. After accepting Jesus, we need to be there to mentor these babies in Christ, helping them grow and develop their faith and answering all their questions until they are ready to go out on their own and disciple others.

Thank You, LORD; we can see You in all things. I pray each of us gladly picks up the mantle and runs the race set before us to take as many people as possible with us to heaven to live with You eternally.

__Hebrews 12:1:__ Therefore let's also, seeing we are surrounded by so great a cloud of witnesses, lay aside every weight and the sin which so easily entangles us, and let's run with perseverance the race that is set before us, "Therefore, since we are surrounded by such a great cloud of witnesses, let us throw off everything that hinders and the sin that so easily entangles. And let us run with perseverance the race marked out for us."

Priceless Moments

2 Timothy 4:7: *I have fought the good fight. I have finished the course. I have kept the faith.*

Isaiah 40:31: *but those who wait for Yahweh will renew their strength. They will mount up with wings like eagles. They will run, and not be weary. They will walk, and not faint.*

March 10th
Daylight Savings Time

"Grandma, Daddy said we had to go to bed early last night because of something called lights time saved, or something like that. Do you know what it is?" "Yes, I do if you mean daylight savings time." "Yes, that's what he said. Why do we do it?" "When we turn the clock ahead one hour in March, it's called daylight savings time, allowing us to make better use of the daylight longer in the evening hours as well as to enable us to sleep more in the darkness and reduce crime. The process is reversed in the fall." "But how can I remember which is which?" "There is a saying, 'Spring ahead and fall back.'" "But who decides when to do this?" "The U.S. Department of Transportation is in charge of the consistent observance in each of our nations different time zones so they can keep track of transportation." "What are time zones?" "You know how we call your aunts and uncles at different times from here, always checking to be sure it's not too early or too late? That consideration is because we live in different time zones."

"When did someone get the idea to try such a thing?" "It was first tried in Thunder Bay, Canada, in 1908. In 1966, President Lyndon B. Johnson signed the Uniform Time Act as a way to conserve energy." "How could this help conserve energy?" "If there is more natural light later in the evening, people would not need to use as much electricity in the home. Surprisingly, Benjamin Franklin suggested daylight savings time in the 1780s to save money on candles. Something called the Sunshine Protection Act was introduced in January 2021, proposing to permanently extend daylight savings time year-round, but it has not been accepted by Congress."

I thought of how time zones are irrelevant to our LORD. He is never interrupted by the changes we make, whether good or bad, down here. Regardless of our location or what we are doing, He is available to hear our petitions and praises 24/7/365.

Thank You, LORD, You are never too busy, sleeping, or on vacation when we call upon You. I pray we return the same consideration by keeping in touch with You as well.

Psalm 121:3-4: *He will not allow your foot to be moved. He who keeps you will not slumber.*
Behold, he who keeps Israel will neither slumber nor sleep.

Psalm 121:5-8: *Yahweh is your keeper. Yahweh is your shade on your right hand. The sun will not harm you by day, nor the moon by night. Yahweh will keep you from all evil. He will keep your soul. Yahweh will keep your going out and your coming in, from this time forward, and forever more.*

Isaiah 40:31: *but those who wait for Yahweh will renew their strength. They will mount up with wings like eagles. They will run, and not be weary. They will walk, and not faint.*

March 11th

The Jeweled Pen

Our granddaughter gave me a jewel-tipped pen for Christmas. She said, "I wanted to give you something I would want myself. As I looked at the different things available, I thought of how much I see you write. I looked at many types of pens but chose this one because it was the prettiest. The other pens didn't have jewels on

Priceless Moments

top of them." I smiled and said, "Thank you so much. It is the perfect gift, and I love it, but not as much as I love you." She was all smiles, jumping into my arms and giving me a big hug. "Oh, Grandma, I love you more than you love me—and you are very welcome."

She went and played for a little while, only to return and ask, "Grandma, after you use the pen for a while, if you don't want it anymore, you can give it to me. I promise you I will take good care of it if you decide you want it back. I might put the jewel in my princess's crown." I was taken aback by her comment. After recovering from the surprise remark, I told her, "Let me try it for a few days, then I will give it back to you." She danced across the floor, singing, "I love you, I love you, I love you, dear Grandma."

I realized how much she loved this pen, the same way God loves each of us so deeply and completely. We pray we earn jewels in our crowns. Yet God did not hesitate to give His Son to set each one of us free from the shackles of sin, not asking for Him back. Rather, God had to turn His back on His Son so the plan of redemption could be realized for all mankind.

Thank You, LORD, for valuing us so much that no price was too high to pay for our ransom. I pray we understand the depth of Your love for us.

1 Corinthians 6:20*: for you were bought with a price. Therefore glorify God in your body and in your spirit, which are God's.*

Titus 2:13, 14*: looking for the blessed hope and appearing of the glory of our great God and Savior, Jesus Christ, who gave himself for us, that he might redeem us from all iniquity, and purify for himself a people for his own possession, zealous for good works.*

1 Peter 1:18-19*: knowing that you were redeemed, not with corruptible things, with silver or gold, from the useless way of life handed down from your fathers, but with precious blood, as of a lamb without blemish or spot, the blood of Christ,*

March 12th
BINGO

We started playing BINGO with the children to help them recognize numbers on their cards and to serve as callers for additional practice saying the numbers. Our first introduction was, "Grandma, we can't play this game. I am not sure of my numbers." With assurance, I said, "That's exactly why we are learning to play BINGO." After the rules were explained, one chip was pulled: N35. Each child was helped to find the letter and number and shown how to put them on the master list. One volunteered, "Can I try to tell you the next one? I think I can do this." She drew, calling, "O something. I'm not sure of high numbers like that." I asked her, "What are the two numbers you see?" She replied, "A '6' and an '8'." She was asked, "When those two numbers are read together, you can say them quickly, and I'll bet you can tell us the number."

She practiced saying them fast as one number and got a look of excitement on her face, saying, "It's "68." I said, "BINGO. I'm so proud of you. Now that you understand how this works, let your brother give it a try." He was very enticed to try—because his sister had. He reached in and pulled out a chip, calling, "'1,' '4,' and '3'," saying the two numbers together until he said, "43." A beaming face looked at me and said, "That's right, isn't it?" A smile spread across my face from ear to ear, answering his own question. "Yes, that's right." The game continued with a few hiccups, but each child gained much-needed confidence in identifying their numbers.

I was amazed to think about how we are taught spiritual lessons. Sometimes we recognize the message immediately; for others, it takes trial and error instruction to comprehend the message we are to receive. Much patience and practice are needed, but God is patient with us until He can say BINGO.

Thank You, LORD, that we recognize Your voice, both when we call for guidance and when we recognize Your voice as the receiver of Your Word. I pray we stay tuned into You for effective two-way communication, both as the caller and as the receiver.

John 10:27: My sheep hear my voice, and I know them, and they follow me.

Psalm 105:1: Give thanks to Yahweh! Call on his name! Make his doings known among the peoples.

Acts 2:21: It will be that whoever will call on the name of the Lord will be saved.

March 13th

Can We Share?

I gave the grandchildren a bag of animal crackers, which were divided into smaller bags, at the playground. A minivan full of children came shortly thereafter. Our kids were sitting and eating their snack when one approached me and said, "Grandma, we have so many little bags of crackers, and we won't eat them all. We all talked and wanted to know if it was OK with you if we shared with the other group of kids. They don't have any snacks with them." I looked over at the other kids watching our kids eat, smiled to myself, and said, "I think that would be a fine idea. Why don't each of you take a couple bags to give to the other children? I'm sure they will truly appreciate it." She ran over to the others and related the message. Soon, each child carried several bags over to the other children.

They soon came running back, bubbling with excitement: "Thank you for letting us do that. The other kids were really excited and kept telling us, "Thank you, thank you, thank you." I felt like our kids sharing with the others gave them as much delight as those who received the treats. I grabbed them into a group hug and said, "This makes me a very proud grandmother to know you've seen the needs of others, wanted to do something about it, saw you had plenty, and took the steps to share. I pray you always look at others needs and decide if you can help them be in a better place for having met you." At this point, the mother of those children came over. "I'd like to thank you for your generosity towards my children. We decided to come to the playground to make up for not having any snacks at home. I prayed for God to help them enjoy this time anyway. Then, your family provided the "missing link" to make it a perfect day. God bless you all." She gave each of us a hug and returned to her children. "See kids," I said, "God can use you anywhere, even the playground."

Thank You, LORD, for unexpected teachable moments that can occur anytime, anywhere, not by coincidence, but in Your perfect timing. I pray we stay attuned to the lessons sent our way and act upon them.

Hebrews 13:16: *But don't forget to be doing good and sharing, for with such sacrifices God is well pleased.*

Matthew 5:16: *Even so, let your light shine before men, that they may see your good works and glorify your Father who is in heaven. "In the same way, let your light shine before men, that they may see your good deeds and praise your Father in heaven."*

Proverbs 11:25: *A generous person will prosper; whoever refreshes others will be refreshed. NIV*

March 14th

<u>My Favorite Lovey</u>

The grandchildren all have their own special *lovey*, a stuffed animal to which they have been attached since birth. When they come for the day or a sleepover, the lovey is always in tow. Our grandson arrived one day without his buddy, a giraffe. His sad

Priceless Moments

little face let me know something wasn't right, saying, "Grandma, I lost G-Raffy camping. I promise I never took him outside, but we couldn't find him for the ride home." He began to sob. I scooped him up in my arms and headed for the rocker, where he snuggled in. After a few minutes, he quieted down to the *sniffle-swallow* cry stage. I quietly said, "Is there anything I can do to help you feel better?" No response. I thought I'd better leave well enough alone. Eventually, he stirred and replied, "I thought about it, and yes, there is something you can do." He grabbed my face with his little hands and asked, "Would you look for another giraffe? I miss my buddy. I've had to sleep with Dinosaur, but it's just not the same."

All I can think of is, "Where do I find a giraffe this time of year? The holidays are over, and giraffes just aren't a popular item to keep around throughout the year." Being his faithful grandma, I prayed, then stated, "I will do my best, honey, to look for another giraffe. But I can't make any promises since I don't know where to look for one this time of year." I can tell he watches adults as he perked up, saying, "I know. You can look on the internet. Mommy says they have everything on there. I would want it to be like G-Raffy, but it really doesn't matter. I would really like to have another giraffe." Now he has set the bar high. I convinced him to get down and play while I searched the net. There's nothing currently available that isn't super tall.

A day later, I walked into the grocery store, and on the clearance pile was a giraffe. It was different, none-the-less, a little boy snuggling-sized giraffe. I sent up a "Thank You, LORD, for providing even the small things." Now he is thrilled to bring Marshmallow to visit.

Thank You, LORD, for assistance with unusual requests, even *lovey* ones. I pray we never hesitate to take all requests, big or small, and place them at Your feet since all things are important to You—even loveys.

James 1:22*: But be doers of the word, and not only hearers, deluding your own selves.*

Priceless Moments

Psalm 107:9: *For he satisfies the longing soul. He fills the hungry soul with good.*

Psalm 94:18–19: *When I said, "My foot is slipping!" Your loving kindness, Yahweh, held me up. In the multitude of my thoughts within me, your comforts delight my soul.*

March 15th
I Really Like Your Hair

Our grandson came for a visit. He walked in the door and immediately said, "Oh, Grandma, I like your hair. Did you do something different with it today? It looks really pretty." I was really caught off guard, not expecting anything like that from a four-year-old. "Thank you, honey. It is so sweet of you to notice. This morning I got up early and cut my hair, getting rid of all the curls so it could be straight." He came over and ran his little fingers through my hair. "It's really soft. I like it better without the curls." Then he buried his nose in my hair, stating, "And it smells so good, too. What did you put on it?" I explained, "Anytime I cut my hair, I put a special conditioner on it to protect the new ends from all the heat from the blow dryer."

He stood there for a few minutes, mulling over my response. "Can you cut my hair and put some of that good-smelling stuff on me so I can smell good, too?" Quick thinking brought this response: "I don't think I can do it right now. Mommy cut your hair last week, so you don't need anything done to it right now." His head dropped, and a look of disappointment crossed his darling little face. I added, "Don't you worry, because I have a good idea." As I took his hand and headed towards the bathroom, a renewed look of hope crossed his face. "Here, honey, take this towel. You're going to need it." Now, confusion played across his face. I got the step stool. He climbed up, and I had him put his head in the sink, then proceeded to wash his hair, finishing up with good-smelling stuff. Delight was his final reaction.

How often do we notice something in or about others, then ask God to do the same for us? Of course, He treats all of us the same with His consistent mercy and love, but He usually desires different things, individualizing our gifts. After we realize our blessing from His hand, we, too, are delighted with His decision(s) for us.

Thank You, LORD, for seeing each of us as individuals needing individualized treatment tailored to our needs. I pray we become so in tune with Your will that we accept Your gifts on our behalf.

2 Corinthians 9:15: Now thanks be to God for his unspeakable gift!

1 Peter 4:10: As each has received a gift, employ it in serving one another, as good managers of the grace of God in its various forms.

Romans 12:5b, 6a: so we, who are many, are one body in Christ, and individually members of one another, having gifts differing according to the grace that was given to us:

March 16th

The Color-Changing Lights

Several years ago, my husband bought a set of three flameless battery-operated color-changing candles. He loves to turn them on and just let them run through a variety of different colors, setting the mood for a peaceful evening. During a sleepover, Papa turned on the lights for the grandchildren. "Wow, look at those lights. Did you know they change colors?" As we watched their fascination, the synchronization of lights kept changing. "Yes," I replied. "We like to sit and watch them change. It seems that once they have

Priceless Moments

been on for a few minutes, they are no longer the same color but start changing into many different colors. If left on long enough, they start to reflect the same color on all three again."

The kids wanted a snack, and I just happened to have colored popcorn. As it was popping, I heard, "Oh, Grandma, you're missing it." I hurried in to see. All around the living room were flickering tea lights from all different candles, casting the most beautiful glow everywhere—ceiling, walls, curtains, furniture, and floor. I inquired, "Where did these come from? They're beautiful." Papa added, "I found these a while ago and decided they would be lots of fun somewhere down the line. And tonight's the night." I realized the microwave had been beeping while I was mesmerized by the lights. I headed back to the kitchen, only to return with colored bowls full of popcorn. Squeals of laughter, commenting, "We should be singing *Jesus loves the little children.*" I asked, "Why?" "Because all these different colors make us feel so special inside and out since Jesus loves everyone, regardless of their skin color."

Colors do influence how a person feels: calming, creating happiness, sharing life, and reminding us of seasons. Mood rings changed color by reacting to temperature in the extremities. Fortunately, Jesus is colorblind in the sense that He looks at our hearts, the inside, not our skin color, the outside.

Thank You, LORD, that we are all precious in Your sight, separated only by those who live for You from those who don't. I pray mankind will discover Your deep love for us and love You in return as their Savior.

Psalm 139:14: *I will give thanks to you, for I am fearfully and wonderfully made. Your works are wonderful. My soul knows that very well.*

Isaiah 1:18: *"Come now, and let's reason together," says Yahweh: "Though your sins are as scarlet, they shall be as white as snow. Though they are red like crimson, they shall be as wool."*

Priceless Moments

Matthew 17:2: *He was changed before them. His face shone like the sun, and his garments became as white as the light.*

March 17th
<u>St. Patrick's Day</u>

"Grandma, we talked about the Irish at school today. I was told my last name is Irish. What do you think?" "They are right, honey. Your last name is Welsh, meaning *foreigner* or *stranger*. It is very fitting since Saint Patrick, originally named Maewyn Succat, was kidnapped and brought to Ireland, where he was sold as a slave to tend animals. He felt this was due to his lack of faith, so he prayed many times a day, developing a strong faith in God. Later, he escaped and went back to Britain, where he trained as a priest before finally returning to Ireland to teach others about his Christian faith. The holiday celebrates his death, considering him the patron saint; the arrival of Christianity; as well as the heritage and culture of the Irish. The Irish flag contains three colors: green, symbolizing Irish nationalism; orange, symbolizing Orangemen of the North; and white, symbolizing peace."

"Wow. That's really cool. Are there other things to go with the holiday?" "Irish Protestants wear orange; Irish Catholics wear green. The four-day celebration centers around items like shamrocks, leprechauns, the *Kiss Me, I'm Irish* Blarney Stone, the green-colored river in Chicago, harps, grand parades, green hats with shamrocks, pots of gold at the ends of rainbows, and Celtic knots. People will eat corned beef and cabbage, soda bread, and beverages dyed green. They will go to musical gatherings called *ceili,* hearing fiddles, pipes, and others as well as dancing. Since this day occurs during Lent, many Irish Catholics abstain from drinking."

The Irish believe in luck, but it is when prayer and preparation meet opportunities provided by God that things happen. I was reminded of an old Irish proverb: *You'll never plow a field by turning it over in your mind.* We must pray and believe, then put feet to those prayers.

Thank You, LORD, that we are able to share meaningful days to honor You. I pray we celebrate You daily, even if there is no designated holiday on the calendar.

Ecclesiastes 3:13: *Also that every man should eat and drink, and enjoy good in all his labor, is the gift of God.*

1 Corinthians 10:31: *Whether therefore you eat, or drink, or whatever you do, do all to the glory of God.*

1 Corinthians 5:8: *Therefore let's keep the feast, not with old yeast, neither with the yeast of malice and wickedness, but with the unleavened bread of sincerity and truth.*

March 18th
<u>See My Fingernails</u>

Our daughters-in-law painted the granddaughters' fingernails. When the nail polish had dried, the girls came running, saying, "Grandma, look at our pretty nails. Our moms painted them for us. We even got to pick the colors we wanted." Excitement definitely filled the air. "They are absolutely beautiful. You must have stayed very still to get them painted and to let them dry." "Oh, we're not done yet. We can choose stickers to put on top of the polish. Once the stickers are on, we are getting clear polish put on top to keep them looking nice for a long time." While walking over to the painting station, I inquired, "And where did you find these fun colors and stickers to do your nails?" They all started talking at once, so it was difficult to get a definitive answer.

I decided not to ask again since it really didn't matter. I did ask, "Can I get my nails done, too? I only want the basics, all one

Priceless Moments

color, and no stickers." Again, the cacophony of voices started. I think they said, "Live a little. Let's have some fun. Each of us can do a couple of your nails, and we'll see what we come up with." I figured I could always get out the nail polish remover later, if needed. "OK, girls. Give them your best work. When you're done, we can take pictures of everyone's nails." For them, anticipation fills the air, as did trepidation for me. Each one grabbed a different color, and they set to work. I just closed my eyes and prayed. I could hear lots of giggling, and finally, "Grandma, open your eyes. You can look now." They were very colorful, alright. I thanked each one and gave them a big hug, even tipping each with a dollar. They were ecstatic.

I realized I needed to accept their gift as joy, like we need to accept God's gift of His precious Son. Jesus bore the markings of stripes on His back, poke marks in His head, and nail prints in His hands and feet—all for us.

Thank You, LORD; our creation is full of vibrant color. I pray we can look at the different hues and be reminded that Your gifts come at different times in our lives, either directly or indirectly, and in many colors.

Genesis 37:3: *Now Israel loved Joseph more than all his children, because he was the son of his old age, and he made him a tunic of many colors.*

1 Chronicles 29:2: *Now I have prepared with all my might for the house of my God the gold for the things of gold, the silver for the things of silver, the bronze for the things of bronze, iron for the things of iron, and wood for the things of wood; also onyx stones, stones to be set, stones for inlaid work, of various colors, all kinds of precious stones, and marble stones in abundance.*

Ephesians 4:7: *But to each one of us, the grace was given according to the measure of the gift of Christ.*

March 19th
<u>Spring Cleaning</u>

I guess it's time to do my spring cleaning—at least that's what the calendar is saying. So, I got out my supplies and started in the kitchen. On the first second of drawing some water, the doorbell rang. I shut off the water and answered the door. "Hi, Grandma. We were driving past your house and asked Daddy to stop. We wanted to see you. Can we stay a little while to visit?" Their joy was contagious. "Sure. Come on in." Addressing the parents, I said, "If you need to do something, go ahead. We'll be fine." They took me up on the offer.

"Grandma, what are you doing? Why do you have all this stuff out?" I explained, "I was going to start spring cleaning." "What's that, and why do you do it?" "It's an opportunity to do a more thorough job of cleaning the house, like wiping down walls, washing curtains and lights, all the bedding, and just giving the house a deep cleaning." "How often do you make yourself do that?" "I try to do this deep cleaning two times per year, in the spring and fall. I'll tell you what, I'll put this stuff away for now and…" Our granddaughter interpreted, "Can we help? I want to strip the beds and dust. I always help Mommy to do that." "And I want to run the sweeper and wash some dishes." "OK, we can clean a little, then play some games. How does this sound to you?" "Awesome, Grandma. Let's get started."

This is like the Christian life. We realize it's time to accept Jesus as Savior, then proceed to let Him clean house, allowing others to help lift the load in learning more about Him so our walk becomes more productive in readying us to be a witness for Him.

Thank You, LORD; we just need to come to You as we let You do the deep cleaning job in our hearts and lives. I pray we can help others realize they don't need to try to clean up their lives before coming to You because this is what You do for us to prepare us for a life of service in Your kingdom.

Priceless Moments

Psalm 51:10: *Create in me a clean heart, O God. Renew a right spirit within me.*

Ezekiel 11:19: *I will give them one heart, and I will put a new spirit within you. I will take the stony heart out of their flesh, and will give them a heart of flesh;*

Acts 15:9: *He made no distinction between us and them, cleansing their hearts by faith.*

March 20th

Spring

"Grandma, come quick. Your plants are peeking through the snow. Will they die if it gets cold again?" I looked, "Oh, the daffodils and tulips are here once again. They grow from bulbs in the soil. God has built into them a biological clock, so they know when to start growing, when to flower, when to drop off and go back to sleep, or when to become dormant until next year. If it gets cold again before they bloom, they may die off for that year as a way of protecting themselves. If it gets unusually warm, the bulbs may be tricked into blooming out of season." "Are there other kinds of bulbs that grow in other seasons?" "Yes, many kinds of lilies and irises grow in summer. Crocuses and dahlias are a few fall bulb plants."

"How often do bulb flowers need to be planted? Could we plant bulbs? Where could we get some?" "Slow down a little. Let's answer these questions first. Spring bulbs get planted once in the fall, summer bulbs get planted in the spring, and fall bulbs get planted in late fall before a heavy frost. Some require sun; others require shade. Some like to be planted in flowerbeds, as a border around your sidewalk or house, in a hanging basket, or in a flowerpot. In order to buy and plant bulbs, you need to decide how many and what flowers you want for each season and how you want to enjoy them, and then plan to plant accordingly. We can get seed catalogs to look at or visit a garden store to see the flowers in bloom. But the most important thing is to get permission from your parents to plant them somewhere at your house." "OK, Grandma, let's go ask and see what they say."

I thought of **1 Corinthians 7:20** in the NIV translation, *Each one should remain in the situation where he was when God called him.* In other words, "bloom where you are planted," where we can be of the most benefit for Him to use us.

Thank You, LORD, for the newness of life when we find You as our personal Savior. I pray this new life, which starts in Your springtime, grows throughout the remaining seasons of life until we've blossomed in Your faithfulness, spreading beauty all around us.

Zechariah 10:1: Ask of Yahweh rain in the springtime, Yahweh who makes storm clouds, and he gives rain showers to everyone for the plants in the field.

1 Corinthians 7:17a: Only, as the Lord has distributed to each man, as God has called each, so let him walk.

Song of Songs 2:11-12: For behold, the winter is past. The rain is over and gone. The flowers appear on the earth. The time of the singing has come, and the voice of the turtledove is heard in our land.

March 21ˢᵗ
Spring Break

I picked our granddaughter up from school one day. She came running, saying, "Oh, Grandma, I'm so excited. We start spring break today. We are off for a whole week. I am so excited because

Priceless Moments

I get to see you every day. Can we have a sleepover?" All I could think of was take a breath before you keep going. But she continued, "My brother is going to be off, too. We want to go for walks, ride bikes, and go out for lunch, if that's OK with you." Wow, a girl who knows what she wants. "Sounds good, but since it's also your brother's time off, we need to find out what he wants to do too."

We just picked up brother, who was also very excited about spring break. His first question was, "Who started spring break anyway? It's an awesome idea." "It was first observed in Europe in the late 19th century before being brought to America in the 1930s. It's also observed in many other countries. Some go to places with music festivals and beach activities. Others travel home to see family or go to warmer places, take family vacations, and hold Easter celebrations since it's close to Easter." "Those all sound like a lot of fun."

I thought of how we tend to make our own plans for our lives without consulting God. We put forth so much effort to make things perfect from our own perspective. Sometimes, God agrees with these plans, but others are slightly or dramatically different from His perspective. Regardless, we need to learn to consult Him, making Him part of our decision-making, so we are more in line with and accepting of His will.

Thank You, LORD; You are just as interested in the small details as You are in the big picture of our lives. I pray we walk so close with You that our goals are always in tune with You.

John 8:47: He who is of God hears the words of God. For this cause you don't hear, because you are not of God.

Romans 8:27: He who searches the hearts knows what is on the Spirit's mind, because he makes intercession for the saints according to God.

1 Peter 3:8, 9: Finally, all of you be like-minded, compassionate, loving as brothers, tenderhearted, courteous, not rendering evil for evil, or insult for insult; but instead blessing, knowing that you were called to this, that you may inherit a blessing.

March 22nd
<u>Partridge In a Pear Tree</u>

The youngsters walked in today singing *The Twelve Days of Christmas*, but not in any particular order. The verse *and a partridge in a pear tree* was repeated over and over without many of the other verses. I asked, "Why do you like to sing only one verse? Do you need some help remembering the words to the other verses?" They giggled, "No, we like to say the word partridge. What is it anyway?" "Good question. A partridge is a medium-sized brown, gray, and white bird, a lot like a pheasant but smaller. These plump birds have short legs and short, curved bills, and they can camouflage themselves or blend in with things around them. This is very useful since they are a game bird, meaning they are often hunted. They mostly stay on the ground, can run quickly, but also have the ability to fly to get away from danger." "What do they eat?" "They eat seeds, leaves, and invertebrates, while their baby chicks eat mostly insects."

The singing resumed. I continued, "In the song, the partridge was the first gift given by *my true love*. As each new verse is added, you would sing from that verse all the way down to the very first one, *A partridge in a pear tree*. "Grandma, I like to sing this one verse because it makes me think of Jesus being the only One in a pear tree, or on His tree. If I sing it over and over, I am singing praises to Him." I hesitated, "Very interesting. Jesus was the only One Who hung on His tree. I'm sure He appreciates your thinking of Him all year long." They just smiled and continued to sing their favorite verse.

For some reason, the kids like to sing Christmas carols all year, which is fine with me. I absolutely enjoy them all, but now look at this secular carol with a new meaning. Children enjoy seeing Jesus in everything they do.

Thank You, LORD, for letting little ones see You in all things like adults see You on every page in the Bible. I pray we can find Your childlike awareness. We can be much happier if we are always looking for and/or seeing You in every step of life.

Isaiah 6:1: *In the year that king Uzziah died, I saw the Lord sitting on a throne, high and lifted up; and his train filled the temple.*

Acts 7:56: *Behold, I see the heavens opened, and the Son of Man standing at the right hand of God!*

Colossians 1:15: *He is the image of the invisible God, the firstborn of all creation.*

March 23rd
I'm a Star Student

Our granddaughter called to say, "Grandma, today I was given an award at school for being a Star Student. My dad, mom, and sister came to see me get my award. It was really exciting. I wish you could have been there." "Oh, honey, I am so proud of you. I wish I could have been there, too. You must be doing good work to show your teacher what a fine mind God has given you. What exactly did you do to become a Star Student?" She spoke rapidly: "A Star Student is one who is Safe, Thoughtful, And Respectful. I do these things by being at school every day and on time; not getting into trouble; doing all my work at school and at home; being respectful to my teacher and my classmates; being responsible, truthful, and honest; showing confidence; saying please and thank you; not interrupting or talking back to my teachers; and keeping my hands to myself." "Wow," I said. "That's a lot of things to do. How do you remember to do all those things?" She giggled, "Oh, Grandma, you're so funny. I just do them because I've learned most of this at home, and now I just do it at school, too."

I couldn't help but think of **Proverbs 22:6**: *Train up a child in the way he should go, and when he is old he will not depart from it.* Schooling truly starts in the home, both with the basics of book AND Bible learning.

Thank You, LORD, for godly parents and Your Word to be a lamp to our feet and a light to our path. I pray we teach our children to let You shine through all their thoughts, words, and deeds.

Daniel 12:3: *Those who are wise will shine as the brightness of the expanse. Those who turn many to righteousness will shine as the stars forever and ever.*

Philippians 2:14-16a: *Do all things without complaining and arguing, that you may become blameless and harmless, children of God without defect in the middle of a crooked and perverse generation, among whom you are seen as lights in the world, holding up the word of life,*

2 Timothy 2:15: *Give diligence to present yourself approved by God, a workman who doesn't need to be ashamed, properly handling the Word of Truth.*

March 24th

Palm Sunday

"Grandma, why do we celebrate Palm Sunday?" "Palm Sunday, the week before Easter, was a very significant event to start the Holy Week. People had come from all over Israel for Passover. It was the time Jesus chose to make His triumphant entry into Jerusalem riding on a donkey." "What all happened on that Sunday? We talked about it at church, but I want to hear it again."

Priceless Moments

"People were so excited to see Him that they laid down their cloaks and palm branches in His path, giving Him the royal treatment, then shouted, "Hosanna to the Son of David. Blessed is He who comes in the name of the LORD. Hosanna in the highest." The people of the city were asking, "Who is this?" The crowds who had gathered answered them, "This is Jesus, the prophet from Nazareth in Galilee."

She thought for a minute, "Why did they not know who Jesus was?" I prayed, then answered, "Since people knew He was of the line of King David, the people hoped He would become their King and defeat the Romans to restore or regain control of the kingdom of Israel. Indeed, Jesus was a King, but His kingdom was not of this world but rather of heaven. Jesus knew the prophecies about His life, death, and resurrection, so on this day He firmly decided He would hang on the cross, or be crucified, to ultimately rise from the dead and redeem mankind."

My mind wandered back to biblical times, thinking of the oppression the Israelites experienced under Roman rule. Today, we experience a similar type of tyranny with Satan as the ruler of this world. Jesus came to set us free—just for asking. He is waiting to enter our hearts at this very moment. Our task is to live for Him because He lives for us.

Thank You, LORD, for being willing to experience the mountain tops and valleys of life as we do. I pray we are accepting and committed to following You, whatever the cost.

Psalm 118:26: *Blessed is he who comes in Yahweh's name! We have blessed you out of Yahweh's house.*

Zechariah 9:9: *Rejoice greatly, daughter of Zion! Shout, daughter of Jerusalem! Behold, your King comes to you! He is righteous, and having salvation; lowly, and riding on a donkey, even on a colt, the foal of a donkey.*

Priceless Moments

2 Kings 9:13: *Then they hurried, and each man took his cloak, and put it under him on the top of the stairs, and blew the trumpet, saying, "Jehu is king."*

March 25th
<u>*Do You Like My Crown?*</u>

Our granddaughter was wearing a crown and asked, "Do you like my crown? I'm wearing it because I want to see how it fits and if you will notice." I smiled and said, "I may not have noticed, so I'm pleased you pointed it out to me." "Oh, Grandma, you are so funny. You notice everything. Do you think it matches my dress? Or do you think it would be better with another dress? I want it to be just perfect." "Now you've piqued my interest. What do you want to be just perfect at, and how does it involve a crown?" She thought, then said, "I want to go to Disneyland this spring. I figure I'd better start looking for things to take. I know the princesses will be wearing crowns, so I want to be sure to fit in. I want my crown to match my dress. Can you help me?" Girls, I thought. "Sure, little princess, with what all would you like me to help?"

I shouldn't have asked. "I've been looking at this top because it has sparkles on it to go with these shorts. I picked out a long pair of pants to match in case it was cold there. I picked this jacket to go with everything else on my bed." My mind is reeling—is she going to Disneyland, or is it just wishful thinking? I asked, "When are you planning your trip?" "Oh, Mom didn't talk to you yet. We're going over spring break and meeting up with our cousins from the other side of the family. I'll miss you. But I've already been trying to decide what to bring home for you." After going through what seemed like her entire wardrobe, I said, "That's so sweet of you. Why don't you surprise me?"

I thought of how some people make extensive plans to go to heaven, but first they need to ask Jesus into their hearts to have the assurance they are saved and going to heaven. God will do all the coordinating; we just need to do our part. No packing is required; when we get there, He will give us white robes.

Thank You, LORD, for Your promises of heaven. I pray we remain faithful to our crowns and white robes.

Isaiah 62:3*: You will also be a crown of beauty in Yahweh's hand, and a royal diadem in your God's hand.*

2 Timothy 4:8*: From now on, the crown of righteousness is stored up for me, which the Lord, the righteous judge, will give to me on that day; and not to me only, but also to all those who have loved his appearing.*

Revelation 6:11*: A long white robe was given to each of them. They were told that they should rest yet for a while, until their fellow servants and their brothers, who would also be killed even as they were, should complete their course.*

March 26th

Marshmallow Bunnies

Every Easter, marshmallow bunnies are a must-have treat, kind of like a rite of passage. The grandchildren spot them in EVERY store, placed at the perfect eye level so as not to go undetected. "Oh, Grandma, they're back." I asked, "What's back?" like I hadn't noticed. "Marshmallow bunnies, they're the best. May we have some, please?" I responded, "Well, let me see, since they're the best and you're the best, I think we should buy one." Shrieks of "Yes" attracted the attention of others. "Excuse me, guys, but you need to turn down the volume. You are attracting unwanted attention from others." By this time, the other shoppers were tuned in as to the reason for their excitement and were chuckling to

Priceless Moments

themselves. They stopped and looked around to see the smiles and hear the laughter.

The children stood frozen in place, trying to figure out what to do. Eventually the embarrassment wore off, and our granddaughter said, "We're sorry for disturbing you while you were shopping, but it's marshmallow bunnies." One kind lady was so impressed with her apology: "Dear children. I remember those days of seeing them on the shelves for the first time each season, too. Sometimes I still get excited and have to buy myself a pack or two. Here, I hope Grandma doesn't mind, but allow me to buy those for you," she said, handing them each a dollar and adding, "Your excitement made my day."

A little embarrassed myself, I, too, thanked her. I realized how the laughter of a child can reach deep into the souls of others. Laughter is indeed good medicine. God must be pleased when He sees us enjoying ourselves in His creation while bringing joy to others.

Thank You, LORD, for children who *let it all hang out*, regardless of where they are. I pray our inner child can surface more often to experience all the good things in our lives, freeing ourselves of the pain and depressed mood of the day, and becoming the fun-loving, happy people You intended us to be.

Proverbs 17:22*: A cheerful heart makes good medicine, but a crushed spirit dries up the bones.*

Genesis 21:6*: Sarah said, "God has made me laugh. Everyone who hears will laugh with me."*

John 15:11*: I have spoken these things to you, that my joy may remain in you, and that your joy may be made full.*

Priceless Moments

March 27th
<u>Coloring Eggs</u>

"I know a good activity to do today. Do you want to hear it?" "Sure," I replied. "You always have great ideas, so let's hear them." "I think we should color some eggs for Easter. I remember doing it last year here and at home. It is so much fun. The best part is we get to eat them later." "Wow, that is an awesome idea. I happen to have a dozen hard-boiled eggs we can use, plenty of food coloring, a clear crayon to draw pictures on eggs before dying them, and newspaper to put down on the table. I even found aprons to wear to protect your clothes." "I bet you were already planning to do this with us, weren't you?" "Let's say I was hoping you would want to complete an activity, so I had different things ready, just in case."

We proceeded to set things up when the phone rang. "Excuse me, kids, I need to take this call." I walked into the next room and took care of business. When I returned, they were sitting uncharacteristically quiet, so I started to look for something amiss. They asked, "What are you looking for, Grandma? We couldn't do anything without you. We wanted to be sure not to lose the privilege of dying eggs. We did draw on some eggs with the clear crayon to be ready to dye them." My heart melted with their compliance: "Thank you so much for your patience because I know waiting is hard sometimes. I am so proud of all of you." The remainder of the project went very well—no spilled colors or dropped eggs. "Now that we are done, can we mix colors to see what they look like?" The next few minutes were spent experimenting with colors in different amounts and combinations. Fun!..

At times, we experiment with things that may not be healthy for us. God is there to see us through the waiting time(s), either holding our hands or providing a caring individual to give comfort and counsel until the challenges are past.

Thank You, LORD, that You know what we need before we do, already preparing help or an answer for such a time as this. I pray we are appreciative and patient, for our trials will only make us stronger.

Proverbs 3:5-6: *Trust in Yahweh with all your heart, and don't lean on your own understanding. In all your ways acknowledge him, and he will make your paths straight.*

Romans 8:28: *We know that all things work together for good for those who love God, for those who are called according to his purpose.*

James 1:6: *But let him ask in faith, without any doubting, for he who doubts is like a wave of the sea, driven by the wind and tossed.*

March 28th
Easter Egg Hunt

"Grandma, Grandma, Grandma, come quick. Dad and Mom had a bunch of Easter eggs that we think are already hidden because they came back in the house without anything in their hands." "Are you serious? Why do you think they would do this now?" "Because tomorrow is Easter, and they always hide eggs for an Easter egg hunt. We colored and decorated some real eggs and some plastic eggs, so they looked really nice. We are going to church tomorrow, then skiing, so there won't be any time to hide or look for hidden eggs then." "You have a good point there. I hear them coming in here, so let's play until they ask you go do something, OK?" "That sounds fun." We played for a while, and they didn't act like anything was going to happen.

Soon we heard, "Hey, guys, do you want to come here for a little? We have something we'd like to show you." Their eyes lit up, and

Priceless Moments

smiles crossed their faces as they both gave thumbs up in the air and ran out the door. I didn't hear what was said to them, but I did hear, "Of course, we'd love to go out and play." I got up and followed them out of the room when I heard, "Grandma, are you coming? The fun is about to begin." I got there in time to hear, "On your mark… Get set… Oh, wait a minute, we forgot to give you your baskets… Go." The kids ran frantically across the yard looking for hidden treasures, giggling and laughing as they went. They returned to the patio after their baskets were full, immediately diving in to see what was hidden in the eggs.

Aren't we like that? We know something is going to happen, yet while it's in progress, time seems to drag on and on. Oh, the waiting for trial and crucifixion before being able to go and properly prepare Jesus' body for burial. But, oh, the joy in finding an empty tomb and realizing the Savior has risen.

Thank You, LORD, for the times You give, take, and give things back better than ever. I pray we see things through to the end to find that the give and take was part of Your plan to strengthen our resolve to follow You in spite of current circumstances.

Luke 24:6-9: *He isn't here but is risen. Remember what he told you when he was still in Galilee, saying that the Son of Man must be delivered up into the hands of sinful men and be crucified, and the third day rise again?" They remembered his words, returned from the tomb, and told all these things to the eleven and to all the rest.*

Luke 24:34: *"The Lord is risen indeed, and has appeared to Simon!"*

1 Peter 1:3: *Blessed be the God and Father of our Lord Jesus Christ, who according to his great mercy caused us to be born again to a living hope through the resurrection of Jesus Christ from the dead,*

Priceless Moments

March 29th

Good Friday

"Grandma, why do we have the day off from school today?" "Today is Good Friday, the sixth day of Holy Week. Prior to Jesus being hung on the cross, He was wrongly accused and sentenced to death by crucifixion, a very painful and disgraceful type of punishment. This day we celebrate Jesus' crucifixion, or being nailed to the cross, from noon to 3p.m. During this time, darkness covered the land. Then, a most fascinating thing happened when Jesus died for our sins. The temple curtain was torn in two from top to bottom, removing the separation of man from God and opening the Holy of Holies to ALL mankind, both Jews and Gentiles. Jesus was removed from the cross, and His body was given to a rich man named Joseph of Arimathea. Joseph wrapped His body in a clean linen cloth, placed Him in his own new tomb, and rolled a large stone in front of it—to keep Him in and men out."

"Why are all of those things important?" "It comes down to the fact that Jesus willingly went to the cross to suffer a shameful death on the cross, a cruel and painful death to pay the price for our sins, a death each of us deserved, yet His love for us was so great that He willingly went to die in our place. He knew His Father's plan was perfect, regardless of the anguish and misery it caused Him for a time. He knew this, too, would pass, resulting in a blessing for the world. Now, it is up to us to remember the price He paid and choose to live for Him."

Thank You, LORD, for love so great and so deep that You freely gave Your life for mankind, including those of us yet to come. I pray we develop this bottomless love for our fellowman, be they a friend, acquaintance, or foe, because we are ALL valuable in Your sight.

***Mark 15:46**: He bought a linen cloth, and taking him down, wound him in the linen cloth, and laid him in a tomb which had been cut out of a rock. He rolled a stone against the door of the tomb.*

***Romans 8:32**: He who didn't spare his own Son, but delivered him up for us all, how would he not also with him freely give us all things?*

***1 Peter 3:18**: Because Christ also suffered for sins once, the righteous for the unrighteous, that he might bring you to God, being put to death in the flesh, but made alive in the Spirit,*

March 30th
<u>The Empty Cross</u>

Before service, our granddaughter looked up in front of the church. She cocked her head to one side, then the other. "Grandma, I never noticed it before, but the cross is empty. Was it always like that?" Her prompting demanded that I, too, look up at the empty cross. I pondered a moment before answering, "I think of Jesus carrying the empty wooden cross to the place where the Romans would crucify Him as an act of humiliation, then take Him down to bury Him, making it, once again, an empty cross. The empty cross shows Jesus is no longer on it, a reminder of His precious gift by dying there once, being raised from the dead once, and leaving the cross permanently empty. The empty cross tells of Jesus' selfless sacrifice of death, burial, and resurrection to bridge the gap between heaven and earth and guarantee those of us who accept Him as Savior will be with Him forever in heaven."

After the service, she asked, "Can I go up to touch the cross?" I didn't see any harm in it, so we went forward. "Wow, Grandma. This thing is heavy. Did the cross Jesus died on look like this one?" "No one knows for sure since the Bible doesn't say, but tradition says when Peter was old, he asked to be crucified upside

Priceless Moments

down because he felt unworthy to be crucified in the same form and manner, head up and feet down, as Jesus was. The Bible does say Jesus told Peter how he would die when he was old." "Do people still get crucified?" she asked. "Unfortunately," I began, "the last I knew, some places in the Middle East still do a few executions."

I'm amazed at how this generation has a deep need to know when our generation would've heard or learned something and said, "Oh," and moved on. This conversation stimulated my curiosity about more in-depth information about Jesus' journey to the cross as well as the cross itself.

Thank You, LORD, the apostles, and historians have documented enough information to stimulate interest in searching out more truth and evidence. I pray our innate sense of curiosity keeps us searching the Word to find more nuggets of truth that will give us a better picture of You.

John 3:16: *For God so loved the world, that he gave his one and only Son, that whoever believes in him should not perish, but have eternal life.*

John 21:18-19: *"Most certainly I tell you, when you were young, you dressed yourself and walked where you wanted to. But when you are old, you will stretch out your hands, and another will dress you and carry you where you don't want to go." Now he said this, signifying by what kind of death he would glorify God. When he had said this, he said to him, "Follow me."*

Acts 5:30: *The God of our fathers raised up Jesus, whom you killed, hanging him on a tree.*

Priceless Moments

March 31st

Easter

"Can you tell us what Easter is all about, Grandma? We like the way you tell us stuff." "I would be delighted to share with you. The world says Easter is about a bunny, festivals, new clothes, coloring and hiding eggs for an egg hunt, baskets full of treats, and maybe church. The other side of Easter has a special message of its own. Jesus chose to be beaten, cursed, denied, and crucified on a cross to bring love and forgiveness to us—the most important gift of all because it restored communion with God. God the Father and God the Son gave the best they had to give, without hesitation, setting the example of selfless love to share with others."

"But, praise the LORD, the story doesn't end there. Jesus' body spent time in the tomb, but His Spirit went to Abraham's Side, a special place for the dead who had followed God. In **Luke 12:4-5**, Jesus spoke about this so the people would realize their choice to seek God or turn away from Him here on earth. Their choice will ultimately determine where they will spend eternity. Early Sunday morning, women went to the tomb. They found the stone rolled away, an angel sitting on top of the stone, and an empty tomb. Jesus was crucified and rose again, so we have the opportunity to spend eternity in heaven with Him. A very important thing to note is that all the events that took place this week fulfilled exactly 100% of the prophecies of Holy Week."

It's important to realize Easter is never "over." Crippling habits are broken—sharing, caring, giving, loving, and sacrificing for each other—because we see Jesus at work in people demonstrating their faith and trust in Him. We must teach everyone the power of the cross and what it stands for as evidence of God's great love for every human being in this world. Gender, race, socioeconomic status—NONE of it matters. What truly matters is our acceptance of Jesus as LORD and Savior to take us through life—good and

Priceless Moments

bad—until we meet Him face-to-face in eternity, the ultimate goal of life.

Thank You, LORD, for providing the bridge between heaven and earth, permanently removing any barrier between us and You. I pray we find You as our Savior to remove the barrier from our side, then keep our eyes fixed on You to find and stay on the narrow road, the only road leading to heaven.

Isaiah 53:4-5: *Surely he has borne our sickness and carried our suffering; yet we considered him plagued, struck by God, and afflicted. But he was pierced for our transgressions. He was crushed for our iniquities. The punishment that brought our peace was on him; and by his wounds we are healed.*

John 3:16-17: *For God so loved the world, that he gave his one and only Son, that whoever believes in him should not perish, but have eternal life. For God didn't send his Son into the world to judge the world, but that the world should be saved through him.*

1 Peter 2:24: *He himself bore our sins in his body on the tree, that we, having died to sins, might live to righteousness. You were healed by his wounds.*

Priceless Moments

April

Children's children are the crown of old men.

Proverbs. 17:6

April 1ST
April Fool's Day

"What is April Fool's Day? Our teacher said we could tell jokes but no pranks." "April Fool's Day dates from the 16th century, when France observed the new year on April 1, a day for parties and dancing. In 1562, Pope Gregory introduced a new calendar where the new year started January 1. People didn't hear about it in the country areas or believe the calendar had changed, so they still celebrated New Year's Day on April 1. Others called them fools, pulling pranks to make them believe something was true when it wasn't. Today, in good fun, people play tricks on others when they least expect it to happen, be they a friend or a stranger. When the innocent victim discovers or realizes they were not told the truth, the prankster yells, "April Fools." Some people will laugh at the joke, but others get mad, so be careful with whom you pull pranks."

"What kinds of things do people do to each other?" "Your Dad loved to tell anyone their shoe was untied or it was raining. Others could be: there is something on your shirt; after lunch, you have food on your face; school's been canceled; your mom is here; something hit your car; watch out for the bird; and things like this. Some people trade salt for sugar, change the time on clocks to the wrong hour, or send someone asking for directions to the wrong place. These types of pranks will draw different kinds of reactions from people. Know whom you are pranking, trying to match the joke to the person so all can laugh when the joke is discovered.

How refreshing and comforting it is to know Jesus never plays pranks on us. He tells us in the Word the way things are, but He never changes what He says for any reason. His intent is never to harm us but to mold and make us into individuals who can *dish it out* and also *take it* with a smile on our faces.

Thank You, LORD, for a sense of humor to break the ice with a new crowd or get familiar faces to laugh in a tense moment. I pray

Priceless Moments

we are sensitive to those around us and do not overstep frivolity to cause others discomfort.

Proverbs 26:18-19: Like a madman who shoots torches, arrows, and death, is the man who deceives his neighbor and says, "Am I not joking?"

Ephesians 5:4: Nor should there be obscenity, foolish talk or coarse joking, which are out of place, but rather thanksgiving. NIV

Matthew 12:36: I tell you that every idle word that men speak, they will give account of it in the day of judgment.

April 2nd
Let's Ride a Bus

It's amazing how an opportunity to ride a bus can swell the young at heart. "Grandma, did you know when I get older, I get to ride a bus to school every day? Right now, Dad and Mom like to take me, so they know I'm getting there safely and to the right classroom. They said, "When you get older, you will enjoy riding the school bus." "Nice for you. I used to ride a school bus for fifteen minutes to get to my elementary school and an hour to get to my high school." "Wow, that's a long time. Did you get tired?" "Not really. I talked with friends and did my homework, so it was done when I got home. When I got older, a lot of times I stayed after school for band practice or some other activity."

"Guess what? Mom said we are going on a trip, and we get to ride on a bus once we get there. I think they don't allow you to drive on the roads; just ride the buses, because the roads are very narrow and there is very little parking for all those cars. I hope we get to ride up front to watch where the driver is going. He usually has the best view of all without other people's heads being in the way of where you want to look. And those heads always move to the place where you want to look." So true. He is spot on with his observations.

What a valuable realization that other people can get in the way of seeing things clearly. We need to stay up front in our walk with the LORD to avoid unexpected distractions and obstacles as much as possible, especially since Jesus is our Pilot and we are the co-pilots, the ones sitting and learning from the Master.

Thank You, LORD, for Your ability to help us see the beauty of the earth from our vantage point in time. I pray we stay up front with You so we can see Your leading in our lives, regardless of the path You have chosen for us to take.

1 Corinthians 3:11: *For no one can lay any other foundation than that which has been laid, which is Jesus Christ.*

John 16:5: *But now I am going to him who sent me, and none of you asks me, "Where are you going?"*

2 Kings 2:11: *As they continued on and talked, behold, a chariot of fire and horses of fire separated them, and Elijah went up by a whirlwind into heaven.*

April 3rd

The Calendar

"Grandma, you have a calendar in every room. Why do you use a calendar, and how did it get started?" She was very observant, I thought. "I keep calendars in every room because I like looking at the pictures for each month. And if I need to know a certain day or date—the main reason we use calendars—I can look it up wherever I am in the house. The first known calendar was from Rome, about 2700 years ago. It had ten months—no January or February. The calendar started with March and ended with December, whose root word "dec" means ten. The first two

Priceless Moments

months were added later and named for Roman gods, as were March and April for a Roman goddess. The sixth- and seventh-months' names, Quintillis and Sextilis, were changed to July and August in honor of Julius Caesar and Caesar Augustus."

"Has the calendar changed in other ways?" "Yes," I answered. "Different countries used different types and different numbers of days. One time, the Aztec Indians had a 25-ton stone calendar. Julius Caesar decided to take the usual 355-day calendar and make it 455 days long, but it confused everyone. The Jewish and Chinese used a 29- or 30-day lunar month, occasionally adding one month after two or three years to correct for weather, growing crops, and livestock. A Catholic Pope named Gregory changed the calendar to reflect the lunar calendar. This calendar will be correct until the year 4317. To keep it in balance, once every four years, an extra day is added to February, which is called a "leap year." They said, "Wow, that's fascinating."

I marvel at their desire to learn new things, always asking for more information. I'm sure God is delighted when we are curious and go to His Word to get answers to our biblical questions. The Bible is always at our fingertips, be it in hard copy, on phones or iPads, or written on our hearts and minds.

Thank You, LORD, for helping us understand that even though things around us change daily throughout our lives, You remain the same. I pray Your steadfast love will guide us throughout the constant change of life, steadying us for the rocky or smooth road ahead.

Deuteronomy 7:9*: Know therefore that Yahweh your God himself is God, the faithful God, who keeps covenant and loving kindness to a thousand generations with those who love him and keep his commandments,*

James 1:17*: Every good gift and every perfect gift is from above, coming down from the Father of lights, with whom can be no variation, nor turning shadow.*

Priceless Moments

Hebrews 13:8*: Jesus Christ is the same yesterday, today, and forever.*

April 4th
My Training Wheel Bike

The time has arrived to watch our granddaughter transition from training wheels to riding the bike on her own. "Everybody, are you watching me? Please don't. It makes me nervous. Dad don't let go of me or my bike. I don't want to fall." She took a deep breath and said, "OK, Dad, I'm ready. Make sure you hold onto the back of my bike." They started down the road together, with Dad pushing and her peddling as fast as she could. Then, the moment of takeoff. She was riding on her own and didn't know it. When she realized Dad was not holding her bike from behind, she started to wobble. "Keep going, honey; you're doing it all on your own, and we're all so proud of you."

After riding a little more, she turned around and rode back to the house. Out of breath, she said, "Did everyone see me? I did it all by myself. I'm so excited." I couldn't help myself. "No, none of us saw it because you told us not to look." Her eyes grew wide as her mouth dropped open, "What do you mean no one saw me? I didn't really mean for you not to watch." "Oh, honey, we saw you and are so happy for you. That was some really good riding. Now we are going to be able to ride wherever we like."

Making transitions from one mode of thinking to another can seem hard and challenging, and we may wobble back and forth until we build up confidence and speed to be able to stay upright. When we realize it is the LORD behind us to give us balance and direction, our path becomes clear. We can move ahead without fear or hesitation because His support and guidance are always keeping us on the path towards heaven.

Priceless Moments

Thank You, LORD, for Your steady hand in teaching us to follow You. I pray we are willing to trust You every step of the way and be led as You deem fit.

John 8:31-32: *Jesus therefore said to those Jews who had believed him, "If you remain in my word, then you are truly my disciples. You will know the truth, and the truth will make you free."*

1 John 2:28: *Now, little children, remain in him, that when he appears, we may have boldness, and not be ashamed before him at his coming.*

Luke 9:23-24: *He said to all, "If anyone desires to come after me, let him deny himself, take up his cross, and follow me. For whoever desires to save his life will lose it, but whoever will lose his life for my sake, will save it.*

April 5th

Trampolines

The grandchildren received a trampoline for Christmas. As the days get longer and the weather gets warmer, interest in jumping has ignited. "Grandma, can we jump for a while before coming inside for supper? Neither one of us has any homework. We will come in when you call and set the table. Is that OK with you?" As per usual, they always seem to have their ducks in a row. "I think you've made a good case," I replied, "so it sounds good to me. You have about thirty minutes, so have fun. I will call one time, and I hope you respond that first time." "We will, we promise."

I went into the house and started supper. A little later I called, "Hey, guys, it's time to come in and set the table." Believe it or not, I heard, "OK, Grandma." They put their shoes back on and headed to the house. Once inside, they asked, "What do we need to set on the table?" "Four forks, two small plates, and two large plates. Your choice of napkins, as we will need them." They set to work and had the table set in record time. "Can we watch the iPad until dinner is ready?" "Sure. I appreciate you keeping your word, so I know you will do it again."

As the children grow a little older, from the toddler stage to a young child, their ability to submit to authority becomes easier for a little while, then sometimes more challenging as they grow into their teen years. Adults are like that as well. We need to learn to submit ourselves to Jesus, then remain devoted, not wavering in our commitment to Christ but growing more submissive as we mature in our faith.

Thank You, LORD, for teaching little ones to listen to and obey authority. I pray we listen to our heavenly Authority, following His example of submission and obedience to His and our Heavenly Father in a steadfast manner.

Proverbs 19:27: *If you stop listening to instruction, my son, you will stray from the words of knowledge.*

James 1:19, 20: *So, then, my beloved brothers, let every man be swift to hear, slow to speak, and slow to anger; for the anger of man doesn't produce the righteousness of God.*

Titus 3:1, 2: *Remind them to be in subjection to rulers and to authorities, to be obedient, to be ready for every good work, to speak evil of no one, not to be contentious, to be gentle, showing all humility toward all men.*

April 6th

<u>Fishing</u>

"Last time all of us were together, we went fishing. Since we are here again, do you think we can go fishing? We brought our

Priceless Moments

fishing poles, and Daddy has his tackle box." "I think this is a question to ask your parents. I know fishing is always at the top of their list. They've turned each of you into an angler." "Grandma, what's an angler? I don't think I've ever heard the word before." "Good question. An angler is a person who fishes with a rod and line as a hobby. At times, you're a fisherman when using nets or traps to catch fish."

"Now I have a question for you. What kind of things are we going to need to go fishing?" "Well, I brought my fishing pole, fishing line, bobbers, hooks, bait, and some special lures. I even brought my high boots in case I got too close to the water, so my feet wouldn't get wet. Sometimes it rains when we're out fishing, so I brought my rain jacket and an umbrella." "Wow, I'm really impressed you came so prepared with all the needed fishing gear and clothing items for any kind of weather." "One time we were out and got caught in the rain. Again, we quickly packed up our gear and went back to the car, but we were soaked. We didn't have any clothes in the car, so we were wet until we got home. Daddy turned on the heater, but it just didn't seem to help enough. So it's better to be prepared than not."

Out of the mouths of babes, telling us to be prepared for every potential situation. We need to remember that Jesus is coming again, and if we're not prepared, we're going to get left behind. But when we are prepared for him to come at any given time, we will be caught up into heaven and live with Them eternally to walk the streets of gold. But, in the meantime, we are to be witnessing to and *catching* the unsaved He puts in our path.

Thank You, LORD, for using children to teach us valuable lessons about life. I pray we never get so caught up in the trappings of this earthly existence that we do not take the time to be prepared for our heavenly home.

Matthew 4:19: *He said to them, "Come after me, and I will make you fishers for men."*

Priceless Moments

Mark 16:15: *He said to them, "Go into all the world, and preach the Good News to the whole creation."*

John 21:5-6: *Jesus therefore said to them, "Children, have you anything to eat?" They answered him, "No." He said to them, "Cast the net on the right side of the boat, and you will find some." They cast it therefore, and now they weren't able to draw it in for the multitude of fish.*

April 7th
<u>The Corner Office</u>

The grandchildren like to come visit me in our office in the corner of the house. Somewhere along the way, they've dubbed it the *corner office*. "Hi, Grandma. How is your day going? We have homework from school today. I was wondering if I could do mine on the desk in the corner office. I like the light that shines in at the desk. It makes it so easy to see my homework stuff. Sis can do her homework at the student desk in the living room." I thought a minute about the good pitch. "Sure, I think that sounds fair. Your sister used the corner office desk last time." Each settled down and promptly completed the assigned homework.

"Grandma, we're both done. Can we play the computer in the corner office? We like the big screen and the different games on it. We promise to be careful and not fight. We know the corner office is a fun place for all of us. If you have time, would you be able to join us for a game or two?" I chuckled and said, "With an offer like this, how could I refuse? What game do you two have in mind?" "Well, we haven't played your favorite game for a while. Do you want to play solitaire doubles? You and Papa can play one side, and we can play the other. Do you think Papa would like to play?" "Now, a question like this needs to be asked to your Papa, not me." "OK. We'll go find him."

Priceless Moments

As I sat waiting for them to return, I pondered how we should be careful not to play games with God. He desires us to be forthright with Him, others, and ourselves. The secret place of the *corner office*, an area away from others, is a place to meet God to listen to His still, small voice or any other means He chooses to talk with us.

Thank You, LORD, for a straightforward Bible full of truthful information to help us understand Your plan for our world and our future. I pray we meet You in the corner office to prepare ourselves to receive Your direction for our daily lives.

Proverbs 3:5-6: *Trust in Yahweh with all your heart, and don't lean on your own understanding. In all your ways acknowledge him, and he will make your paths straight.*

James 1:5: *But if any of you lacks wisdom, let him ask of God, who gives to all liberally and without reproach, and it will be given to him.*

Psalm 91:1: *He who dwells in the secret place of the Most High will rest in the shadow of the Almighty.*

April 8th
<u>Colors of the Rainbow</u>

"Hey, Grandma. Do you have a minute to help me learn the colors of the rainbow in order? Our teacher said we can earn bonus points if we can correctly say them tomorrow. You seem to know all kinds of neat ways to learn stuff." I had to chuckle and say, "Of course, I can help you learn them. First, let's go over the colors. I will print them as a list on a piece of paper so you can see them as well as hear them. The colors are red, orange, yellow, green, blue, indigo, and violet. Now, look at the first letter of each color. What do you see?" "There is an 'r,' 'o,' 'y,' 'g,' 'b,' 'i,' 'v.'" "That's absolutely correct. If you put the first three letters together, what do they spell?" She looked at them a little bit, then said, "Roy?" "That's right, princess. The next part is silly. Biv is the last of the three letters. If you say "Roy," put "g" in the middle and "biv" at the end; the colors are in order."

She wrote Roy—g—biv on her own piece of paper. She thought of color names to fit the acronym, saying them out loud. After several tries and being encouraged to look at a picture of a rainbow in her mind, she listed the seven colors in order, without error. "Oh, thank you so much. I can say these tomorrow and pick something out of the treasure box. The last time I looked in the treasure box, there was a rainbow-colored key chain. I think I'll pick this one and put it on my backpack as a reminder of God's promise to Noah and us about not flooding the earth again." I replied, "That sounds like an awesome idea. I will be excited to see it tomorrow when you get home."

How many times do we think of things and relate them back to God? These children have been taught from the beginning about God, seeing Him in anything and everything in their lives—it's second nature to them. No matter if we were taught early in life or have recently accepted Jesus as our Savior, we must endeavor to eat, sleep, and breathe Jesus 24/7 until it becomes second nature to us as well.

Thank You, LORD, for promises that appear and reappear as visual reminders of Your constant faith and abiding love. I pray we are looking for Your hand in all things to give us reminders of Your loving care for us.

Genesis 9:13*: I set my rainbow in the cloud, and it will be a sign of a covenant between me and the earth.*

Isaiah 1:18*: "Come now, and let's reason together," says Yahweh: "Though your sins are as scarlet, they shall be as white as snow. Though they are red like crimson, they shall be as wool."*

Priceless Moments

Revelation 4:3*: And the One who sat there had the appearance of jasper and ruby. A rainbow that shone like an emerald encircled the throne. NIV*

April 9th
Catch the Gecko

Our son's property is home to many geckos, seen at all times of the day. When we are outside, you hear, "Catch the gecko before it gets away. There it goes, climbing up the side of the patio. Don't let it get away." I said, "All hands on deck. We need to catch the critter before it gets away. It's a matter of life and death." "Oh, Grandma, don't be so dramatic. We will see more of them as we do so every day. If we catch one, can I keep it?" "I think that's a question to ask your parents, not me. They make good pets since they are easy to take care of, are easy to tame, and don't mind being held."

"Grandma, what else do you know about geckos?" "Surprisingly, geckos are considered nocturnal, or nighttime lizards, but we see them here all day long. They come out when the weather gets warmer and drier." "How do they climb the walls?" "They have sticky pads on the bottoms of their feet to help them climb. Usually, they will only bite if they feel threatened, but most of the time they will run from you—like they are doing now. Geckos climb over walls of buildings to find insects, their favorite food, but will also eat worms and small birds." "How long do geckos live?" "Their average lifespan is between two and nine years, depending on where they live, how much food they find, and how well they stay away from their predators or other animals that like to eat geckos."

Watching the kids chase the geckos reminded me of our different types of behaviors and spiritual gifts: serving, organizing, keeping track of needs, teaching or leading, giving financial or other gifts (time, food, clothing, etc.), and being full of mercy. I hope we don't need to be *caught and tamed* to be of service to our LORD.

Thank You, LORD, for all types of gifts. I pray we see the value in each one, endeavoring to stay on the LORD's side while using them and not running around under our own strength. May we be aware of our gifts and pray that You will provide opportunities to use them.

Leviticus 11:29: *Of the animals that move about on the ground, these are unclean for you: the weasel, the rat, any kind of great lizard, the gecko, the monitor lizard, the wall lizard, the skink, and the chameleon. NIV*

Numbers 32:23: *But if you will not do so, behold, you have sinned against Yahweh; and be sure your sin will find you out.*

1 Corinthians 1:4-6: *I always thank my God for you because of his grace given you in Christ Jesus. For in him you have been enriched in every way—with all kinds of speech and with all knowledge— God thus confirming our testimony about Christ among you.*

April 10th

Can We Go To the Library?

"Can we go to the library today? It's been a long time since we've gone to story time. They always read neat books, and we learn a lot." "You're right, and that's a marvelous idea. It has been a while, and today is the day for story time. Did you know our country's Library of Congress in Washington, D.C., established in 1800, is the largest library in the world?" "Wow, it must be a big place." "Yes, it is. It has over one hundred thirty-eight million items housed on bookshelves that cover around six hundred fifty miles." "What kinds of items are in the library?" "Good question.

Priceless Moments

Besides books, there are other types of printed materials like Bibles, American history documents like speeches and proclamations, newspapers, periodicals, maps, manuscripts, sheet music, photographs, telephone directories, comic books, recordings, DVDs, cassette tapes, and much more."

We loaded up and headed towards the library. "Grandma, how does our library here compare to the Library of Congress?" "Our library here was established in 1897 by members of two local women's clubs to start a free library that would be open to the public. The original library grew over the years, receiving monies from private individuals and various organizations, outgrowing several buildings until it moved to a renovated Safeway grocery store building in 1974, where it remains today." "That's awesome. Wouldn't it be fun to get groceries and books at the same place? You know, one-stop shopping." They giggled at being so clever. "OK, we're here. Let's go enjoy story time."

After thinking about all the items at the Library of Congress, my favorite is the Gutenberg Bible, one of three perfect copies on vellum existing in the world, purchased in 1930. Available all these years… Yet D.C. is drifting farther and farther away from the tenets of God.

Thank You, LORD; we are privileged to have Your Word in print in our own homes. I pray we are willing to read it daily, not keeping it under glass for show but as a roadmap for our lives. May we also be praying for our elected leaders to experience the Master's hand to guide them in making godly decisions for You and our country.

Isaiah 41:10: *Don't you be afraid, for I am with you. Don't be dismayed, for I am your God. I will strengthen you. Yes, I will help you. Yes, I will uphold you with the right hand of my righteousness.*

Priceless Moments

Jeremiah 1:9: *Then Yahweh stretched out his hand, and touched my mouth. Then Yahweh said to me, "Behold, I have put my words in your mouth."*

Acts 2:33: *Being therefore exalted by the right hand of God, and having received from the Father the promise of the Holy Spirit, he has poured out this, which you now see and hear.*

April 11th
<u>*A Kleenex, Please*</u>

The kids seem to have colds or stuffiness any time of the year. I heard, "May I have a Kleenex, please?" followed by sneezing and, "Hurry, please. The box of Kleenex near me is empty." Of course, it is, so I grabbed toilet paper, saying, "I'll be right there." When I entered the room, I heard, "I can't use that; it's not a Kleenex." I explained, "I need to go find another box, but I don't want to take the time right now. This will work just fine for now. Here, let me help you." Refusing, she said, "No, I need a Kleenex. Please hurry." The situation was dire, so I proceeded to wipe her nose myself. "Grandma, that's gross. How could you do this to me?"

Somewhat amused yet conflicted, I said, "Honey, toilet paper is another form of Kleenex. They were at my fingertips when you called, sounding desperate, I might add, so I hurried to your rescue with this clean option." She settled down, so I added, "Did you ever see someone using a handkerchief, the original Kleenex? They can be washed after use, saving on garbage." Intrigued, she asked, "Do you know anybody who uses a handkerchief?" I smiled and said, "Yes, Papa uses handkerchiefs all the time. Also, they keep his nose from getting sore." I watched as a deep thought crossed her face, "Do you think I could have a handkerchief?" "Sure. Let me go find you one."

I thought of times when we are insistent in prayer with God when we want something to be our way, yet God answers with a twist or with something completely different. Initially, we may be upset, but in the end, we realize God had a much better option for us—we just didn't know it yet. (And, yes, I replaced the box of Kleenex.)

Thank You, LORD, for not giving us what we want but what we need. I pray we end our prayers with "not my will but Your will be done," since You have known what we truly needed all along.

Jeremiah 29:11: *For I know the thoughts that I think toward you," says Yahweh, "thoughts of peace, and not of evil, to give you hope and a future."*

1 Thessalonians 5:18: *In everything give thanks, for this is the will of God in Christ Jesus toward you.*

Hebrews 13:20-21: *Now may the God of peace, who brought again from the dead the great shepherd of the sheep with the blood of an eternal covenant, our Lord Jesus, ^{21} make you complete in every good work to do his will, working in you that which is well pleasing in his sight, through Jesus Christ, to whom be the glory forever and ever. Amen.*

April 12th

My Favorite Story

"Hey, kiddos, it's time for bed. Please brush your teeth and put on your jammies. I'll meet you on the couch." I heard some hustle and bustle going on, indicating the request was being carried out. Soon they came running, saying, "We talked it over, and we would like you to read our favorite story about Jesus. We just love to hear it." "I would be delighted to read about Jesus, but which particular story do you want? There are so many good ones, but I want to know which one is truly your favorite." Whispering went on between the two of them, exchanging "No, not that one," or

Priceless Moments

"Maybe," until I heard, "We want the one about Jesus when he was a boy, and His parents couldn't find Him after they had already started home."

Eyes filled with expectation focused on me. I opened my Bible to **Luke 2:41-49**, reading the account of a twelve-year-old found to be missing among the relatives on their way home from Passover. "Why did Jesus say He had to be in His Father's house?" they wanted to know. "Jesus knew God was His Heavenly Father, so He wanted to be in His Father's house. He also knew He needed to be obedient to His earthly parents, so He returned home with them without any questions."

Oh, for the zeal of little ones wanting to hear more of Jesus and then wanting to hear how Jesus went to church and listened to His parents. I pray they never outgrow their desire for You.

Thank You, LORD, for including a story of a young Jesus and how He was hungry for more of You. I pray our faith grows from the childlike faith to a deep, abiding love—where we still listen to and want more of You.

Luke 2:49: *He said to them, "Why were you looking for me? Didn't you know that I must be in my Father's house?"*

Luke 2:51-52: *And he went down with them, and came to Nazareth. He was subject to them, and his mother kept all these sayings in her heart. And Jesus increased in wisdom and stature, and in favor with God and men.*

Philippians 2:8: *And being found in human form, he humbled himself, becoming obedient to the point of death, yes, the death of the cross.*

Priceless Moments

April 13th
Scrabble

"Grandma, do you have any different games we can play? I'd like to try something different." "I sure do. Have you played a game before called *Scrabble*?" "No, what is it? How do you play it?" "Alphabet letters are on little tiles. They are mixed up, and each person chooses a tile. The one closest to the letter 'A' goes first. Each person chooses ten tiles to place on their game rack, keeping them hidden from everyone else. The first person spells a word, placing it on the "start" block on the board and adding up the numbers on the tiles to get a score. They will draw enough tiles to replace those used for their word. The next person will use one of those letters from the first word to build another word, either by adding to the word or using one of their letters to spell a different word, and then count up their score. There are other things, but they are not important right now.

"What is the history behind this game?" "It was created in the 1930s during the Great Depression by an unemployed architect named Alfred Butts as a variation of another game, called *Lexiko*, played without a board, playing letters in a crisscross fashion. Players earned points based on the length of the word they created. Later, it was renamed *Criss Cross* to describe the way words were placed on the table, then trademarked as *Scrabble* in 1948 by James Brunot. Actually, today is National Scrabble Day.

Reflecting on the game, I thought of how sometimes there are simple words to spell, but other times there are no possible combinations of the hand we are dealt. Yet, our hand is reliant on what our fellow players lay down. I'm thankful God doesn't make us play *Scrabble* to win our salvation. His rules are very easy to follow, with no hidden twists or turns lurking in each round—being saved and then sanctified.

Thank You, LORD, for providing salvation, something we can all achieve, but not by being dealt a certain hand but rather by dealing our hand to You to make something beautiful out of our lives.

Matthew 7:21-23: "Not everyone who says to me, 'Lord, Lord,' will enter into the Kingdom of Heaven, but he who does the will of my Father who is in heaven. Many will tell me in that day, 'Lord, Lord, didn't we prophesy in your name, in your name cast out demons, and in your name do many mighty works?' Then I will tell them, 'I never knew you. Depart from me, you who work iniquity.'"

Romans 12:2: Don't be conformed to this world, but be transformed by the renewing of your mind, so that you may prove what is the good, well-pleasing, and perfect will of God.

1 Thessalonians 5:21-22: Test all things, and hold firmly that which is good. Abstain from every form of evil.

April 14th

Water Puddle Boots

Our grandchildren have a fascination with water puddles—what kid doesn't? One particularly rainy day, the grandchildren asked, "Can we wear our water puddle boots and go outside today? Wouldn't it be lots of fun splashing around out there, especially since we don't get water puddles every day?" I thought it sounded like fun, too. "OK, rain boots and raincoats for everyone." "Grandma, are you coming out with us?" I chuckled, "Of course. You don't want me to miss out on all the fun, do you?" They shook their heads, saying, "But you're a grownup. I didn't think you would do something like this." "You've got me there," I responded, "but I'm actually just a big kid at heart."

Once outside, I heard, "Let's get Grandma." They ganged up on me, splashing me from both sides. The kid in me was surfacing as I decided, "OK, kiddos. Remember, if you can dish it out, you'd better be able to take it, too." I let them chase me as I led them to the biggest puddle in the area. I yelled, "Jump." Of course, they weren't ready for a good splash. While still holding my hands, they yelled, "Jump." Anticipating this move, we all jumped and sent water in all directions. "That was fun. Let's do it again." Knowing we were soaked anyway, I said, "Sure, but make it a good one." When we went inside, we looked like we'd stood under the shower with our clothes on—but it was worth it.

I realized, again, how much fun water puddles can be. It dawned on me how we need to immerse ourselves in God's Word, being drenched in the fullness of His glory and soaking in every word God provides for us. Our inner child can learn so much more when we are open to all the possibilities only He can provide.

Thank You, LORD, for good times shared with family and friends. I pray we see You in the showers of blessings You provide for us daily and that we are never too grownup or sophisticated to appreciate the abundantly given gifts from Your hand—including rain and puddles.

Job 37:6: For he says to the snow, "Fall on the earth" likewise to the shower of rain, and to the showers of his mighty rain.

Genesis 7:4: In seven days, I will cause it to rain on the earth for forty days and forty nights. I will destroy every living thing that I have made from the surface of the ground.

Hosea 10:12: Sow to yourselves in righteousness, reap according to kindness. Break up your fallow ground; for it is time to seek Yahweh, until he comes and rains righteousness on you.

April 15th

What Is Income Tax

"Dad and Mom were talking yesterday about paying their income tax. What is that, and why do they have to pay it?" "Income tax is what we pay on the money we earned last year. This money gives

Priceless Moments

the government the funds needed to build roads; protect our country, called national defense; provide benefits for veterans and military retirees; pay out money the recipients already paid in for social security, a forced governmental retirement savings plan; pay down our national debt; and sponsor other giveaway programs sponsored by the government that no one has paid into to get their benefits later."

"How did such a thing ever get started?" "Our U.S. Constitution originally did not allow for its citizens to be taxed. Our country observed other countries taxing their people, so they adopted the idea from France in 1862 during the Civil War. It was put aside for a few years until Congress decided to bring it back in 1894, and then it was declared unconstitutional. By 1913, the 16th Amendment to our Constitution brought back the tax, setting a fixed rate of 1%. Now we have to keep records of earnings and spending to complete tax forms by April 15th each year. As of today, most people pay around one-fourth of their earned money for different types of taxes.

I thought about how hard we have worked for our money and endeavor to be good stewards of what God has entrusted to us, yet once it leaves our hands, the same stewardship principles are not followed. After taxes and before paying bills, if Christians would cheerfully give a ten-percent of their tithe to God plus freewill offerings, He promises He will bless His people.

Thank You, LORD, for the promises in Your Word. I pray we understand that You tell us if we do our part first, then You will fulfill Your part of the promise to us. The proper sequence of actions is needed.

Romans 13:1-2: *Let every soul be in subjection to the higher authorities, for there is no authority except from God, and those who exist are ordained by God. Therefore he who resists the authority withstands the ordinance of God; and those who withstand will receive to themselves judgment.*

Priceless Moments

Mark 12:17: Jesus answered them, "Render to Caesar the things that are Caesar's, and to God the things that are God's."

Malachi 3:10: Bring the whole tithe into the storehouse, that there may be food in my house, and test me now in this," says Yahweh of Armies, "if I will not open you the windows of heaven, and pour you out a blessing, that there will not be room enough for."

April 16th
Hi, Grandma, It's Me

When our granddaughters are riding from home to church, school, or shopping, and vice versa, they like to call Grandma. "Hi, Grandma, it's me. We're on our way home from gymnastics, and I wanted to call and see how you were doing. We did this kind of roll and that kind of jump. And I was the only one of all the kids who listened." "Oh, honey. It is so good to hear from you. I'm so proud of you. I love hearing those good reports." She proceeded, "We just saw a bald eagle in a tree. People were pulled off the road to watch them. What's really neat is that we learned about bald eagles at the library. Did you know they lay their eggs in a big nest way up high and sit on them to keep them warm? When they get too warm, they get off the eggs and let them cool down so that they can still hatch." "That's fascinating."

I asked, "Has your dad shown you a website where you can watch the eagles, from building the nest and laying of two or three eggs until they hatch into baby eagles called eaglets? It is really fun to watch and lets you see all the things you were just telling me about happen in the nest." "Oh, Daddy, can we look for this on the internet? I would like to watch them and hopefully see the baby eaglets hatch. Maybe we can take a few pictures that I can show the other kids the next time we go to the program at the library."

I find myself thinking it's the same with God, "Hi, God. It's me again." We need to be sure to keep the line of communication open from our end because God's line is never too busy, but rather, always on speaker ready to take our call.

Thank You, LORD, for a hotline to heaven. I pray we take advantage of the privilege to just say hi, to thank and praise You for the beautiful day, not always asking for something.

Psalm 17:6: *I have called on you, for you will answer me, God. Turn your ear to me. Hear my speech.*

Colossians 3:15: *And let the peace of God rule in your hearts, to which also you were called in one body, and be thankful.*

Jeremiah 29:13: *You shall seek me, and find me, when you search for me with all your heart.*

April 17th
Battery-Operated Tea Lights

"Grandma, can we decorate with those little battery-operated lights you have? I'd like to see them all lit up and change colors." "You know what? I like to watch those myself. They are called tea lights. I can get them, but I will need lots of help to set them up in the living room. Then, I'll need someone to turn them on and off every evening. Will you be able to help me do that?" The hissing started, "Yesssss, yesssss, yesssss. How soon can you go get them?" "If you're ready, I'll go get them now." They were squealing with delight as I walked out of the room to the storage closet. Also, I saw a set of three-tier color-changing candles and decided to bring them out as well.

The kids had already moved some things around to make room for the tea lights. "Where did you get those big lights? Do they run on batteries, too, or do you need to plug them in?" Our grandson picked one up, turning it all around, and then stated, "These run on batteries. Do you have any of this size to make them work?" I looked at the bottom of the candles and said, "Each one of these need three AAA batteries. I'll go back to the storage closet and get the batteries we need." I returned, "Here you go. Help me put them in so you can turn them on."

We enjoyed the beautiful glow, which made me ponder, "Our God is alive; no batteries required." We don't need to turn Him on or off because He is the ONLY living God; all others are made of wood or stone. One important lesson is that these batteries are useless just lying around in the closet. We need to put them in something for them to be beneficial. God and His Word are like the one important lesson in these batteries—we need Them in us to work properly or come alive.

Thank You, LORD, that we are privileged to serve You. I pray we can rest in You to recharge our "batteries" to remain energized to work for the kingdom.

Matthew 11:28: Come to me, all you who labor and are heavily burdened, and I will give you rest.

Romans 12:11-12: Never be lacking in zeal, but keep your spiritual fervor, serving the LORD. Be joyful in hope, patient in affliction, faithful in prayer. NIV

Isaiah 40:30-31: Even the youths faint and get weary, and the young men utterly fall; but those who wait for Yahweh will renew their strength. They will mount up with wings like eagles. They will run, and not be weary. They will walk, and not faint.

April 18th

You Didn't Say Goodnight

Our daughter-in-law called and said, "You need to talk to your grandson." He was sobbing, "Grandma, you didn't say good night to me. I wanted to give you a hug and a kiss, but you were gone

Priceless Moments

already." "I was there for supper, helped clean up the kitchen while you got a bath, then left. I feel terrible. Oh, honey, I'm sooooo sorry. I thought you were already in bed, so I didn't want to wake you. Honey, I'll tell you now. Good night, and I love you very much. I will try not to miss a night again!" Through the remaining sobs, "OK, Grandma. I missed you saying good night. Please, I don't want to miss my good-night hug and kiss again."

The next day, I made a point of holding our little man and saying, "I want to tell you how much I love you and apologize for missing out on our special time last night. I will try my very best not to forget again. Will you forgive me?" He smiled and said, "Oh, Grandma, I need to tell you good night because I love you so much. When you were gone, I was afraid you wouldn't know that." "Dear, sweet child, I know how much you care, but I also know how important it is to you to express yourself to me. If we need to, let's say goodnight early so we both can sleep better. Deal?" "Deal."

That night I pondered how we miss a night here and there speaking to God to express our love and adoration, until eventually we stop, thinking, "He won't miss me saying good night… and then good morning.' When we understand how valuable these expressions of love are, we return to letting God know what He means to us.

Thank You, LORD, for Your long-suffering nature when we drift from giving You hugs and kisses every night. I pray we understand these are expressions of devotion to You, which bring us into a deeper relationship with our Heavenly Father.

1 John 4:9-11: By this God's love was revealed in us, that God has sent his one and only Son into the world that we might live through him. In this is love, not that we loved God, but that he loved us, and sent his Son as the atoning sacrifice[a] for our sins. Beloved, if God loved us in this way, we also ought to love one another.

Priceless Moments

Ephesians 4:15: *but speaking truth in love, we may grow up in all things into him who is the head, Christ,*

1 Peter 5:7: *casting all your worries on him, because he cares for you.*

April 19th
Military Dog Tags

My husband keeps his military dog tags hanging on the wall. The grandchildren have noticed them but haven't asked questions. When changing the month, the tags are removed to flip the calendar. "Grandma, why do you take those metal things down every time you change the calendar, then put them back up when you're done? What are they for? Why do you have them?" "Wow, that's a lot of questions. I'll try to answer them. These metal things are called dog tags. Papa was given these when he was in the U.S. Navy. I take them down so I can turn the page on the calendar to the new month. I put them back up because Papa knows where to find them. All military personnel are given two dog tags to wear under their uniforms in case of an emergency. Each tag contains their name and information about them, so they were used primarily for identification. Today, they are more of a symbol of his military service since most information is kept on computers."

They were absorbing the information when they asked, "Can we each look at one? Are they heavy to wear?" "Here you go," I said, handing each one a dog tag. "You can run your fingers across the information embossed into the metal or pressed into it." "I have another question: what type of metal is this? It's very light." "You are correct. There is a long history of how dog tags came about. Anything from sewing their names in their jackets, a soldier pin, a round metal disc, or a paper tag attached to their uniforms and belongings. Eventually, a half-dollar-sized disc was worn around the neck. For identification purposes, each soldier was now issued two dog tags. They used to be made out of stainless steel, but the newer ones are made out of aluminum, like these in your hands."

As we talked, I thought of how God would identify us as members of His army. A song says, *"They will know we are Christians by our love,"* a reflection of the love of Jesus willingly dying for us and our sins.

Thank You, LORD, for changing hearts and showing where our allegiance lies. I pray we demonstrate enough evidence to be convicted as Christians by every person we meet.

Matthew 7:16-17: By their fruits you will know them. Do you gather grapes from thorns or figs from thistles? Even so, every good tree produces good fruit, but the corrupt tree produces evil fruit.

John 13:34: A new commandment I give to you, that you love one another. Just as I have loved you, you also love one another. By this everyone will know that you are my disciples, if you have love for one another.

Romans 8:16.17: The Spirit himself testifies with our spirit that we are children of God; and if children, then heirs: heirs of God and joint heirs with Christ, if indeed we suffer with him, that we may also be glorified with him.

April 20th

Antique Cars

"Did you see that car, Grandma? It doesn't look anything like the ones we see on the roads here." I looked quickly to see the car to which he was referring. "Ah, that's a Model T Ford, named after its creator, Henry Ford." "Wow, how do you know that?" "When Papa and I were first married, we owned an antique car. Our landlord, the person we rented from, owned many antique cars as

Priceless Moments

well. He taught us about and showed us many different cars. He actually owned one of those cars, like you just saw." "What all do you know about it?" "Well, I know Mr. Ford wanted to make a simpler, cheaper model than the other fancier cars he'd already made. At first, it came in three colors: red, gray, or green; then only a dark green; and the next year, they were all blue. The year he started a moving assembly line, they only came in one color, saying, "Any color the customer wants, as long as it's black."

"Cool. Do you still have your old car? I don't remember seeing it here." "Unfortunately, no. We moved and had to sell it, so our landlord bought it." "What was it like?" "Our 1932 Ford had suicide doors, or coach doors, which means both the front and rear doors opened in the middle. They were considered a safety hazard since back seat passengers could get trapped or injured if their door were hit by another vehicle. The windshield wipers rarely worked, but it had the best radio ever. The coolest part was that it had a rumble seat in the back instead of a trunk. The seat came up when you lifted the trunk lid to form the back of the seat."

I thought of how our sins are only black; there are no little white lies or gray areas of truth. Sin is sin, regardless of its severity, all requiring to be covered with the red blood of Jesus to make us white as snow.

Thank You, LORD, that Your crowning creation is redeemable by the blood of the Lamb. I pray we all humble ourselves and be blessed as we accept the greatest Gift ever given to mankind.

Job 34:22: *There is no darkness, nor thick gloom, where the workers of iniquity may hide themselves.*

2 Peter 2:17: *These are wells without water, clouds driven by a storm; for whom the blackness of darkness has been reserved forever.*

Psalm 51:7: *Purify me with hyssop, and I will be clean. Wash me, and I will be whiter than snow.*

Priceless Moments

April 21st

Kites

"Hey, guys, have your parents ever told you to go fly a kite?" "Have they ever told us what? I don't understand what that means." I chuckled and said, "Telling you to go fly a kite is their way of being nice when asking you to go do something else." "Have you ever been told to go fly a kite?" "Yes, I have. I remember my older brothers telling me that when their friends were at our house. You know what I did then—I went to the garage and got my favorite kite and enjoyed the time outside flying my kite. Often, my younger brother would come out and join me because they told him the same thing. We would have contests to see who could keep their kite up the longest. Those were really fun days."

"Can you tell us about kites and how they are used?" "Sure can. Sit down, and I'll tell you about flying high. Kites can be made of silk, plastic, canvas, strong paper bags, or nylon, covering a wooden or plastic frame and a long, funny tail. Kites had mythical and religious beginnings, being used in scientific experiments, to carry weather measuring instruments, tow people across water, and now for fun." The little ones disappeared for a few minutes, returning with two kites. "Grandma, can you tell us to go fly a kite?" I had to bait them. "Why would I want to do that? I don't want to push you away." "But, Grandma, we want to fly kites, and we need your help. You know how to make them work."

Memories of kites soaring and swooping, dipping in downdrafts, and hours of fun floated through my mind. Our Christian walk experiences mountain and valley times as well. We come in all shapes, sizes, and uses, as do kites.

Thank You, LORD, for pleasant childhood memories of fun and Your faithfulness. I pray we focus more on the good times and view the valleys as challenges rather than catastrophes. The way we conduct ourselves in and out of the home is viewed by family, friends, neighbors, co-workers, new acquaintances, and strangers, influencing their decision to "fly" with You or "swoop" with Satan.

Isaiah 40:31: *But those who wait for Yahweh will renew their strength. They will mount up with wings like eagles. They will run, and not be weary. They will walk, and not faint.*

Obadiah 1:4*: "Though you mount on high as the eagle, and though your nest is set among the stars, I will bring you down from there," says Yahweh.*

Jeremiah 49:22: *Behold, he will come up and fly as the eagle, and spread out his wings against Bozrah. The heart of the mighty men of Edom at that day will be as the heart of a woman in her pangs.*

April 22nd

<u>Baseball</u>

"Have you ever played baseball, Grandma? My Dad said he played baseball for many years when he was a boy." "Yes, I did, but just with my brothers and cousins. And, yes, your Dad played for many years." "What kind of a player was he?" "He could hit almost anything thrown his way. He had a strong arm that could get the ball thrown just where he wanted it to go." "Did he ever hit a home run?" "Yes, he did. I remember one time he injured his foot. His coach wasn't going to let him play, but your Dad convinced him he could hit a home run. The coach agreed. True to his word, he got up to bat and hit a home run. He hobbled to first base, at which point a substitute came in to run the remaining bases to home."

He was mulling something over in his mind and finally asked, "Can you teach me about baseball so I can learn to play? I'd like to hit a home run like my dad." "OK. Let's start with the basics. There are four bases: home, first, second, and third. As a player,

Priceless Moments

you, the batter, stand in the batting box to receive a ball thrown from the pitcher on the other team. You swing at balls that cross the plate, called the strike zone. If you miss, it's called a strike. If the ball is too high, too low, or outside the batting box, it's called a ball. Each player gets four balls and three strikes per turn. Three strikes and you're out; four balls and you get walked to first base. To score a run, you must run all the bases without getting out." "That's a lot of information. Maybe we can go out and work through this much, then learn some more later." "I agree. Let's go."

Baseball reminds me of being a Christian. We are born (first base), grow up, accept Jesus at some point (second base), become sanctified (third base), and slip into eternity in the arms of our LORD (home.).

Thank You, LORD, for leading us each step of the way to our heavenly home. I pray we read and study our Bibles to know the "rules" to follow to be assured of finishing the "game" with a home run across heaven's "home plate."

Matthew 7:13-14: "Enter through the narrow gate. For wide is the gate and broad is the road that leads to destruction, and many enter through it. But small is the gate and narrow the road that leads to life, and only a few find it. NIV

1 John 5:13: These things I have written to you who believe in the name of the Son of God, that you may know that you have eternal life, and that you may continue to believe in the name of the Son of God.

Mark 16:16: He who believes and is baptized will be saved; but he who disbelieves will be condemned.

Priceless Moments

April 23rd

Earth Day

"Can you explain Earth Day to me? Our teacher said we're going to talk about it in school tomorrow." "Ah, getting a jump on the lesson, I see. Good for you. Earth Day, inspired by Arbor Day, when settlers in Nebraska were encouraged to plant trees, is something we do every year on April 22 to make people worldwide aware of caring for and protecting the environment. Each year there is a new theme to focus on one aspect of the event to take place on one day or throughout the coming week." "What kind of things do people do?" "Good question. Some things done during this time are planting trees, picking up trash along the roadside, emphasizing recycling and conservation or not wasting resources, educating people to use recyclable containers instead of disposable ones for their snacks and lunches, things like that." "That's a lot of stuff, but what can we do to help?"

I pondered her question, then responded, "When you go for walks to enjoy the beauty of nature, take a bag with you to pick up trash along the path; participate in a neighborhood cleanup; make a bird feeder out of things from around your house, like toilet paper tubes, popsicle sticks, and pinecones; help plant a garden of flowers or vegetables and herbs, to name a few. Does this give you any ideas of things that you could do?" "Oh, I know something we could do as a family. I may not be able to do things the bigger kids do, but I would love to go for a hike or a bike ride and pick up trash." "Great idea. That would be a fun family activity."

I thought every day should be Earth Day since the LORD initially intended for us to be its caretakers. Our lives should also be an "Earth Day," continually ridding ourselves of the trash that accumulates in our lives and can weigh us down and hinder our walk with the LORD.

Thank You, LORD, for never cutting us off from cleaning up our lives. I pray we walk close with You, listening to the Holy Spirit give us insight into areas to be confessed and swept clean.

1 John 1:9*: If we confess our sins, he is faithful and righteous to forgive us the sins, and to cleanse us from all unrighteousness.*

Colossians 3:25*: But he who does wrong will receive again for the wrong that he has done, and there is no partiality.*

Romans 12:2*: Don't be conformed to this world, but be transformed by the renewing of your mind, so that you may prove what is the good, well-pleasing, and perfect will of God.*

April 24th
Let's Plant a Tree

"We talked about Arbor Day and Earth Day today. You talked about Earth Day yesterday, right, Grandma? Arbor Day is when families or groups of people get together to plant trees in their yard, in parks, or in the forest. Our teacher said there are many benefits to planting trees. She told us to plant them, water them, cut off dead branches, add supports to help them grow straight and strong, and surround them with material to keep animals away from them so they don't kill them." "It sounds like you were really listening. How did you remember all this information?" "A man from the forest people came to our class and showed us how to plant a tree and how to take care of it."

I thought for a minute, then responded, "I guess we could plant a tree in our front yard. When it grew bigger, it would provide some shade for the house to keep it cooler in the summer. But I wouldn't know the first place to start looking for trees to plant." A little pause: "Oh, Grandma, I almost forgot. The man gave each of us a card from where he works so we would know where to get trees and answers for any questions we might have." "OK, you've convinced me. Let's plant a tree."

Priceless Moments

May we find ourselves "planting trees" like growing people as Christians, "watering" them with the Word, keeping their "roots" moist, pruning "limbs" that grow or sprout in the wrong direction, surrounding them with "material" to keep away the wolves in sheep's clothing, adding "supports" where needed to keep them growing and maturing in their Christian walk. We need to be as enthusiastic as children to present the good news to others.

Thank You, LORD, for other Christians who plant the seeds of Jesus in people's hearts, others to water and cultivate, and others to bring the increase into the kingdom. I pray we are not concerned about the area in which You have called us to serve but work wholeheartedly to do our part where we are planted as You guide us to lead others to You.

Jeremiah 17:7-8: *Blessed is the man who trusts in Yahweh, and whose confidence is in Yahweh. For he will be as a tree planted by the waters, who spreads out its roots by the river, and will not fear when heat comes, but its leaf will be green, and will not be concerned in the year of drought. It won't cease from yielding fruit.*

1 Corinthians 7:17: *Nevertheless, each one should retain the place in life that the LORD assigned to him and to which God has called him. NIV*

James 1:3-4: *knowing that the testing of your faith produces endurance. Let endurance have its perfect work, that you may be perfect and complete, lacking in nothing.*

April 25th

<u>What's a Secretary?</u>

"Do you know what a secretary is, Grandma? Mom said something about her secretary, but I didn't understand what she

Priceless Moments

meant. I knew you could tell me." "Sure, we can talk about it. Basically, a secretary is the person who makes the office run smoothly and is the center of communication. This man or woman has to know how to organize, keep the boss up-to-date on the when and why of what's happening in the office, know how to type, and perform other related duties." "What are other related duties?" "This means they have to be a receptionist, the one who answers the telephone, greets people who come to their office, alerts the person with whom they have an appointment, takes care of the mail, organizes meetings takes minutes of meetings by writing down what was said, types the minutes, then sends copies to whoever might need them." "This person does a lot of work." "What happens if the secretary is sick or goes on vacation?" "Like the rest of us, you do as much of your work ahead of time, hoping to have the necessary things done before that happens. Secretaries are so appreciated that a special day was created in 1952 to honor all office staff. It's called Administrative Professionals Week. It's a great way to say how much their faithfulness is appreciated each and every day of the year—to give them flowers, a gift, and take them out to lunch. Everybody needs to know... they are truly appreciated."

I thought about how secretaries are an underpaid and underappreciated sector of the workforce. It's truly the secretary who makes the boss look good. When unexpected things kept turning up, my secretary went above and beyond to make sure the impossible was done. She was indispensable and truly appreciated. And I did everything to let her know I felt this way.

Thank You, LORD, for people who give their all on the job. I pray, because You gave Your all for us, that we give our all for Your kingdom—because thanks will never be enough.

Matthew 5:10: Blessed are those who have been persecuted for righteousness' sake, for theirs is the Kingdom of Heaven.

Mark 1:15: and saying, "The time is fulfilled, and God's Kingdom is at hand! Repent, and believe in the Good News."

Luke 4:43: But he said to them, "I must preach the good news of God's Kingdom to the other cities also. For this reason I have been sent."

April 26th
The Rainbow-Colored Whisk

"I like your rainbow-colored things in the crock on the counter, Grandma. Can I look at one? What do you do with it?" As I'm turning in her direction, I'm thinking, "What are you talking about?" Like in the game *I Spy*, I spied the rainbow-colored whisks in the kitchen crock of utensils. Choosing one from the crock and handing it to her, I asked, "Are you talking about this?" "Exactly. What is it?" "It's called a whisk, for whipping or stirring eggs or batter to combine them together. Would you like to try using it to understand what it does? We can make some chia pudding." "Oh, really. Yes, let's do that, please and thank you."

We gathered all the ingredients on the counter. "Now, here is the bowl to make it in. I will tell you how to do it, and you can make it all by yourself. It's a simple recipe, and I have every confidence you will do a fine job." "What do I do first?" "Well, is this going to be for just you, or do you want to make some for everyone?" "Can we do it for everyone for dessert?" "I like how you think. You measure out three cups of almond milk, two-thirds cup of chia seeds, and one-fourth of a cup of honey, then use the whisk to mix it all together." "Wow, this is fun. I like using the whisk, especially since it has all the colors of the rainbow."

She made me think of how much appreciation we should have for God's beautiful choice of colors and His special promise to Noah and mankind with the rainbow. Incorporating those beautiful colors into our lives can bring to mind God's glory and faithfulness to us every day—because God never breaks a promise.

Priceless Moments

Thank You, LORD, for constant reminders of Your goodness and faithfulness. I pray we look for Your hand at work in all we say and do, giving You praise for always being there for us in the little things that bring so much pleasure.

Genesis 9:13-15: *I set my rainbow in the cloud, and it will be a sign of a covenant between me and the earth. When I bring a cloud over the earth, that the rainbow will be seen in the cloud, I will remember my covenant, which is between me and you and every living creature of all flesh, and the waters will no more become a flood to destroy all flesh.*

Ezekiel 1:28: *As the appearance of the rainbow that is in the cloud in the day of rain, so was the appearance of the brightness all around. This was the appearance of the likeness of Yahweh's glory.*

Revelation 4:3: *And the One Who sat there had the appearance of jasper and ruby. A rainbow that shone like an emerald encircled the throne. NIV*

April 27th
My Sunglasses

"Grandma, where did you get those cool sunglasses? Did you know they change colors when you wear them outside?" "Thank you. I'm happy you like them. Papa bought them for me because he knew how much we all liked rainbows and would enjoy seeing the colors change." "Nice, but how do they do that?" "When the material in the sunglasses senses a big change in temperature, the inks or dyes in them make them change colors." "Do they only change from one color to another, or can they change to many different colors?" "Surprisingly, several different dyes can be used in one product. Here, let me show you. I have a color-changing bag. Let's take it out into the sun and watch the white and black flowers to see what they do."

We took the bag outside to soak up some sun. "Cool, Grandma. It didn't take long for the garden to change from those two colors to a full one of different-colored flowers. I never thought anything like this could happen from just going outside. How long will these colors stay on the bag?" "The color change starts to fade almost instantly but can last for up to five minutes before completely returning to the original colors of black and white." "Does this have anything to do with glow-in-the-dark things like my sleeping bag and backpack?" "The process is different. Maybe we can talk about it another day."

I find that the more questions the little ones ask, the more interested I become in understanding more about the world around me, like the amazing products we find in stores. God has certainly helped man discover all kinds of things He placed in creation for our enjoyment.

Thank You, LORD, for all the intriguing things You provide to bring us delight. I pray we never lose our sense of wonder and curiosity about the many treasures You have provided for us to explore, create, and enjoy.

Zephaniah 3:17*: Yahweh, your God, is among you, a mighty one who will save. He will rejoice over you with joy. He will calm you in his love. He will rejoice over you with singing.*

Isaiah 61:10*: I will greatly rejoice in Yahweh! My soul will be joyful in my God, for he has clothed me with the garments of salvation. He has covered me with the robe of righteousness, as a bridegroom decks himself with a garland and as a bride adorns herself with her jewels.*

Isaiah 25:1*: Yahweh, you are my God. I will exalt you! I will praise your name, for you have done wonderful things, things planned long ago, in complete faithfulness and truth.*

Priceless Moments

April 28th
The Sleeping Bag

"Grandma, did you remember when you said you would tell us about my glow-in-the-dark sleeping bag and backpack? I've been waiting all day to hear about it. It's fun to go to bed at night and see the dinosaurs glowing. But when I wake up, they aren't glowing anymore. Why is that?" "The parts that glow in the dark are made from materials called phosphors. These phosphors absorb energy when the light is turned on and then slowly release their stored energy in the form of green light. The glow will gradually get less and less as the energy is released or used up, until it's all gone. That's why your sleeping bag no longer glows in the morning."

I could see the mental wheels turning once again. "Oh, so I would have to leave the light on longer to keep it glowing all night?" "I don't think it works like that, buddy. The material can only absorb so much charge, regardless of how long the light is on. It will hold the charge until the light is turned off, then they will start glowing to release the charge. Once it uses up all the stored energy, the glow is gone. Same thing with the backpack. The stars and horses can only absorb so much energy. Once the light is turned off, they will start releasing their charge until the glow disappears. A fun idea is to charge them up, then go in a dark room or closet, even during the daytime, and watch the process take place. Once you see how the glow starts to lessen, you will have a better understanding of how the charge is released. What do you say we go try it now?" "Yes, yes, yes, now."

I really enjoyed watching the bright glow fade during our time together. Unfortunately, some Christians seem to fade in their commitment to Jesus, being drawn to things "of the world" instead of things "out of this world."

Thank You, LORD, for the glow You put on our faces after accepting You as our personal Savior. I pray we never allow this

Priceless Moments

glow to diminish over time, but stay "charged up" in the light of Your glory.

Exodus 15:11: *Who is like you, Yahweh, among the gods? Who is like you, glorious in holiness, fearful in praises, doing wonders?*

Psalm 19:1*: The heavens declare the glory of God. The expanse shows his handiwork.*

1 Timothy 1:17*: Now to the King eternal, immortal, invisible, to God who alone is wise, be honor and glory forever and ever. Amen.*

April 29th
Do You Have an Umbrella?

"Oh, no. It just started to rain, and I have to walk to the school bus. Do you have an umbrella in the house? If so, may I borrow it for today?" "Of course. I have one that folds up to the point where it will fit in your backpack. Let me go get it, and I'll show you how it works." I went to the closet and pulled out the umbrella and showed her how to remove the outer sleeve, open the tie wrap, put it up and down without bending the ribs or the metal arms, close it with the tie wrap, and replace the outer sleeve.

"Did you know that umbrellas are made by hand? They are called canopies because of their shape and design. There are usually eight ribs that are sewn or attached to the eight panel sections that are attached to a pole, sometimes called a shaft. The shaft can have a straight handle or a curved handle and be made from wood, fiberglass, aluminum, or steel. The tip of the outside of the umbrella is called a ferrule. The sections can be plain, like one color, or printed with any type of design. The first umbrellas were made of silk and called parasols, but now the material can be vinyl, or a material coated with a waterproof finish. They are easy

Priceless Moments

to put up, dry quickly, and fold down easily. Umbrellas are used for more than just rain. They can protect us from the sun at the beach, while walking outside, on the golf course, and other places to protect equipment, as well as be part of a tightrope walker to help them keep their balance.

I've always heard rainy days can be showers of blessings. Lately, it has been pouring, so God is really blessing us after our dry spell. These blessings help the gardens grow, producing food and flowers, all to bless mankind. Kids enjoy jumping in and running through the water puddles, and fishermen delight in the emerging fishing worms.

Thank You, LORD, for sending us rain in due season and showering us with blessings—with or without rain—as You deem fit. I pray we are found worthy of Your blessings on a daily basis.

Ezekiel 34:26-27: *I will make them and the places around my hill a blessing. I will cause the shower to come down in its season. There will be showers of blessing. The tree of the field will yield its fruit, and the earth will yield its increase, and they will be secure in their land. Then they will know that I am Yahweh, when I have broken the bars of their yoke, and have delivered them out of the hand of those who made slaves of them.*

Isaiah 44:3: *For I will pour water on him who is thirsty, and streams on the dry ground. I will pour my Spirit on your descendants, and my blessing on your offspring:*

2 Corinthians 9:8: *And God is able to make all grace abound to you, that you, always having all sufficiency in everything, may abound to every good work.*

Priceless Moments

April 30th
April Showers...

"Grandma, what are April showers? I heard you say something like that before." "Yes, there is a saying, "*April showers bring May flowers.*" The full saying is "*March winds and April showers bring May flowers and June bugs.*" We can talk about the first part today, OK?" "Sure, it sounds good." "Then, here it goes… April showers refers to rain during the month of April, usually when the jet stream, or wind, of the weather moves northward and brings heavy downpours of rain and strong winds inland from the Atlantic Ocean. Showers mean the weather will change a lot during the day, with rain off and on throughout the day, compared to rain that falls for hours at a time before stopping."

"That's interesting, Grandma. I never heard anyone make a difference between rain and showers before. Does it have any different type of meaning?" "The month of April is often thought of as springtime, a time for things to start to bloom. When you look around, you see flowers like daisies and sweet peas peeping up through the ground and trees starting to bud. The other interesting thing happening in April is that you start taking off layers of clothes, like heavy winter coats exchanged for light spring coats, shorts for long pants, sneakers for boots, and baseball caps for winter hats." "I never knew so many things changed in April. I liked hearing about this."

Springtime is a chance to shed heavy clothing for warmer weather, enjoy longer days of light, see the newness of life springing up all around you, cookouts, breathe fresh shower-washed air, and put smiles on everyone's faces because the fresh air is good for your teeth and mental health.

Thank You, LORD, for the newness of spring. I pray we appreciate Your gift of the changing seasons to remind us You are in control of nature and our lives. May we enjoy each season of the year and each season of our lives that You grant us.

Priceless Moments

Genesis 8:22*: While the earth remains, seed time and harvest, and cold and heat, and summer and winter, and day and night will not cease.*

Ecclesiastes 3:1*: For everything there is a season, and a time for every purpose under heaven:*

Psalm 74:16-17*: The day is yours, the night is also yours. You have prepared the light and the sun. You have set all the boundaries of the earth. You have made summer and winter.*

May

*God,
you have taught me
from my youth.
Until now,
I have declared
your wonderous works.*

Psalm 71:17

Priceless Moments

May 1ˢᵗ
...Bring May Flowers

"Oh, boy. Do we get to learn about May flowers today? I sure hope so." "Absolutely. I knew you would be waiting, so I'm ready for you. Here we go… Do you know why April showers bring May flowers?" "I don't know, but I think you'll tell us." "You're right. All the rain showers we receive in April, our traditional rainy month, bring a lot of much-needed water to the ground to enable the flowers to bloom. As the month of April progresses, the initial April showers can be in the form of snow or ice. As the days begin to get warmer and longer, the showers change to rain. Another meaning to the phrase is that all the rain may be unpleasant to many but hang in there; something enjoyable can come of it, like being rewarded with the beautifully abundant flowers that will come in May. Also, those who learn patience to endure the rains of April will have something to look forward to by being rewarded with the beautiful aromas of May."

"My Dad always told us this joke: 'If April showers bring May flowers, what do May flowers bring? Do you have an idea what the answer is?" "No. That's a hard one. Tell us the answer, please." "Mayflowers bring Pilgrims. Do you remember who the Pilgrims were?" "Yes, Grandma. The Pilgrims were the people from England who came across the ocean in a boat called the Mayflower and landed in a place called Plymouth Rock. We learned about them because they had a Thanksgiving dinner with the Indians." "Excellent," I replied. "Do you remember why they left England?" "Yes. They left England so they would no longer be punished for the way they worshiped God."

I wondered how we weather challenging situations when things seem at their darkest. When we hold on there, with God's leading, and get through the toughness of "April," we will come out the other end into the rewarding days of "May"—an abundance of joy and relief to have weathered the storm.

Thank You, LORD, for carrying us through the difficult times and walking beside us after the trials cease. I pray we realize You never leave us nor forsake us, but stick closer than a brother through thick and thin.

Song of Solomon 2:11-12: *For behold, the winter is past. The rain is over and gone. The flowers appear on the earth. The time of the singing has come, and the voice of the turtledove is heard in our land.*

Isaiah 40:8: *The grass withers, the flower fades; but the word of our God stands forever.*

Luke 12:27: *Consider the lilies, how they grow. They don't toil, neither do they spin; yet I tell you, even Solomon in all his glory was not arrayed like one of these.*

May 2nd
Fake It Until You Make It

"Grandma, can I ask you a question?" "Yes, you may. What's on your mind?" "Have you ever had someone say something about you that's not true? When you have considered them a friend, how do you respond to them?" "If I were in your place, I would not treat my friend any differently until I knew for sure they were talking about me and why. Many times, people talk about someone, and we think it's about us, but we have actually heard them talking about someone else." "OK, but how do I be nice to them until I know for sure what is true?" "There is a phrase, "Fake it until you make it," meaning you need to pretend to still be friends until you find out the truth. Pray. Your friendly actions can bring an apology or reveal they were talking about someone or something else."

Priceless Moments

Several weeks later, our granddaughter asked, "Grandma, can I talk to you?" "Sure, honey. What would you like to talk about?" "Do you remember when I heard friends say something mean about me behind my back?" "Yes, I do. Were you able to still treat them with respect? Did you find out what actually happened?" "Thanks to you, I prayed and tried faking true friendship until I learned the truth. I learned one of their class projects was to create a story. They were talking about it when I overheard them last week. They shared their ideas with me today to see what I thought of them. I was so relieved to know it wasn't me. You're telling me to fake my real friendship until I knew the truth, which saved my best friendship. Thanks. I love you." "You're welcome, love."

Joy filled my heart when I realized she prayed about her actions and responses to those "talking about her." Prayer should always be our first line of defense. God provides clarity and direction in questionable matters. We need not make snap decisions; we need to have all the answers before we act.

Thank You, LORD, for giving sound judgment when a clear mind is desired. I pray that You are our first line of defense before making any kind of decision or reacting to unsubstantiated thoughts, words, or deeds.

Proverbs 3:5-6: Trust in Yahweh with all your heart, and don't lean on your own understanding. In all your ways acknowledge him, and he will make your paths straight.

1 Corinthians 10:13: No temptation has taken you except what is common to man. God is faithful, who will not allow you to be tempted above what you are able, but will with the temptation also make the way of escape, that you may be able to endure it.

Philippians 4:6: In nothing be anxious, but in everything, by prayer and petition with thanksgiving, let your requests be made known to God.

Priceless Moments

May 3rd
<u>*Temper Tantrum*</u>

Little ones often experience temper tantrums when they become frustrated due to not getting enough attention, not getting a special treat or toy, not wanting to do a requested task, being hungry, or being tired. Their frustration from a lack of words, skills, or knowing how to express themselves appropriately can lead to physical, verbal, or a combination of both disruptive and unpleasant reactions or behaviors in any given situation.
"Grandma, I know the rules, but I don't want to clean up the toys. I'm tired of doing it all the time." A toy is thrown. My instinct to "stay calm and distract him" kicked in. I knew I had to be consistent, so I had to help him change his behaviors. Here was an opportunity to let him make a choice. "I'm sorry you feel this way, but if you start to clean up, I'll pitch in and help you. Once this is done, it will be snack time. Or aren't you hungry for a snack?" He wasn't having it.

Initially, I prayed for wisdom for myself and a sense of peace for him. Realizing tantrums are not intentional, I said, "Did you see the new tire swing outside?" in a really silly voice. He stopped, looked at me, not knowing what to do, and said, "What tire swing?" Again, I talked in a silly voice, "I fooled you. So, little man, are you a soloist or a double at clean-up?" That broke the ice for him: "Grandma, you're so silly at times. Let's do it together so we can have a snack. I'm getting a little hungry." Meltdown averted. We calmly talked about why throwing the toy was inappropriate behavior. He apologized before I asked him to do so: "I'm sorry, Grandma. Please forgive me." "Yessiree, little man. I appreciate and accept the apology. This calls for a snack—after we clean up. Let's go." "OK."

How many times do we have an adult temper tantrum because we are not getting what we want—also resulting from frustration or anger with your friend, spouse, coworker, or God? LORD, help us, please, and thank You.

Thank You, LORD, for Your gracious response to our times of challenging behavior. I pray we bring everything to You before reacting so a calm head can prevail to avert wrong responses that cause hard feelings.

Psalm 37:8-9: *Cease from anger, and forsake wrath. Don't fret; it leads only to evildoing. For evildoers shall be cut off, but those who wait for Yahweh shall inherit the land.*

Psalm 127:3-5: *Behold, children are a heritage of Yahweh. The fruit of the womb is his reward. As arrows in the hand of a mighty man, so are the children of youth. Happy is the man who has his quiver full of them. They won't be disappointed when they speak with their enemies in the gate.*

Proverbs 15:1: *A gentle answer turns away wrath, but a harsh word stirs up anger.*

2 Timothy 2:22: *Flee from youthful lusts; but pursue righteousness, faith, love, and peace with those who call on the Lord out of a pure heart.*

May 4th

The Crusty Old Lady

One day, while watching the grandchildren—they don't like it called babysitting—our granddaughter got upset with something I said to her, and she called me a crusty old lady. I was taken by surprise at the name-calling as well as wondering what a crusty old lady was. After deliberating silently, I decided to ask the question I wondered about: "What is a crusty old lady?" She thought for a minute, then replied, "I don't know. What do you think it means?" Before answering her question—and to give me an idea as to where this may have come from—I asked her, "Where did you hear this?" Again, she had no answer.

Priceless Moments

Pondering my own definition, I replied, "I'm mean, grumpy, angry, annoyed, yelling without cause, not fun to be around, or not doing something you want me to do. Maybe I'm smelly; I wear dirty old clothes; I have an unhappy look on my face." I was out of options. I had no idea what it meant. But as I was giving my response, her little jaw started dropping, and her eyes got bigger and bigger. She said, "But, Grandma, you're none of those things. You're kind, loving, and have a smile most of the time. I know you have to get stern sometimes, but it's because you only want what's best for us and to follow God's will for our lives."

I had to stop and realize that, even though they don't always act like they're listening to our "words of wisdom," something is indeed getting through. Our "preaching" and living out God's Word in front of them had made enough of an impact for her to recognize we all need discipline, yet we only want what's best for them, and when done in love, we will unlock the door of open communication to tackle tougher subjects in the future.

Just like with God, sometimes we may not always understand what is said or done or why it was said or done, but He is doing it for our own good. We need to keep all channels open for God to communicate with us, wherever we may be and whatever our needs may be. He knows before we even ask, but we have to be sensitive to His still, small voice leading and guiding us along our path in life.

Thank You, LORD, for helping us get through tough, challenging times. Although we may not understand the "life lesson," we know that when our hope and trust are in You, we will stay calm in the midst of our circumstances.

Romans 8:28: *We know that all things work together for good for those who love God, for those who are called according to his purpose.*

Priceless Moments

Psalm 9:9-10: *Yahweh will also be a high tower for the oppressed; a high tower in times of trouble. Those who know your name will put their trust in you, for you, Yahweh, have not forsaken those who seek you.*

Philippians 4:19: *My God will supply every need of yours according to his riches in glory in Christ Jesus*

May 5th

Cinco De Mayo

"Hey, Grandma, do you know what Cinco de Mayo is?" We learned about it in school today. It means the 'Fifth of May,' a day to celebrate the culture, history, and traditions like food, music, and dancing of our Mexican friends who live in America. One of the girls in our class is from Mexico, but she lives here now. She said a battle happened because their country had no money to pay France what they owed them, so they came to get their money anyway. This holiday celebrates the Mexicans defeat of the French at the Battle of Puebla in 1862. She said they make decorations of red, white, and green, Mexico's national colors, to carry at their school's parade in Puebla. There were even men dressed in military uniforms at the parade. She said sometimes people confuse this victory in a battle with their Independence Day, but they became a nation over fifty years before this battle. She counted from one to one hundred in Spanish."

"Wow, it seems like she could share a lot with you about her former country." "Yes, and our teacher told us more things, too. She said there are more than one hundred fifty Cinco de Mayo celebrations held across the U.S. and in other countries. Did you know the U.S. helped the Mexicans win because we sent money and guns to help them force the French to leave? She said they have street festivals with all kinds of food, like tacos, fajitas, and some others I can't remember. She helped us make some decorations to put up in class for our own celebration, and then we got to take our own home when class was over. Do you want to see what I made?" "Sure. I'm guessing this is the flag of Mexico. You did such a nice job. I'm sure your parents will be excited to hear all the things you've shared with me."

I thought of how well the Mexican-American girl knew her former country's history. In America, sadly, many young people and adults take little to no pride for our country, wishing to forget or rewrite our history.

Thank you, LORD; our final battle will be a victory for Your side. I pray we study to learn Your Word, the signs for the future, and how to defeat the enemy. I pray we proudly wear Your mark on our hearts for all to see through our mannerisms, words, deeds, and treatment of others, be they kind or deplorable.

2 Kings 6:16: *He answered, "Don't be afraid; for those who are with us are more than those who are with them."*

Psalm 27:3: *Though an army should encamp against me, my heart shall not fear. Though war should rise against me, even then I will be confident.*

Revelation 11:15: *The seventh angel sounded, and great voices in heaven followed, saying, "The kingdom of the world has become the Kingdom of our Lord, and of his Christ. He will reign forever and ever!"*

May 6th

<u>Can We Pray?</u>

It's 3:30 AM, and I hear a whimper from another bedroom in our house. Immediately, I get up and head toward the crying. "Grandma, I had a bad dream. Can we pray? I know if we ask Jesus to be with us, He will take away my fear." "Dear sweet boy,

Priceless Moments

it will be a privilege to pray with and for you." I held his little trembling body close and said, "Dear Heavenly Father, we bring this special little life to you, asking You to calm his fears. Yet, even more, we ask You to fill his heart with knowledge of You and Your graciousness to and for us. Let him experience You at a deeper level of commitment as he grows. Thank You for hearing our prayer and filling this room with Your presence." At the end of the prayer, I heard the soft "pah" escaping his lips as I laid him down to sleep soundly in our Master's arms.

I returned to bed but couldn't get back to sleep. As I lay praying for him, I found myself changing my focus from him to life: family, friends, our church, our country, and our world in a different light. I realized we have so much head knowledge that seldom gets transferred to heart knowledge to take us into a deeper spiritual walk with our Heavenly Father. Feeling the need for this myself, I spent the remainder of the nighttime hours in humility before our Father God.

Thank You, LORD, for an always open phone line to Heaven. I pray we move beyond the surface prayers of "please do this" and "please do that" for me or others to a deeper spiritual prayer of "What can I do for You?" and "Your will be done." using us as directable servants full of faith to help accomplish Your will for eternity.

Ephesians 3:20,21*: Now to him who is able to do exceedingly abundantly above all that we ask or think, according to the power that works in us, to him be the glory in the assembly and in Christ Jesus to all generations forever and ever. Amen.*

Colossians 3:12*: Put on therefore, as God's chosen ones, holy and beloved, a heart of compassion, kindness, lowliness, humility, and perseverance;*

2 Chronicles 7:14*: if my people, who are called by my name, will humble themselves, pray, seek my face, and turn from their wicked* *ways, then I will hear from heaven, will forgive their sin, and will heal their land.*

May 7th
<u>I Didn't Mean To Say That</u>

"You make me so mad I could spit. Stay away from me." It was a voice I didn't recognize. I'm like, "What did you just say? Were you talking to me?" A shocked look crossed her face, like "Busted." I recognized her as a friend from school. She said, "No, to her." pointing to our granddaughter. I asked, "Can we talk about it?" The little girl said, "She won't let me have the toy, and I want to play with it." I probed, "Did you ask her if you could play with it, if she could share?" She looked very surprised and said, "No, I didn't. I don't have one like it at home, and I wanted to play with it." "Let's sit down together and talk about it."

"I think it's great to have a chance to play together. Sharing is very important, but so is being polite to each other and asking each other to share. A valuable lesson for all of us to learn is how God created us. He gave us two ears and one mouth, so we could listen twice as much as we talk. We need to be kind to others, showing interest in what they are saying to validate the reason they are sharing. They may just need a listening ear or need to vent their frustration so they can move past whatever is bothering them. Interestingly, silent and listen are spelled with the same letters." She responded, "That's cool." Turning to our granddaughter, she said, "I'm sorry. Next time, I'll ask you to share." I wrapped my arms around both girls and asked, "What can we all share?" A thoughtful moment passed, and they said, "Faith and friendship."

The unfortunate thing is, once something leaves our mouth, we can never take it back. We can apologize up and down, but whatever we said still resonates with the person to whom it was said. The key is to truly listen wholeheartedly, communicating love and respect, so any potential misunderstanding may be avoided, as well as to pick up on a need or concern they unwittingly expressed in conversation.

Thank You, LORD, for designing our bodies to reflect how we should interact with others. I pray we are effective listeners, uplifting concerned speakers, and sharing the gospel. If someone takes issue with this, at least a seed was sown. Above all else, may we be attentive in our two-way communication with You by being good listeners.

Matthew 17:5: *While he was still speaking, behold, a bright cloud overshadowed them. Behold, a voice came out of the cloud, saying, "This is my beloved Son, in whom I am well pleased. Listen to him."*

Proverbs 1:5: *Let the wise listen and add to their learning, and let the discerning get guidance. NIV*

Luke 10:16: *Whoever listens to you listens to me, and whoever rejects you rejects me. Whoever rejects me rejects him who sent me.*

May 8th

<u>Play-Doh</u>

"Grandma, did you buy new Play-Doh yet? Did you remember we threw ours out from last year because it dried out?" I smiled, heading to the closet and pulling out a bag of fresh Play-Doh. "Are you looking for something like this? This may be just what you need. I thought the weather was getting warmer and you'd be ready to go out and play on the patio again. I said to myself, "Self, in order for those adorable little tykes who keep showing up at our door to have fun outside, they'll need new supplies this year. And, guess what? I listened to myself and bought Play-Doh."

Priceless Moments

They giggled all the way to the hall closet to get their flip flops, grabbed the bag of goodies, and said, "Thanks." and headed out the door—with me right behind them. Little did they know I was way ahead of them. They found the Play-Doh tools, drinks, and snack already on their kid-sized picnic table, waiting for them. "Oh, Grandma, thanks. You must have known we were coming." "Let me think. You brought a suitcase, and your parents are going away for a few days. They said you'd be here by 10 a.m., so I had a pretty good idea. Such a surprise, right? "That's so funny. You're so silly. Are you going to help us make something or use the tools to create from there?" "I really had no plans, but I want to enjoy watching you create. Now, what do you say we have a mid-morning snack before playtime?" "Yes, snacking always sounds good to us." "I'm so sorry you are not pleased with your supplies and snack. I'll try to do better next time." "Oh, Grandma, it's just perfect. You always seem to be one step ahead of us, knowing what we would like."

Watching the delight in their eyes and the thanks they express is very exciting; it never gets old. God must feel like that when we thank Him for anticipating what we need and going above and beyond to surprise us with things He feels are best for us.

Thank You, LORD, for taking delight in us. I pray we are worthy of the blessings and joy You bestow upon us, rejoicing over us with gladness. May we return the favor and delight ourselves in You.

Psalm 37:4: *Also delight yourself in Yahweh, and he will give you the desires of your heart.*

Romans 5:1,2: *Being therefore justified by faith, we have peace with God through our Lord Jesus Christ; through whom we also have our access by faith into this grace in which we stand. We rejoice in hope of the glory of God.*

Priceless Moments

Zephaniah 3:17: *Yahweh, your God, is among you, a mighty one who will save. He will rejoice over you with joy. He will calm you in his love. He will rejoice over you with singing.*

May 9th
<u>Cookie Cutters</u>

Papa likes unique-shaped cookies for all occasions; thus, he has a collection of cookie cutters in all shapes and sizes. We pull out those symbolic of the different holidays and have fun making cookies with the grandchildren. "Oh, boy, we get to bake cookies today. I see the cutters sitting on the counter. What flavor are we going to make?" OK, she hit the ground running. "I thought we'd look at them for a while to decide if we really want to make cookies or not." "Grandma, you know we always want to make cookies; besides, it gives us something to take to the neighbors. They always love to see us coming because we always have treats in our hands."

I pondered her response, saying, "Truer words were never spoken. What kind of cookies should we make?" "I like the soft, thick sugar cookies. They are good with or without decorations. They're also good to have as a snack with a cup of tea. Do you have any ginger-lemon tea to go with them?" "Hey, that sounds like a winning combination. I'm sure we have that flavor of tea bags in the pantry. Who all wants to help?" All munchkins say, "Me." "Very well, then. Hands washed, aprons in the hutch, and all hands on deck to make some tasty treats." "Grandma, when we're done, can we each have a cookie and a cup of tea for snack?" "I'm so glad you volunteered to help eat them, or Papa and I would have to eat them all by ourselves."

God doesn't see us as cookie-cutter-shaped, decorated, or plain. He sees each one of us as a very unique individual and special in

His sight, be we red, orange, yellow, black, or white; tall, short, plump, skinny, etc.

He made each one of us for His purpose. It's our job to find out what our purpose is.

Thank You, LORD, for diversity. If we were all cookie-cutter people, life would not be as exciting due to the minimal differences that make the world go around. I pray we find delight in our differences, which mold us into the unique individuals You intended us to be.

Psalm 119:73-74: Your hands have made me and formed me. Give me understanding, that I may learn your commandments. Those who fear you will see me and be glad, because I have put my hope in your word.

Isaiah 64:8: But now, Yahweh, you are our Father. We are the clay and you our potter. We all are the work of your hand.

Matthew 10:29-31: Aren't two sparrows sold for an assarion coin? Not one of them falls to the ground apart from your Father's will. But the very hairs of your head are all numbered. Therefore don't be afraid. You are of more value than many sparrows.

May 10th
Noah's Ark

As a family, we went to visit Noah's Ark in Williamstown, Kentucky. The grandchildren were wide-eyed and full of questions throughout the entire experience. "Why is it so big? How did all those animals get here? Is this where the ark landed? How come the restaurant is separate from the ark? How come they have a gift shop? Who did they sell stuff to?" All interesting questions. "The ark did not land here. It landed somewhere in the mountains of Ararat, in Armenia, in Asia, across the world from here. God had

Priceless Moments

Noah build this big boat to hold all of the animals He would send to Noah and his family, as well as supplies like food and water, and bedding for every living thing on the ark. The restaurant and gift shop were not on the original ark but are here to make it easier for families to get something to eat and to take home something, like a souvenir or stuffed animal, to remember their visit here."

"God gave Noah a big job to do; it took him over one hundred twenty years to build it. He was faithful to talk and preach to the curious passersby, telling them of God's upcoming flood, something new to all of them." After checking out the ark, we headed outside. 'Wow, Grandma, look at the cool playground, animals, and street food places. Can we play, pet the animals, and get something to drink?" "Sure." "Did the animals on the ark look like these?" "I'm not sure they looked exactly the same, but they were close enough to recognize a giraffe as a giraffe, a rabbit as a rabbit, and so on. I can tell when you get to heaven you are going to ask God every detail." We all had a good laugh and enjoyed the trip.

I was struck by the enormity of the ark, the attention to detail, the charts, pictures, and live-looking beings throughout the ark. I realize things could have been different in the original ark, but this certainly gives one a good idea of what it must have been like.

Thank You, LORD, for modern man being interested enough to share a vision of what the ark may have been like. I pray we understand the depth of Your love to find an obedient family to carry out Your design to spare Your ultimate creation of man and animals.

Genesis 6:3*: Yahweh said, "My Spirit will not strive with man forever, because he also is flesh; so his days will be one hundred twenty years."*

Genesis 6:14*: Make a ship of gopher wood. You shall make rooms in the ship, and shall seal it inside and outside with pitch.*

Priceless Moments

Genesis 7:1: *Yahweh said to Noah, "Come with all of your household into the ship, for I have seen your righteousness before me in this generation.*

May 11th
<u>Mom's the Word</u>

The grandchildren were talking about what they wanted to do for Mommy on Mother's Day. Ideas flew back and forth for quite some time. I cautioned, "Time to change the subject since your mother will soon be here. Remember, 'Mom's the word.'" Blank looks were sent in my direction—you know, the 'deer in the headlight look.' Our granddaughter said, "What are you talking about? I've never heard that one before. What does it mean? Are we to tell Mom she's weird?" "Let me start here, little man. The saying 'Mom's the word' means to keep silent or quiet so as not to 'spill the beans' or tell the other person you want to keep a secret from. 'Mom's the word' tells those who want to keep a secret to change the subject, so you don't accidentally tell your special surprise."

"Is this the same thing as lying?" "To keep a secret for a special surprise, like a birthday party or gift, is OK. But when you do it to cover up the truth to protect yourself or someone else, that is a lie. Lies will only weigh you down and are usually only found out by accident, bringing a harsher punishment. In this case, honesty is ALWAYS the best policy.

God wants us to be upfront with Him immediately about any wrongdoing on our part. He already knows what sin(s) we've committed, so clean the slate and start over with a heartfelt confession. God has a high standard, so we should follow our Heavenly Father's example and hold ourselves to this same standard. We will fail, but we should still strive for His example of perfection.

Priceless Moments

Thank You, LORD, for setting the bar high for us to work towards on a daily basis. I pray we understand You are perfection, untouched by sin. We should strive to be the best we can be every day by growing closer to You, listening to Your voice leading us toward forgiveness, and having a deeper desire to be more like You.

Matthew 5:48: *Therefore you shall be perfect, just as your Father in heaven is perfect.*

James 3:2: *For we all stumble in many things. Anyone who doesn't stumble in word is a perfect person, able to bridle the whole body also.*

Revelation 15:4: *Who wouldn't fear you, Lord, and glorify your name? For you only are holy. For all the nations will come and worship before you. For your righteous acts have been revealed.*

May 12th
Mother's Day

"Are we going to take Mommy out to dinner for Mother's Day? I think it would be fun to go to McDonald's. We don't go there very often, so I think she would really enjoy it. What do you think?" I thought to myself, 'Yes, every mother's dream is a beautiful sit-down dinner at McDonald's.' I controlled myself and said, "This could be one option. I'll list some others I've been thinking about, and you can let me know what you think about them," proceeding with my list. They looked at each other, whispered some comments back-and-forth, then said, "No, I think she would really like McDonald's best."

Not wanting to be the rotten apple, I said, "Maybe we can think about this and see if we can come up with some way to incorporate or include something you want to do for Mommy and things I think I would like to do for Mommy. We all thought for a while, and then I said, "I have the perfect idea. Why don't we take Mommy out to McDonald's for breakfast before church, go to church, then take her out to the restaurant of her choice after church?" Silence filled the room until one brave soul finally said, "Grandma, I think that's the perfect idea. She would love to go out for breakfast and dinner, so there's no cooking or dishes to clean up. We have one more question for you. Would you be able to help us make a homemade Mother's Day card for Mommy? Daddy helped us buy one from the store, but we wanted to make her one ourselves." "I think that sounds like a marvelous idea. Let's go get supplies and get the cards made now so we have them done for Mother's Day."

I thought about compromise. It's good in these situations, but compromise over spiritual matters is a more delicate situation. Is the color of the carpet or walls of the church matter—or is it 'Gospel by the Book?' Certainly, the sanctuary décor can be a matter of prayer, but God's word is non-negotiable.

Thank You, LORD, for godly mothers on their knees praying for their children and grandchildren. I pray we carry the torch, with Your guidance, into the next generations to keep our families centered on You.

Genesis 3:20: *The man called his wife Eve because she would be the mother of all the living.*

Deuteronomy 4:9: *Only be careful, and keep your soul diligently, lest you forget the things which your eyes saw, and lest they depart from your heart all the days of your life; but make them known to your children and your children's children—*

Isaiah 66:13: *As a mother comforts her child, so will I comfort you, and you will be comforted over Jerusalem. NIV*

Priceless Moments

May 13th
I'm Student of the Week

Our granddaughter came flying in the door, saying, "I'm *Student of the Week*, see." I turned around to see a crown on her head, a sash, a diploma-like paper, and a banner in her hand, all proclaiming her as *Student of the Week*. "Wow, what an honor. What does it mean, and how did you get it?" "I've been a good listener and a good helper for my teacher since school started. All week, I get to tell my classmates something about myself, so they get to know me better. I've already made a new friend because we like a lot of the same things." "What kinds of things have you and will you share with your class?" "I told them about my family and the things we like to do. Tomorrow, I'll tell them about my favorite book. One day, each person will write something they like about me. I might get to sit up close to my teacher's desk one day. I get to be the line leader all week."

"Wow. It sounds like a great honor to be an awesome, responsible student." "My teacher said when someone else is Student of the Week, they will get to do the same kinds of things as me. She wants to treat us all as special, yet all the same, so no one has hurt feelings. I think this is a really great way to let everyone in class see what it's like to have their classmates look up to them. I know I like to hear them say they appreciate me, and they like how I lead the class to different things, like lunch, recess, gym, music class, library, and leaving school at the end of the day. I know I probably forgot some things, but I feel really special right now. I want the other kids to feel that way, too." "You are very special, honey, and we are all very proud of you. High five."

God likes to put His spotlight on us as well. We are all very special to Him, each being His student of the week—in the same week, every week. He looks deep inside, to the very soul of our being, and sees everything others cannot see. When we keep a close walk with Him, He will reveal the areas needing attention.

Thank You, LORD, for seeing us for who we are—the good, the bad, and the ugly (Ennio Morricone), yet You still desire a close relationship with us. I pray we heed Your correction with understanding and put it into action in our lives to become more like You.

Job 32:8*: But there is a spirit in man, and the Spirit of the Almighty gives them understanding.*

Proverbs 20:27*: The spirit of man is Yahweh's lamp, searching all his innermost parts.*

John 15:26*: When the Counselor has come, whom I will send to you from the Father, the Spirit of truth, who proceeds from the Father, he will testify about me.*

May 14th
Can We Go Visit Someone?

"Can we go somewhere and visit someone today? We haven't done this for a while. People are so much fun to talk with and share about Jesus with. Can we make Rice Krispie treats to take with us?" "Sure, that sounds like a good idea." The children love to go visit people in the neighborhood, taking some type of food to share with them. "Where should we go first? Do you know of anyone who needs some company right now?" "Well, let me think. Yes, I do. They have not been feeling well and have not left the house for a while. They are doing better now, and I'm sure your bright, smiling faces will bring rays of sunshine to them."

Treats were prepared, and we went down the street. We knocked on their door. Sad, tired faces brightened to see the kiddos. "Grandma said you are just starting to feel better, so we brought you some treats. Can we come in and visit for a little while?" Who could turn down these treats—kids and food? The kids shared what they've been doing at home, at school, and on their spring break vacation, and plans to finish up their school year. The more they talked, the more our hosts smiled and asked the kids questions. Next thing I know, I look at my watch and go, "Oh no. I need to go; it's time I get you guys home." Our host said, "It's OK; you don't need to be in a hurry; we're enjoying your company. But we understand. Please do come again soon."

I thought we needed to share more than just food during our visits. People love to hear what the children have to say, so the children talk about what they do in Sunday school, children's church, Awanas, Good News Club, and family devotions.

Thank You, LORD, for uninhibited children who freely speak their minds to other about Your goodness. I pray we follow their lead and openly share our faith, devotional life, and church activities with others. But, most importantly, invite them to be a part of Your kingdom.

Acts 1:8*: But you will receive power when the Holy Spirit has come upon you. You will be witnesses to me in Jerusalem, in all Judea and Samaria, and to the uttermost parts of the earth.*

2 Timothy 4:2*: preach the word; be urgent in season and out of season; reprove, rebuke, and exhort with all patience and teaching.*

Romans 10:9*: that if you will confess with your mouth that Jesus is Lord, and believe in your heart that God raised him from the dead, you will be saved.*

May 15th

A Banana Sandwich

Ah, the joys of childhood for all of us were brought back to mind when I heard, "Grandma, I'm really hungry. Do you have anything

Priceless Moments

good to eat?" I replied, "The answer to your question is one you will have to determine yourself. But I can tell you what we have, or you can look for yourself; it's up to you." Roving eyes canvassed the pantry, refrigerator, and counters, at which point his face lit up. "Grandma, you have bananas. Do you have any bread, bagels, or English muffins?" I chuckled, saying, "You've just looked everywhere here. Did you see any of those?" A glint in his eye lit up his face as he headed back to the refrigerator. "Yes, those big bagels will be perfect, but can we toast them to warm them up? I prefer mine to be warm." "You know what? The toaster oven will be the perfect tool for you. Let's cut one and see what happens."

The necessary ingredients were gathered, and we cut the bagel. "You're turn. Place the bagel in the toaster oven, and then I'll turn it on. While it toasts, you can peel the banana and cut it how you want." When he had finished this part, a 'ding' sounded, so we got the warm bagel and put it on his plate. He proceeded to spread peanut butter on both halves, layer on the banana, and finish by putting the 'lid' on it. "I'm ready to enjoy. Do you want to take a bite?" "No, thank you, but it was very kind of you to offer. I hope it hits the spot." He said, "What do you mean by that?" Stifling a chuckle, she said, "I hope it makes your taste buds and belly happy." "Me, too."

It is simply delightful to see a child's eye filled with delight, but it will only be temporary. The banana sandwich will soon be gone, and he'll return in search of something else. We need to move from being happy in the moment to sustaining lifelong joy, regardless of our circumstances.

Thank You, LORD, for happiness and joy. I pray we realize happiness is more short-term, for the moment, while joy results in a more permanent state achieved through worship, prayer, Bible reading, communion with family and friends, and rejoicing in You.

Priceless Moments

Romans 15:13: *Now may the God of hope fill you with all joy and peace in believing, that you may abound in hope, in the power of the Holy Spirit.*

Psalm 16:11: *You will show me the path of life. In your presence is fullness of joy. In your right hand there are pleasures forever more.*

1 Peter 1:8-9: *Though you have not seen Him, you love Him; and even though you do not see Him now, you will believe in Him and are filled with an inexpressible and glorious joy, for you are receiving the goal of your faith, the salvation of your souls. NIV*

May 16th
<u>Police Officers</u>

"Guess who visited us in our classroom today?" "I don't know, but I'll make a guess it was… humm, a fireman." "Well, no. It was a police officer. He was all dressed up in his uniform. He talked to us about his job and how he keeps people safe." "Nice. What else does he do for his job?" "He makes sure people follow our laws, like not speeding or turning around where they shouldn't; helps out in case of emergencies, like a car accident or someone falling; fires; and keeps our homes and businesses safe by stopping criminals from stealing or breaking into places." "Did he say what they do to carry out their job?" "Yes, he did. Some guys drive around in police cars, others ride motorcycles or bikes, and others walk. They all wear a badge, so we know they are policemen; they carry a gun; and they always tell us they are there for us."

"That's a lot of helpful things they do for us. Can you think of anything else they do?" "Not really." "Have you seen a policeman directing traffic to help fire trucks, ambulances, and rescue trucks get to the scene of an accident or fire? Or has someone pulled over on the side of the road to stop them from speeding and hurting others and themselves? They have sirens and lights on their cars to

Priceless Moments

let people know to stop or move over to the side of the road. Besides the people in uniform, there are officers in street clothes, called detectives." "Cool. Aren't they the ones who help the police by going undercover to get more information?" "Yes. Excellent response. How did you know that?" "I read it in a Dick Tracey book."

It's awesome to learn some interesting facts by reading a book or listening to a "classroom visitor" talk. God provided the best book ever to speak to us while reading Scripture, through Jesus and the Holy Spirit, through our pastors and Bible study teachers, life group interactions with other believers and seekers, creation and nature, music, difficulties and circumstances, our conscience, and spending quality time with Him in prayer.

Thank You, LORD, for enabling us to "hear" Your voice in so many ways. I pray we always check the responses against Your Word to ensure they are in agreement and will bring glory to You.

Psalm 4:8: *In peace I will both lay myself down and sleep, for you, Yahweh alone, make me live in safety.*

2 Corinthians 11:4: *For if he who comes preaches another Jesus, whom we didn't preach, or if you receive a different spirit, which you didn't receive, or a different "good news", which you didn't accept, you put up with that well enough.*

Revelation 22:18-19: *I testify to everyone who hears the words of the prophecy of this book, if anyone adds to them, may God add to him the plagues which are written in this book. If anyone takes away from the words of the book of this prophecy, may God take away his part from the tree of life, and out of the holy city, which are written in this book.*

Priceless Moments

May 17th
The Jeep

"Wow, did you see that cool Jeep, Grandma? I think they are really neat looking." "Initially, the Jeep was considered a GP, or general purpose vehicle—the go anywhere, do anything vehicle. The 'G' stood for the Ford government contract vehicle and the 'P' for its 80-inch wheelbase. When the G-P are slurred together, the word 'jeep' is heard. The Ford GP was used by the military in 1941 during World War II. A publicity stunt of driving a Willys Quad GP up the steps of the U.S. Capitol and calling it a Jeep. Being overheard by a newspaper columnist who's published in newspapers all over the U.S. From that day on, it was called a 'Jeep.'"

"Cool. Do you know anyone who owns a Jeep?" "Not currently. Did you know your Dad's first vehicle was a Jeep? It was a 1987 maroon-colored Cherokee with a dark interior. As a matter of fact, this was the vehicle that Daddy had to take Mommy to the prom." He looked confused, then said, "I thought Daddy's Jeep was silver?" I marveled and said, "You are absolutely correct. He had a second one, a 2004 Jeep Liberty in silver. I'm surprised you remember it." "Not really, Grandma, but I saw a picture of it on your phone."

I loved the look of association on his face, knowing his parents drove a Jeep. This must be how our Heavenly Father feels when we recognize Him as the Ruler of our lives. He is a general-purpose God, one whose *general purpose* is for us to make heaven our future home. The recollection of His work in our lives and acknowledging it to others must thrill His heart since another one of His creations "has come home."

Thank You, LORD, for Your presence enveloping every area of our lives. I pray we always feel the joy experienced when we first surrendered our lives to You and the growing satisfaction of each day being sweeter as the years go by.

Priceless Moments

Psalm 92:12-14: *The righteous shall flourish like the palm tree. He will grow like a cedar in Lebanon. They are planted in Yahweh's house. They will flourish in our God's courts. They will still produce fruit in old age.*
   They will be full of sap and green,

Proverbs 15:20: *A wise son makes a father glad, but a foolish man despises his mother "A wise son makes a father glad, but a foolish man despises his mother.*

Mark 3:13: *He went up into the mountain and called to himself those whom he wanted, and they went to him.*

May 18th
Armed Forces Day

"What is Armed Forces Day, and why do we celebrate it?" "It is a special day set aside to honor our active duty and honorably discharged proud patriots who've served in our military forces. Other nations around the world also celebrate their military on different days. Armed Forces Day is a separate holiday from Veteran's Day and Memorial Day. All these military appreciation days are events intended to express appreciation for men and women who currently, and sometimes previously, served in the different branches of the military. It's celebrated on the third Saturday of May. Each branch of the armed forces had its own special day, but this day is for celebrating the unification, or bringing together, of the Armed Forces under the Department of Defense in 1949." "How do we celebrate this day?" "Although it is not a federal holiday, it is often celebrated with parades, air shows, open houses, and receptions across the country."

"Who made this day a holiday?" "President Harry S. Truman established this day to educate civilians, those not in the military,

Priceless Moments

about the role of our armed services and the types of jobs they do, 'praising the work of the military services at home and across the seas.' He continued, 'It is vital to the security of the nation to establish of a desirable peace.' President Truman served in the National Guard, the Army, and the Army Reserve, so he had a great understanding of the importance of showing appreciation for those people serving in our military.

I thought of how we have military personnel, active and veterans, in our families, just like we have Christians in our families. Members of both "branches" give their best for our country—on this earth and in our heavenly home—to receive security and benefits before receiving an honorable discharge at the end of our commitment.

Thank You, LORD; every day serving You is a special day. I pray that as active-duty members of Your "military," we do more than just talk about You as our Commander-in-Chief, but praise You for Your presence with us as well as our fellow Christians around the world.

Proverbs 3:27: *Don't withhold good from those to whom it is due, when it is in the power of your hand to do it.*

Matthew 23:11-12: *But he who is greatest among you will be your servant. ¹² Whoever exalts himself will be humbled, and whoever humbles himself will be exalted.*

Luke 6:38: *Give, and it will be given to you: good measure, pressed down, shaken together, and running over, will be given to you. For with the same measure you measure it will be measured back to you.*

May 19th
<u>Papa's Military Picture</u>

"Why is Papa's picture next to a man in a different set of clothes? They kind of look alike," he said, pointing to pictures on the wall. I replied, "Interesting observation, little man. This is a picture of Papa in his U.S. Navy uniform when he was in the military. The picture beside him is of his dad, your great-grandfather. He served in the U.S. Army and is wearing an Army uniform." "Why do they have to dress differently and wear different hats?" Good observations. "Each branch of the military service has its own style of uniform as well as a motto and song."

He thought for a minute and asked, "How many different military branches are there?" "There are six active branches: the Army, Navy, Marine Corps, Coast Guard, Air Force, and Space Force. There are six reserve branches, as well, for those six active branches as well as the National Guard." "What are the reserves?" "The reserves are those who have served and are ready to help the active-duty branches as needed. Papa served two years in the reserves after he was honorably discharged."

I realize that once we become Christians, we serve in God's army. We put our faith in Jesus and live according to His Word as revealed by the Holy Spirit. We are called to be soldiers living under the LORD's command to counter evil, showing and living the tremendous love that flows from God's heart to all mankind. We "look like Him" as we bear His image given to us from creation, then His characteristics and nature after our salvation.

Thank You, LORD, for the privilege of serving in Your earthly army. I pray we man our station, ready to fight the enemy at every turn, being prayed up and studied up to fight spiritual warfare for the freedom of all people to experience all the blessings God has in store for us. Paul said we must fight the good fight, finish the race, and keep the faith (**2 Timothy 4:7**).

Priceless Moments

Genesis 1:26*: God said, "Let's make man in our image, after our likeness. Let them have dominion over the fish of the sea, and over the birds of the sky, and over the livestock, and over all the earth, and over every creeping thing that creeps on the earth."*

Colossians 1:15*: He is the image of the invisible God, the firstborn of all creation.*

Philippians 2:6-8*: who, existing in the form of God, didn't consider equality with God a thing to be grasped, but emptied himself, taking the form of a servant, being made in the likeness of men. And being found in human form, he humbled himself, becoming obedient to the point of death, yes, the death of the cross.*

May 20th

Can I Help?

The grandchildren enjoy doing things like running the sweeper, dusting, doing dishes, and making beds to help out around the house, just because. They don't expect to get anything from it; they just want to be helpful. Today is no exception. They literally walked in the door and asked, "Hi, Grandma. Do you need any help today to clean your house? We thought if we asked right away, we could help you fix dinner. By the way, what are we having for dinner?" "I have chicken, so I'm debating between Cuban chicken, chicken Milanese, or chicken Parmesan casserole. What do you think?"

Neither child said anything. Our granddaughter perked up, saying, "Can we make apricot chicken in the instant pot? If so, I can cut up the apricots." "And I can cut the carrots while you cut the chicken," piped in our grandson. We can throw it all in the pot and let it cook. We can set the table while you make the rice. Then dinner will be ready. Do you like this idea?" "I'd say you guys are terrific. Best idea I've heard, I'll say. Let's get cooking."

Priceless Moments

We find we get further with the grands wanting to help when we purposefully move more slowly and let them help at their pace, even letting them start or complete work on tasks without asking them to do so. The ultimate comment is, "Hey, thanks. You did a terrific job." "Wow, you worked faster and did a better job than me." "I like how you did that. I never thought to do it that way. Can you show me how to do it your way?" Oh, this is so hard for me. What am I going to do?" I love their uninhibited desire to help.

Thank You, LORD, for our built-in internal motivation. I pray we find the childlike motivation to explore Your Word, getting the most out of our study and private time with You. May we find a way to help others grow.

Jeremiah 31:33: "*But this is the covenant that I will make with the house of Israel after those days,*" *says Yahweh: "I will put my law in their inward parts, and I will write it in their heart. I will be their God, and they shall be my people.*

Matthew 19:26: Looking at them, Jesus said, "With men this is impossible, but with God all things are possible."

1 Corinthians 15:58: Therefore, my beloved brothers, be steadfast, immovable, always abounding in the Lord's work, because you know that your labor is not in vain in the Lord.

May 21st

The Mouse Trap

"Hey, Grandma, do you have a mouse trap? We'd like to play with one." "Excuse me, what did you say? I don't think it's a good idea to play with a mouse trap. Besides, we don't have that type of

Priceless Moments

problem here, so we don't have any." I was shocked at such a request. The kids responded, "No, no, no, not that kind of mouse trap. We heard some kids talking about a mouse trap, and we're trying to figure out what they meant." I dusted off the cobwebs of my brain, saying, "Ah, I think I may have an idea. Give me a moment." I walked into the living room—two kids in tow—to dig in a cupboard. Their heads were so close to mine that I could barely see inside.

Finally, I saw what I was looking for—a game called *Mouse Trap*. Pulling it out, I said, "Is this what you have in mind? Let's take a look inside the box." Puzzled looks appeared as the game was assembled. At last, the mice and trap were put in place. The lights went on. "I get it. The mouse they were talking about catching is one of these (picking up the red mouse) under the cage thing. It looks like fun. Can you tell us how to play it, then play a game with us?" I hesitated, then said, "Sure, but I need to read the directions, as I honestly can't remember ever playing this with the kids." We figured it out and were hooked.

It's amazing how our language has several different things that can lead us to wrong conclusions. It's great to know there are no contradictions within His Word. It's up to us to delve into the Word to find the answers we're looking for and to discover more than we ever dreamed was there.

Thank You, LORD, for a Bible to stimulate our desire to learn more about You and the world You created. I pray we increase our knowledge as well as our desire for more of You, your earthly history, and our future with You.

Hosea 4:6: My people are destroyed for lack of knowledge. Because you have rejected knowledge, I will also reject you, that you may be no priest to me. Because you have forgotten your God's law, I will also forget your children.

John 16:13: However when he, the Spirit of truth, has come, he will guide you into all truth, for he will not speak from himself; but whatever he hears, he will speak. He will declare to you things that are coming.

2 Timothy 3:16*: Every Scripture is God-breathed and profitable for teaching, for reproof, for correction, and for instruction in righteousness,*

May 22nd
<u>Battleship—Who's Move?</u>

After breakfast, I asked the grandchildren, "Do you want to play a game called Battleship?" "Never heard of it. How do you play it?" she asked. I replied, "We each get a grid like this with two sections: one will be used for your moves, the other for the person with whom you're playing. You call out a row and column combination from the grid to try and sink the other person's ships. Here, let me show you." I proceeded to work through the game until it made sense. When we finished, he asked, "How did this game get created?" "If I remember correctly, the original pencil and paper game was created around World War I. About twenty-five years later, the game changed to a plastic game like this before being made into video games and an app to be downloaded to your phone or iPad. Small travel games to take wherever you go are for sale in stores."

"Can we play a game now? You and I will hide our ships without looking, then see how it goes. I think I understand how to use the grid for my ships and how to mark off the spaces I call out for you. I don't remember all the names of the ships, but I know there were five. Can I sit on this side of the table? If I need help, will you answer my questions?" "Absolutely, little man." We played several calls of *fire* before hearing this: "Who's move is it, Grandma? I know I shot and hit one of your ships, but I can't remember if you played or not." And so it goes for the remainder of the game.

Years ago, I remember playing this with our kids—always a hit—pun intended. Thankfully, God does not try to hit us with fire; rather, He works to mold and shape us into works of art that show others good examples of how He is working and changing our lives and forming useful workers in His kingdom.

Thank You, LORD, that after we make the first move to choose You for eternity, it's then Your turn to reveal Yourself to us and show us the direction You want for our lives.

Deuteronomy 20:3b, 4: *Don't let your heart faint! Don't be afraid, nor tremble, neither be scared of them; for Yahweh your God is he who goes with you, to fight for you against your enemies, to save you.*

1 Corinthians 10:13: *No temptation has taken you except what is common to man. God is faithful, who will not allow you to be tempted above what you are able, but will with the temptation also make the way of escape, that you may be able to endure it.*

2 Thessalonians 3:3: *But the Lord is faithful, who will establish you and guard you from the evil one.*

May 23rd

<u>The Dancing Bear</u>

"Grandma, can we play one of Papa's musical dogs or bears? They are so much fun, especially when we get them all playing at one time." "I think playing them one at a time is more fun since you can enjoy the music and the singing since you can understand the words." "That's true, but it's also fun to make noise." Chuckling, I grabbed and tickled him, saying, "I thought you liked to make noise all by yourself without the bears." He just giggled and twisted in my arms. I remarked, "Why don't you give me a great big hug and we can talk about it?" He said, "Sure. I'll squeeze the stuffin' out of you, and you'll say 'yes,' right?" I told him, "You're too cute and lovable for your own good." He laughed and said, "Thanks, Grandma," proceeding to give me a wonderful hug.

"To answer your next question about which one to play, can I try Papa's dancing bear? It's so much fun to dance to this fun music." Now he's anticipating me, so I'll throw him off. "Let me ask you, 'Do you think it's the animated dancing bear or the music that makes you want to dance?'" "Gee, Grandma, I never thought about it that way. When I think about it, both the dancing bear and the music make it fun to play." "Thank you for the answer. That's what I thought, because both make me want to play it as well. Why don't we have some fun? Race you to the plant table to play the bear." Of course, I had to let him win.

I reflected on the benefits of music in a person's worship, be it during good times or when your spirit needs a lift. Singing is actually commanded in Scripture, allowing one to combine the word with memorable tunes to stay with us throughout our lives, strengthening ourselves spiritually while taking a stand against Satan, the original heavenly song leader.

Thank You, LORD, for different options in music to bless our souls as well as to sing praises to You. I pray the gift of song enhances our worship, whether or not we can carry a tune.

Ephesians 5:18-19: *Don't be drunken with wine, in which is dissipation, but be filled with the Spirit, speaking to one another in psalms, hymns, and spiritual songs; singing and making melody in your heart to the Lord;*

Colossians 3:16: *Let the word of Christ dwell in you richly; in all wisdom teaching and admonishing one another with psalms, hymns, and spiritual songs, singing with grace in your heart to the Lord.*

Acts 16:25: *But about midnight Paul and Silas were praying and singing hymns to God, and the prisoners were listening to them.*

Priceless Moments

May 24th

<u>What?</u>

"Hey, Grandma, come quick. Why is your plant lying on the floor? The dirt is everywhere." A shocked "What?" escaped my lips as I raced into the living room. Trying to keep myself calm, I checked the floor and found a broken plant in the midst of a scattered pot's worth of dirt. No object was found to be the culprit for its demise. I asked, "Does anyone have an idea of how this happened? I'm not angry. I just want to know what happened so we can be sure it doesn't happen again." Eyes all around the room exchanged glances, but no one peeped a word.

I knew I couldn't be accusatory, but I just wanted to know what happened. One brave child came into the kitchen and said, "Grandma, no one did it on purpose. It was an accident. We were playing together and got really involved in the game. We all reacted at the same time, jumping up. We lost our balance and fell into the plant stand. We caught the other plants but must have missed this one. We didn't know if we should try to clean it up or call you. We decided to call you in so we didn't make it worse." She was on the verge of tears, so I put my arms around her. "Thank you for being honest with me. I truly appreciate it. I'll let all of you know that calling me in was the right thing to do. Cleanup will be so much easier to get it off the top of the carpet."

I couldn't help but think about how we need to go to the LORD immediately after we've created a mess. We could try to clean things up ourselves, with the possibility of making the situation worse. Or, we could go to our Heavenly Father to face the consequences of our actions, be they painful or learning opportunities to help us grow in You.

Thank You, LORD, that we experience consequences to enable us to experience Your grace. I pray we learn from our mistakes and from Your discipline, because we learn more quickly from our errors than from our accomplishments.

Ecclesiastes 8:11: *When a sentence for a crime is not quickly carried out, the hearts of the people are filled with schemes to do wrong. NIV*

Proverbs 1:31: *Therefore they will eat of the fruit of their own way, and be filled with their own schemes.*

Matthew 6:14–15: *For if you forgive men their trespasses, your heavenly Father will also forgive you. But if you don't forgive men their trespasses, neither will your Father forgive your trespasses.*

May 25th

My Dream

A favorite question to ask children is, "What do you want to do when you grow up?" I decided it was time to ask the granddaughters this question, too. One granddaughter answered, "I want to be a dancer. I can already stand on my toes." Another, "Maybe a doctor." One more, "I want to be a teacher." Yet another, "A mommy." Our grandson said, "I want to be like my dad." I said, "Those are all good occupations. It will be interesting to see if you keep those thoughts as you grow and experience different types of jobs." "Grandma, what did you want to be when you were our age?" "Wow, that was a long time ago. As I remember, I wanted to be a musician because I always liked to sing."

"So, did you change your mind about what to do when you grew up?" "It is so nice of you to ask. As a matter of fact, I did change my mind. When I was ready to go to college, I was told my desire for music was more of a hobby than an occupation. After reading about other things to take in college besides music, I agreed I should pick something else." "Did you enjoy the change of job?" "Yes, I did. I felt God was in charge of my choice of what to study. I've always enjoyed working with people, and my jobs centered around people first."

Rethinking my life's work was one of the best moves I've ever made. By changing directions to follow His will, He provided me with lifelong Christian friends and the love of my life. They have influenced my life for You beyond anything I could ever imagine.

Thank You, LORD, for being faithful in guiding our lives into areas You deem best for us. I pray we stay sensitive to changing directions whenever and as often as possible, if and when You determine You could use us more effectively elsewhere. I want to be what my dad wants me to be.

Proverbs 16:9: *A man's heart plans his course, but Yahweh directs his steps.*

Psalm 32:8: *I will instruct you and teach you in the way which you shall go. I will counsel you with my eye on you.*

Jeremiah 1:7-8: *But Yahweh said to me, "Don't say, 'I am a child;' for you must go to whomever I send you, and you must say whatever I command you. Don't be afraid because of them, for I am with you to rescue you," says Yahweh.*

May 26th

The Treasure Box

The younger grandchildren talk about picking things out of the treasure box at school on Fridays for good behavior or doing good throughout the week. When asked what good things were rewarded, they answered, "Showing kindness, paying attention in class, coming to school, and being on time, stuff like that." "I'm so proud of you for being able to choose a prize for doing things Jesus wants you to do as well. What kinds of prizes do you choose from?" "Pencils, stickers, squishy things, key chains, foam

Priceless Moments

airplanes, balls, bracelets, stuff like that. Some of it's really cool, others are really lame." "Wow, if I had a chance to choose cool stuff, I'd have good behavior, too." "Grandma, next Friday, do you want us to find something in the box for you?" "Oh, you are much too kind. You will have earned the prize, so I think you should choose something for yourselves."

I thought a minute, then asked, "If we had a treasure box here, what kinds of things would you like to do to earn the privilege of choosing a treasure?" I heard, "Grandma, a treasure box would be nice, but what kinds of things would you put in it?" I hadn't expected the tables to be turned, but I always give them an answer. "I think I would put in credit slips for completing your chores, showing kindness to one another, dates with Grandma, stickers for your sticker books, LEGOS, or money for piggy banks. You could save the credits earned for bigger prizes or spend them each week as you earn them." "Sure, that sounds good. Let's build a treasure box."

I wondered how many of us need a positive behavior plan to motivate us for daily reading, studying, and praying. I realized we do have a treasure box, but not in our earthly home. Our treasures are waiting for us up in heaven.

Thank You, LORD, for kind hearts that mirror Your own. I pray we demonstrate these positive behaviors with everyone we meet.

1 Corinthians 13:4-7*: Love is patient and is kind. Love doesn't envy. Love doesn't brag, is not proud, doesn't behave itself inappropriately, doesn't seek its own way, is not provoked, takes no account of evil; doesn't rejoice in unrighteousness, but rejoices with the truth; bears all things, believes all things, hopes all things, and endures all things.*

Micah 6:8*: He has shown you, O man, what is good. What does Yahweh require of you, but to act justly, to love mercy, and to walk humbly with your God?*

Priceless Moments

Colossians 3:12*: Put on therefore, as God's chosen ones, holy and beloved, a heart of compassion, kindness, lowliness, humility, and perseverance;*

May 27th

<u>Memorial Day</u>

Today is a special day to honor all military soldiers who died in American wars. President Lyndon Johnson and Congress declared Waterloo, NY, the birthplace of Memorial Day in 1966. It originally started with a ceremony on May 5, 1866, three years after the Civil War, to honor veterans who fought in that war, calling it Decoration Day. The nation decorated the graves with flowers because flowers would be in bloom all over the nation. This federal holiday is considered the beginning of summer and is celebrated by family gatherings, parades, and community programs to honor the deceased veterans of the past year. The American flag is flown at half-staff until noon only on Memorial Day. The date changes every year to celebrate it on the last Monday of May.

There is a vast amount of information about previous celebrations prior to a national declaration, but the current way of honoring our fallen veterans has changed very little. Today, special services, parades, and decorating the graves with flowers remain a national tradition, a way of giving back by those of us who remain, celebrating our freedom and opportunities due to their sacrifice. To date, over 1.1 million Americans have died in the country's wars. Poppies are the official symbol of remembrance sold this holiday weekend.

I can't help but think of how God must have felt when He sent His Only Son to the troubled country of Israel, knowing He was signing His Son's death warrant on the cross. Fortunately, today,

Priceless Moments

Christians have picked up the torch to continue to remember the sacrifices both God and Jesus made on our behalf.

Thank You, LORD, for Your sacrifice on the cross to fight and win the battle against the enemy, Satan. I pray we continue to remember Your sacrifice and be willing to sacrifice our time, energy, schedule, and even our lives for Your cause.

John 3:16: For God so loved the world, that he gave his one and only Son, that whoever believes in him should not perish, but have eternal life.

Romans 5:8: But God commends his own love toward us, in that while we were yet sinners, Christ died for us.

Mark 10:45: For the Son of Man also came not to be served, but to serve, and to give his life as a ransom for many.

May 28th

The Teddy Bear

"I have a teddy bear named Freddie. I take him everywhere I go because he's my favorite." I was intrigued, so I asked, "What can you tell me about Freddie? I'm interested to learn more about him." "Oh, Grandma, feel him. He's so soft and furry, and his face is sweet. He has different-colored paws. He has a little heart on his bottom, which just makes me smile. When I'm sad, he always listens to all I have to say. He never judges me by telling me I'm wrong. He and I pray together in the morning when I get up and at night when I go to bed. We pray at meals, too, so I can feed him. He never complains about anything. He's such a faithful friend. Sometimes I wish he could talk and tell me what it's like to get a bath in the washing machine or to tumble in the dryer. I know he gets tired, so I put him down for a nap. I don't nap with him because I'm too big for that now."

"It sounds like he's a terrific companion to have. What does he do during the day when you're away?" "Sometimes I take him to school to play with the other kids. They like to bring their favorite stuffies to school, too." "What other kinds of stuffies does Freddie get to play with at school?" She smiled and said, "Freddie likes to play with Paula the panda, George the koala, and Allen the teddy bear. He's not as cute as mine but he's nice. There are others there, but these are his and my favorites."

I thought God has favorites, too—the righteous, anyone who has accepted His Son as their Savior. They have plans to take us on the most wonderful trip we have ever been on—straight to heaven, be it at our death or in the rapture, whichever comes first.

Thank You, LORD, for Your known plans for our future. I pray we work hard to increase the number of people going to heaven in the future because I know You have a special place prepared for each one of us in Your mansion.

Proverbs 15:29*: Yahweh is far from the wicked, but he hears the prayer of the righteous.*

Galatians 3:27-28*: For as many of you as were baptized into Christ have put on Christ. There is neither Jew nor Greek, there is neither slave nor free man, there is neither male nor female; for you are all one in Christ Jesus.*

1 Peter 3:12*: For the eyes of the Lord are on the righteous, and his ears open to their prayer; but the face of the Lord is against those who do evil.*

May 29th

What's a Tithe?

"The pastor was talking about giving a tithe. What is it?" Excellent question. "The idea of a tithe came from **Genesis 15:10**: *'Then*

Priceless Moments

Abram gave him (Melchizedek, king of Salem) a tenth of everything.' If you had ten pennies, a tenth would be one of those pennies, leaving you with nine pennies to spend as you want. Beyond the tithe are offerings, money, or possessions freely given beyond the tenth. Money and possessions are talked about more in the Bible than salvation and prayer, so God knew this area was one we really needed to understand to keep our priorities in line with His will for our lives. Everything we have belongs to God, and He loans it to us to use wisely to help build His kingdom. The longest book in the Bible, **Numbers 7**, deals with giving."

"In Old Testament times, people gave God tithes from their land and animals to support the priests. Today, tithes are given from money earned on things like jobs. God honors those who give generously, humbly, and freely, all with the proper attitude, as a voluntary act of worship and stewardship. He's not standing there with His hand out, yet He wants you to give consistently so He can bless you for your right-heart attitude. It is best to give God the first of your money, tithes, and offerings to honor God before your own needs. Your personal gift should come from what you have earned, not something Mom or Dad give you to put in the offering. He views your generous gift, no matter the amount, as a matter of your heart, a sacrifice freely given to Him to build His kingdom. He will say of you, *"Well done, my child,"* and so will I."

I reflected on a non-mandatory tithe, yet I couldn't help but think that when God gave His best, He gave 100%. Most of us give something, but is it ten percent—or less? Are there offerings freely given as well? What we do with our money is an indication of whether or not we're living for God or the deceiver—Satan.

Proverbs 3:9-10: *Honor Yahweh with your substance, with the first fruits of all your increase: so your barns will be filled with plenty, and your vats will overflow with new wine.*

Malachi 3:10: *Bring the whole tithe into the storehouse, that there may be food in my house, and test me now in this," says Yahweh of*

Armies, *"if I will not open you the windows of heaven, and pour you out a blessing, that there will not be room enough for."*

2 Corinthians 9:6-7*: Remember this: he who sows sparingly will also reap sparingly. He who sows bountifully will also reap bountifully. Let each man give according as he has determined in his heart, not grudgingly or under compulsion, for God loves a cheerful giver.*

May 30th
RV Fun

"Grandma, Grandma, Grandma, come quick. We need to show you something." Wow, something's really important to them—better hurry. A quick trip downstairs, shoes on, and out the door to two adorable grandchildren. Each held out a hand and said, "Close your eyes." Obediently, I took their hands and closed my eyes. I was led up the steps and across the driveway. For the life of me, I'd no idea where they were taking me. I heard, "Open your eyes." I was standing in front of their RV. "Go on in." I walked up the stairs and heard, "Surprise. We've made you a lunch of peanut butter and jelly wraps, carrot sticks with hummus, and nature's best. Do you remember what nature's best is?" "Of course, I do. It's water."

During lunch, they shared, "We had so much fun getting this ready for you. We know you like to travel with us, so we thought we'd get ready for the new season. Did you like our surprise?" Looking at their beaming faces, I responded, "I really loved it, but not as much as I love you. Also, I was very surprised you took so much time to do something so nice for me. You are very special, thoughtful children." They looked at each other and giggled. "Grandma, would you mind helping us clean up? We want to leave it as clean as we found it." How sweet, I thought.

Priceless Moments

"Absolutely. And... I'll even help you do the dishes." They looked at each other, high-fived each other, and said, "Yes."

I thought of how fantastic it would be if we had sustained excitement like this over our acceptance of Jesus as our personal Savior. This type of excitement is so catchy; just think of how many people we could win for the LORD. Our faces will set the stage for sharing Jesus with all we meet. Remember, seeing is believing.

Thank You, LORD, for realizing that our outward actions and reactions do have an influence on others. I pray we consider our reactions in front of others since our faith is always on display as others are always watching and thinking about whether what we have is something they want to have as well.

Ephesians 4:2: *Be completely humble and gentle; be patient, bearing with one another in love. NIV*

Philippians 2:14: *Do all things without complaining and arguing,*

Colossians 3:23, 24: *And whatever you do, work heartily, as for the Lord, and not for men, knowing that from the Lord you will receive the reward of the inheritance; for you serve the Lord Christ.*

May 31st

The Jesus Revolution

The movie *The Jesus Revolution* caught the attention of everyone who saw the trailer, read the promotional information, or heard about it from friends. The grandchildren were fascinated with the information shared, asking many questions to satisfy their curiosity. "How could a preacher and the people at church not accept someone who wants to hear about Jesus? Why did the church people say they wouldn't go to church there anymore if the preacher let people who were different come to their church? I thought the church was for anyone, so we could teach them about Jesus. If we don't invite them to come, how will they hear about the good news? In our Good News Club, they are teaching us to be honest and kind and what to say to others."

"Wow, you have a lot of questions. I'll try to answer them. Yes, Jesus is for everyone, regardless of where they live, their skin color, or their culture. People who have always been in a church that's not growing get used to the same thing over and over. When challenged to reach out beyond their closed group and their comfort zone, they feel unsure about changes and things they don't understand. At this point, they need to take their fears and concerns to Jesus in prayer so He can teach them the things you are learning about in the Good News Club."

I couldn't help but think of Chuck Smith, pastor of the church that appeared very proper yet was closed to others who didn't fit in. Once Chuck started to open his heart and mind to those different from him, the Jesus movement really got a kick in the pants and started to accept others different from themselves, opening up their hearts to the LORD.

Thank You, LORD, for people willing to step out of their comfort zone and experience You on a different level. I pray we all can open our minds and hearts to those in need.

Mark 16:15: *He said to them, "Go into all the world, and preach the Good News to the whole creation.*

2 Timothy 4:2: *preach the word; be urgent in season and out of season; reprove, rebuke, and exhort with all patience and teaching.*

Romans 10:17: *So faith comes by hearing, and hearing by the word of God.*

June

These words, which I command you today, shall be on your heart; and you shall teach them diligently to your children, and shall talk of them when you sit in your house, and when you walk by the way, and when you lie down, and when you rise up...

Deut. 6:6-9

Priceless Moments

June 1ST

Praise God for the Rain

We like to take our children out for dinner to celebrate anniversaries, birthdays, and *just because* occasions at a location of their choosing—within our general area. Tonight, we were going out to dinner in our local town to celebrate the birthday of our daughter-in-law. Let's back up a moment to fill in a very important piece of the puzzle. Our area had been experiencing a drought, so the grandchildren and I had been praying for rain almost every day since it started. Today was no exception. Earlier this day, we were praying for rain again.

The timer rang, indicating it was time to go meet their parents. As we pulled into our parking spot downtown, a few raindrops fell on the windshield. The kids squealed, "God answers prayer." As we got out of the car, they continued praying, so I grabbed an umbrella. I told them, "We are exercising our faith by taking our umbrella." At that moment, the skies broke forth in buckets full of rain, so up went the umbrella. Again, the peals of laughter turned into praising God for the rain—for at least six blocks from car to restaurant. We were anything but quiet in our praise, attracting the attention of EVERYONE who passed by. Most people were receptive, and some joined in. Others gave strange looks, but no one scoffed. We reached the restaurant when the windows of heaven opened, making it hard to see out the window. Our granddaughter said grace, "Thank you for Mommy and for answering prayer for all that glorious rain. Thank You; some people on the street joined in our praise. Thank You; we had to use the umbrella. You can keep the rain coming, because we still need it. Amen."

I realized how exciting it was for the kids to see their prayers answered so quickly and so abundantly, as well as to ask for the rain to continue. Childlike faith is where we all need to start—and return to again and again when our faith waivers—because children have a knack for unquestionable faith.

Thank You, LORD; the grandchildren were unashamedly praising You regardless of the people around us. I pray they continue to recognize You for giving the rain, knowing all glory goes to You.

Matthew 5:16: Even so, let your light shine before men, that they may see your good works and glorify your Father who is in heaven.

Hebrews 13:15: Through him, then, let's offer up a sacrifice of praise to God continually, that is, the fruit of lips which proclaim allegiance to his name.

1 Corinthians 10:31: Whether therefore you eat, or drink, or whatever you do, do all to the glory of God.

June 2nd

The "Meany"

Have you ever been tormented by someone for no reason, at least not known to you? Our granddaughter was having a tiff with her little brother, but I could not figure out why, so I asked, "Honey, has your brother done something to upset you? If so, please tell me, and we can all talk about it together." The silence hung so heavy in the room that she could not lift her head. I gently put my hand under her chin and again asked, "Is everything OK? I'm here to help you if you need me." No response, so I left the room to get her some Kleenex because she had started to cry. I heard her say, "You meany."

When I returned, she wiped her eyes, blew her nose, and then said, "He was playing with something I wanted. When I asked him nicely to give it to me, he said 'no.'" Oh, great, I thought. He is usually the one who would give you the shirt off his back if he could. I scooped her up in my arms and sat her on my knee. "Do you remember our rule about 'move your feet, lose your seat'?

And that it applies to seats as well as toys, right? So, if he had it first, he has the right to continue playing with it or to give it to you." She crossed her arms and went 'hrump.' I softly asked her, "Who is controlling your heart and emotions right now?" The arms relaxed as the tears began to flow. Very quietly and meekly, she said, "That meany Satan. In Jesus' name, get away from me, Satan." She got up, went over to her brother, threw her arms around him, and apologized. He must have felt bad, as well, because he also apologized and gave her the toy.

I felt so heartened to know she realized Satan was the cause of her reacting inappropriately towards her brother. Better yet, she rebuked Satan, then took the higher road, swallowed her pride, and apologized.

Thank You, LORD, for being able to witness these little hearts being so sensitive to Your leading. I pray we, too, learn to recognize the source of our grief as well as the source of our joy.

Luke 11:4: Forgive us our sins, for we ourselves also forgive everyone who is indebted to us. Bring us not into temptation, but deliver us from the evil one.

Ephesians 4:32: And be kind to one another, tender hearted, forgiving each other, just as God also in Christ forgave you.

Colossians 3:13: Bear with each other and forgive one another if any of you has a grievance against someone. Forgive as the LORD forgave you. NIV

June 3rd
The Telephone Book

"Grandma, do you have a telephone book? I want to know if there's a telephone number in there for God. I know we always talk to Him when we pray, but I want to talk to Him as a friend."

Priceless Moments

"Oh, honey, that's an awesome thought to want to talk to God as your friend. Know that He is your friend, but you never need a phone number to call or talk to Him. Jesus is your friend; someone you can talk to as well as pray to anytime of the day or night for any reason." "But how do I know He hears me?" "He will speak to our hearts, giving us a sense of peace."

"The Bible tells us God always hears our prayers the first time. Our prayers are so important to Him that He keeps them in golden bowls in heaven. He will answer them if we pray within His will for our lives and ask for the right things. Sometimes He delays the answer because the time may not be right. If we pray for things that will not be good for us, His answer will be "no." If we feel God has not answered our prayers, we are told to keep asking, seeking, and knocking for God's will in our lives. We always have the opportunity to share our prayer request(s) with others, asking them to join us in prayer. Scripture tells us that where two or more are gathered together in His name, He will be with them.

I couldn't help but praise God that no telephone book is needed to reach Him. No matter where we are—at home, work, or deep in the woods—our "cell reception" is always 100% accessible, and there is never a busy signal. And our prayers are treasured so much that God places them in a golden bowl in heaven.

Thank You, LORD; we have a hotline to You regardless of our circumstances or where we are. I pray we think to pray first before doing anything else, so we stay within Your will for our lives.

Psalm 145:18: *Yahweh is near to all those who call on him, to all who call on him in truth.*

1 Thessalonians 5:16-18: *Always rejoice. Pray without ceasing. In everything give thanks, for this is the will of God in Christ Jesus toward you.*

1 John 5:14: *This is the boldness which we have toward him, that if we ask anything according to his will, he listens to us.*

June 4th

Bumps, Bruises, Cuts, and Scars

Our grandson was riding his bike on a dusty, stony road when he encountered a stone that did not move out of his way. Needless to say, he did a swan dive over the handlebars, landing in a heap of "bike, child, dirt, stones, blood, and tears." First things first, he had a wellness checkup on the spot. Scraped elbows, banged-up knees, and a wounded pride were the casualties. He was scooped up and comforted.

When it came time to clean his wounds, he didn't want to endure the additional pain of the peroxide cleansing the open wounds. He was told he could deal with it now and get it over with, or later when infection would set in and require more extensive cleaning. Being a smart young man, he chose to "just get it over with" so he could move on and forget about it. He was told he could hold my hand and cry until it was all over—he did. As the cleansing proceeded, he was told he would have "battle scars" to prove he had come through the ordeal triumphantly. After the situation was over, he didn't want to get back on his bike and go for a ride—ever again. We talked about how God would be with him and keep him safe, even if he got a few more "battle scars."

God reveals Himself to us in like manner. We fall down through some type of small or devastating experience. We, too, have the choice to deal with it now or later. God is always there to hold our hand and assure us that He will be with us through it all. No amount of cleansing will ever be too great when He is by our side. Like little children, we should surrender to the early cleansing so we don't have to carry around years of burdens or guilt. They will only weigh us down and fester until we come clean before God. He will do the best heart-cleansing job one could ever experience. For each additional bump or boulder along the way, God is there, encouraging us to come to Him for immediate cleansing of our wounds.

Priceless Moments

Thank You, LORD, for your promise to never leave us or forsake us. May we always be open and willing to come to You for all of our bumps, bruises, cuts, and scrapes along the rocky pathway called life.

Revelation 7:17*: for the Lamb who is in the middle of the throne shepherds them and leads them to springs of life-giving waters. And God will wipe away every tear from their eyes.*

Isaiah 41:10*: Don't you be afraid, for I am with you. Don't be dismayed, for I am your God. I will strengthen you. Yes, I will help you. Yes, I will uphold you with the right hand of my righteousness.*

Jeremiah 33:6*: Behold, I will bring it health and cure, and I will cure them; and I will reveal to them abundance of peace and truth.*

June 5th
<u>Grandma, Hold My Hand</u>

I so enjoy going on walks with our grandchildren. Their observations are so fresh and detailed, unlike their grown-up counterparts, who have become so unobservant, just overlooking the variety of treasures to be found along the path. Children see the bugs on the grass, the buds on flowers, the blossoms on the tree—you get the picture. In all sincerity, I don't remember how long it's been since I last tuned in to the little joys of nature. Anyway, on our most recent walk, the little ones found treasures: beads from a broken bracelet, a shed snakeskin, acorns, pretty colorful leaves, bird nests, sticks, special stones, water puddles, pine cones, and the list goes on. "Grandma, did you see all the treasures we are finding? Can we take them home?"

They love to see and touch things, as well as bring them home. Diplomacy became the word of the day: "We need to let things be in their natural environment for the animals to use later." That only goes so far when dealing with four- and six-year-olds. Needless to say, we bartered: "Let's look at all your treasures and select only a few to take home. If you will be able to pare down the items to be taken home, we could come back tomorrow to see if any of the animals came and took some of the things left behind for their own use." They thought about it for a minute, then talked between themselves. "OK, Grandma. We will only take two items each, as we can come back tomorrow in hopes that the remaining items could still be here." "Good deal."

This made me think of how, at times, we try to barter with God. He wants us to do this, but we want to do that. We want to go here, but God wants us to go there. We want to talk to this person, but God wants us to talk to someone else. Ultimately, our choice is to follow God's leading in our lives or to walk away and do our own thing. May we be willing to give God's way a try BEFORE walking away, realizing His way is perfect.

Thank You, LORD, for letting us exercise our God-given free will. I pray we use the God-given wisdom inside each one of us to choose God's direction for our lives.

Psalm 139:9, 10*: If I take the wings of the dawn, and settle in the uttermost parts of the sea, even there your hand will lead me, and your right hand will hold me.*

Psalm 73:23*: Nevertheless, I am continually with you. You have held my right hand.*

Isaiah 41:13*: For I, Yahweh your God, will hold your right hand, saying to you, "Don't be afraid. I will help you."*

Priceless Moments

June 6th

Papa Always Knows What To Say

Papa is a very special person to our grandchildren. They crawl all over him, and he would tickle, kiss, and hug them. The smiles and laughter they share will keep them enjoying each other's company for hours on end, doing whatever the grandchildren want to do. They build with blocks, read stories, toss little balls back and forth, and play with cars and trucks. The kids like to splash in the kiddie pool on the back patio. Papa taunts them, "OK, guys, now don't splash me." Of course, that just encourages them to splash, so he has an excuse to splash them back.

When the grands would ask any type of question, Papa would always give them an answer. When skinned knees or elbows, stubbed toes, or funny bones occur, he says how much he loves them and that it will be OK before they get married. The kids didn't understand the last comment, but they snuggle in his comforting arms. When they start to relax, he jokes around, helping them forget the "boo-boo" pain. He asks them what they want to do next, and they start to tickle him. Peals of laughter ring throughout the house as the frivolity continues. Sometimes I'm not sure who the kids are or who the adults are.

Ah, what a loving exchange to observe. My mind's eye can see God demonstrating the same kind of tender care for us when we are hurt, helping us to forget our troubles by sharing His love and plan for our lives. Since He knows what we need, He is there to help us move past the hurt into joy.

Thank You, LORD, for Your loving exchange with us regardless of our circumstances, leading us through times of pain and suffering and into better times ahead. I pray we keep looking up for those comforting words and guidance at some of the most challenging times of our lives.

Revelation 21:4*: He will wipe away every tear from their eyes. Death will be no more; neither will there be mourning, nor crying, nor pain, any more. The first things have passed away.*

Psalm 34:18*: Yahweh is near to those who have a broken heart, and saves those who have a crushed spirit.*

Isaiah 41:10*: Don't you be afraid, for I am with you. Don't be dismayed, for I am your God. I will strengthen you. Yes, I will help you. Yes, I will uphold you with the right hand of my righteousness.*

June 7th

Swimming

"It is so hot out today. Can we go swimming?" One can see beads of sweat running down their red cheeks as they enter the house. The mercury hit 80° today, a rapid climb from yesterday. "You know what," I said, "that sounds like a refreshing idea. Where do you have in mind? It's too early for the local swimming pool or splash pad to open for the season." "Can we go down to the pond and splash around? We've been taking swimming lessons and really want to practice what we are learning." "Wow, that sounds awesome. What kinds of things have you been learning?" A long pause and thoughtful looks on both faces

"Since we are comfortable in the water, our teacher talked about being safe around the water, be it at a pool or at the beach." "What kinds of things keep you safe around the water?" "Stuff like no running, not going into the pool alone, not going into the water without water wings, stay in the shallow end, stuff like that. We've been learning how to breathe while floating—to hold our breath with our heads under water for five seconds. Mom and Dad had us in a hot tub and had us pick up toys from the bottom of the tub. That was so much fun and has really helped us do things in class.

Priceless Moments

Hopefully we can learn more here and become good swimmers like they are."

I pondered how swimming may be one of those activities that's been around since the beginning of time. Splashing in the water is fun for almost everyone; it's so cool and refreshing. God created such a perfect world full of possibilities in each area of creation—we just need to expand our horizons to find them.

Thank You, LORD, for the multiple uses of water—life-sustaining; fun in and out of it; for cleaning our bodies, clothes, dishes, etc. I pray we express thanks to You for such a multi-purpose world with such endless possibilities.

Isaiah 25:11*: He will spread out his hands in the middle of it, like one who swims spreads out hands to swim, but his pride will be humbled together with the craft of his hands.*

John 21:7*: That disciple therefore whom Jesus loved said to Peter, "It's the Lord!" So when Simon Peter heard that it was the Lord, he wrapped his coat around himself (for he was naked), and threw himself into the sea*

Acts 27:43*: But the centurion, desiring to save Paul, stopped them from their purpose, and commanded that those who could swim should throw themselves overboard first to go toward the land;*

June 8th
<u>Let's Plant Pumpkins</u>

"Grandma, can we plant some pumpkins? I think it would be cool to see how big they get." "That could be a fun idea. We don't have a big enough space at our house, so you would have to ask your parents. If they say OK, here is what you need to know: Pumpkins are considered a winter squash, a type of vegetable but technically a fruit that has many uses. They like to be planted where they get sun all day long with lots of room to spread out and grow, as well as a place for a long growing season, which is considered between seventy-five and one hundred days. Since they grow well in North America, where we live would be an ideal location to grow some."

"When could we start to grow some? I can hardly wait." "First, you need to decide if the pumpkins are for eating or craving at Halloween. Also, what color or colors do you want?" "What do you mean by what colors do we want? Pumpkins are orange." "Yes, but they can be white, red, pink, and blue, as well as smooth, bumpy, oval, flattened, or round." "Wow, that's awesome. When we're done, can we look up those colors on your phone?" "Sure, we can. Now, we could plant seeds inside by placing them in newspaper pots or peat pots, like we used for the flowers. "OK, let's decide on what to use them for and colors. We can't wait to get started."

Oh, the enthusiasm of young hearts, a trait I wish more Christians would continue to foster in their lives, so we can truly understand the phrase "Sweeter as the years go by, sweeter as the years go by, richer, fuller, deeper, Jesus' love is sweeter, sweeter as the years go by." Then our faces can show what our hearts know.

Thank You, LORD, for the varieties and types of pumpkins that describe mankind. I pray we allow our differences to complement each other as an opportunity to return Your creation to its intended design.

Genesis 1:27: *God created man in his own image. In God's image he created him; male and female he created them.*

Proverbs 1:15-16: *My son, don't walk on the path with them. Keep your foot from their path, for their feet run to evil. They hurry to shed blood.*

Galatians 3:28: *There is neither Jew nor Greek, there is neither slave nor free man, there is neither male nor female; for you are all one in Christ Jesus.*

Priceless Moments

June 9th

<u>Children's Day</u>

"Last week, our Sunday School teacher said we were going to talk about Children's Day next week. What is it?" "Excellent question. Remember, we celebrated Mother's Day a couple of weeks ago and are planning on Father's Day next week? Well, we also get to celebrate you guys, too. Celebrated on the second Sunday in June, this is a day to honor children." "When did it start? "It started in 1857 when Reverend Dr. Charles Leonard, from Chelsea, Massachusetts, held a special service in which he dedicated himself to and for the children, baptizing them. It was first called Rose Day, then Flower Day, and finally Children's Day. An International Children's Day was proclaimed in Geneva, Switzerland, in 1925. Soon other countries also adopted the celebration."

"Why do people feel it is important to have a Children's Day?" "Children are the society and future of every country. Many children face difficult times growing up, like missing a parent, living in a poor family, or having mental or physical health problems. This special day encourages adults to spend time making memories with their children, helping them feel important and a necessary part of our lives. Also, it gives adults a chance to realize they need to reach out to help another child or children by being a "big brother or sister," providing money, food, clothing, toys, coaching a little league sports team, being a scout leader, being a Sunday School teacher, and things like that."

It is so important to celebrate the purity and innocence of our children. They need to feel like princes and princesses in our lives—every day—but especially on their designated day. They should go out to breakfast, go to church, have a picnic lunch with their favorite foods—whatever it takes to make them feel just as special as they endeavor to make us feel on our special day.

Thank You, LORD, for Your gift of children. I pray we realize the little treasures in our lives will become more precious every day when we raise them in the fear and admonition of You. May our quivers be full of them.

Psalm 127:3-5: *Behold, children are a heritage of Yahweh. The fruit of the womb is his reward. As arrows in the hand of a mighty man, so are the children of youth. Happy is the man who has his quiver full of them. They won't be disappointed when they speak with their enemies in the gate.*

Proverbs 22:6: *Train up a child in the way he should go, and when he is old he will not depart from it.*

Matthew 18:10: *See that you don't despise one of these little ones, for I tell you that in heaven their angels always see the face of my Father who is in heaven.*

June 10th

S'mores

Kids came flying in the door, yelling, "Yes, we get to make s'mores. Grandma, can you help us get the things we need to make them? Some are too high on the shelves for us to reach." I had to have some fun with them, asking, "What are s'mores, and what is needed to make them?" Shocked looks crossed their faces as they just stared at me. "Come on, Grandma, s'mores are the greatest food ever around a campfire. We need graham crackers, marshmallows, and chocolate bars. Hey, wait a minute, you knew what they were because you make peanut butter squares to use in place of chocolate." I started to laugh. "Of course, I know what they are. I was just checking to be sure you remembered since it's been a long winter until camping season. And, yes, I made a fresh batch of peanut butter bars. I hid them in the freezer for such a time as this. Come on, let's do this."

Priceless Moments

We put the items on a tray along with plates, drinks, and a damp washcloth. "Why are we taking out a wet washcloth?" Again, I chuckled, "Ah, do you remember last year when a certain young lady got marshmallow and chocolate in her hair and all over her hands and face? I'm just being prepared so I don't have to make a special trip back inside to take care of removing the cold and setting up marshmallows and chocolate. It's just much easier this way. Can you think of anything else we'll need?" "Nope." "OK, then, off to the table with the goods. Marshmallow sticks are on the bench—and let's have some fun."

I love camping activities with little ones. When we didn't have time to go away for a weekend, we would camp in the backyard, locking up the house behind us. Other times, we would join a caravan of our church buddies and families to enjoy the great outdoors together. Nothing beats devotions around a campfire, followed by s'mores, pizza, and fruit pies from pie irons.

Thank You, LORD, for happy memories forged around the great outdoors, provided by You. I pray we take every opportunity to go outside and enjoy all of the beauty and fun things You have provided for us, regardless of the season.

Psalm 33:5: *He loves righteousness and justice. The earth is full of the loving kindness of Yahweh.*

Psalm 96:11-12: *Let the heavens be glad, and let the earth rejoice. Let the sea roar, and its fullness! Let the field and all that is in it exult! Then all the trees of the woods shall sing for joy.*

John 1:3: *All things were made through him. Without him, nothing was made that has been made.*

June 11th

Family Time

"Grandma, can we have some family time? We like to spend this time together because we have so much fun with you guys." "And we enjoy spending quality time with you as well. What is your favorite part about family time?" "We enjoy reading books, watching a movie together, playing games, putting together puzzles, talking about what we did today and what we hope to do tomorrow, what we're going to do on vacation together, stuff like that. What's your favorite part about family time?"

"Well, my favorite part is getting to hold you when we read books or watch a movie. We enjoy listening to you talk about your activities, but most of all, we love to hear you share what you are learning about Jesus. It warms our hearts to see how your knowledge of Jesus is growing and how much Scripture you have been learning. Keep those truths about Jesus forever in your heart and mind. Look to God and pray about everything, and let Jesus lead you in all things. When friends try to tell you that believing in Jesus is a waste of time, remember that Satan will use wayward friends to try to pull you away from Jesus. At this point, pray for them, asking them to go to church with you, but find Christian friends."

I remembered back to when I was a child and would sit upon my grandparents' knees and hear them tell me about their love for Jesus. Those family moments are forever imprinted upon my heart, and I desire to do the same for our grandchildren.

Thank You, LORD, for setting the example of how parents treat their children. I pray we are the kind of grandparents (and parents) who lovingly share our faith with our families. May they see that You have kept and sustained us, being faithful, through all the challenges of our lives.

Priceless Moments

Deuteronomy 6:7: *and you shall teach them diligently to your children, and shall talk of them when you sit in your house, and when you walk by the way, and when you lie down, and when you rise up.*

Proverbs 22:6: *Train up a child in the way he should go, and when he is old he will not depart from it.*

Ephesians 6:1-3: *Children, obey your parents in the Lord, for this is right. "Honor your father and mother," which is the first commandment with a promise: that it may be well with you, and you may live long on the earth."*

June 12th
The Eagle's Nest

"Did you guys see the bald eagle's nest on top of the electric lines? There is a camera in the nest. We've been able to watch mom and dad build a new nest because a windstorm knocked the old one down. They used large sticks to make the outside of the nest, then lined it with small sticks and covered it with grass, moss, and their own feathers—anything that made it soft to lay their eggs. I learned they both bring the building stuff to the nest, and then the female does most of the building. They make sure they can see all around the nest to provide safety for their eggs. We watched the eggs until they hatched into baby eaglets; that's what baby eagles are called. When they grew to the point where they were ready to fly and be on their own, their parents started pulling the soft stuff out of the nest. This encourages them to leave the nest. Did you know any of that?"

"Most of that is new, Grandma, so can you tell us anything else?"
"Sure. We've also watched a pair of eagles build and use their nest. They usually build nests, called an aerie, in live or dead trees near rivers or lakes in forested areas. Some even nest on the ground or on cliffs. This area will provide shelter, drinking water,

and food, making it an ideal location for raising their children. The nests can be up to thirteen feet deep and eight feet wide and can weigh as much as one ton, making them the largest nest of any North American bird. They start to build the nest between one and three months before the female lays the eggs. The nests generally start out small but will get bigger each year as the pair uses them year after year. Eagles are a symbol of God's care and concern for His people. Eagles are swift, strong, and have excellent vision."

I thought about how eagles are mentioned thirty-three times in Scripture. Moses compared God to an eagle but chose to reflect on the gentle, caring side of God (**Isaiah 31:5**), a different perspective to ponder.

Thank You, LORD, for Your love in stirring our nests and encouraging growth and independence in You. I pray we heed Your love and encouragement to leave the comfort and safety of a baby Christian and become like Your other characteristics of being bold and powerful for the kingdom.

Deuteronomy 32:11-12: As an eagle that stirs up her nest, that flutters over her young, he spread abroad his wings, he took them, he bore them on his feathers. Yahweh alone led him. There was no foreign god with him

Ezekiel 17:3: The Lord Yahweh says: "A great eagle with great wings and long feathers, full of feathers, which had various colors, came to Lebanon, and took the top of the cedar."

Isaiah 40:31: but those who wait for Yahweh will renew their strength. They will mount up with wings like eagles. They will run, and not be weary. They will walk, and not faint.

Priceless Moments

June 13th

Stickers

I sat cutting apart stickers from an overabundance of address labels and junk mail, sorting them into four piles, when the grandchildren walked in the door. "Oh, Grandma, thank you for all the new stickers. I used all the ones I had before and wasn't sure if or when I would get more. Also, the notebook you gave me to put all the stickers in is full. Do you have another notebook with a red cover? I would like to keep the same color so I know right away which one is mine. The other kids' books are getting full, too. Maybe you could look for their colors of notebooks and have them ready when they're needed." "Wow, honey. You've really thought about all of this. I'm really impressed that you have all the answers to questions I hadn't thought of yet. Give me a minute, and I'll go now and look at the colors of the notebooks in the closet."

After taking a quick check in the closet, I found three of the four colors needed. "Guess what I found? Three notebooks in the right col…." "Is one red? I really hope so." I chuckled and said, "Yes. As I was trying to say, one of the notebooks was red. Here you go." Squeals of delight escaped her lips. "Oh, thank you, thank you, thank you." She gave me a great big hug, grabbed the notebook, and took off into the living room to her awaiting stack of stickers.

Flashbacks to days gone by when my mother gave the four of us the same type of collection of stickers to play with brought a smile to my face. Although things are constantly changing, there are also lots of things that stay the same. The love of God is freely given to us, but it is never hidden in a notebook but on the pages of our hearts. No matter where we go, those "pages" are always with us, ready to be opened as needed.

Thank You, LORD, for constantly giving us "stickers" on our hearts. I pray we recognize your gifts and allow them to peel back the concerns, fears, and disappointments that steal our joy, leaving us with a beautiful picture of Your love.

Proverbs 4:23: *Keep your heart with all diligence, for out of it is the wellspring of life.*

Philippians 4:19: *My God will supply every need of yours according to his riches in glory in Christ Jesus.*

Hebrews 10:16: *"This is the covenant that I will make with them: 'After those days,' says the Lord, 'I will put my laws on their heart, I will also write them on their mind;'"*

June 14th
Flag Day

"Another holiday—what does this one mean, Grandma?" "If you're talking about Flag Day, it's a special day to remember when the flag of the United States was accepted by the Second Continental Congress in 1777." "Was the flag always the same as it is now?" "Actually, at that time there were only thirteen colonies, so the flag was designed to represent the current makeup of our country as follows: the flag had thirteen white stars in a field of blue in the upper left corner and thirteen stripes that ran across, alternating between red and white with red at the top and red at the bottom. Each star and stripe represented one of the original thirteen colonies, separate from our mother country, England. The original flag was created by Betsy Ross."

As I watched the wheels turning," the following obvious question was asked: "What do the colors represent, and how is the flag different now?" "Red represents valor or courage. White is for hope, purity, and the cleanliness of life. Blue is the color of heaven, in reference to God, loyalty, and sincerity. The star stands for dominion, or control, of our own country. The stars are from heaven, red from our mother country, separated by white stripes for posterity and liberty. It was nicknamed *Old Glory*, representing patriotism, respect, a sense of duty, opportunity, privilege, and liberty and justice for all. As more states were added to our nation, the flag was updated to reflect those changes. Now we still have thirteen stripes for the original thirteen colonies, adding a new star for each new state." "Wow, our flag tells us a lot of stuff"

I reflected on the curiosity of those wanting to understand the meaning of our flag and what it represents. We all need to refresh our memory on its symbolism; more people would see God's hand behind these men who gave us freedom, granted solely by the hand of our gracious God.

Thank You, LORD, for freedom of country but also freedom from sin. I pray we "refresh" ourselves daily in body, soul, and spirit with the freedom You have given us through Your death on the cross, a gift we are not worthy of but graciously accept from Your hand.

Psalm 119:45*: I will walk in liberty, for I have sought your precepts.*

2 Corinthians 3:17*: Now the Lord is the Spirit and where the Spirit of the Lord is, there is liberty.*

Galatians 5:13*: For you, brothers, were called for freedom. Only don't use your freedom for gain to the flesh, but through love be servants to one another.*

June 15th

My Little Chair

The grandchildren came over to spend the day with us. I told them, "We have a surprise for you both." Their eyes lit up and got as big as saucers. "What is it?" they asked in unison. I said, "This summer, I'd like to spend our devotional time outside on the patio. Papa was out shopping and came home with a surprise that we can use out there." We took them out and showed them two folding youth-sized chairs for them to sit on. They were so excited. They asked, "Can the baby sit in one of these?" I replied, "Not yet. She's still too young to trust in one of these. She could very easily upset it and get hurt." "Oh, no, we wouldn't want that to happen, Grandma. I've fallen on cement before, and it really hurts." She proceeded to show us her scar.

After a few minutes of sitting and enjoying their chairs, our granddaughter asked, "Do you think Jesus had a little chair something like this to sit in?" I thought a minute, then said, "Since His earthly father was a carpenter, I would feel safe in saying that he made Jesus a little chair of His own. In those days, all of their furniture was handmade. Jesus, as He grew, would have worked with His earthly father in the family shop to help make other chairs for His brothers and sisters, just like you work with your dad. It's interesting to think about Jesus working alongside His earthly dad, maybe to make Himself a new chair when He outgrew the first one."

I thought of my own carpenter father making us toys, toy boxes, and shelving, as well as building homes for us and others. People always wanted something different. Yet Jesus' standard never changes. He is a one-size-fits-all Savior. He is not concerned with our outside presentation but rather with the inside condition of our hearts.

Thank You, LORD, for Your consistent standard of being saved—admitting we are sinners, confessing our sins, and asking you into our hearts and lives. I pray that after the initial forgiveness is given, we endeavor to show your work of grace in our lives through the things we do for You.

Malachi 3:6a: *For I, Yahweh, don't change;*

Hebrews 13:8: *Jesus Christ is the same yesterday, today, and forever.*

Priceless Moments

Hebrews 1:3: *His Son is the radiance of his glory, the very image of his substance, and upholding all things by the word of his power, who, when he had by himself purified us of our sins, sat down on the right hand of the Majesty on high*

June 16th
<u>*Father's Day*</u>

"Grandma, did you know today is Father's Day? We made Dad a special card at school, then we made him a card at home. Why do we celebrate Father's Day?" "Good question. Over one hundred years ago, a woman was sitting in a church service listening to a Mother's Day message. Her mother had passed away giving birth to her last sibling; thus, her father had raised all of them alone on a farm in the state of Washington. She thought about her father, Mr. Smart, an American Civil War veteran who had done everything for his children, sacrificing everything to keep them together, demonstrating a selfless love for his family. She decided to let him know how special he was to her, so she organized the very first Father's Day in 1910, choosing June, the month of his birth."

"That was really awesome; she did that for her dad. What is something we could do to show how much we love our dad and appreciate him?" "Excellent question. Some things we used to do for our dad were to buy or make him a present—no neckties since that seemed to be the most common gift a father would receive. We would make up special certificates for how we could spend time with him doing something he wanted to do with each of us. That always seemed very special to him, and he always enjoyed that. Plus, we made him breakfast in bed and took him out to his favorite restaurant after church. Sometimes we went for a walk, played family games, watched a movie, and things like that. If there was enough wind, we'd go fly kites." "Can we do something like that for our dad?" "I'm sure you can, but we need to talk to your mom first." "Ok, that sounds like a plan."

Talking about fun things we did for our dad brought to mind many fun times together as a family. God created families to love, care for, and share the good and bad together, not to build walls and refuse to talk with each other. We have such a short time here on earth that we shouldn't waste one moment of our God-given time together.

Thank You, LORD, for creating families. I pray we understand Your divine purpose for placing us in the family of Your choosing. There are lessons to be learned that only our particular family can teach us. Father knows best.

Ephesians 6:4: You fathers, don't provoke your children to wrath, but nurture them in the discipline and instruction of the Lord.

Proverbs 1:8, 9: My son, listen to your father's instruction, and don't forsake your mother's teaching: for they will be a garland to grace your head, and chains around your neck.

Psalm 103:13: Like a father has compassion on his children, so Yahweh has compassion on those who fear him.

June 17th

Solar-Dancing Toys

Our grandchildren are fascinated with solar-dancing toys. We have them in the living room by the windows, so each afternoon we hear and see them dancing away in the sunlight. "Grandma, we have to stop what we're doing and go watch the toys dance." All activities are stopped as we make the trek to watch the delight of the children. Comments like, "Oh, look at this. The hula girl is really shaking her hips." "The monkey is swinging so hard that he almost knocked himself over." "The dinosaur is really moving, almost like he's getting ready to run." When the sun goes behind a cloud, it signals that it's time to return to previous activities.

Priceless Moments

"Grandma, do you think there will be solar toys in heaven? I would really like to watch them all the time."

I paused and prayed for wisdom before saying, "I really don't know. I'll bet God has so many other awesome things for us to watch that will be so much greater than the solar toys. If they are there, they will be dancing all the time, as Jesus will be our source of light, keeping it glowing all the time." "What I mean is, how can He be the source of light?" "**Revelation 22:5** tells us, *'There will be no more night. They will not need the light of a lamp or the light of the sun, for the LORD God will give them light. And they will reign forever and ever.'*" "Wow, that's really cool, Grandma. But will we need sunglasses to look at Him?" "Only time will tell, little one."

It's amazing how something as simple as a dancing toy shows God's love. He provided someone with the ability to make them dance, and He provided the sun to make them dance. God's hand is in everything good. Unfortunately, some people take good things and find a way to use them for evil.

Thank You, LORD, for still being present in our world. I pray we grow stronger in our faith and remain steadfast in our love and devotion to You, seeing You in all that we do.

Genesis 1:4: God saw the light, and saw that it was good. God divided the light from the darkness.

John 8:12: Again, therefore, Jesus spoke to them, saying, "I am the light of the world. He who follows me will not walk in the darkness, but will have the light of life."

Matthew 5:14-16: You are the light of the world. A city located on a hill can't be hidden. Neither do you light a lamp and put it under a measuring basket, but on a stand; and it shines to all who are in the house. Even so, let your light shine before men, that they may see your good works and glorify your Father who is in heaven.

Priceless Moments

June 18th
<u>The New Dining Room Light</u>

When we moved into our new house, my husband had a difficult time seeing his plate during meals since the builder had installed a dark-colored light on one side of the table. Our son decided to change out the light for a much brighter, white-colored light, centering it over the table, making it easier for ALL of us to see to eat, do crafts, etc. For the next year, the grandchildren commented every time we sat down to eat, "My Daddy did that," pointing up to the light. After a while, the comments became less frequent and then seemed to fade away. Occasionally, one of them would comment, "You know, we still remember that Daddy changed the light so Papa and the rest of us could see to eat."

We were eating one of our Thursday family breakfasts when our granddaughter looked up and said, "I remember that. Daddy changed the light for us so we could all see." Once again, we were all aware that the light had been changed, looking up and commenting, "Yes, he did, and we are all so thankful to him and appreciate the good work he did and for centering it over the table." He sat there smiling and said, "You are all welcome." I said, "Who changes the light in our hearts and minds to light the path of our lives so we can see where we are traveling in our journey on this earth?" They both shouted, "Jesus."

God must feel appreciative of our thanking Him for centering Himself above our world, removing the dimness from our lives, and replacing it with His bright light so we can stay on the path to find our way to Him. Many times, the way will seem dark, but as with the children, they remembered to look up once again and found the light still hanging there for our benefit and pleasure.

Thank You, LORD, for always providing Your light for us to follow. I pray we always keep our eyes lifted up to stay in the light of Your love. If our path seems to be growing dim, it's time to "plug in" to Jesus to recharge our spiritual "batteries" to keep us on the lit path to heaven.

John 1:5*: The light shines in the darkness, and the darkness hasn't overcome it.*

Proverbs 3:5-6*: Trust in Yahweh with all your heart, and don't lean on your own understanding. In all your ways acknowledge him, and he will make your paths straight.*

Isaiah 48:17*: Yahweh, your Redeemer, the Holy One of Israel says: "I am Yahweh your God, who teaches you to profit, who leads you by the way that you should go."*

June 19th
Juneteenth

"Grandma, have you ever heard of Juneteenth? I remember talking about it several days ago in school, but I don't remember what it was all about." "The history of Juneteenth actually started on the eve of January 1, 1863, or "Freedom's Eve," when slave and free African Americans met in private homes and churches to wait for news that President Abraham Lincoln had freed them through the Emancipation Proclamation." "What is that?" "This proclamation or announcement gave freedom to all the slaves in the Confederate or Southern states. It wasn't until Congress passed the Thirteenth Amendment that slavery was abolished or done away with in the United States. On June 19, 1865, Union army troops came to Galveston Bay, Texas, to let the black people who were slaves there be freed through an executive order. These freed slaves soon called this day "Juneteenth."

"So, Grandma, are you saying that Juneteenth wasn't just a one-time thing but that it took many different times to free the slaves for good?" "You are correct. Laws are talked about and revised many times until everyone is satisfied with the law before it is accepted, and everyone is told to obey it." "Did passing this law keep African Americans free?" "Unfortunately, many people are prejudiced, meaning they dislike or distrust this group of God's people." "Why do people act like that?" "Prejudices develop when people look at or see things differently; their society group forces prejudices on them; or they blame someone different from themselves for something bad that's happened." "Wow, it sounds like we really need to pray for these people." "Well said."

We were raised to be blind to skin color, that we all bleed the same since God created all men equal, just like in the Declaration of Independence. Discrimination arises in our upbringing and is learned from people with whom we keep company. I am so thankful for our freedom in Christ.

Thank You, LORD, for creating mankind in Your image and likeness. I pray we follow Jesus' example of not tolerating racism, prejudice, or discrimination but displaying love, joy, and peace to Jew and Gentile alike.

Deuteronomy 10:17: *For Yahweh your God, he is God of gods and Lord of lords, the great God, the mighty, and the awesome, who doesn't respect persons or take bribes.*

Ephesians 4:32: *And be kind to one another, tender hearted, forgiving each other, just as God also in Christ forgave you.*

Galatians 3:28: *There is neither Jew nor Greek, there is neither slave nor free man, there is neither male nor female; for you are all one in Christ Jesus*

June 20th

Fly, Fly Away

"Did you know we are all flying to Alaska this summer? We get to play with our cousins, and climb mountains, and do other things already planned. We get to stay in a few different houses along the

Priceless Moments

way. It's going to be so much fun. I can hardly wait." "Yes, I did. Your parents got us all tickets at the same time, so we can sit together on the plane. It will be over six hours of flying time, so if we sit together, we can talk, watch a movie, play games, read a book, or sleep. We can also watch the clouds to see what shapes they make, all things to help the flight seem to go more quickly." "What movies can we watch? What games?" "The flight plays several movies, but we won't know what they are until we get on the plane. If you have one or two loaded on your iPad, you could watch those. I've already packed a couple of your favorite card games and a book I've been reading."

Silence always makes me wonder what the next set of questions will be. "How many people will be on our flight? Do people like to visit Alaska?" "At this point, I don't know how many people are on the flight. Not everyone signs up for seating assignments, so we'll find out when we board the plane. Not everyone on the plane will be visiting there because they may be returning home from visiting our area. Some people may be flying there to catch another flight to another location. Everyone is doing their own thing and going where they need to or want to go. We can talk to people on the plane and get some good answers to your questions."

I can only imagine what our *flight* to heaven will be like: no bumpy take-offs or landings, no air pockets or bad weather causing bumpy rides, no overbooked flights, no crying babies, no upset passengers. Just a peaceful sleep until the LORD's return to take us to heaven to be with Him forever.

Thank You, LORD, for the assurance of eternity with You. I pray we are always looking up and being prepared for Your return. In the meantime, we need to learn about Your future plans for mankind.

1 Corinthians 15:51: *Behold, I tell you a mystery. We will not all sleep, but we will all be changed, in a moment, in the twinkling of an eye, at the last trumpet. For the trumpet will sound and the dead will be raised incorruptible, and we will be changed.*

1 Thessalonians 4:14, 16: *For if we believe that Jesus died and rose again, even so God will bring with him those who have fallen asleep in Jesus. For the Lord himself will descend from heaven with a shout, with the voice of the archangel and with God's trumpet. The dead in Christ will rise first,*

Daniel 12:2: *Many of those who sleep in the dust of the earth will awake, some to everlasting life, and some to shame and everlasting contempt.*

June 21st

Summer

Ah, summertime. A time to play, relax, and enjoy the sunshine and fresh air. "Grandma, what does summertime mean to you?" "I think of many things, like school's out and I get to spend more time with you. It's a time for swimming, picnics, bike riding, and horseback riding. Nature has trees budding, flowers peeking their heads up through the ground, fishing on the lake, and lemonade. I enjoy the gentle rain showers, thunderstorms, fluffy clouds just floating by, flying kites, jumping rope, and just plain being outside." "What kind of things do you like to do outside besides what you just told us?" "Well, there's walking in the garden, hiking, walking to the playground, amusement parks, camping, family reunions, swinging in the hammock, jumping on the trampoline, climbing trees, and exploring new areas. I guess the outdoor activities could be endless."

"Neat. If you have to only pick one thing, what would be your one-time all-favorite thing about summer?" "My favorite would be to go camping and watch the campfire spark towards the sky, see the colors dancing within the fire, and feel the warmth it provides. I would get out the marshmallow sticks and enjoy roasting hot

Priceless Moments

dogs or sausages, making mountain pies, and making s'mores. There's nothing better than a golden brown, gooey marshmallow melting inside two graham crackers. It makes me hungry just to think about it. In the winter, our dad used to toast marshmallows over the stove and make us s'mores all winter long. As a matter of fact, we did that for our kids as well." "Can we try that sometime?" "No time like the present, I always say, so let's do it." "Yummmm."

The joys of reliving childhood memories with the grandchildren. God has given us so many different ways to share our love and memories with the next generation and beyond, particularly His Word. It's like the proverbial pebble thrown in the pond; the Word keeps expanding its reach as we are obedient to share the good news with those in our inner circle and beyond.

Thank You, LORD, for experiences that become good teaching moments. I pray we realize things happen to us for a reason so we can use them to share with others, either to plant a seed or to strengthen their belief in You.

Exodus 9:16*: But I raised you up for this very purpose, that I might show you My power and that My Name might be proclaimed in all the earth. NIV*

Romans 8:28*: We know that all things work together for good for those who love God, for those who are called according to his purpose.*

1 Thessalonians 5:11*: Therefore exhort one another, and build each other up, even as you also do.*

Priceless Moments

June 22nd
The Summer List

"Now that school is over for the year, what things would you like to do this summer? I have two requests: that we do devotions and go for a walk every day we're together. I would also like to play speech and phonic games, math games, and reading games. We can be sure you don't lose any ground in terms of what you've learned this year at school." "Absolutely, Grandma. We would also like to ride bikes, play on the swings, jump on the trampoline, and go to the park. We may think of something else later, but those are at the top of the list." "Well, I think you just about covered everything that you like to do anyway. If something new comes up, I'm sure we can add it to the list."

I thought about all the ways we could accomplish both sets of goals when I heard, "Hey, Grandma, could we play BINGO to review numbers and write some of our own stories to read?" "I think that is an awesome way to have fun as well as to review and keep your skills fine-tuned. If you come up with any other terrific ideas, we can add those to the list. I'm so proud of you for thinking of creative ways to learn and enjoy our summer."

Summer can be a time of relaxation on the education front, so finding fun ways to keep their skills sharp can be challenging. When fun ways are used to stay at "the top of their game," we're all winners. Same with our relationship with Jesus. We need to not get lax with our habits that foster spiritual growth.

Thank You, LORD, for preparing study and reading plans in written and computer formats. I pray that in our busy lives, we take advantage of these time savers to keep us in Your Word and growing in Your Spirit.

***Luke 17:5**: The apostles said to the Lord, "Increase our faith."*

Priceless Moments

Psalm 92:12-14*: The righteous shall flourish like the palm tree. He will grow like a cedar in Lebanon. They are planted in Yahweh's house. They will flourish in our God's courts. They will still produce fruit in old age. They will be full of sap and green,*

2 Peter 1:5-6*: Yes, and for this very cause adding on your part all diligence, in your faith supply moral excellence; and in moral excellence, knowledge; and in knowledge, self-control; and in self-control perseverance; and in perseverance godliness.*

June 23rd
Time for Vacation

"When does summer really begin? We hear many different times given, but they are never the same." "Well, the calendar says the summer solstice is finally here as of June 21, indicating the longest time of daylight in the year. In general, summer starts for different people depending on their circumstances. For example, after teachers and students have their last day of school, summer vacation begins for them. The change from cooler to warmer weather makes people feel like summer has arrived, making it time for ice cream to cool us down. And it's time for a family vacation. Going to the beach is an awesome place for a vacation. You can play in the sand, swim, have cookouts, and have picnics."

"A vacation means spending time away from your responsibilities to have fun and bond with those around you. Vacation time gives families an opportunity to be together more and get to know each other better without being rushed to do homework or other school activities. An added bonus is that vacations can take you to new places or be a stay-cation in your own backyard. You can travel from a cold area to a warm area, or vice versa; stay in a cabin, a tent, an RV, a hotel, Airbnb, or with family or friends. You can go back to the same place every year or travel to different locations every year. You can go at the same time or at different times throughout the year." "Awesome. I'm glad our parents like to go different places and do different things all year long."

Looking through photo albums and thinking of previous vacations can also provide a sense of escape from routines without leaving the comfort of your own living room. Reading about the various travels and experiences of Bible heroes tells of their commitment to serve the LORD wherever they went.

Thank You, LORD, for a beautiful creation to explore. I pray we, like the saints of old, mix Your business with pleasure, sharing the gospel wherever You take us, being unashamed of blessing our food, giving thanks for all Your goodness and mercy, and planting seeds of desire in others to know what makes us "tick."

***Matthew 11:28**: Come to me, all you who labor and are heavily burdened, and I will give you rest.*

***Ecclesiastes 3:13**: Also that every man should eat and drink, and enjoy good in all his labor, is the gift of God.*

***Proverbs 16:9**: A man's heart plans his course, but Yahweh directs his steps.*

June 24th

Sand Castles

"Grandma, have you ever built a ssandcastle before? When we talked about going on vacation to the beach, that's one of the things we didn't talk about." "Yes, I have. When your dad was little, we had molds they could use to put the wet sand in to form different phases of a sandcastle. Other times, we would scoop sand together and try to shape something different with our hands." "Where did the idea of building sandcastles come from?" "The art of building sandcastles started over five hundred years ago, in the 14th century, when a man named Belarus Das created sculptures in

Priceless Moments

his native land of India. By the 19th century, sandcastle sculpting was seen on beachfronts and boardwalks, with people throwing coins in the sculptor's direction."

"Can you explain why people like to play so much in the sand?" "It's exciting and fun to see what you can make before the surf from the water eventually reclaims its sand by washing it away. This lets you start all over again. This time, you can build a moat, like a trench, around the castle to collect the water, making it harder for the water to reach the castle. Another fun thing is to walk up and down the beach and see the different sand creations others have made. Be sure to take your camera to take pictures so you can see your favorites over and over again as well as to get ideas for building your next sandcastle." "Sure thing. I got a new camera for Christmas, so that sounds like lots of fun."

Building things has always been "lots of fun." I remember building a different type of castle with memory verses called building blocks for developing a productive Christian life. Fortunately, this castle is one that never washes away—no moat required. Our castle is built on the Roman Road found in Scripture.

Thank You, LORD, for setting the example of growing in wisdom, stature, and favor with God and man. I pray we follow Your example and teach it to our grandchildren as the building blocks of a productive Christian life.

Jeremiah 12:2: You have planted them. Yes, they have taken root. They grow. Yes, they produce fruit. You are near in their mouth, and far from their heart.

1 Samuel 2:26: The child Samuel grew and increased in favor both with Yahweh and also with men.

2 Peter 3:18: But grow in the grace and knowledge of our Lord and Savior Jesus Christ. To him be the glory both now and forever. Amen.

Priceless Moments

June 25th

Where To Now?

It seems we are always on the road, running somewhere. As the grandchildren got in the car, they asked, "Where are we going now? Who has what activity? Do we have everything we need?" I chuckled out loud and said, "Yes, we are on the road again, and this time it's to go to your swimming lessons. Your mother had your bags laid out, so I have your suits, goggles, and towels. When we get to the pool, you will have time to change your clothes in the locker room. I'll place your shoes and clothes back in your bags and leave them in the pool area for your mom to pick up when she comes to pick you up. I will stay and watch your practice to see how much you have learned and improved your swimming skills."

I sat for a while and watched them progress through their swimming lesson, seeing incremental improvements over time. The teacher was very patient and encouraging, showing the desired skill over and over until it was understood and became their own. Giggles and laughter were greeted with each accomplishment, followed by glances to the stand where I sat to ensure I had seen their goals being met. I applauded and gave thumbs up each time to encourage them along their journey to becoming efficient swimmers.

I thought of how thankful Christians are to know "where to go now." We make progress in our Christian life when we have a mentor showing us the way, teaching us to read our Bibles effectively, how to find answers to questions that we have, and ultimately how to lead others to Christ. Some of us make progress slowly, needing repeated instruction, while others seem to just absorb information readily and progress rapidly through the training process to be able to mentor others. But all this is accomplished through prayer and fasting.

Thank You, LORD, for the best learner's manual in the world—the Bible, Your Basic Instructions Before Leaving Earth. I pray we are good students who study to learn Your Word, hiding it in our hearts.

Psalm 119:11*: I have hidden your word in my heart, that I might not sin against you.*

Isaiah 26:3*: You will keep whoever's mind is steadfast in perfect peace, because he trusts in you.*

Romans 10:9-10*: that if you will confess with your mouth that Jesus is Lord, and believe in your heart that God raised him from the dead, you will be saved. For with the heart, one believes resulting in righteousness; and with the mouth confession is made resulting in salvation.*

June 26th

Kick, Kick, Kick, Kick

Our youngest granddaughter really likes to play after getting her diaper changed. We've found that riding a bike with her legs keeps her giggling. We pedal forward, pedal backwards, then straighten her legs, saying "kick, kick, kick, kick" to go swimming. She absolutely loves it. The more we've done it, the quicker she straightens her legs and laughs until we say "kick, kick, kick, kick." At this point, we sing a little ditty, like "We're pedaling forward to go for a ride to the park. We're passing the town and the people, and finally we arrive at the park. We play a little, then pedal the bike backwards to see where we've been, past the people and the town, until we get back home." At this point—and sometimes before I'm ready—she straightens her legs and starts kicking, then claps her hands for herself.

The other day, I was changing her diaper when the phone rang. I continued changing her diaper while I talked with the other person—on speaker—about their kids kicking a soccer ball. The baby immediately stiffened her legs and started kicking them. At first, I didn't get the connection between her kicking her legs and the word "kick" was said again and she started kicking again. I realized just how much she was learning, remembering, and being able to recall to act appropriately as needed.

I thought, as Christians, how much are we absorbing from the lessons we are learning—or unlearning? Does a word you hear trigger a negative or positive response? Are we letting go of all the bad habits acquired before accepting Jesus and replacing those habits with Christian habits of Bible reading, study, learning Scripture, praying, and sharing with others what we are learning?

Thank You, LORD, for giving us the ability to change our behavior after accepting You as our personal Savior. I pray we stay in tune with Your Word and Your will for our lives.

Psalm 5:3: *Yahweh, in the morning you will hear my voice. In the morning I will lay my requests before you, and will watch expectantly.*

Hebrews 5:13, 14: *For everyone who lives on milk is not experienced in the word of righteousness, for he is a baby. But solid food is for those who are full grown, who by reason of use have their senses exercised to discern good and evil.*

1 Peter 2:2-3: *as newborn babies, long for the pure milk of the Word, that with it you may grow, if indeed you have tasted that the Lord is gracious:*

June 27th

<u>Smoothie Time</u>

One afternoon, the grandchildren decided it was snack time, calling out, "Smoothie time, Grandma." Their favorite treat is a smoothie that includes everything but the kitchen sink. They run to

Priceless Moments

the kitchen, open the refrigerator, and pull out the usual options there, then start on the freezer options, deciding what fruit to pick. I decided to give them a minute of independence since this wasn't their first rodeo. By the time I decided to go to the kitchen, I heard one say, "Let's get out the blender, too." It was already sitting on the counter as I rounded the corner.

As per my usual teasing self, I asked, "Who wants goldfish pretzels?" The eyes rolled, heads tilted to one side, and in unison they said, "Grandma." I started to laugh, and they joined me for a little frivolity before handing me the items for the smoothie. "Can I give you all the stuff from the refrigerator, and she can give you all the stuff from the freezer?" she asked. "I think that's an excellent idea since the items are fairly even in number." In filling the blender, I realized they hadn't missed anything they liked. When items were added, they took the used ones and put them back in their proper locations. Everything was blended and poured, and the filled cups were taken to the table. Comments like "This is the best one yet." and "More, please, and thank you." were heard.

I can see God picking out all the things He wants us to have and laying them out for our enjoyment. It is up to us to partake of them and to be appreciative by telling Him, "Thank You."

Thank You, LORD, for Your watchful care and provisions in our lives. I pray we are mindful to realize we did not make these good things happen all by ourselves; rather, You provided each and every one of them for us to enjoy.

Isaiah 1:19: *If you are willing and obedient, you will eat the good of the land;*

Ecclesiastes 9:7: *Go your way—eat your bread with joy, and drink your wine with a merry heart; for God has already accepted your works.*

John 6:35: *Jesus said to them, "I am the bread of life. Whoever comes to me will not be hungry, and whoever believes in me will never be thirsty."*

Priceless Moments

June 28th

<u>*My Favorite Song*</u>

"Grandma, do you know what my favorite song is? We used to sing it all the time before I started school." "Let me think a minute because we used to sing so many songs. I guess you are going to have to tell me." "OK, but I know you're going to realize it once I tell you. It's *Jesus loves Me*. Do you remember that now?" "Oh, of course, I should have known. Can you tell me why it's your favorite song?" "I don't know. I guess it's because the song means a lot to me because it's about Jesus, it's easy to sing and to remember the words, I like the music, and it helps me feel better when I'm sad. And I can remember the hand motions that go along with the song."

"Those are all very good reasons to like a song. The thing I like most about this song is the message that JESUS loves me, Jesus LOVES me, Jesus loves ME. Either way you look at emphasizing those three words, it all comes down to JESUS LOVES ME. And we know that because the Bible tells us so. It is true that whoever reads it will earn of His love. We are told the words to many different songs the Israelites sang, letting us know that singing is important because it praises God. Most of our Christian songs are based on Scripture. When others hear you singing these songs, you are actually teaching them about Jesus."

One of the first songs the little ones learned was *Jesus loves me*. Jesus has been faithful to them by listening to, reading about, and memorizing Scripture. What an example for adults. So many Christians never open their Bibles, let alone read and study the Word to understand God's love letter to us. We can't really know God without reading His love letter to us. He wants us to B natural, not sharp or flat.

Thank You, LORD, for children who set the example for adults about spiritual matters. I pray we realize we can know our LORD and Savior intimately by studying His Word since it contains direction and answers to our questions about our future.

Zephaniah 3:17*: Yahweh, your God, is among you, a mighty one who will save. He will rejoice over you with joy. He will calm you in his love. He will rejoice over you with singing.*

Colossians 3:16*: Let the word of Christ dwell in you richly; in all wisdom teaching and admonishing one another with psalms, hymns, and spiritual songs, singing with grace in your heart to the Lord.*

Acts 16:25*: But about midnight Paul and Silas were praying and singing hymns to God, and the prisoners were listening to them.*

June 29th
Peek-A-Boo

"Oh, Grandma, she likes to play peek-a-boo with me. I cover my eyes or hide behind the couch or coffee table, and then she looks all around to find me. I uncover my eyes or pop up from behind the furniture, and she just giggles and laughs out loud. Let me show you; watch me." He proceeds to cover his eyes with his hands. The little one tried to look around his hands until he uncovered his eyes and said, "Peek-a-boo! I see you." She looked at him and started laughing again. He was so tickled with himself that he kept repeating the activity until he got tired of it. She kept looking at him as he moved around the living room, playing with other toys—but not her. She lost sight of him, straining to look over things to find him, but with no luck.

She and I played with the toys on her treasure tray, a tray containing items of various colors, shapes, textures, materials, smells, and sounds. She chose one of her favorite items, a miniature beach ball. We played with it for a while until we heard, "Peek-a-boo. I see you." She stopped playing, looked around until she found him, then started laughing and clapping. He had popped up from behind the coffee table. Her surprise and delight in the fun made them both very happy.

I thought about how we try to play peek-a-boo with God, hiding in different places for varying lengths of time, hoping He won't see what we're doing. Regrettably—or fortunately—God sees everything. We can't hide from Him, no matter how hard we try.

Thank You, LORD, for Your long-suffering nature toward mankind. I pray we don't try to play games with You but rather be forthright and real in Your presence, popping up in church, Bible study, small groups, and on our knees.

Zechariah 8:5: *The streets of the city will be full of boys and girls playing in its streets.*

1 Corinthians 9:25: *Every man who strives in the games exercises self-control in all things. Now they do it to receive a corruptible crown, but we an incorruptible.*

Philippians 3:14: *I press on toward the goal for the prize of the high calling of God in Christ Jesus.*

June 30th
Family Reunions

I absolutely love family reunions. It is such a joy to see siblings, nieces, nephews, aunts, uncles, and cousins. It's amazing to think that after not seeing most of our family members for a year, when we get together, it's like no time has passed at all. We talk about the events of the last year, like new births of children or grandchildren, graduations, weddings, vacations, and reminiscing about all of the great stuff we did when we were kids. "Hey, cuz, how are you doing? It seems like forever since I've seen you. How are the kids and grandkids? Sit down and let's talk." "Wow, hi to you." We exchanged hugs. I heard whispering in my ear, "Hey,

Priceless Moments

Grandma, why are you giving her a hug? I don't know who she is." I whisper back, "It's OK; she's my cousin. Now that we're grown up, we only get to see each other once a year at the family reunions."

The grandkids are now old enough to be independent and "meet" the rest of the family. While I chatted with all my cousins, catching up, showing pictures, and filling in the gaps between hasty texts, we noticed all sets of grandchildren meeting each other, finding commonalities, and bonding with their extended family members. We also noticed them introducing the kids they do know to the kids they had not met before. Throughout the day, we kept eyes on all the kids, but they only "touched base" when it was time to eat. Amazingly, no one came over and said they were bored. A wonderful day was had by all. Now we are truly one big, extended, happy family.

I so enjoyed renewing friendships with family members. I thought of how we would be like the grandchildren, meeting many new people in heaven, now our brothers and sisters in Christ, bonding for eternity and praising our LORD.

Thank You, LORD, for family reunions. I pray we work diligently on earth to take more people with us to heaven so we can spend eternity getting to know each other in the heavenly choir.

James 5:11*: Behold, we call them blessed who endured. You have heard of the perseverance of Job, and have seen the Lord in the outcome, and how the Lord is full of compassion and mercy.*

Revelation 7:9a*: After these things I looked, and behold, a great multitude, which no man could count, out of every nation and of all tribes, peoples, and languages, standing before the throne and before the Lamb.*

2 Peter 3:13*: But, according to his promise, we look for new heavens and a new earth, in which righteousness dwells.*

Priceless Moments

July

*We will not hide them
from their children,
telling to the generation to come
the praises of Yahweh,
his strength,
and his wonderous deeds
that he has done.*

Psalm. 78:4

Priceless Moments

July 1ˢᵀ
I'm Thirsty

"I'm so thirsty, Grandma. Do you have anything to drink?" "Of course. Maybe we should take a break from playing to have a drink and a snack." Squeals of laughter and "Yes" preceded a race for the kitchen. Once inside, the refrigerator door flew open as they rummaged through the liquid offerings. "Nothing looks good in here." "Then what can we do to quench your thirst?" Their eyes rolled around in the thinking process as they processed the question. Her eyes lit up, saying, "I know. We haven't made lemonade for a long time. We saw about six lemons in there. Do you need them for anything else?" Smiling inside, I replied, "You know, I have no particular plans for them. Making lemonade will be a good use for them. Let's see how to make lemonade."

We worked to clean and cut the lemons. "Why are you washing and cutting those?" "I'm getting them ready for you to squeeze the juice out of them. God made their skin and juice to be used in many ways. Today, they're being used for our thirst quencher. Now, who wants to squeeze them?" "Grandma, show us how to squeeze them." "Sure, here we go." After a demonstration, volunteers were asking for a turn. Each child squeezed several halves until all the juicing was done. "Now what?" "We'll add a little sugar and stir to mix it in." While each took a turn stirring, one asked, "How can you use the skins?" "You scrape or cut the outer layer, called zesting, to use in recipes. Soon the nectar was poured into glasses. The thirst quencher was enjoyed by all.

We should become thirsty for the Word of God, preparing our hearts to drink in His goodness through His Word—from creation until our spiritual restoration in Revelation. This will add a layer of zest to our lives.

Thank You, LORD, for earthly things to enjoy through Your creation. More importantly, I pray we take the steps needed to "squeeze" every ounce of goodness from Your love letter to feed our souls, preparing us to drink of the joys of heaven throughout eternity.

John 6:35*: Jesus said to them, "I am the bread of life. Whoever comes to me will not be hungry, and whoever believes in me will never be thirsty.*

1 Corinthians 10:3-4*: and all ate the same spiritual food; and all drank the same spiritual drink. For they drank of a spiritual rock that followed them, and the rock was Christ.*

2 Peter 2:17*: These are wells without water, clouds driven by a storm; for whom the blackness of darkness has been reserved forever.*

July 2nd
It's a Girl

Oh, the joy of hearing, "You're going to be grandparents again." The thrill, anticipation, and hope this happy news brings. Questions like, "When is the baby due? How have you been feeling? Who all have you told?" crossed my lips. Huge smiles and giggles accompany the response, "No one else yet. We want to enjoy this time for ourselves, but I just had to tell somebody—and you are it. So, Mum's the word." "Got it. My lips are sealed."

Eventually, family members, friends, and co-workers were told the happy news. As time passed, the blessed day arrived. The phone rings. "Congratulations, Grandma. It's a girl. We are still deciding on her name. She is healthy, and we are both, well, all three of us are doing fine. Daddy has been so good and attentive to her. She has a head of dark hair and a full, round face. And she looks like her dad." Stats, where are the stats? I asked, "What was the time of birth, how much did she weigh, how long was she, and what color

Priceless Moments

were her eyes?" You know, the other important things I also wanted to know.

Aren't we like that with God—tell me everything I need to know, NOW! But, as the saying goes, "All good things come to those who wait." This is where patience and persistence in prayer, Bible reading, and Bible study give us a glimpse into God's desires for us, allowing for a less antsy wait upon the LORD.

Thank You, LORD, for the wonder and gift of new life; in Your opinion, the world should go on. I pray we cherish each day of life You give, making the most of it for Your Kingdom. May this new life remind us of Your unfailing love and our need to teach her about You.

***Psalm 139:14-16**: I will give thanks to you, for I am fearfully and wonderfully made. Your works are wonderful. My soul knows that very well. My frame wasn't hidden from you, when I was made in secret, woven together in the depths of the earth. Your eyes saw my body. In your book they were all written, the days that were ordained for me, when as yet there were none of them.*

***Psalm 119:73-74**: Your hands have made me and formed me. Give me understanding, that I may learn your commandments. Those who fear you will see me and be glad, because I have put my hope in your word.*

***Psalm 127:3-5**: Behold, children are a heritage of Yahweh. The fruit of the womb is his reward. As arrows in the hand of a mighty man, so are the children of youth. Happy is the man who has his quiver full of them. They won't be disappointed when they speak with their enemies in the gate.*

Priceless Moments

July 3rd
The Raspberry Factory

"Oh, no. Grandma, she keeps trying to spit at me. Why does she do that?" I laughed out loud, responding, "I guess the raspberry factory is open." "What do you mean by that? She's spitting at me." "Actually, she's sticking her tongue out and making a funny sound and blowing bubbles, which is called blowing raspberries. It's an important part of her development, a milestone, and a way for her to learn to communicate with us and develop language and social skills. She listens to us talking to her—how loud we talk and the pitch of our voice—and then tries to copy those sounds, giving her lips and tongue some exercise. At this point, we need to repeat those sounds and behaviors back to her to encourage her to talk." "Cool. But why does she spit so much when giving the raspberries?" "Good question. The spitting is called drooling and is a result of more fluid in her mouth, called saliva, to help her break down foods she is starting to eat as well as to help her swallow and keep her mouth clear of the food. Soon it will also help protect the baby teeth."

A long pause… "What is saliva? I know the word but don't understand what it means." "Saliva is the fluid or liquid in our mouth to keep it from drying out, to help swallow food, and to protect our mouth from infection." "OK, then we should encourage her to give us the raspberries?" "Yes. When we encourage her, we can all have fun together while helping her grow and learn new skills. We need to look at her and make eye contact so she can learn to change her surroundings by the sounds she makes." "I guess it is kind of fun. Let's encourage her to be silly and learn at the same time." "Good idea."

Watching children blow raspberries reminds me of baby Christians and how they observe other Christians to emulate their methods while learning the skill of sharing their faith in their own way. God may blow raspberries at us when we become prideful spiritually, trying to get our attention. We need to assume the prayer posture of humility to overcome our pride.

Thank You, LORD, for providing us with a family of God. I pray we observe seasoned Christians to learn tried and true skills for studying our Bible, sharing our faith, and teaching others about Your forgiveness and saving grace.

***Proverbs 16:5**: Everyone who is proud in heart is an abomination to Yahweh: they shall certainly not be unpunished.*

***Proverbs 16:18**: Pride goes before destruction, and an arrogant spirit before a fall.*

***Romans 11:20b-21**: Don't be conceited, but fear; for if God didn't spare the natural branches, neither will he spare you.*

July 4th

Independence Day

Thoughts of Independence Day, which occurs on the Fourth of July in the United States of America, are a joyous celebration as well as many questions from the grandchildren—who knew, right? "Grandma, are you coming to our house for a picnic?" Ah, for a change, it's my turn to ask the questions. "I'd love to come, but why are you having a picnic?" "I don't know." "Do you know what the date is?" "No. I don't look at it much since school's out for the summer." So, it's up to me to fill in the blanks. "I'll bet it's July 4th on the calendar, making it Independence Day." "What's Independence Day?" Ah, the tables are turned. "Good question, young lady. It's the day we celebrate the birthday of our nation." "Do you mean just like we celebrate Jesus' birthday at Christmas?" "Exactly. Our nation was founded by godly men based on godly principles. Many of the laws and documents they set up came from Scripture."

Priceless Moments

A confused look crossed her face. "How can they do that? Won't God get mad if we use His Word that way?" "Actually, the exact opposite is true. God wants us to use His Word as often as we can, so we don't forget Him or His Word. One of our founding fathers and second president, John Adams, said, "Suppose a nation in some distant region should take the Bible for their only law book, and every member should regulate his conduct by the precepts their exhibited…What a Eutopia—What a Paradise this region will be! … I have examined all religions, and the result is that the Bible is the best book in the world."

I reflected on a statement by Samuel Adams when he called on the State of Massachusetts to pray that… "The peaceful and glorious reign of our Divine Redeemer may be known and enjoyed throughout the whole family of mankind." Let it be so, LORD Jesus.

Thank You, LORD, for godly founding fathers who were not intimidated to incorporate their faith into our country's founding documents. I pray we, as a nation, return to these successful principles to not only govern our great country but also our daily lives.

Romans 13:1-2: *Let every soul be in subjection to the higher authorities, for there is no authority except from God, and those who exist are ordained by God. Therefore he who resists the authority withstands the ordinance of God; and those who withstand will receive to themselves judgment.*

Daniel 2:21: *He changes the times and the seasons. He removes kings and sets up kings. He gives wisdom to the wise, and knowledge to those who have understanding,*

1 Peter 2:13: *Therefore subject yourselves to every ordinance of man for the Lord's sake: whether to the king, as supreme;*

Priceless Moments

July 5th
Fireworks

"We're going to watch fireworks tonight, Grandma. Do you want to go with us?" I replied, "Ah, fireworks. Such beautiful colors exploding up and across the sky to entertain and delight the eyes, touching something deep within the soul." "Why do you say that? Sometimes they're just so loud I have to bury my head in the blanket and cover my ears." "But what about the times you look up and marvel at the different shapes, colors, and two- or three-stage displays within one firework explosion? How about the ones taking place on the ground in the shape of flags, waterfalls, or vehicles?" "Oh, I like all of those, particularly if they are the silent fireworks, you know, the ones that make very little noise." "I totally understand what you're saying. Little children, tame and wild animals, and some people have trouble with their ears during a fireworks display."

"Can you tell me what fireworks are anyway? Where did they come from?" "Fireworks were invented in China. They took something similar to a toilet paper tube and filled it with combustibles, a type of burnable material, to make noise, light, smoke, and different colored flames and sparks of red, orange, yellow, green, blue, purple, and silver. Many different tubes can be combined and sent into the air by lighting a fuse or a string attached to a skyrocket. After the explosion, you can see pieces of the blown-up empty tubes floating like confetti to the ground.

I thought about how God gives us many different types of fireworks in the form of sunrises, sunsets, and lightning storms. He also sends other beautiful displays in the form of rainbows and the spectacular Northern Lights—all created through the spoken word of God.

Thank You, LORD, for all the beautiful variety of color displays in creation. I pray we see the beauty in all of Your handiwork, giving You credit regardless of whom we encounter, reaffirming that it is indeed credited to You.

Psalm 19:1: *The heavens declare the glory of God. The expanse shows his handiwork.*

Ephesians 2:10: *For we are his workmanship, created in Christ Jesus for good works, which God prepared before that we would walk in them.*

2 Peter 3:7: *But the heavens that exist now and the earth, by the same word have been stored up for fire, being reserved against the day of judgment and destruction of ungodly men.*

July 6th
Hey, That's My Seat

We have several special chairs for the grandchildren so they can sit around the campfire with the adults, as well as chairs for them to play on in the house. Each chair is a little different from the others, and each child claimed one as their own. One day I heard, "Hey, you're sitting in my seat. Move now or I'll tell Grandma." The offender got up, apologized, and walked into the living room to sit down on Papa's recliner. Again, I hear, "Hey, you're sitting in my seat. I was sitting there before I went into the kitchen. Move now or I'll tell Grandma." A rattled voice replied, "I moved the first time you asked, but now I am entitled to sit here." She responded, "But I was there first." A more confident voice replied, "Remember the rules, move your feet, and lose your seat." The other young gal came back out to the kitchen, deflated and almost in tears.

I dropped what I was doing and walked over to her. I sat down at the dining room table, scooped her up in my arms, and helped her work through her emotions. When she was in control again, I said, "I realize how hard it is to not have what you want, but we should put others needs before our own. Rules never change just to suit your needs. Actually, this morning I heard you telling one of the other kids the same rule: "Move your feet and lose your seat."

Rules apply equally to all of you." "Yes, Grandma, I understand. I will apologize to her as well. Jesus will be happier with me when I do." "Honey, I think that is a wonderful idea."

I thought about the rules, then the commandments in the Bible, which also need to be followed to the best of our ability. The rich young ruler lived a good, clean life but was unwilling to give everything he had to the poor.

Thank You, LORD, for Your consistency in everything You did in thought, word, and deed. I pray we follow the two greatest commands faithfully as they fulfill the original Ten Commandments.

Matthew 22:37-40: Jesus said to him, "'You shall love the Lord your God with all your heart, with all your soul, and with all your mind.' This the first and great commandment. A second likewise is this, 'You shall love your neighbor as yourself.' The whole law and the prophets depend on these two commandments."

Matthew 25:44: Then they will also answer, saying, "Lord, when did we see you hungry, or thirsty, or a stranger, or naked, or sick, or in prison, and didn't help you?"

John 8:31-32: Jesus therefore said to those Jews who had believed him, "If you remain in my word, then you are truly my disciples. You will know the truth, and the truth will make you free."

July 7th

Snack Time

"Hi, Grandma. What's for a snack? I'm starving. It's been a long day." "Well, hello to you, too. Can I have a hug first before you starve to death?" Laughter filled the house as she ran over and gave me a hug. "Now, can I have a snack?" "Why don't I get

Priceless Moments

something ready while you tell me about your day. I think it sounds like a fair exchange; do you agree?" "Oh, Grandma, you're so silly. Sure, I'll tell you what we did. We talked about numbers, letters, and stuff like that. Our teacher likes to ask us questions like you do, so I'm getting used to thinking of things to answer. See the pretty picture I drew today? I want you to hang it up on your refrigerator, so you don't forget me." "Oh, honey, thank you, and I'd never forget you. I love your choice of colors. I'd be honored to hang it up so both Papa and I can enjoy it. What made you decide to draw our whole family?"

As we were talking, a snack of carrots, snap peas, and hummus was prepared. I handed it to her as she answered, "We talked about the importance of people in our lives. The first response I had was to draw all of our family," she said, munching away on a carrot. "I drew a second one for Daddy and Mommy to hang on our refrigerator. See, I think about snacks all the time because we're all eating apples." I laughed out loud, stating, "You are just like your dad. When he was a kid, he also had a one-track mind focused on food. At least you all like fruits and vegetables—good, wholesome food provided by God Himself." She chuckled as she munched away.

It's happy times remembering our family growing up and seeing good times reflected in our grandchildren. May we cherish those memories as we make new ones with the next generation, being careful to never take them for granted. Families are indeed one of the greatest blessings from the LORD.

Thank You, LORD, for wholesome food to accompany Your wholesome Word. I pray we recognize how blessed we are to partake" of Your daily bread of life to keep us physically and spiritually fit.

Genesis 1:29: God said, "Behold, I have given you every herb yielding seed, which is on the surface of all the earth, and every tree, which bears fruit yielding seed. It will be your food.

Priceless Moments

Ecclesiastes 9:7*: Go your way—eat your bread with joy, and drink your wine with a merry heart; for God has already accepted your works.*

John 4:34*: Jesus said to them, "My food is to do the will of him who sent me and to accomplish his work."*

July 8th
Founding Fathers

"Grandma, what are the founding fathers? I've thought about this term since we talked about it several days ago." "The founding fathers were a group of leaders who worked to unite the original thirteen colonies through the War of Independence from Great Britain to create our nation and develop the framework and write policies for the United States of America." "What kind of papers did they write?" "They helped write the Declaration of Independence, Articles of Confederation, and the Constitution of the United States. These men displayed true patriotism in the form of leadership, longevity, and statesmanship."

"How many founding fathers were there, and who were they?" "Interesting questions. There were the major founding fathers (and ages on 7/4/1776): James Monroe (18), Aaron Burr (20), Alexander Hamilton (21), James Madison (25), John Jay (30), Thomas Jefferson (33), John Adams (40), Paul Revere (41), George Washington (44), and Benjamin Franklin (70). There were fifty-six signers of the Declaration of Independence and thirty-nine signers of the United States Constitution. Also, two women played important roles: Abigail Adams and Mercy Otis Warren. At the time, these individuals ranged in age from eighteen to seventy.

It's amazing to realize how young most of these men were when they crafted such a godly framework for our country. Wouldn't it be awesome if our young people—and older people—would grasp such dedication to our LORD, fostering a deep commitment to biblical principles and endeavoring to include them in every aspect of their lives?

Thank You, LORD, for individuals willing to risk it all for the sake of the gospel. I pray we catch that dedication and devotion for Your kingdom, living it out in front of our families, friends, acquaintances, neighbors, and total strangers. May our faces shine like Moses after we've been in Your presence, sparking opportunities to share Your greatness and love.

John Adams: "The Bible contains the most profound philosophy, the most perfect morality, and the most refined policy that ever was conceived upon earth."

Elias Boudinot: "Were you to ask me to recommend the most valuable book in the world, I should fix on the Bible as the most instructive, both to the wise and ignorant."

John Jay: "Let us therefore persevere steadfastly in distributing the Scriptures far and near, and without note or comment. We are assured that they are profitable for doctrine, for reroof, for correction, for instruction in righteousness." **(2 Timothy 3:16)**

Thomas Jefferson: "The doctrines of Jesus are simple, and tend all to the happiness of man… Had the doctrines of Jesus been preached always as pure as they came from His lips, the whole civilized world would now have been Christian."

July 9th
<u>Patriotic Marshmallows</u>

Oh, man, here we go again. I just spied patriotic marshmallows—and so have they. "Oh my goodness, Grandma, do you see that?" she said, pointing to the red, white, and blue marshmallows on the shelf. "They're flag-colored marshmallows." Excitement is brimming everywhere and, once again, attracting attention. "We

Priceless Moments

could make more red, white, and blue Rice Krispie treats. Can we?" I know how their precious little ones think. "It sounds like a fun idea, but once you melt these marshmallows, the colors would blend together, probably making a purple or violet color." "Seriously, Grandma, how do you get that answer?"

Let's fall back on previous experiences here. "Do you remember when we dyed Easter eggs? What happened when mixing the colors and different amounts of the colors in separate bowls?" Wheels were spinning as they thought about the experiment. "We've got all different shades of colors." An "aha" moment as they grasped the reality of it all. "Ding, you're right, Grandma. Those colors would blend together and be completely different than those pretty marshmallow colors. There's a lot of white, so the shade would probably be lighter than we think it would be." "I'm impressed you figured it out on your own. Looking back at what you've done before and how it worked out can help us answer questions we have now. Because you enjoyed making treats before, I'll tell you what. Why don't we buy a bag of these and find out exactly what color they will be? Then we still get to eat the treats." "That's an awesome idea. Thanks."

Experiences teach us more than we can imagine since we can draw on them for future reference. Many times, God puts these in our path to prepare us for a more challenging trial in the future.

Thank You, LORD, for teachable moments that prepare us for greater challenges ahead. I pray we look to You for guidance and answers to meet each new challenge with You as our guide. If this is a test like Job experienced, may we stay committed to serving You throughout these occurrences.

Proverbs 4:5*: Get wisdom. Get understanding. Don't forget, and don't deviate from the words of my mouth.*

2 Timothy 3:16*: Every Scripture is God-breathed and profitable for teaching, for reproof, for correction, and for instruction in righteousness,*

Priceless Moments

James 1:2, 3*: Count it all joy, my brothers, when you fall into various temptations, knowing that the testing of your faith produces endurance.*

July 10th
The Rolling Pin

Baking day has rolled around once again, and I decided to try something new with them. Ingredients and supplies needed to make pies were gathered. "Who likes pie?" A deafening "Yes" resounded in the kitchen. "What kind of pie should we make?" I heard a unanimous "apple." "Then apple it is. Who wants to help make pie crust?" Hands all around went high in the air. "OK, here's what we'll do. Half of you can make the dough, and the other half can roll out the crust. For the next batch, we will switch jobs. Each was assigned a task, and the dough-makers set to work. "The dough is made, now what?" "Great job. Now I will show all of you how to roll out the dough." I started to roll when questions were asked. "Why do you roll that round thing with handles over the dough? What is it supposed to do to it?" "Well, this round thing with handles is called a rolling pin. It is used to flatten the dough evenly so it can be placed in a pie plate before adding the filling." "Ahs and oohs" were heard as they understood the purpose of some "new" (to them) kitchen equipment.

Eager helpers soon had crusts rolled out, switched jobs, and had dough made for lids on the pies. The apple peeler saw each set of hands peel, cut, and core all the apples needed for the pies. The kids separated them into groups for each pie, measured the filling ingredients, and sliced the apples—under my watchful eye. Soon the pies were assembled and ready for the top crusts. The other group rolled them out, and all of them worked to seal the two crusts together. "Now what, Grandma? When do we get to eat them?" "We're taking these to the picnic, so I guess your answer is after you eat your meal and are ready for dessert." By now the oven was preheated, and several pies were popped in the oven to bake. Oh, yes, they turned out great.

It's refreshing to see little ones so eager to try new things, especially when doing it together along with the promise of taste-testing at the end. Isn't this like our LORD, willing to work with and teach us along the way to bring us to the end of the project called life when we get to enjoy the end reward with Him in heaven?

Thank You, LORD, for Your patience in teaching us new skills. I pray we are diligent to listen, learn, and then practice the new skills to lead others to You.

Exodus 4:12: *Now therefore go, and I will be with your mouth, and teach you what you shall speak.*

Jeremiah 32:33: *They have turned their backs to me, and not their faces. Although I taught them, rising up early and teaching them, yet they have not listened to receive instruction.*

John 8:28: *Jesus therefore said to them, "When you have lifted up the Son of Man, then you will know that I am he, and I do nothing of myself, but as my Father taught me, I say these things.*

July 11th
Boating Down the River

"Grandma, come quick and look out the window. There are people in boats on the river. Summer is coming, and it's time to break out our boat, too. Seeing those lucky people out there makes us want to go now." "That sounds like so much fun. What is your favorite part about going out on the boat?" "I can't say I have just one. I like to jump in the water and swim, shoot the water guns, camp along the river, and eat on the boat or somewhere along the river." "What do you like best about the river?" "I like to watch for fish in the water as well as fish jumping. I like seeing the houses along the river. And I like spending time with all of you. I guess I have a couple of favorites, too."

We were quiet for a few minutes until I heard, "How many times did Jesus ride on a boat?" "The actual answer is one nobody knows for sure. One thing we do know is that boats played an important part in His ministry. The Bible tells us of a time when Jesus fell asleep on a boat when a storm came up on the sea. The disciples were afraid and awakened Him. At this point, Jesus calmed the storm. Another one says He pushed off from the shore and taught the people on the shore. Still another says Jesus had His disciples get into a boat and sent them on ahead of Him. Later, He walked on the water to the boat and climbed in.

I reflected on Jesus creating opportunities to preach to as many people as possible, yet how often do we try to reduce our sharing opportunities to as few as possible?

Thank You, LORD, for setting the example for us to reach out of our comfort zones to reach as many people for You as possible. I pray You give us opportunities to expand our circle of influence for Your kingdom.

Matthew 14:32: *When they got up into the boat, the wind ceased.*

Mark 3:9: *He spoke to his disciples that a little boat should stay near him because of the crowd, so that they wouldn't press on him.*

Luke 5:3-4: *He entered into one of the boats, which was Simon's, and asked him to put out a little from the land. He sat down and taught the multitudes from the boat. When he had finished speaking, he said to Simon, "Put out into the deep, and let down your nets for a catch."*

July 12th
<u>Etch-A-Sketch</u>

A toy we played with as children has been greatly improved for this new generation, going from turning little knobs on opposite ends of the board to a magnetic drawing pen. I watched with interest as the grandchildren worked with their pens to create—or at least attempt to create—a unicorn. "Why won't this work? Why won't it do what I want it to do? Grandma, help me, please, or my drawing will be ruined." I felt it would definitely be ruined if I tried to help. When it came to art, I got the short end of the crayon stick. Our kids always said my stick figures were unrecognizable, and she wants a unicorn.

But, to appease her, I took the pen, paused to whisper a prayer for some artistic flare, then attempted to help, saying, "I will do my best. Can you tell me how you want it changed to match the picture in your mind?" She responded, "Well, it still doesn't look like a horse. Can you fix it first?" Although I could only make a few additions to streamline the body, it started to look more like a horse. We worked together on it for a little while until it actually started to resemble the desired unicorn. She became more hopeful with each stroke, "It's working; it's working now. Thank you." And I got a big hug and kiss.

Often times, we try to do things on our own without involving God in the process; only to find things are not going the way we had planned. When we pause to pray, bringing Him in as our partner, things begin to change in us, and we start to resemble our Creator. The more we study and learn, keeping Him close by our side, the more we grow to be like Him and become what He desires us to be.

Thank You, LORD, for Your patience with our slowness to learn to call on You at the very beginning of each day. As You work with us, may each stroke from Your hand create the desired masterpiece in each of us.

Genesis 1:26a*: God said, "Let's make man in our image, after our likeness.*

Exodus 35:35*: He has filled them with wisdom of heart to work all kinds of workmanship, of the engraver, of the skillful workman, and of the embroiderer, in blue, in purple, in scarlet, and in fine linen, and of the weaver, even of those who do any workmanship, and of those who make skillful works.*

Psalm 104:24*: Yahweh, how many are your works! In wisdom, you have made them all. The earth is full of your riches.*

July 13th
<u>*Church Bells*</u>

As we were walking into a new church while on vacation, the church bells began to ring. Our grandson immediately covered his ears, saying, "Grandma, those are too loud. They are hurting my ears." Granted, they were loud, but as I listened to the beautiful tones, I recognized the tune. The melody was simply delightful, so I said, "Ah, little man, I'll bet if you listen a little you will be able to sing along with the chiming bells." He took his hands from his ears and listened until he heard the melody, then his face lit up. "Oh, Grandma, I know that tune. It's one of the songs we sing with you during devotions each morning." He proceeded in through the door, humming the tune to himself.

Throughout the service, he kept looking around the sanctuary as if he were going to discover some secret cave or hideout. As we were leaving the building, the bells began to chime again. This time he was scanning the area, looking for something. "Honey, what do you keep looking for in and out of the church?" "I'm looking to see where they keep the bells. I haven't been able to find them anywhere." It makes sense to me, so I said, "Did you look clear up to the top of the building to a place called the belfry?" He was looking up, but not waaaayyy up, so I helped him tilt his head up. As he looked, he could see the bells swing in and out of the belfry. His face lit up, "Grandma, do you see that? They are playing the most beautiful music as they swing back and forth. Do you hear that? I'm so glad you asked me to listen and showed me where the bells are. I will never forget this moment. Thank you so much."

The joy on his face at that moment is the kind of joy that should be plastered on every Christian's face. We have the best music since many songs are taken right from Scripture, helping us to hide God's Word in our minds and hearts. We need to look up, listen to, and sing along with uplifting tunes so our outside and inside can both praise the LORD.

Thank You, LORD, for the joy of music to relax the soul, lift the spirit, promote sleep, and improve mental alertness and mood. I pray we turn to Your gift throughout the day as a means to help ourselves and others worship You.

Psalm 71:23: *My lips shall shout for joy! My soul, which you have redeemed, sings praises to you.*

Psalm 95:1: *Oh come, let's sing to Yahweh. Let's shout aloud to the rock of our salvation!*

Hebrews 2:12: *I will declare your name to my brothers. Among the congregation I will sing your praise*

July 14th

Toying With Your Food

Thursday night is family dinner night at our house. The children know if they clean their plates there will be some kind of dessert—especially if it's a baking day and they'd help make it. "Grandma,

Priceless Moments

what can we help you with to make dinner?" "Volunteers. I love it. I haven't had time to cut the ends off of the fresh green beans. Do you want to help?" Needless to say, they all came running. "Let me get out some knives and cutting boards plus a stool for someone to stand on, then I'll show you what to do." Everything was ready and the sous chefs began their work. "What an amazing job everyone has done." "What are you going to do with them? Are we going to eat them like this or will you cook them." "I'll steam them, add butter and crushed garlic, stir it all together, and add bacon bits." "Can we do that now?" "No, we'll wait closer to dinner since it only takes five minutes."

We were able to play the rest of the morning until I popped chicken and twice-baked potatoes in the oven. Dinner time rolled around, and they were busy playing, so I cooked the beans. Parents had arrived and everyone came to the table. One little girl was playing with her food, so I asked, "Are you feeling OK? This is one of your favorite meals and you've barely touched your food." "Oh, I'm OK, just disappointed." "May I ask why you're disappointed? You've had a good day playing with your cousins and you helped with the beans." "I know, but there is no reason to eat since there's no dessert tonight because we didn't make any and there wasn't anything in the fridge." I smiled, "But you don't know what's in the freezer." All their eyes lit up and cleaned their plates. (I know, I know, you want to know what was for dessert—pumpkin roll.)

It's amazing how we can assume things without having all the facts. Once we figure out or learn everything we need to know, the whole picture changes and we move into compliance with God's will.

Thank You, LORD, for accepting our humanness and our need-to-know attitude. I pray we grow in our faith to the point where we can do what You have asked us to do without needing a reward for our compliance.

Priceless Moments

Colossians 3:23-24: And whatever you do, work heartily, as for the Lord, and not for men, knowing that from the Lord you will receive the reward of the inheritance; for you serve the Lord Christ.

Philippians 2:14-15: Do all things without complaining and arguing, that you may become blameless and harmless, children of God without defect in the middle of a crooked and perverse generation, among whom you are seen as lights in the world,

Psalm 128:2: You will eat the fruit of your labor; blessings and prosperity will be yours. NIV

July 15th
The Back End Booty Dance

From a very young age, our grandchildren have always loved to dance to music. On one particular occasion, my cell phone rang, playing a really great tune for dancing. Our granddaughter had just pulled herself up to the coffee table when she heard the music. She started smiling and squealing with delight as her little booty started swaying to the music. When it stopped, she looked around, trying to find out why. Realizing what she wanted, I went into the ring tones and started playing a few. Not one brought as much delight as the initial song. When this particular tune came up on the list, her little face lit up with recognition as the little booty started to sway to the beat once again. This went on until she became tired and wanted a nap.

While enjoying a bottle before napping, the phone rang again. Yep, you guessed it, with the coveted tune. Her little booty started swaying back and forth in my lap, not missing a beat—or a drag on her bottle. Once the music stopped, so did her swaying. But it was a die-hard on the other end of the line. They immediately called back, starting the booty swaying once again as long as the music persisted. Although they did not get an answer the first two times, they called again. They must have thought, "The third time's the charm." Anyway, we had one more rendition of the back-end booty dance as she finished her bottle and fell asleep to her beloved tune—with a smile on her face.

I smiled as I thought of how delighted God would be if we got that excited when He called us. I went on to think of how He can call repeatedly and yet get no answer from us. I became thankful that He is persistent in calling out to His own. Although we may be "too busy" to answer, God is never too busy to listen to us. He treasures our prayers so much that they are kept in golden bowls in heaven.

Thank You, LORD, for long-distance calls that don't need a phone line. I pray we always answer Your call the first time, being ready to do Your will, regardless of the request.

Luke 11:9: *"I tell you, keep asking, and it will be given you. Keep seeking, and you will find. Keep knocking, and it will be opened to you.*

Psalm 145:18: *Yahweh is near to all those who call on him, to all who call on him in truth.*

Revelation 5:8: *Now when he had taken the book, the four living creatures and the twenty-four elders fell down before the Lamb, each one having a harp, and golden bowls full of incense, which are the prayers of the saints.*

July 16th

<u>*Daddy's Picture*</u>

Our grandson was walking down the hall past our *hall of fame* pictures of our own children from birth to college graduation. He stood in front of the pictures for a long time, then finally spoke. "Grandma, who are those kids with you and Papa? I don't know

Priceless Moments

any of them. And why do you guys look so different?" Interesting, I thought. We've looked at pictures before but must not have looked much at these. "Honey, those are pictures of your dad, uncle, and aunt as they were growing up." "But I don't see my daddy. Nothing up there looks like him, my uncle, or my aunt. How can it be them?" "These pictures were taken at different times in their lives as they were growing up, just like you are doing now. Remember how we looked at some of your pictures and you didn't always recognize yourself? Here, let me show you. Here are your dad, uncle, and auntie (pointing to and naming them in each picture)."

He looked at them again and said, "I thought that one picture was me with you and Papa. I guess I look like my dad, just like everyone keeps telling me. But that's a good thing because my dad's a really neat person, and he takes me places, lets me ride in the truck, and plays games with me." "You are a very lucky little man because some daddies don't have time or won't make time for their kids." "How can they be like that? Didn't God put each one of us in the family because He felt we could all benefit from being together?" "That's exactly correct, honey. God knows who needs to be taught what lessons and which family can teach them best to each other. A lot of times the parents even learn from the children, so your good behavior can have an influence on all members of your family."

This conversation brought to light just how much God wants us to be members of His family. He's thrilled to do things for us because He loves us, not because we deserve it. The more we seek to do His will, learn of Him, and share Him with others, the more we begin to look like Him, becoming a special reflection of our Father figure.

Thank You, LORD, that we can turn our lives over to You and become members of Your family. I pray we strive to grow in Your grace, looking more like You every day we walk on this earth. But most importantly, when others look at us, they see the "glow" of You on our faces that gets brighter every day.

Genesis 1:27*: God created man in his own image. In God's image he created him; male and female he created them.*

2 Corinthians 3:18*: But we all, with unveiled face seeing the glory of the Lord as in a mirror, are transformed into the same image from glory to glory, even as from the Lord, the Spirit.*

Ephesians 4:24*: and put on the new man, who in the likeness of God has been created in righteousness and holiness of truth.*

July 17th
Can We Fix This?

"Papa, can you fix this?" Our granddaughter came walking into the room, tears streaming down her cheeks, and holding out her hand. It was a broken doll. As she choked back the tears, she said, "Papa, can you please help her? She isn't just any doll; she's my most *favoritest* doll ever." And the tears started to flow again like a river. "Come here, honey, and let me take a look at it. Oh my, she's had a terrible fall. Can you tell me what happened?" As he examined the doll, she choked back the sobs and said, "We were riding my bike when we hit a rock, and it threw my bike. Fortunately, I had on a helmet, but she wasn't wearing hers. To make things worse, I landed on her while she sacrificed herself to break my fall." Papa felt her pain, as evidenced by the gentle manner in which he responded to her. "Come here, honey. I have an idea, but I'm going to need your help to make it work."

As her sobbing slowed, she looked up hopefully and said, "Papa, I'll do whatever I can to help you out." "OK, then, let's head downstairs to the doll repair shop. Many moons ago, I did a similar repair to one of your aunt's dolls." The two of them disappeared downstairs for about an hour. I could hear them talking, playing music, and laughing as they worked. Soon footsteps were heard as they ran back upstairs. This time her face shone with excitement, and Papa's face showed signs of relief. "Look, Grandma, look. We did it. Papa knew exactly what he was doing, and he made it fun, too. Thank you, and I love you, Papa." "I love you too, sweetheart. Come back anytime, and we will see what we can do." "Thanks, Papa; you're the best.'

The joy on both their faces for a successful repair is nothing compared to our Heavenly Father mending our broken hearts over relationships and friendships. We cry to Him, and He responds with love and compassion.

Thank You, LORD, for Your open arms to hear us when we petition You. I pray we have our ears and hearts open to receive Your help and answer to our needs, regardless of Your response, because Father knows best.

Isaiah 40:31: *but those who wait for Yahweh will renew their strength. They will mount up with wings like eagles. They will run, and not be weary. They will walk, and not faint.*

Isaiah 61:7: *Instead of your shame you will have double. Instead of dishonor, they will rejoice in their portion.*
Therefore in their land they will possess double. Everlasting joy will be to them.

Jeremiah 17:14: *Heal me, O Yahweh, and I will be healed. Save me, and I will be saved; for you are my praise.*

July 18th

Let's Have Ice Cream

"Hey, Grandma, do you hear that music? Where is it coming from? I've never heard that kind of music before. Does somebody play that around here very often?" "I didn't hear the music when you did, so I need to listen for a moment to hear what you're talking about. Please and thank you." I signaled for them to be quiet for a moment, and I listened, only to recognize the music he was talking about. "I don't know if you've ever seen one before, but that music is coming from an ice cream truck that drives through the neighborhood once a week. Are you interested in ice cream?" Definite "yeses" were heard all around. "Do you think we should go out and see if it's still here?" Again, "yeses" were heard all around. "OK, everybody get your shoes on while I go get some money to pay for a special treat. No running or pushing while each takes their turn, understood?" The third time, "yeses" were heard all around. I guess the third time truly is the charm.

We walked out the door in an orderly fashion, and I signaled the ice cream truck driver to come back. "OK, let's try youngest to oldest in a line. Each of you can give your order as long as there is no complaining about the reversal of age. "Grandma, that's only fair since it takes them longer to eat theirs than it does the older kids." "I'm in trouble. You're starting to see through my logic." They all laughed, including the ice cream truck driver. Each received their treat and immediately started enjoying the delectably satisfying frozen wonder on the way back to the house. "Let's eat these inside so they won't melt as fast. You can go back out to enjoy the breeze out here after you're done eating and have washed your hands." "OK, Grandma," was heard all around.

Ah, a special heat-busting treat on a hot summer day that can be enjoyed by all. What a fun way to learn to put the needs of others above yourself and still come out on the winning side. God expects us to look at our treatment of others from the vantage point of how we wish to be treated—surely changes one's perspective.

Thank You, LORD, for calling us to have true J-O-Y by the way we honor them: J for Jesus; O for others; and Y for yourself. I pray we realize that although we put ourselves last, Jesus notices our priorities and rewards our faithfulness to Him and our fellowman.

Priceless Moments

Matthew 7:12: *Therefore, whatever you desire for men to do to you, you shall also do to them; for this is the law and the prophets.*

Romans 12:10: *In love of the brothers be tenderly affectionate to one another; in honor preferring one another;*

Philippians 2:4: *each of you not just looking to his own things, but each of you also to the things of others.*

July 19th
My Special Cup

"Grandma, have you seen my special cup? I looked in the cup cupboard, and it isn't there." OK, which little voice was that—and why are they climbing up on the counter to find a certain cup? Off to the kitchen I go to investigate the situation and be sure everyone is safe. "Oh, my, my. What do we have here? I see a lot of mugs out, but I don't understand why. Can anyone fill me in on this?" Giggles erupted everywhere. "Do you remember the last time we were here? You said we could make chai tea the next time we came over? Well, this is the next time, and we are thirsty for chai. Can we make it now? We tried to be helpful and get out the mugs, but we couldn't reach the chai mix, or we would have gotten that out for you as well. We were careful. They held onto me while I crawled up on the stool and handed them down the mugs." They were so proud of themselves that I couldn't be stern.

They watched me for my response. I stood there tapping my lips, then said, "I guess there's very little left for me to do. I'd better get the water heated and get down the mix." Looks of delight crossed their faces as I swung into action, tickling little bellies as I moved across the kitchen. "But, Grandma, where is my special cup? I still didn't find it. I know you only keep mugs in one cupboard." I smiled and said, "Ah, sweetie, but you're mistaken. Maybe someone else used it and put it in the dish…" "The dishwasher. I never thought of the dishwasher. But that means it's dirty, yuck."

"Ah, once again, you're mistaken. I just ran the dishwasher, and everything is clean and dry. If little hands empty it, my big hands will finish our chai, and we can sit down to enjoy this delicious brew." The special cup was found, and the dishwasher was emptied. The chai was good.

Something is just so satisfying that you can do almost anything to possess it. Just like becoming a Christian. Jesus fills our hearts with so much love that we are able to complete unpleasant tasks to gain the ultimate reward, like confessing we are sinners, asking forgiveness from others, and changing old habits into godly ones.

Thank You, LORD; the end goal of accepting You into our lives brings the joy of heaven into view. I pray we are willing to sacrifice whatever He asks of us to gain the greatest reward in all the world.

Matthew 5:12: *Rejoice, and be exceedingly glad, for great is your reward in heaven. For that is how they persecuted the prophets who were before you.*

Hebrews 11:26: *He regarded disgrace for the sake of Christ as of greater value than the treasures of Egypt, because he was looking ahead to his reward. NIV*

Daniel 12:3: *Those who are wise will shine as the brightness of the expanse. Those who turn many to righteousness will shine as the stars forever and ever.*

July 20th
<u>The Tree House</u>

"On our way home from church, we saw some kids playing in a house in a tree. Have you ever seen that before?" Yes, I have," I replied. "It's called a tree house or fort built around or in a big tree." "Why do people build houses in trees? Wouldn't that be

Priceless Moments

hard to do?" "Interesting questions. Many people build houses in trees to avoid danger from weather or animals or to keep food away from animals. Some other places were built around trees to provide support for the walls of their structures. Today, most are built for fun as play areas for kids, a hide-out, a quiet place to work or study, or used as a tree stand during hunting or watching animals." "OK, then, how do you get up in the tree?" "Several options are just climbing the tree, a ladder, or steps."

Quiet, thoughtful looks prevailed for the moment. "Do you know anyone who has a tree house?" "Not here. When we were kids, our dad read us a story about the *Swiss Family Robinson,* who were shipwrecked and built a tree house to live in until they were rescued. We thought it sounded like fun, so Dad built us a tree house in the woods behind our house. It was a lot of fun." "Do you have that book now? Can you read it to us, too?" "Sorry, guys, but I do not have this particular book. We could always go to the library and borrow it, if you like." "Yes, please. How soon can we go get it?" "I think now is about as good a time as any, so let's go."

It was fun thinking about good times as a child. But I wonder how many times we "build tree houses" in our lives to escape reality, hoping to keep ourselves "safe." This is where trust comes in: bringing our "concerns" and laying them at the feet of Jesus, trusting Him to keep us safe.

Thank You, LORD, we do not have to build tree houses for "safe keeping." I pray we turn to You for protection and guidance in difficult times, growing our faith as a witness to those around us.

Proverbs 1:33: *but whoever listens to me will live in safety and be at ease, without fear of harm.*

Psalm 12:5: *"Because of the oppression of the weak and because of the groaning of the needy,*
   I will now arise," says Yahweh; "I will set him in safety from those who malign him."

Priceless Moments

2 Thessalonians 3:3-5: *But the Lord is faithful, who will establish you and guard you from the evil one. We have confidence in the Lord concerning you, that you both do and will do the things we command. May the Lord direct your hearts into God's love, and into the perseverance of Christ.*

July 21st
Tiny Little Fingers

There's nothing more precious than a newborn baby, fresh from heaven. Their innocence is unfathomable, and their trust is incomprehensible. As our newborn granddaughter lay in my arms, she wrapped her tiny little fingers around my big index finger. Although so helpless, she was so willing to reach out and become acquainted with her new surroundings. Those baby blues were struggling to focus, yet her little fingers were reaching out to say, "Hey, world, here I am; love me. I've come to bring you joy—and a few sleepless nights, but I'm worth it all. What I need from you, more than anything, is to accept me and allow me to grow up to follow your example of love and acceptance so I can see you as a reflection of Jesus. I pray you find me more valuable than your new car, home, job, and pleasures of this world. No matter how you look at it, I am a part of you, and I desire to feel your love and affection each time you hold me."

"Take a moment to reflect on the joys I am going to bring you over our future that we have to share together. I will eventually look at and focus on you, making your heart soar. I will smile, probably gas at first, but soon there will be a genuine recognition of the connection we are developing between us. My eyes will dance and sparkle with delight when you play with me, trying to get me to look at and smile at you again. Soon I'll roll over, crawl, and sprout a few funny things in my mouth that keep my tongue busy trying to guess what they are. You'll be over the moon with joy when I pull myself up on things, walk around things, and take my first solo steps towards you. That's just for starters. I can't tell you anymore right now because I'm sleepy. Love you and good night."

Babies bring out the best in us, just like Jesus wants to do. If we would wrap our fingers around Jesus, trusting Him explicitly, like babies do for their caregivers, what a wonderful world this would be.

Thank You, LORD, for babies; in Your opinion, the world should go on. I pray we develop a deep respect for life, fighting to save the unborn so they and we can experience a little piece of heaven together here on earth.

1 Samuel 1:27: I prayed for this child, and Yahweh has given me my petition which I asked of him.

Psalm 127:3: Behold, children are a heritage of Yahweh. The fruit of the womb is his reward.

James 1:17-18: Every good gift and every perfect gift is from above, coming down from the Father of lights, with whom can be no variation, nor turning shadow. Of his own will he gave birth to us by the word of truth, that we should be a kind of first fruits of his creatures.

July 22nd

Picture Perfect

As the kids were lining up for a family grandkids picture, I said, "Smile, you're on candid camera." One alert munchkin asked, "Grandma, what does that mean? I've never heard that before." They all froze, waiting to hear the explanation. "It used to be a TV show where the show's creators would play jokes on people who weren't expecting them. Today, it's said to be funny to ask others to smile for the camera. It's like when you want us to smile to

Priceless Moments

have our picture taken and you say, "Say cheese, or cheesecake, or pickles." "Grandma, why do you take so many pictures anyway?" "Good question. Pictures are a fun way to remind us of the people, places, and things we did when we were together—a vacation, things you are working on for a school project, or some of the funny things we've done. It's a way to help our memories be available to look at over and over when we have the time or need the picture to say what we had done."

They thought about the explanation. Finally, one cherub asked, "Do you think God takes pictures of us so He can remember everything about us?" "Interesting question. God knows everything from the beginning of time through the end of the world and on into eternity. He does not have a need for pictures because everything is recorded in His mind." "Do you think God took pictures of Jesus on the cross and in the grave? Do you think God was surprised by anything that happened to Jesus?" "God would not have been surprised because, since the beginning of the world, Jesus' death and resurrection were part of His plan to save mankind after the fall of Adam and Eve." "Wow, He really does see everything picture-perfect." "Yes, He does."

Jesus's love for us is picture perfect, with no flaws—without the pranks. The problem comes on our end when we screw up our faces, give others bunny ears, or refuse to cooperate with His will for us.

Thank You, LORD, that all things in Your world are picture-perfect. I pray we learn to look at our lives through the lens You use to look at our lives. These could be two completely different "pictures," so we need to determine Your will for our lives to follow Your picture-perfect plan.

Psalm 18:30*: As for God, his way is perfect. Yahweh's word is tried. He is a shield to all those who take refuge in him.*

Proverbs 16:7*: When a man's ways please Yahweh, he makes even his enemies to be at peace with him.*

Priceless Moments

1 John 4:18*: There is no fear in love; but perfect love casts out fear, because fear has punishment. He who fears is not made perfect in love.*

July 23rd
Can You Take the Time…?

"Grandma, I wanted to come over to see you today. Can you take the time to work on a science project with me? My parents are both at work, and I want to get it done early so I've got time to draw a few pictures." "Hummm, let me look at my appointment book. I keep everything in there, so I don't miss anyone's activities." I walked over and looked at the book, knowing full well that I was available. "Well, look at that; I'm free." "Oh, good. When can we start? I brought over a few things I thought we could use. If we need something else, you'll probably have what's needed. If not, we can go to the store. Is that OK with you?" "Sure, honey. The first thing you need to do is tell me about the project you would like to make." "Our teacher brought in a few caterpillars that hang upside down on a branch and will soon turn into butterflies. I am supposed to make a habitat for a butterfly."

To be sure she understood what she was making, I said, "Wow, what's a habitat?" "A habitat is a place, called a shelter, where an animal lives and keeps their food, water, and anything else they might need to survive. We learned that animals can live in the mountains, the grass, forests, deserts, or the water." "What kind of habitat do butterflies live in?" "Butterflies can be found in all habitats but water." "What do they need to grow?" "They need milkweed to breed and flowering plants to eat. Did you know butterflies use their feet to taste things? If their wings get wet, they stay still until they dry out. They live under leaves to hide from things that want to eat them and to stay out of the rain." "This is fascinating. So, what kind of habitat do we need to build?" "I am taking a shoe box, cutting off the top, poking holes in the sides, and filling it with different kinds of plants that are brightly colored and smell strong." "OK, then. Let's get busy."

Just like the caterpillar, we hang our lives on the promises of God to make us a new creation when we accept Him as LORD and Savior. As a caterpillar, we die to sin; as a butterfly, we live in Christ. Like the butterfly, may we remember the things we learned as caterpillars—and not repeat them.

Thank You, LORD, for the transformation You have planned for those who accept You as LORD and Savior. I pray we realize how much You desire to redeem us from hanging as lost to flying free in forgiveness.

Ezekiel 36:26: I will also give you a new heart, and I will put a new spirit within you. I will take away the stony heart out of your flesh, and I will give you a heart of flesh.

2 Corinthians 5:17: Therefore if anyone is in Christ, he is a new creation. The old things have passed away. Behold, all things have become new.

Ephesians 4:22-24: You were taught, with regard to your former way of life, put off your old self, which is being corrupted by its deceitful desires; to be made new in the attitude of your minds; and to put on the new self, created to be like God in true righteousness and holiness. NIV

July 24th
Blowing Bubbles

A favorite activity of any kid at any age is to blow bubbles. Papa was shopping one day and came home with a six-pack of bubbles for each grandchild. I was a little surprised until I learned they were on clearance for one dollar each. When the kids were together, Papa brought out the bubbles. Shrieks of laughter exuded

Priceless Moments

from each cherub to the point that neighbors were wondering what was happening—And if they could come over and enjoy the mayhem, too. "Grandma, can we blow bubbles in any direction we want? Will the neighbors get mad at us?" Isn't it refreshing to see little ones concerned about others? "No, the neighbors won't get mad. And, absolutely. Blow as many as you want in any direction you want. If anyone comes over, we have plenty to share."

Some blew bubbles, others flicked them back and forth to make tiny bubbles, and others blew slowly to make ginormous bubbles. If they got bored blowing bubbles, they started chasing bubbles. The laughter was infectious. The adults were laughing almost as hard at them as they were at the bubbles. As in every good activity, "Grandma, I'm hungry." "Me, too." "Me, three." "OK," I said, looking at my watch. "Oh, my, it's supper time." (Fortunately, dinner had been working hard cooking itself in the crockpot while we played carefree in the backyard.) "Everyone go sit down, and I'll bring dinner out here." While they ate, Papa and I cleaned up the empty bottles.

Bubble mania had ensued for several hours, emptying over half of the treasure trove. But all the fun and family time were worth so much more than the bargain bubbles. I thought of how we need to get so invested in reading, studying, sharing the good news, and fellowshipping with others so their lives can also "bubble over" with joy.

Thank You, LORD, for family, fun, fellowship, and food to cement relationships. I pray we use these times to enjoy the good, clean activities, sharing Your love to bring glory to Your Name.

***Ecclesiastes 5:18**: Behold, that which I have seen to be good and proper is for one to eat and to drink, and to enjoy good in all his labor, in which he labors under the sun, all the days of his life which God has given him; for this is his portion.*

***1 Thessalonians 5:21-22**: Test all things, and hold firmly that which is good. Abstain from every form of evil.*

Colossians 3:17: *Whatever you do, in word or in deed, do all in the name of the Lord Jesus, giving thanks to God the Father, through him.*

July 25th
<u>The Gifts</u>

Have you ever received a gift from your grandchild and had them take it back again? I have: "Grandma, here is a special gift for you. I made it at school. My friend wanted me to give it to him, but I told him it was for someone special—you. Now close your eyes and hold out your hands—no peeking." I complied, feeling something being placed in my hands. I waited…. "Now you can open your eyes." I looked and said, "Oh my. The picture is just beautiful. Can you tell me about it?" He proceeded, "Our teacher said we could have free time to make something for someone special. She laid out paper, crayons, and a bunch of other stuff I didn't take. I drew you a picture of… sorry, I forgot something… I'll be back." He took the drawing, headed to our children's desk, and began to work.

About five minutes later, he returned and said, "Here it is again. I forgot to add something I knew you would like. See here, I added a picture of Jesus talking to the superhero so that guy would know Jesus is in charge." I responded, "The addition of Jesus to anything makes it extra special—just like you. I love it—and you. Thank you." "Grandma, can we hang it on the refrigerator? This way everyone can see Jesus is in charge." "What a perfect idea. Let's go put it up now."

God gives good gifts to us all the time, starting with His breath of life breathed into man to become a living being, giving us parents, siblings, friends, spouses, and families of our own—especially grandchildren. But the greatest gift was His Son, Jesus.

Thank You, LORD, for being willing to give Your life so freely for us, no strings attached, only a desire that we would freely come to You and accept Your gift as King of our lives. I pray our goal in life is to remain faithful as we lead others to the saving knowledge of Your sacrifice for us.

Luke 6:38: *Give, and it will be given to you: good measure, pressed down, shaken together, and running over, will be given to you. For with the same measure you measure it will be measured back to you.*

2 Corinthians 9:7: *Let each man give according as he has determined in his heart, not grudgingly or under compulsion, for God loves a cheerful giver.*

Proverbs 11:25: *The liberal soul shall be made fat. He who waters shall be watered also himself.*

July 26th
The Washing Machine

You know those times when you're in a hurry, so you put both small loads into one big load? I thought it was a great idea until I heard, "The washing machine is making a really funny sound, Grandma. Did you hear it do it?" I went back to the laundry room and checked the washer. By now it had stopped on its own, flashing ten minutes left to go. I looked inside the drum, which was full of water. "Grandma, can you fix it?" "I certainly will do what I can, but I am not a repair person." I tried restarting the machine, which seemed to work for about five minutes before stopping again. I tried the *spin only* to no avail. "Grandma, what are you going to do? There is so much water in there; how can you get rid of it?" Good question. I called a man from our church, also a repairman, to see how soon he could come—tomorrow afternoon. I booked him and started to ring out the entire load of clothes as best as I could, proceeding to put them in the different sinks to drain some more.

Tomorrow finally came. All morning long, I rang out the heavier clothes to help them keep dripping their excess water. By then, the good clothes were dry enough for the dryer, so I finished them off. When the doorbell finally rang that afternoon, the technician ran some diagnostics. I learned that a major part was plugged with dirt from the water, keeping the sensor from realizing it needed to drain the water. Unfortunately, this part needed to be ordered and would take about a week to come in. The only upside is that has been by now everything from the last load was dried, folded, and put away. A week later, the phone rang with wonderful news—the replacement part had arrived and was soon put in its new home.

I thought of how we try so many different things to make life satisfying, but nothing seems to work. When we accept Jesus, as our master technician, He doesn't need to run diagnostics or order parts, but is able to clean us up from our sins through our confession, burying them in the sea of His forgetfulness.

Thank You, LORD, for being the Great Technician Who can fix any problem. I pray we don't waste our lives on quick fixes but rather turn to You for a permanent fix that offers eternal life.

Jeremiah 30:17: *"For I will restore health to you, and I will heal you of your wounds," says Yahweh; "because they have called you an outcast, saying, 'It is Zion, whom no man seeks after.'"*

Psalm 147:3: *He heals the broken in heart, and binds up their wounds.*

Ephesians 3:20-21: *Now to him who is able to do exceedingly abundantly above all that we ask or think, according to the power that works in us, to him be the glory in the assembly and in Christ Jesus to all generations forever and ever. Amen.*

Priceless Moments

July 27th

Papa Bear

"I like your Baby Bear pajamas. Are they new, or is this just the first time I'm seeing you wear them?" "I've had them for a little while, but I usually wear the unicorn ones." "I see. You've got several different styles of unicorn pajamas, and I like them all. What made you decide to switch it up and wear these?" "Well, I had a bath last night, and I wished I had something different to wear to bed. As I was going through the pajamas in my drawer, I saw these again. I was very excited because my wish came true. It just felt good to be wearing something different for a change. And when I got up this morning, I was in no hurry to get dressed so I could wear them a little longer."

I thought a little bit and finally asked, "What makes this pair of pajamas so special to you?" "I remember seeing pictures of these in a paper that came in the newspaper. It showed a man wearing Papa Bear pajamas, a woman wearing Mama Bear, a girl in Sister Bear, a boy in Brother Bear, and a baby in Baby Bear." "Interestingly, I remember seeing those featured in an ad around Christmas time. I thought they were really cute. I went to get everyone in your family a matching set, but they sold out quickly, and none were left." "That's OK. But what makes these so special to me is imagining all of us in them." 'Yes, that would have been a lot of fun."

I thought about how God is our Papa Bear, fiercely protecting all us cubs when we call upon Him. Others should know we belong to Him because we wear our Baby Bears everywhere we go. We are also identified by our words, actions, places we visit, and compassion we show to others. We will be known as Christians by our love.

Thank You, LORD, for changing our lives and making us new creatures in You. I pray people can look at us and know we belong to You without having to question our behaviors.

2 Thessalonians 3:3*: But the Lord is faithful, who will establish you and guard you from the evil one.*

Deuteronomy 31:6*: Be strong and courageous. Don't be afraid or scared of them; for Yahweh your God himself is who goes with you. He will not fail you nor forsake you.*

1 Corinthians 10:13b*: God is faithful, who will not allow you to be tempted above what you are able, but will with the temptation also make the way of escape, that you may be able to endure it.*

July 28th
<u>*The Spillway*</u>

One day we were visiting a local dam and talked about going to look at the spillway. Soon I heard, "Grandma, what do you mean by going down to the spillway to feed the fish? I've never heard that word before." "A spillway is the most important part of the dam since it is designed to let a sudden rise or surge of flood water flowing into it from upstream flow over the dam and downstream to keep the dam from overflowing. In other words, when the water rises above this spillway, it is quickly able to flow over it to protect the bank of the dam." "Why don't they keep that water to use later since it seems most places are always in a drought?" "Excellent question. Many times, the excess water is diverted or sent to different places to be used for irrigation or to produce electricity at a hydropower plant. Water below the spillway has a high level of oxygen for the fish to survive."

"Cool. Can we ever see the fish go over the spillway?" "Depending on where the spillway is located in the dam wall, if there is six inches or more of water going over the spillway, young fish are usually the ones to go over the spillway. Chances of seeing them go over are better after a rain since this is the time fish become more active in looking for food." "Why did you say young fish? Is there a difference between young and old fish?" "In a

Priceless Moments

sense, yes. Landowners, lake owners, and dam owners can use a "parallel bar" barrier that is placed across the spillway to keep the adult grass carp fish, who like to leave during high spillway flows, from going over the spillway." "Is there any way to have a dam or pond without a spillway?" "Good thought. Many are designed with underground gates or valves that can be opened to also help deal with flood waters." "Neat. Can we go visit more dams and see how they build their spillways?" "Good idea, but we will need to talk to your parents."

Looking at all the water flowing over the spillway made me think of how the LORD's love flows to us in a never-ending stream. How fast and how much depends on the streams of prayers we send to Him.

Thank You, LORD; Your love is never ending. I pray we find You in every situation, looking beyond the never-ending disappointments and troubles to find peace and comfort by abiding in You.

Romans 5:5: *and hope doesn't disappoint us, because God's love has been poured into our hearts through the Holy Spirit who was given to us.*

1 John 3:1: *See how great a love the Father has given to us, that we should be called children of God! For this cause the world doesn't know us, because it didn't know him.*

1 John 4:16: *We know and have believed the love which God has for us. God is love, and he who remains in love remains in God, and God remains in him.*

Priceless Moments

July 29th
Filing Papers

The grandchildren arrived one morning, calling out, "Grandma, where are you? I don't see or hear you anywhere." "I'm in the office filing some paperwork." "Why are you doing that? Is it something you have to keep?" "As a matter of fact, it is paperwork for the next tax year. If I put it in the proper file folder, I'll know exactly where to find it next year." "Hey, that's some good thinking." "Thank you. It's one of the tricks I learned early on to keep organized and be able to pull together all the information needed to get taxes finished and filed in a timely manner." "What other kinds of things do you file?" "Things like newspaper clippings, health information, car repair, dentist visits, guarantee information." "Do you keep a folder for your van repairs, too?" "Good listening. I did put that thought together in my mind for the car and van. Actually, they each have their own folder. Also, I keep a running list on my phone of repairs, tire rotations, oil changes, new tires, and stuff like that, so if we're somewhere and I need it, I have it with me even when I can't check it at home." "Wow, that's a really good idea."

A few minutes passed, and she asked, "Can you help me make some folders? I would like to organize some papers I have in my room." "Sure, I'd be delighted to help you" "What all am I going to need?" "For starters, we can use one of the plastic storage boxes in the garage, so you can also keep them in one place. Next, I'll get some of our extra file folders out of the closet. You need to think of the things you want to file so you can write their names on the tops of the folders. Things can be changed as needed, thrown away, and new folders created. Why don't you make a list of file folder names, and I'll go get the storage box and the file folders ready for our project. Next time we're at your house, you can start your own filing system."

Once we become Christians, we should rethink our filing system. File away unacceptable behaviors and habits and replace them

Priceless Moments

with God-pleasing activities. Be selective in your activities with non-Christian friends, but never stop praying for them.

Thank You, LORD, for providing a way to leave the old life behind. I pray we TOTALLY clean house of our sinful past, becoming such profoundly changed new creatures that all who encounter us desire the same.

Ephesians 4:22-24: *You were taught, with regard to your former way of life, to put off your old self, which is being corrupted but its deceitful desires; to be made new in the attitude of your minds; and to put on the new self, created to be like God in true righteousness and holiness. NIV*

Isaiah 43:18: *Don't remember the former things, and don't consider the things of old.*

Philippians 3:13, 14: *Brothers, I don't regard myself as yet having taken hold, but one thing I do: forgetting the things which are behind, and stretching forward to the things which are before, I press on toward the goal for the prize of the high calling of God in Christ Jesus.*

July 30th
<u>For Every Child</u>

"Oh, Grandma, we had the most wonderful lesson last Sunday in children's church. We learned that Jesus was crucified for every child, even the one who is mean and hits people and never has anything nice to say to anybody." "Wow, can you tell me more? This sounds very interesting?" "They told us Jesus showed respect to these people by establishing rules to follow, responding to their behavior in a loving manner, recognizing their need, and responding with friendship. They said these are ways to treat a bully in a way that will help support them in making a change in their behavior. The saying is "recognize, respond, and report," then get an adult to teach them how to be appropriate through friendship and how to control their anger. The most important thing we are to remember is not to bully anyone in return, and not to watch someone bullying another person. We are to show them a positive way to treat others, including them in activities and showing them how we treat each other in a way that honors Jesus."

I was surprised to realize she had retained so much information. "Do you ever see anyone being bullied?" "No, the girls I'm friends with are nice to each other. But I did hear one of the girls say she was bullied by a boy in an older class." "Have you ever been bullied?" "No. I pray every day that Jesus will take care of me and my friends to keep us safe as well as to help me think and do my best to make Him proud of me." "You just made my heart leap for joy at realizing how Jesus would react to you praying for the behavior of others, good or bad. That is a sign of a really good friend. I hope they realize what a loving and caring young lady you are growing up to be. I want you to know just how proud you make me feel to see you putting Jesus first in your life."

God tells us that when our sins are forgiven, He takes them and sends them very far away, burying them in the sea of His forgetfulness (**Micah 7:19**), never to be brought up again to cause problems in our relationship but to have it restored.

I'm reminded of how many opportunities God provides for us to seek forgiveness for our sins, no matter how great or small. We must realize it is up to us to initiate calling out to Him to obtain that forgiveness.

Thank You, LORD, for Your continual presence in our lives. I pray we keep our hearts and minds clear daily of any potential dislike of others since it can develop into hate depending on which "emotion" we feed.

Psalm 51:2: *Wash me thoroughly from my iniquity. Cleanse me from my sin.*

Priceless Moments

Ephesians 4:32: *And be kind to one another, tender hearted, forgiving each other, just as God also in Christ forgave you.*

1 John 1:9: *If we confess our sins, he is faithful and righteous to forgive us the sins, and to cleanse us from all unrighteousness.*

July 31ˢᵗ
<u>Details, Please</u>

"Grandma, are we going there sometime?" "Going where, honey?" "You know, there?" "I'm sorry, sweet child, but I have no idea where 'there' is. Can you tell me something about this place? We can play a game called 'twenty questions' to see if we can figure out if we are going 'there' sometime. How does that sound to you?" "It sounds like fun." "OK. First question: have you been there before?" "Yes." "Is it close to here or far away?" "I don't know because I don't drive." "Fair enough. Was I there with you?" "No." "Was it a long time ago or just recently?" "It wasn't too long ago. I was still in school." Yes. Narrowed down to one year. "Did you go by airplane, train, bus, or RV?" "We were in an airplane, then in a rented van." Ah, spring break vacation. "What kinds of things did you do?" "We went to the beach and played in the sand, built sandcastles, and swam in the ocean. We visited some kind of park and rode rides." "Did you see anyone you knew?" "Yes, Auntie and her family also took an airplane to come and meet us." Ah, I can feel success is close to solving the mystery of "there." Disneyland!...

At this point, a strange look crossed her face. I hesitated to ask, but here it goes. "What's on your mind, honey?" "I'm not sure if one of my answers is correct." Oh, dear. Here we go again. "Which one are you questioning?" "Now that I think about it, they didn't fly, they drove." OK, now where else has she been? "Did you see anyone else there?" "Yes, we saw the other Papa and Grandma." "Are you sure you saw them?" "Yes, we stayed with them."

Priceless Moments

BINGO. "Are you talking about when you went to Hilton Head?" "Oh, yes, Grandma, that's it. I just couldn't think of its name. The more you asked me questions, the more I began to remember things about the trip. Thank you for helping me to remember." "You're welcome."

I wonder how many times we approach God with the twenty questions mentality. This approach will never help us since God knows what we need before we do.

Thank You, LORD, that no situation is too difficult for You. I pray the first thing we do is reach out to You in a forthright manner about what is truly on our hearts and minds.

Psalm 34:4: *I sought Yahweh, and he answered me, and delivered me from all my fears.*

Jeremiah 33:3: *Call to me, and I will answer you, and will show you great and difficult things, which you don't know.*

Matthew 7:7-8: *Ask, and it will be given you. Seek, and you will find. Knock, and it will be opened for you. For everyone who asks receives. He who seeks finds. To him who knocks it will be opened.*

Priceless Moments

Priceless Moments

August

*All your children
will be taught by Yahweh,
and your children's peace
will be great.*

Isaish. 54:13

August 1ST
I'm Not Bad

"Grandma, that lady just said I'm a bad little boy. I got upset with her and told her I'm not bad; I just have bad behavior at times. She just looked at me, her mouth dropped open, then she walked away." "Oh, dear. What happened to make her say such a thing?" A sheepish look crossed his face as it dropped down to his chest. "I said to her, 'Oh. You crossed in front of me and almost made me fall.' Then she said, 'You shouldn't have walked in front of me.' I told her, 'I was just standing here like my grandma asked.' What did I do that was wrong? I listened to you and stood there minding my own business when she walked into me." As I was about to answer him, a female stranger approached us. I couldn't discern the reason for her coming our way, but our grandson hid behind me—then I knew the "why."

The woman stopped. She looked at both of us, so I said, "Hello. May I help you?" She stood there a moment, then said, "Does he belong to you?" "Yes, he's my grandson. Can I help you?" Now a sheepish look crossed her face as she lowered her head. "I'm sorry. I said some unkind things to your grandson a moment ago. As I was walking away and reflecting on what I thought was his rudeness towards me, I realized I was the one who caused the incident by walking into him. I was totally out of line to accuse him of being bad. It was his response that shook me to the core. I realized people are generally kind, but we all have our moments of bad behavior. He taught me a lesson I will never forget." Then she knelt down and addressed him, saying, "I'm sorry I hurt your feelings. Please forgive me for being rude to you." He came out from behind me and said, "OK, I forgive you, but you should ask Jesus to forgive you, too." Out of the mouth of babes.

This incident often replays in my mind. Many times, we are rude to Jesus because of our own shortcomings. May we have the internal fortitude to realize our shortcomings and ask for forgiveness.

Thank You, LORD, for a conscience to make us aware of our actions. I pray we are attuned to listening to Your voice and seek forgiveness from you and anyone else we may have offended in the process.

Romans 12:2*: Don't be conformed to this world, but be transformed by the renewing of your mind, so that you may prove what is the good, well-pleasing, and perfect will of God.*

Philippians 4:6-7*: In nothing be anxious, but in everything, by prayer and petition with thanksgiving, let your requests be made known to God. And the peace of God, which surpasses all understanding, will guard your hearts and your thoughts in Christ Jesus*

Lamentations 3:22-23*: It is because of Yahweh's loving kindnesses that we are not consumed, because his compassion doesn't fail. They are new every morning. Great is your faithfulness.*

August 2nd
I Do It Myself

Our grandchildren enjoy playing with the larger Lego-style building blocks. We often talked about keeping the items balanced so they would be able to remain upright throughout the building process. One particular day, while enjoying one of our building projects, our granddaughter said she was going to build a masterpiece. Initially, all was going well. She was keeping the building balanced for a while, but then got her mind off the total picture by focusing on its height instead of its balance. The masterpiece was becoming lopsided, creating problems keeping it upright. Several times I offered to help her rebalance the project, but she either ignored me or declined. The last time I asked, she replied in exasperation, "I DO IT MYSELF." When she couldn't hold it up any longer and still keep building, she said, "Grandma, can you please help me? I'm sorry I didn't let you help sooner." When she let go for me to help, the "masterpiece" went crashing down. She sobbed and ran into my arms to be comforted. After she regained control of her emotions and was able to play again, we worked together to rebuild her "masterpiece." Oh, of course, she asked me to "take a picture" so she could show her parents and her brother—which we did.

I was reminded of how we respond to God while doing one of our own projects. We have a picture in our minds of what we would like to do—of course, with God's guidance. But, as we work through the project, following all of God's leading, we get sidetracked, lose our focus on the Master Creator, and decide to wing it instead. Often God offers to lend a hand, but our attitude of *I've got this* gets in the way of completing our perfect masterpiece. After things come crashing down around us, we, too, run to God for comfort and affirmation. After we make things right with God, we, too, can start over to make the perfect masterpiece, maybe a little different from our original design yet good in its own right. And, of course, take a picture—even if only in our minds—of the wonderful things we can accomplish when we do it all together with God.

Thank You, LORD, for being there to help us pick up the pieces of our masterpiece and still make something beautiful with Your creative hand guiding the process. I pray we keep our eyes fixed on You throughout our lives to keep all areas of our lives balanced within Your will.

Jeremiah 18:1-4: *The word which came to Jeremiah from Yahweh, saying, "Arise, and go down to the potter's house, and there I will cause you to hear my words." Then I went down to the potter's house, and behold, he was making something on the wheels. When the vessel that he made of the clay was marred in*

the hand of the potter, he made it again another vessel, as seemed good to the potter to make it.
Psalm 139:14: *I will give thanks to you, for I am fearfully and wonderfully made. Your works are wonderful. My soul knows that very well.*
Philippians 4:13: *I can do all things through Christ, who strengthens me.*

August 3rd
The Clocks, Bells and Chimes

We have many different items in our house that ding, clang, and make noise. As the grandchildren were growing and becoming aware of the different sounds, they would look at or in the direction of the "sounding" item. The items in particular that caught their attention are the dining room clock, the living room anniversary clock, and the doorbell. The more the grandchildren focused on these, the more it piqued the interest of my husband and me. We watched the kids jerk their heads in the proper direction as the "chosen" item resounded throughout its location. Anything from clapping, smiling, a look of surprise, or running to watch the item occurred each time. Day after day, these three things peaked everyone's interest, but we could not come up with a reason why.

One day the clock in the dining room had just chimed when the doorbell rang, and then the anniversary clock rang. Four of us looked at each other, very aware of them all ringing back-to-back. Papa said, "It can't be, but I think it's so." I looked at him and said, "That's it. You're right. How long has this mystery haunted us—until now?" Our granddaughter said, "Did you hear that? I think I know the answer to the 'mystery' we keep talking about." Our grandson chimed in, "Me too. I know the answer." We all started laughing, saying together, "They all play the same tune." I went outside and rang the doorbell. Sure enough, it was the same tune played by all three items. We laughed so hard since none of us had realized it over all these months, even though we sensed a connection between them.

I thought of how our LORD uses many different things to get our attention. It's awesome to finally understand His leading to get us headed in the direction that will bring honor to His name.

Thank You, LORD, for not giving up on us when we are confused. I pray we continue searching for answers as You give us clarity in life's direction.

Psalm 32:8: *I will instruct you and teach you in the way which you shall go. I will counsel you with my eye on you.*

Proverbs 16:9: *A man's heart plans his course, but Yahweh directs his steps.*

Jeremiah 1:7-8: *But Yahweh said to me, "Don't say, 'I am a child;' for you must go to whomever I send you, and you must say whatever I command you. Don't be afraid because of them, for I am with you to rescue you," says Yahweh.*

August 4th
Let's Do Devotions

"Grandma, what is your favorite thing to do with us?" I thought, "Well, that's a loaded question, because I adore all the grandchildren and love doing what they like to do." But I knew I had to pick one thing. I responded, "My favorite thing is doing devotions with you." Of course, the proverbial "why" must be asked, so I said, "Because I know how much you enjoy the stories, the videos, songs, and coloring activities. You always want to do more than we have time to do." "You're right, Grandma, that is one of our most favorite activities ever, too." "What is your favorite thing to do with me?" "I like that you have us work through reading the Bible and doing the Bible app. We get to learn about all of them before we start over again. I like it when we start by putting on the full armor of God. We learned about it in preschool. We even learned about the fruits of the spirit, like love, joy, peace, patience, kindness, goodness, faithfulness, gentleness, and self-control. **Galatians 5:22**."

"Wow, I'm really impressed with how much you have learned about the Bible." "I love learning about God because He takes care of us all the time." "What kinds of things should we remember to do every day?" "We should pray for family, friends, enemies, our churches, and those in leadership, whether or not we agree with them." "Yes, young man, you are spot on with the way God wants us to live. Daily devotions keep us closer to God and give us less of a chance to stray from God or to have our thoughts influenced by Satan's demons or others he has already led astray. Friends are usually the people he starts with, so be careful what you listen to from them. Then always pray about your decisions to ensure they line up with God's will for your life."

I thought about the spiritual training our grandchildren were getting between home and the Christian school. It is important to train or teach the youngsters BEFORE they are influenced by the "world," which teaches them to question and hate God, and to pray for them daily and when God brings them to mind.

Thank You, LORD, for providing Scripture to guide us through life. I pray we follow Your Word, learning to bring our thoughts into agreement with Your roadmap for our lives.

***Psalm 1:2**: but his delight is in Yahweh's law. On his law he meditates day and night*

***Romans 15:4**: For whatever things were written before were written for our learning, that through perseverance and through encouragement of the Scriptures we might have hope.*

***2 Timothy 3:16-17**: Every Scripture is God-breathed and profitable for teaching, for reproof, for correction, and for* *instruction in righteousness, that each person who belongs to God may be complete, thoroughly equipped for every good work.*

August 5th
The Hot Tub

My husband and I have always talked about getting a hot tub, but we have never committed to doing it. When all the little ones were present, we were asked, "Papa and Grandma, when are we going to get a hot tub? There is plenty of room for one on the patio. And we promise to see that it gets used as often as we can." Ah, spoken like miniature adults. I wonder whom they've heard talking. We pulled out some information we'd collected and shared it with the adult kids and grandkids. The adult children were very serious in their selections. "I like this one because…" "No, I think this is better because…" "But, this one offers…" "I'm looking at the options. There definitely should be a cover to keep the heat in. That way, it won't take as long to heat up each time." Not one of them chose the same product.

Meanwhile, the grandkids were looking at the pictures. "Oh, I like this one because it's blue." "This one looks like the colors swirl in it." "True, but this one has lots of jets. I'll bet we can move them around to the point where we want them to be." "I don't care about the color. I think this one is too small. We couldn't all be in it at the same time." "Hey, did you see this one has some cool seats in it? Enough for all of us." But the best response of them all was, "All the best hotels have this kind with lots of seats, jets, and a thermometer to be sure it is hot enough. Oh, and it has a cover, too. Well, it has to be this one because this is the best hotel I've ever been to."

It is amazing how each generation has such varied opinions. And the little ones are not keeping up with the Joneses; they've stepped up to hotels. When did we decide all the amenities were necessary in order to be satisfied with your purchase.

Thank You, LORD, for not requiring us to keep up with the Joneses. I pray our material needs are based on what You desire us to have. The only way we will discern this is to seek Your will through prayer.

Job 8:7: *Though your beginning was small, yet your latter end would greatly increase.*

Proverbs 24:14: *Know also that wisdom is like honey for you: If you find it, there is a future hope for you, and your hope will not be cut off. NIV*

Jeremiah 29:11: *"For I know the thoughts that I think toward you," says Yahweh, "thoughts of peace, and not of evil, to give you hope and a future."*

August 6th
Let's Pray for Peace

"According to the Bible, we are to pray for the peace and protection of Jerusalem. Grandma, why is that an important thing for us to do?" "Well, honey, from the time Jesus was born and grew up, He was not accepted as their long-awaited Messiah. They were looking for a military king to free them from the Roman government, but instead they got a preacher who became their suffering servant. So they continued to look for someone who would fit their perception of a Messiah. All the while, Jerusalem has experienced very little peace across history." "Why have they not had peace?" "Satan hates God and His people so much that he stirs up hatred towards them at every opportunity he gets. Our prayers are a way of seeking God's heart and favor toward all men. The apostle Paul said we should pray for those individuals we dislike since it is part of our responsibility as Christians. This type of prayer brings about peace and helps His people to do well in living a peaceful life."

After a few minutes, the following question popped out of his mouth: "So I'm to pray for people I like as well as those I don't like, right? Could you give me an example?" "Sure. One thing that is very important in our world today is people talking badly about our political leaders. The Bible tells us in **Romans 13:1**: *"Everyone must submit himself to the governing authorities, for there is no authority except that which God has established. The authorities that exist have been established by God."* Therefore, God chooses good and bad leaders as a way of waking us up and leading us back to Him. He also commands us to pray for ALL of them." "What can we do to help?" "We need to pray for the enemies' plans to be unsuccessful but for God's perfect plan to be fulfilled. Also, we need to pray for the Jewish people to recognize and accept Jesus as LORD and Savior, their Messiah, so they can take the lead in helping others find Jesus as well."

This is a good reminder for us to reach out to our brothers and sisters through prayer. We need to realize we're all the same underneath our outer shells of different faces, figures, and races, but we are all still children of God. What makes us "not the same" is our personal relationship with Jesus Christ.

Thank You, LORD, for making all men and women equal in Your eyes. I pray we all feel the need to turn to You and bring our family and friends to the saving knowledge of Jesus Christ.

***Psalm 122:6**: Pray for the peace of Jerusalem. Those who love you will prosper.*

***Philippians 4:6-7**: In nothing be anxious, but in everything, by prayer and petition with thanksgiving, let your requests be made known to God. And the peace of God, which surpasses all understanding, will guard your hearts and your thoughts in Christ Jesus.*

John 10:10*: The thief only comes to steal, kill, and destroy. I came that they may have life, and may have it abundantly.*

August 7th

<u>*Lighthouses*</u>

One of the things Papa likes to collect are lighthouses. There are lighthouses all around every room of our house. Our grandchildren like looking at them and asking, "Grandma, why does Papa like lighthouses? He has them everywhere: in calendars, wall hangings, pictures, ornaments, even on the tablecloth." I said, "The answer is very interesting. Lighthouses, built in dangerous places overlooking the sea, are very tall and have foghorns and bright lights shining day and night. The purpose of a lighthouse, a landmark for boats or ships, is for ship captains to watch it as a guide to come into and out of harbors, as well as to warn boats of dangerous areas like rocky coastlines or shallow areas." "Are there any other things they can use to guide them in the water?" "Good question, honey. Buoys, radar beacons, nautical charts or maps, and now GPS also provide assistance to keep mariners, seafarers, or people out on the water, safe. Actually, today is National Lighthouse Day."

"How did Papa get interested in lighthouses?" "Papa served for four years in the United States Navy after high school. He said, "Being a big destroyer ship and being chased by the enemy made his faith stronger. I knew I had to rely on God for my safety as well as that of my fellow crew members. I always thought about a song that had a lighthouse in it whose last phrase was, 'If it wasn't for the Lighthouse, where would this ship be?' I knew I had to rely on the best Lighthouse ever." "What is the best lighthouse ever?" "Papa was calling Jesus our earthly Lighthouse throughout life because many things in this world are dark." "Like Satan, right?" "Exactly. We can follow Jesus as He guides us day and night through the rough times in our lives because He stands firm, just like the lighthouses held steady by anchors placed deep in solid rock to hold them up when hit by strong wind and waves."

Jesus is our lighthouse, faithfully standing firm and flashing His warning light to get our attention, to avoid danger, or to come this way to follow Him. He is always on duty, so it is up to us to be watching for His light.

Thank You, for being our faithful Guide throughout the challenges in our lives. I pray we keep our eyes fixed on the Lighthouse so we can travel through the pitfalls and joys of life with confidence in Your leading.

John 8:12: *Again, therefore, Jesus spoke to them, saying, "I am the light of the world. He who follows me will not walk in the darkness, but will have the light of life."*

Psalm 43:3: *Oh, send out your light and your truth. Let them lead me. Let them bring me to your holy hill, to your tents.*

Revelation 21:23: *The city has no need for the sun or moon to shine, for the very glory of God illuminated it, and its lamp is the Lamb.*

August 8th

<u>The Cookie Jar</u>

We have a cupcake-shaped cookie jar sitting on the refrigerator. Little eyes check it out every time they come in the kitchen. Curiosity finally got the best of our grandson, so he asked, "Grandma, what do you keep in that cupcake up there? (pointing up) I never saw you take it down. Are there cupcakes in it?" I looked and smiled. "Do you think we should take it down and have a look inside?" His face lit up with anticipation: "Yes, we should do that—now." Again, I smiled, reached up, and took down the cupcake. I asked, "Do you really want to see the treasure inside?" "Oh, Grandma, please. Can you hurry? I can't wait to see all those, uh, cupcakes."

Drum roll, please… As I slowly removed the lid, he got down to get a peek inside before it was completely removed. Consternation crossed his face as he said, "What are those?" Again, I smiled and said, "This is where Papa keeps his matchbook collection. He collected them from around the world while he was in the Navy. Uncle Sam, a nickname for our government, gave him a boat ride on a big ship around the world. On those trips, he liked the unique designs on the ones from overseas, so he started collecting them." His disappointment changed to interest as he examined the different styles.

I couldn't help but think of how our Christian lifestyle must look to non-Christians. Their taking a peek at what we do and where we go hopefully encourages them to take a full-on look at our daily lives. When we portray Jesus accurately, the seeker will come to find and accept Jesus for themselves.

Thank You, LORD, for Christians not only looking different but also showing a different lifestyle, one that should entice and draw others to Your people. I pray we embrace the uniqueness of Christian individuals as a means of reaching more people for You.

John 15:19: *If you were of the world, the world would love its own. But because you are not of the world, since I chose you out of the world, therefore the world hates you.*

Romans 12:2: *Don't be conformed to this world, but be transformed by the renewing of your mind, so that you may prove what is the good, well-pleasing, and perfect will of God.*

Proverbs 3:1-6: *My son, don't forget my teaching; but let your heart keep my commandments: for they will add to you length of days, years of life, and peace. Don't let kindness and truth forsake you. Bind them around your neck. Write them on the tablet of your heart. So you will find favor, and good understanding in the sight of God and man. Trust in Yahweh with all your heart, and don't lean on your own understanding. In all your ways acknowledge him, and he will make your paths straight.*

August 9th
What's an Interview?

"Grandma, I heard one of the teachers at school talking about going for an interview. What's an interview? I didn't want to ask her because I didn't want her to think I was listening, so I thought I'd ask you." "No problem. An interview is when you have a conversation with someone. Usually, one person will ask questions for another person to answer. The one asking the questions is called the "interviewer," and the person answering questions is called an "interviewee." She politely interrupted, "Excuse me, but why do they do this back-and-forth stuff?" "Good question. A person may be looking for a job, so the potential employer wants to find out this person's skills, work experience, and goals to determine if they are the right one for the job. Also, the one looking for a job can learn if this company would be a good fit for them."

"Another reason for an interview is to find out what a political candidate would hope to achieve if elected to office; to learn more about a writer or famous person; to obtain information for a newspaper article or TV show; or for the police to find out what an observer or suspect knows about something they are investigating." A moment of silence was broken when our granddaughter asked, "Do you think I will ever be interviewed?" I looked her in the eyes and said, "If your school has a newsletter or newspaper, you may be asked a few questions to get your opinion on the question of the day. When you are older and want a job, I'm sure you will be interviewed. Only God knows the real answer to your question. Your most important interview will be when you stand before God someday."

Wow, what a thought to realize we may be "interviewed" by God when we reach the pearly gates. Fortunately, Jesus will be there to tell His Father that we are one of His own and that our admission or acceptance into heaven is secure. We had already answered the "interview question," "Do you believe in Me?" "YES."

Thank You, LORD, for being there to bear witness of Yourself when we were seeking a "better position" in life. I pray that as people observe our lives, they find us worthy of "interviewing" us about our beliefs and changed lives.

Philippians 4:19: My God will supply every need of yours according to his riches in glory in Christ Jesus.

Psalm 84:11: For Yahweh God is a sun and a shield. Yahweh will give grace and glory. He withholds no good thing from those who walk blamelessly.

Revelation 3:8: I know your works (behold, I have set before you an open door, which no one can shut), that you have a little power, and kept my word, and didn't deny my name.

August 10th
Ants On a Log

"Grandma, can we have ants on a log for a snack?" I asked, "You want what? I've never heard of eating ants on a log. I can't imagine going out and finding a log that you can eat as well as ants to put on it. Can you tell me how we're going to do that?" "Oh, my, silly Grandma. Do you really not know what that is, or are you giving us a hard time?" I laughed and said, "I've never heard of ants on a log for snacking. Please enlighten me. What is it? If it's healthy, you can have it for a snack." "It's OK. We use stuff from the kitchen. We need you to get us some plates, please."

Priceless Moments

They talked among themselves, apparently dividing up the items to collect, bringing a variety of stuff and putting it on the counter.

"OK. This is what we do. We each get a long piece of celery and wash it, drying it off with a paper towel. The knife is used to spread peanut butter on the celery. The raisins are put on top. Last of all, we get to eat it." I looked at the assembled creation in front of me and thought, "Yummm." "Come on, Grandma, don't just look at it; try it." Without hesitation, I ate the whole thing, licking my fingers at the end so as not to waste any of the goodness. I commented, "I am so relieved to know there are different kinds of ants and logs available. Well, we'll have to do this again sometime." They just giggled and put their own ants on their logs.

Sometimes, my overactive imagination creates lots of giggles for the kids. But I wonder how often we make God laugh, frown, or get really upset with us over the things we say and do. I'm sure He has a sense of humor because He made me and a lot of others like me who enjoy bringing a smile to people's faces.

Thank You, LORD, for levity, which, when used appropriately, can lighten a somber mood or break the ice in a tense situation. I pray You give us insight and discretion in all situations when using this tool.

2 Corinthians 1:17: *When I therefore was thus determined, did I show fickleness? Or the things that I purpose, do I purpose according to the flesh, that with me there should be the "Yes, yes" and the "No, no?"*

Ephesians 5:4: *Nor should there be obscenity, foolish talk of coarse joking, which are out of place, but rather thanksgiving. NIV*

1 Thessalonians 5:16-18: *Always rejoice. Pray without ceasing. In everything give thanks, for this is the will of God in Christ Jesus toward you.*

Priceless Moments

August 11th
Hey, Mister, That's Bad For You

We were walking down the street when the kids said, "Eewh, what's that smell? It smells like something died. It really hurts my nose and burns my lungs." We looked around to see a man walking behind us. He was smoking a cigar. Our granddaughter turned around and said, "Hey, mister, that's bad for you. Don't you know it can cause cancer and make you cough a lot, besides making your breath and clothes stink?" I was horrified and also concerned about how he would respond to her chastisement. He stopped and just stared at us—all the while I was praying for our safety. Before I could steer us away from the situation, she continued, "Jesus can help you quit that nasty stuff. You just need to ask Him into your heart and then ask Him to take away your bad habit."

The man threw down his cigar and stomped it out before walking up close to us. He asked, "May I address her for a moment?" He was being very nice about it, and I felt at peace with him being there, so I said OK. He knelt down in front of her and said, "Little girl, thank you for talking to me." His voice was gentle, and his manner was respectful. "I remember being young once and making the same comments about adults around me who were smoking. I had forgotten that experience until now. I picked up the habit because my friends started to smoke and dared me to smoke too. I never really thought about the problems smoking could cause me, but when you pointed out a few to me, it really made me think. Also, I want to apologize for hurting your nose and lungs. I promise you I will quit and commit my life to Jesus. I learned about him as a boy before I ran with a wild crowd. Please keep your faith and commitment to Jesus." She gave him a hug before he walked away.

I remember experiencing the same sense of burning eyes, lungs, and nose around cigarette smoke. I've shared this with them, now realizing just how much she has absorbed. This situation reminded me of how important it is to teach them young about Jesus, not expecting them to learn about it as adults—when it might be too late.

Thank You, LORD, for Your protection in precarious situations and for recalling Your teachings. I pray this man—and others challenged to seek You—follow through to confess and accept Your forgiveness and grace.

Proverbs 22:6: *Train up a child in the way he should go, and when he is old he will not depart from it.*

Isaiah 54:13: *All your children will be taught by Yahweh; and your children's peace will be great.*

Proverbs 1:8-9: *My son, listen to your father's instruction, and don't forsake your mother's teaching: for they will be a garland to grace your head, and chains around your neck.*

August 12th

<u>The Empty Bottle</u>

Our young granddaughter has been enjoying the novelty of having four front teeth, granting her the ability to bite off and chew a variety of foods. Before each rendezvous with her new-found passion for food, she enjoys a bottle of milk. Today was no different. As I was putting a bib on her, she became impatient, grabbing the bottle before I could lay her back in my arms. She sucked it away with great passion until it was drained—good to the last drop. But the bottle may have been finished, but she wasn't. She insisted on keeping the bottle in her mouth—sucking air—while I was trying to remove it from her mouth and hands. I succeeded in gaining possession of the bottle while she wailed. Her cousins came rushing to her rescue, saying, "Grandma, what are you doing to her? Why is she crying so hard?" "Well, I was

Priceless Moments

feeding her a bottle. When the milk ran out before she was ready to stop drinking, she continued to try to drink, but I had to stop her before she filled her belly with air and got a tummy ache."

They thought about my response and then replied, "Oh, baby, please don't cry. Grandma was just trying to keep you from getting sick. She loves you so much and only wants what's best for you. If you need it, she can get you some more milk." I had to smile at their gentle manner and amount of concern for her. I suggested, "Why don't we take her out to get some solid food? She has cheese, vegetable soup, strawberries, bananas, and yogurt to eat." "Oh, boy, can we help feed her?" "Of course, both she and I would appreciate your help." As we walked toward the highchair, she got excited as she understood what it meant—solid food.

I thought of how we sometimes respond to God when we feel He hasn't answered our prayers and petitions by the time we thought He should have, just like the baby. Once another or better option becomes available, we are more satisfied with the outcome.

Thank you, LORD, for timing that is always spot on and in our best interests. I pray we are patient enough to wait for Your perfect timing to send us what You feel is best.

Psalm 27:14: *Wait for Yahweh. Be strong, and let your heart take courage. Yes, wait for Yahweh.*

Isaiah 40:31: *but those who wait for Yahweh will renew their strength. They will mount up with wings like eagles. They will run, and not be weary. They will walk, and not faint.*

Lamentations 3:25: *Yahweh is good to those who wait for him, to the soul who seeks him.*

Priceless Moments

August 13th
Please, Don't Yell At Me

When I was picking up our granddaughter from school one day, I heard, "Please don't yell at me. I didn't do it, and I don't know who did. Just leave me alone." She came running around the corner of the school building in tears. "Oh, Grandma, my friend accused me of taking her special pen, but I didn't do it. I know stealing is wrong. Besides, I wouldn't do that to her because she's my friend. What should I do?" "Let's go back to your classroom and help her look for it, OK? By doing this, it shows you are truly her friend. And hopefully we can find the pen to prove you wouldn't steal from her." We headed back to the classroom.

As we walked into the classroom, she took a deep breath and said, "Hi. We came back to help you look for your pen. When did you have it last?" An angry voice responded, "Over at the art table, but I already looked there." I suggested we look at ourselves and move everything just to be sure. Every piece of paper was moved. "Oh, look, Grandma. Here it is, at the bottom of this pile of papers." She picked up the pen and ran over to her friend. "Look what we found over there under a pile of papers on the art table." Her friend's mouth dropped open as she looked up. "I'm so sorry I blamed you. I must have forgotten to pick it up when we were done with our project." Our granddaughter gave her a hug, saying, "It's OK. I prayed for Jesus to help us find it, and He did."

I was impressed that she prayed for guidance to help her friend. What a good reminder that we need to pray first and then listen for Your still small voice for guidance, confident that You will reply. A. W. Tozer said, "It's the nature of God to speak." He wants to give us clear responses so we know His will for us in every situation.

Thank You, LORD, for not yelling at us. I pray we stay tuned in, listen carefully to Your leading, and respond to Your conviction of our wrongdoings or a job well done.

Ephesians 4:31-32: *Let all bitterness, wrath, anger, outcry, and slander be put away from you, with all malice. And be kind to one another, tender hearted, forgiving each other, just as God also in Christ forgave you.*

1 Kings 19:12: *After the earthquake a fire passed; but Yahweh was not in the fire. After the fire, there was a still small voice.*

1 Corinthians 6:17: *But he who unites himself with the LORD is one with Him in spirit. NIV*

August 14th
Let's Have Pizza

"What would you like for supper? I have a coup…." "Pizza, pizza, let's have pizza. We want Papa's favorite pizza with double pineapple and ham. That's the only kind of pizza we really like anymore." To see if they were listening or dreaming of pizza now, I asked, "If you can tell me how many French fries it takes to circle the earth, then we'll have pizza." Response, "What did you say? How would we know the answer?" I told them, "I was just checking to see if you were listening. And the answer is, drum roll please (they obliged) 393,779,549." "Really, who would know that answer and who would really care." My response was, "There are people with lots of time on their hands who think up these questions and proceed to find an answer.

We ordered the "pizza of choice" and waited for it to be delivered. "Grandma, what other silly facts do you know about food? You can tell us while we wait for the pizza." "OK, here it goes. Firsts of different foods: pizza in 1889, sandwich in 1760, potato chips in 1853, hot dogs in 1871, hot dog buns in 1904, ice cream cones in 1994. The first of these restaurants, Mc Donald's, opened in 1940; Kentucky Fried Chicken in 1952; Denny's was established as

Priceless Moments

Danny's Donuts in 1953; Burger King in 1954; Pizza Hut in 1958; Taco Bell in 1962; Arby's in 1964; and Wendy's in 1969. The biggest pizza was 122'8" in 1990; the longest banana split was 4.55 miles long in 1988; the biggest donut 16' across and 16' high in 1993; the largest cookie contained over 3 million chocolate chips was 1001 square feet in 1993." Ding-dong, saved by the bell.

We are fascinated by food of any size, shape, or color. Too bad people do not have the same desire to learn more about the Bible, it's firsts, biggest, and best… There is so much fascinating information within its covers to keep us reading day and night.

Thank You, LORD, for Your daily provisions of grace and mercy. I pray we never lose sight of Your desire to provide for us physically and spiritually, but we have to make the first move to seek Your face.

Job 38:41: Who provides for the raven his prey, when his young ones cry to God, and wander for lack of food?

2 Corinthians 9:8: And God is able to make all grace abound to you, that you, always having all sufficiency in everything, may abound to every good work.

2 Peter 1:3: seeing that his divine power has granted to us all things that pertain to life and godliness, through the knowledge of him who called us by his own glory and virtue,

August 15th
Full Armor Of God

"Grandma, can we say the Full Armor of God again today? I really like to say it, but I have a lot of questions." "OK, we can certainly say it again after we answer your questions. What would you like to know?" "Well, the only picture I've seen of someone wearing armor is Goliath. What are all of those pieces used for, and what do they mean to us?" "Excellent questions. We can talk about each piece separately. First, the belt of truth: The Roman soldiers had to wear a belt for a place to put their weapons close to their bodies, just as we should keep God's Word to enable us to handle whatever comes our way. Second, a breastplate of righteousness: The soldiers wore the breastplate to protect their vital organs, like the heart and lungs, and to prevent being killed. Just like righteousness, or right living, knowledge of God's Word can help us discern or understand good from evil, helping us make better choices in line with His Word. Third, sandals of the gospel of peace: Soldiers protected their feet by wearing sandals. Sandals help us walk to take the good news of Jesus to all different places at all times, even through spiritual battles. Fourth, shield of faith: Soldiers soaked their shields before battle to protect them from flaming arrows. Strapped to their arms, they could deflect arrows and knock over enemies with force. Thus, our faith, an unstoppable force, can protect and guard us as we fight back against Satan. Fifth, the helmet of salvation: Soldiers wore helmets to protect their heads from direct attacks from enemy arrows, rocks, or direct blows. For us, the helmet can keep out bad thoughts or mind pictures, allowing truth from God to fill our minds instead. Lastly, the sword of the Spirit, or the Word of God, is our only offensive weapon. Soldiers used their swords to kill their enemies or cut through just about anything in their way. We need to read and study our Bible to know right from wrong, seek God's direction for our lives, defend what we believe, and be prepared to witness as well as answer questions from those seeking to know more about God. The Bible is our most important weapon against Satan."

We need to start every morning by putting on the full armor of God to prevent the enemy from making an inroad into and taking over our lives. We need to keep our faith rooted in God's Word so we are able to fight battles, both defensive and offensive, for our LORD. Remember, I alone am a minority; me plus God is a majority.

Thank You, LORD, for using visual and written pictures to help us understand Your truth. I pray we apply these truths to our lives every day in our homes, workplaces, churches, and at play—everywhere we go.

Ephesians 6:11*: Put on the whole armor of God, that you may be able to stand against the wiles of the devil.*

2 Corinthians 6:7*: in the word of truth, in the power of God; by the armor of righteousness on the right hand and on the left,*

Hebrews 4:12*: For the word of God is living and active, and sharper than any two-edged sword, piercing even to the dividing of soul and spirit, of both joints and marrow, and is able to discern the thoughts and intentions of the heart.*

August 16th

Carpenters

"Do you know what a carpenter is, Grandma? I heard Dad talking about doing carpentry work with his friend." "Sure. I have always said, 'My Heavenly Father was a carpenter—He "built the world," my Big Brother Jesus was a carpenter, my earthly father was a carpenter, and I married a carpenter. I guess we need to teach our children the trade—which we did." "Wow, that's a lot of carpenters that you're related to. Do I know any of them?" I had to smile. "Yes, honey, you know God, our Heavenly Father; you know Jesus, your Big Brother; and Papa, my husband. Your great-grandfather, my dad, went to be with Jesus before you were born." "Do you think my dad will teach me how to build things?" "I'm sure he will. Your Dad always enjoyed helping Papa work on things around the house. And now he works on fixing and building things around your house."

Priceless Moments

I thought a minute, then said, "I've heard your dad teaching you the names of different tools so you know which ones to hand him when he asks. You are doing very well with getting him the one he needs. I even saw him let you use the hammer and the screwdriver." "You're right. He has been teaching me all along. I really like to spend time with him and help him do things. I call it our guy time. Dad just smiles at me." It is so rewarding to see our grandchildren working alongside their parents to learn the carpentry trade as well. These are useful skills that will always come in handy at some point in life.

Another very useful skill is teaching them to use the full armor of God. Each weapon in the Christian's arsenal is of vital importance and should be put on first thing in the morning so they are prepared for spiritual warfare at any juncture in their daily lives. Along with Bible study, we are prepared to meet the enemy head-on.

Thank You, LORD, for the faithful ones before us who meticulously wrote down Scripture through the inspiration of the Holy Spirit. The full armor is worn daily, as well as using the "lamp" to provide "light" and protection along our paths of life.

Psalm 119:105-106: *Your word is a lamp to my feet, and a light for my path. I have sworn, and have confirmed it, that I will obey your righteous ordinances.*

Matthew 13:55: *Isn't this the carpenter's son? Isn't his mother called Mary, and his brothers James, Joses, Simon, and Judas?*

2 Kings 22:5b-6a: *Let them give it to the workmen who are in Yahweh's house, to repair the damage to the house, to the carpenters, and to the builders, and to the masons, and for buying timber and cut stone to repair the house.*

August 17th
My Secret Mission

Our grandson likes to explore everything and everywhere. On that day, he said, "Grandma, I'm going on a secret mission. Do you want to come?" Who could refuse such a special invitation? So I said, "Absolutely. Where are we off to, and what is our mission?" As he has been told, on occasion he responded, "Easy with the questions. This is on a need-to-know basis. As soon as I figure it out, I will let you know." Such a response says, "He hasn't got a clue." But I graciously said, "Yes, sir. I am ready to serve as you lead the mission." "OK, then follow me." He produced two walkie-talkies and gave me one, saying, "Just in case."

We walked out of the house onto the patio. He signaled for me to stop, then he crept up to the corner of the house, slowly peeking around. I heard, "All's clear. Let's move." I came up behind him and waited for instructions. "I'm going to sneak over to the garage. Cover me." And he was off. I saw him motion for me to follow, so I did. "Now, I'm going to sneak around the garage. You wait so you are safe." It was several minutes until, over the walkie-talkie, I heard, "It's clear. Come up to meet me at the corner of the house. Over and out." My mission was clear, so off to the corner of the house I went. He signaled to be very quiet, so I obeyed. Grabbing my hand, he said, "For your safety, close your eyes, take my hand, and let me lead you to the next part." This sounds like fun. I knew where I was, so, sure, why not? He was slow and careful, finally stopping and saying, "Surprise, open your eyes." Before me, I saw lunch on the table. He did all this with the help of his father.

At the close of the successful quest, I recalled how Jesus fulfilled many prophecies to complete His mission here on earth, following the commands of His Heavenly Father. He was always obedient to the Person in charge, completing each necessary step to redeem mankind; in the future, we will feast with Him in heaven.

Thank You, LORD, for the special mission given to Your Son, which He successfully completed. I pray that, when we are called upon to complete a special mission, we follow Your lead, going when and where directed, to receive the reward at the end of the journey.

Matthew 28:19-20: *Go and make disciples of all nations, baptizing them in the name of the Father and of the Son and of the Holy Spirit, teaching them to observe all things that I commanded you. Behold, I am with you always, even to the end of the age." Amen.*

Mark 16:15: *He said to them, "Go into all the world, and preach the Good News to the whole creation.*

Deuteronomy 31:8: *Yahweh himself is who goes before you. He will be with you. He will not fail you nor forsake you. Don't be afraid. Don't be discouraged.*

August 18th

<u>The Bouncy House</u>

"Grandma, have you seen those things we get to jump around in? We went to a friend's birthday party, and they had one. Mom said we could rent one for my birthday party." "That sounds like a lot of fun. Those are called bouncy houses—things blown up with air, or inflated, to keep them up while you jump. They are like an enclosed portable trampoline." "Do they all look the same, or are they different?" "Good question. They usually come as castles, houses, or slides. They're fun because they can be taken down and easily transported, or moved, from one place to another, like church, amusement parks, festivals, and, yes, your house for a birthday party. When the party or other activity is over, they are deflated, or let the air out, rolled up, and stored until needed again."

Priceless Moments

She got really quiet in her thinking mode, then said, "Where will she be able to get a bouncy house?" I told her, "Some businesses rent them, or you can buy one for yourself at Sam's, Home Depot, online at Amazon, or places like that." "I hope she buys one so we pick out the one we want and can use it anytime we want. We can have friends over and have a good time sharing our special toy. We'll need Daddy to set it up and turn on the air supply so it will fill up so the fun can begin."

I realized she just made a good case for having your own Bible. It would be available to use anytime you want, be easy to open, share with others, or do anything else, then close up when you are finished. It is easily transportable and comes in different versions and print sizes to suit your needs. You have already "set up" Scripture, providing the "supply" of life's direction to enable us to live a clean, fun life in You. The Good Book is the perfect gift.

Thank You, LORD, for the steadfast love You have promised in Your Word. I pray our trust in You grows daily as we continue to open and apply Your Word to remain faithful to the hope proclaimed in Your gospel.

Hebrews 10:23: *Let's hold fast the confession of our hope without wavering; for he who promised is faithful.*

2 Timothy 2:15: *Give diligence to present yourself approved by God, a workman who doesn't need to be ashamed, properly handling the Word of Truth.*

Galatians 6:9: *Let's not be weary in doing good, for we will reap in due season, if we don't give up.*

August 19th
More, Please and Thank You

The grandchildren have all been taught to use courtesy words: please, thank you, you're welcome, etc. They're good at using them—most of the time. As with all efforts at positive reinforcement, gentle reminders are given, followed by a please and thank you. The eyes roll, with or without various degrees and decibels of groans, and are accompanied by a "fit-like" twist or turn of the body. Begrudgingly, the anticipated please and/or thank you will follow. One day, our granddaughter asked, "Why do we have to always say those words?" Fair question, so I responded with a question of my own: "How do you feel when you've done something nice for someone and they don't acknowledge your terrific efforts, let alone say 'please, thank you, or you're welcome?"

Just then, God provided a teaching moment for both of us. A woman walked by and accidentally dropped one of the letters she was carrying. Our granddaughter spotted the letter, picked it up, and ran after the woman. She said, "Excuse me, but you dropped your letter. This person gave her a disgusted look, grabbed the letter, and said, "Run along now," shoeing her away. Thunderstruck, she turned to me and said, "Oh, Grandma, I see what you mean. We need to pray for her." So, we stopped in the middle of the sidewalk and prayed for God to touch that woman's heart and make it kind towards others.

Ah, the dreaded courtesy words that are missing from most people's vocabulary these days. Sometimes, I find myself saying them under my breath for the ungrateful individuals for whom something nice was said or done. But here, I felt brokenness for our little one. Yet she surprised me with her thoughtfulness towards a very unkind, rude person—pray for her. She did not take it as an affront, but as an opportunity to pray for her. How a child shall lead them, by words and example. I found myself reflecting on how Jesus was mistreated, yet He taught to "turn the other cheek."

Thank You, LORD, for the tenderness of a child's heart who is listening to Your voice. I pray we are as attuned to Your still small voice giving us direction in our actions and responses to others as the children are.

Matthew 5:38-39: "*You have heard that it was said, 'An eye for an eye, and a tooth for a tooth.' But I tell you, don't resist him who is evil; but whoever strikes you on your right cheek, turn to him the other also.*"

Titus 3:1–2: *Remind them to be in subjection to rulers and to authorities, to be obedient, to be ready for every good work, to speak evil of no one, not to be contentious, to be gentle, showing all humility toward all men.*

Philippians 2:3: *doing nothing through rivalry or through conceit, but in humility, each counting others better than himself;*

August 20th
A Stronger Crab

Two of the grandchildren were playing with the baby's 'Cute Crab', a crawling toy with light and sound designed to encourage infants to hold up their heads, move their eyes and bodies, crawl, etc. It was great fun to watch them interact with the toy. But the baby was getting a little upset watching them chase her toy, and she was not included. "Why is she getting upset, Grandma? She is down here with us, watching us play. She should be happy." I responded, "Because she likes to try to catch the crab when it walks towards her, and she is not able to do so right now because you are stopping it from coming her way or blocking her view of it."

Priceless Moments

The older two soon got the idea to use the moving crab to knock down a tower they had built. Of course, right. The crab made many attempts to run into the tower belonging to an "evil city," being "guided" by the kids using its ability to sense and avoid potential obstacles, thus "aiming" it at the tower for direct hits. Our grandson became frustrated with its misses and said, "Grandma, we need a stronger crab." Eventually, the crab ran out of battery life and needed to be recharged.

Their antics reminded me of how people will try to guide their lives into things they think will give them pleasure and joy, only to realize things of this world can never satisfy or accomplish for them their heart's desire. The truth is, our God is stronger than any earthly blockade and can knock down all "evil cities" in our lives. He never runs out of "battery life," so He is always ready and able to help when we call upon Him.

Thank You, LORD, for your eternal power source guiding us, be it using others as a "sensory mechanism" to redirect us, a guardian angel, the Holy Spirit, or your word. It is very comforting to know that once we give our hearts and lives to You and stay charged up daily in Your Word and prayer seeking guidance, you will honor our request to stay close and guide us through whatever method is necessary to keep us on the path to You.

Proverbs 3:5-6*: Trust in Yahweh with all your heart, and don't lean on your own understanding. In all your ways acknowledge him, and he will make your paths straight.*

Psalm 40:4*: Blessed is the man who makes Yahweh his trust, and doesn't respect the proud, nor such as turn away to lies.*

Proverbs 28:26*: One who trusts in himself is a fool; but one who walks in wisdom is kept safe.*

Priceless Moments

August 21st
Starving Children

The grandchildren seldom have food preferences, but once in a while, it rears its ugly head. It was lunchtime when the food they liked was served. "I don't want to eat that; I don't like that." I couldn't help myself: "Since when? You ate it for supper last night and were raving about how much you liked it." "Well, that was last night—but I don't like it today." They got up from the table and started to walk away. Trying to be diplomatic, I said, "OK. But understand that if you don't eat your lunch, there will not be an afternoon snack." I knew I had an ace up my sleeve because we had already talked about snacks, and it was going to be one of their favorites—a fruit smoothie.

Very begrudgingly, they marched back to the table and slowly ate their lunch. I decided it was time they heard about "starving children in Africa." I remember being told this when I was a kid and didn't want to eat something. So, I explained to them that there were actually children in the world who would give anything to have any type of food given to them. Heads popped up, and in unison, they basically said, "You're joking us. Kids don't really starve." I explained, "Many children not only don't have food, they don't have enough clean water, clothing, medical care, or sometimes only one parent." Needless to say, their food quickly disappeared.

After lunch, we settled on the couch together. I went on to relate how many people in our country and around the world are starving in other ways: for love, money, jobs, a roof over their heads, or no car, but the saddest are those starving for God's Word. Puzzled faces greeted the last comment. They knew what missionaries were, so I explained that they share God's Word in places where many people have nothing but the chance to learn about and accept Jesus as their Savior, ending the starvation in their souls.

Thank You, LORD, that we live in an area where Your Word is preached straight from the Bible, not in a misguided, twisted version of a "feel-good, prosperity lesson" about life. Sometimes, Your Name may not even be mentioned. I pray we're a sermon in our shoes everywhere we go and in everything we do, feeding others with and through Your Word.

Matthew 4:4: But he answered, "It is written, 'Man shall not live by bread alone, but by every word that proceeds out of God's mouth.'"

Revelation 7:16: They will never be hungry or thirsty any more. The sun won't beat on them, nor any heat;

Matthew 5:6: Blessed are those who hunger and thirst for righteousness, for they shall be filled.

August 22nd
Gone in 60 Seconds— 30 Seconds—10 Seconds— 0 Seconds

In feeding our 5-month-old granddaughter, I always have to chuckle when she decides she is hungry. Sometimes, she gives a timely warning so the bottle can be heated, and then we get comfy in the recliner, put on a bib, and get a bottle to her mouth. Other days, she is like the movie *Gone in Sixty Seconds*. Still, there are the days when she loses her patience somewhere between the "I'm hangry" cry and the last phase of "bottle in mouth." Today, from the minute she indicated hunger, ALL patience was gone. We checked the diaper several times, bounced, danced, sang, and looked at her favorite items around the house for what seemed like 30 minutes, when actually it was only 5 minutes, long enough to warm the bottle.

Priceless Moments

Still expressing her distain at how long it was taking to get to the recliner, I hurriedly put on the bib, popped the cap off the bottle, and headed it in the direction of her mouth. But, no, she wasn't having it. She continued to fuss and make her disapproval known until she was good and ready to partake of the nectar of life. Once she was satisfied she had made her point, she accepted the bottle and downed it in what seemed like 60 seconds.

I thought of how many times we react to God and His provisions for us in similar ways. Sometimes, He provides for us in His time, and we are satisfied with that. Other times, we fuss, fret, and fume with varying degrees of intensity because God hasn't met our timetable when we have petitioned Him for something. The same way with the bottle, a certain amount of time is needed to heat the milk to her liking. She is not very happy if the milk is not warm enough. With God, only He knows how much time will be needed to prepare His answer to our request to be the best for all of us. God is never late, seldom early, but always on time.

Thank You, LORD; we have the privilege of making our requests and needs known to you. I pray we have the patience and fortitude to continue praying for an answer and waiting patiently until You deem the time is right.

Psalm 27:14: *Wait for Yahweh. Be strong, and let your heart take courage. Yes, wait for Yahweh.*

2 Peter 3:9: *The Lord is not slow concerning his promise, as some count slowness; but he is patient with us, not wishing that anyone should perish, but that all should come to repentance.*

Psalm 34"17 *The righteous cry, and Yahweh hears, and delivers them out of all their troubles.*

August 23rd
A Promise

"Grandma, what do I do if I made a promise to somebody and I broke it? I didn't mean to, but it just slipped out of my mouth before I realized I had said it. I don't want my friend to think I can't be trusted." "I understand how sometimes we can say things without thinking first, but it still breaks a promise. The first thing you should do is talk to Jesus about your situation. Then you should treat your friend with respect and ask them if you could sit down and talk. Tell them, 'I'm sorry if this will hurt you, but I accidentally told the secret I was supposed to keep.' Let them know that their friendship means a lot to you, and you hope that they will forgive you and that your friendship can continue. They may be upset with you for a while, but if you are sincere, hopefully they will get over it soon and trust you again."

After a few moments, he asked, "But what if he never trusts me again?" "I would continue to pray about the situation and ask Jesus to heal your friendship. If the other person doesn't want to be friends anymore, you continue to show respect and a friendly manner towards them. If you keep the right heart attitude, Jesus will provide you with other friends. Then you must decide if what someone wants you to keep secret is a good thing or a bad thing. For example, they like this girl, or someone is hurting them at home. The first one is OK to agree to a secret, but the second one should be told to a trustworthy adult to get them help so the abuse stops."

I remember making "pinky promises" with my siblings and friends many moons ago. But even more important is the promise of serving Christ and the marriage vows we take with our spouses. The latter are the two most important decisions we will ever make in our lives.

Thank You, LORD, for the promises in Your Word, which You always keep. I pray we respect You and others enough to keep our promises with them, even sharing them to let others know just how important these promises are to You.

Ecclesiastes 5:5: *Do not let your mouth lead you into sin. And do not protest to the temple messenger, 'My vow was a mistake.' NIV*

Psalm 145:13: *Your kingdom is an everlasting kingdom. Your dominion endures throughout all generations.*
Yahweh is faithful in all his words, and loving in all his deeds.

Matthew 5:33: *"Again you have heard that it was said to the ancient ones, 'You shall not make false vows, but shall perform to the Lord your vows,'*

August 24th
Time For School

Ah, the start of a new school year. I can hear it now: "Good morning, guys. It's time to get up for your first day of school. Your clothes are laid out, and your breakfast is ready. After you get dressed, please come downstairs and eat." Excitement filled the air as they bounded out of bed, dressed quickly, and raced downstairs to their favorite breakfast of scrambled eggs, bacon, and hash browns. They chattered excitedly about their new teachers, who their classmates would be, and what kind of things they would be learning this year. "Can we go to school early to find our cubbies and see who all will be in our class? We certainly don't want to be late on our first day."

Their Mom said, "I'm so happy to see how excited you are to go back to school. I know you'll both do great. You've learned a lot of things this summer through our travels and working with Grandma. You've already visited your classroom and met a few of the other kids in your class at the LORD's house. My desire for you is that you be good listeners, be respectful of others, and do your best every day to reflect Jesus in your life to everyone you meet." Devotions and prayers were completed, teeth were brushed, new shoes were donned, lunch boxes were placed in new backpacks, and they were ready to head out the door to a new school year.

I remember those days of each new school year. I also remember my parents praying over us before we went out the door to face the secular world of education that we would be bold enough to stand up for our faith and not be bullied into accepting non-Christian indoctrination.

Thank You, LORD, for the excitement we feel when we accept You as our LORD and Savior. I pray the excitement of this new life in Christ never gets dull, but that our reading, studying, and fellowshipping with other Christians help us grow into a deeper relationship with You.

1 Chronicles 29:9: *Then the people rejoiced, because they offered willingly, because with a perfect heart they offered willingly to Yahweh; and David the king also rejoiced with great joy.*

Nehemiah 12:43: *They offered great sacrifices that day, and rejoiced; for God had made them rejoice with great joy; and the women and the children also rejoiced; so that the joy of Jerusalem was heard even far away.*

Matthew 5:12: *Rejoice, and be exceedingly glad, for great is your reward in heaven. For that is how they persecuted the prophets who were before you.*

August 25th
Do You Think They Liked Me?

"Oh, Grandma, kindergarten was so much fun today. But I'm worried they may not have liked me. Everyone was so quiet."

Priceless Moments

"Were they just quiet to you, or were they quiet with everyone?" "Let me think… I think they were quiet with everyone." "Since it's so early in the school year, I think everyone is getting used to the new teacher, routine, and classmates. Many of the kids may not have been in school before and are not used to the structure of the classroom. They may even be missing their parents and siblings, so they have very little to say right now until they become more comfortable with this new situation." "Hmmm, I never thought about it like that before." "Here may be a way to help understand it. Do you remember your first week or two of preschool? Did you feel comfortable with everything right away, or were you a little concerned about a few things? If you were concerned about a few things, how long do you think it took you to feel comfortable with being in preschool?"

He pondered the question for quite some time, as if he were looking through his "memory banks" to find the answer. "Well, that was a long time ago, but I do remember feeling a little scared at first because I didn't know what to expect about being in school. I know my sister has told me some things, but I have to do it myself to really understand what it's all about." "So true, young man. Each person can respond to the same situation in very different ways due to their previous experiences and temperament, or behaviors and attitudes about new experiences." "I don't quite understand all of that, but it seems to make some sense."

It seems every child goes through the phase of what do people think of me? Do they like me? Do they want to be my friend? It's Satan trying to confuse us by having us question ourselves, which brings on doubt and confusion. Yet we have a Friend Who is faithful, true, and steadfast and Who can eliminate our self-doubt.

Thank You, LORD, for tolerating our human frailties. I pray that when the first seed of doubt starts to take root, we turn to You for affirmation and a good "weeding" session.

Psalm 60:11: *Give us help against the adversary, for the help of man is vain. Through God we will do valiantly, for it is he who will tread down our adversaries.*

John 16:33: *I have told you these things, that in me you may have peace. In the world you have trouble; but cheer up! I have overcome the world."*

1 Peter 5:9: *Withstand him steadfast in your faith, knowing that your brothers who are in the world are undergoing the same sufferings.*

August 26th
Bed Time

No matter a person's age, sometimes bedtime is a challenge. For adults, it's completing work that must be done before the new work day or getting stuff ready for kids to go to school the next day. For children, there is something on their mind that keeps them from falling asleep. Are they upset about something, concerned about a test, or concerned about having bad dreams? Our problem comes when they say, "Grandma, I promise I'll go right to sleep if you let me stay up to watch a part of a movie, play a game, or read another book. I know I haven't always kept my promise, but I will this time, please—and thank you."

I wanted to be diplomatic, so I said, "How about this: you go to sleep now, and when you get up, we can watch a little more of a movie, play another game, or read another book? If you show me you can do as I ask, then next time I may consider honoring your request. I would like to see you show me respect consistently, just as I show you respect consistently when you ask me for a favor. I really don't want to send you to bed earlier or take away the privilege of doing the fun things during the day." She thought a second and replied, "OK, you are fair to us, so I'll go to sleep now. I know you'll keep your side of the bargain tomorrow."

Priceless Moments

How many times do we find ourselves trying to bargain with God? God remains consistent in His responses to us, working to shape our behavior to ultimately be a blessing to Him and to others we encounter in our daily lives.

Thank You, LORD, for being a faithful, loving Parent Who sets limits and sticks to them. I pray we recognize our attempts to manipulate You and learn to follow Your path for us rather than our own wants and desires.

Philippians 1:21: For to me to live is Christ, and to die is gain.

Jeremiah 10:10: But Yahweh is the true God. He is the living God, and an everlasting King. At his wrath, the earth trembles. The nations aren't able to withstand his indignation.

Colossians 1:10-12: And we pray this in order that you may live a life worthy of the LORD and may please Him in every way: bearing fruit in every good work, growing in the knowledge of God, being strengthened with all power according to His glorious might so that you may have great endurance and patience, and joyfully giving thanks to the Father, Who has qualified you to share in the inheritance of the saints in the kingdom of light. NIV

August 27th

Where Are My Pals?

A new school year has started, and the little ones are returning to a new teacher and classroom of peers. As our granddaughter entered the classroom, she whispered, "Where are my pals? I don't see anyone I know. I only met the teacher when we had an open house at school. Oh, this is going to be just awful." I led her back out of the classroom and said, "Let's pray. Dear LORD, we ask you to be with this precious child of Yours right now, showing Your kindness to her by providing her with a room full of new friends

Priceless Moments

and new opportunities to show them Your love. We thank You for the new experiences that will come her way. Fill her heart with Your peace, we pray. Amen." "Thank you. I feel better already because I know Jesus will be with me and take care of me."

She took my hand as we walked in silence back to the classroom. As she entered the door, a little girl came running up to her, saying, "I got worried about you when I saw you come in the room only to leave again. I prayed for God to give you peace and bring you back here. I felt a peace from Him, like He was saying we are going to become good friends." Her whole demeanor changed. She straightened her posture, put a smile on her face, and told me goodbye, happily following her new friend into this new situation orchestrated by our LORD.

Amazingly, God already, in His goodness, knew a little heart would be broken to feel alone in a new situation, but He had a plan that included a new Christian friend who started praying for her before they even met. Oh, how great is our God and so worthy of our praise. By the way, these two girls became best friends.

Thank You, LORD, that You know what lies ahead for all of us. I pray we stay humble and pray before entering any situation, having You go before us to prepare the way that will bring honor and glory to You.

***Deuteronomy 31:8**: Yahweh himself is who goes before you. He will be with you. He will not fail you nor forsake you. Don't be afraid. Don't be discouraged.*

***Isaiah 52:12**: For you shall not go out in haste, neither shall you go by flight: for Yahweh will go before you; and the God of Israel will be your rear guard.*

***Isaiah 45:2**: I will go before you and make the rough places smooth. I will break the doors of bronze in pieces and cut apart the bars of iron.*

Priceless Moments

August 28th
The Touch Lamp

I walked into the living room and noticed the touch lamp on the piano was on. I wondered if the electricity had gone out or just blinked. Our granddaughter walked in the room, saying, "Hey, Grandma, that light on the piano is really neat. I can touch it, and it turns on, first with a really low light, then with a bigger light until it gets really bright. If I touch it again, it goes off. Why does it do that?" At least now I know why the light was on. "It's called a touch-sensitive lamp because the metal senses that you have touched it. In other words, your finger acts like flipping the light switch, turning a knob, pushing a button, or having it hooked up to a timer to turn on and off at the same time every day." "What happens if the light bulb stops working?" "They use a special bulb that is dimmable. If you do not have one, it will work as a regular lamp.

Her face lit up. "I get it. It's like when Daddy uses a smart switch and turns it on with his phone. He likes to do that because he can turn lights on and off at our house without us being there. At Christmas, he hooked up the trees and a wreath outside, and our Christmas tree came on when he was ready. It is really cool to see them go on and off all by themselves. Did you know Daddy even hooked up our heat to his app so he could turn it up before we got home or turn it down if he forgot before we left the house? Someday, I'm going to ask him to do that at my house. Do you think he will do that?" "Honey, if they are still using those types of switches, I'm sure he would be delighted to put them in your home."

I thought of how the light of Jesus is a steady, constant light, never wavering or changing in intensity. We don't turn Him on and off with the touch of our hand or phone. Rather, we "turn" Him on in all His brightness when we "turn over" our lives to Him, asking Him to be our Light and our Guide.

Thank You, LORD, for being the Lighthouse in our lives. I pray we stay lit for You, never growing dim or turning off, always shining our brightest because your internal power source is living within us.

Psalm 27:1: *Yahweh is my light and my salvation. Whom shall I fear? Yahweh is the strength of my life. Of whom shall I be afraid?*

1 John 1:5b-6: *God is light, and in him is no darkness at all. If we say that we have fellowship with him and walk in the darkness, we lie, and don't tell the truth.*

Psalm 119:105: *Your word is a lamp to my feet, and a light for my path.*

August 29th
I Can Help

While doing dishes, I had many volunteers: "Can I help?" was echoed. I said, "OK, let's divide and conquer." Of course, I heard, "What do you mean by that? We came to help." "Well, I could use your help to clean up the kitchen, run the sweeper, dust, and fold towels. If each one of you helps by doing one of the tasks by dividing up the larger amount of work for one person into smaller, manageable parts, we are taking the work load and conquering it, or getting it all done. Who wants to help?" They are always ready to help, shouting out, "I want to sweep." "I want to do dishes." "I want to fold towels." "Oh, good, I get to dust." Each picked their favorite task and completed it well.

With good helpers, the large task was completed in record time. "Thank you for the wonderful job each of you did in helping me. The Pennsylvania Dutch have a saying, *"Many hands make light work."* We divided the work and completed, or conquered, the tasks. Who would like to walk over to the playground for a picnic?" That's all I got out as they scattered to the pantry and refrigerator to gather all we would need. I finished, "And ride some rides?" "Yes, yes, yes" was heard all around. Everything was loaded into the picnic basket and placed in the cooler they'd already placed inside the wagon. "OK, gang, sunglasses and sunscreen for everyone before we leave." Although they were not happy about this request, they complied. "Off we go, and each of you can have a turn pulling the wagon."

How fun to think they understand that if they help, there is always a reward waiting at the end. Same with God—we accept Jesus, then witness for Him and make more disciples. Our reward: taking as many as we can to heaven with us to live with Jesus throughout eternity.

Thank You, LORD, for instructing us in Your will for us to share the gospel with others. I pray that as we divide the task with fellow brothers and sisters around the world, we can conquer Satan, reaping a greater harvest for Your kingdom.

Galatians 6:7: *Don't be deceived. God is not mocked, for whatever a man sows, that he will also reap.*

Luke 10:2: *Then he said to them, "The harvest is indeed plentiful, but the laborers are few. Pray therefore to the Lord of the harvest, that he may send out laborers into his harvest.*

Matthew 3:11b, 12: *He will baptize you in the Holy Spirit. His winnowing fork is in his hand, and he will thoroughly cleanse his threshing floor. He will gather his wheat into the barn, but the chaff he will burn up with unquenchable fire.*

Priceless Moments

August 30th
The Cactus Plant

When our granddaughter was younger, she fell into a cactus plant. She and her family arrived for Thanksgiving, only to notice other guests had brought us a cactus plant. She was very leery of it, asking, "Grandma, can you put the cactus plant up on the refrigerator, so I won't get hurt again? I remember how much it hurt the first time." I explained, "This is a Thanksgiving cactus called a *zygocactus*. It does have jagged-looking leaves, but it doesn't have any sharp needles on it; only the pretty pink flowers." The doorbell interrupted our conversation. More guests have arrived for dinner, bearing a prickly pear cactus.

All I could think was, "What a teaching moment." We welcomed the guests and thanked them for the cactus, placing it next to the first cactus. "Honey, take a good look at both cacti. What do you notice is the same about both?" She said, "They are both green and both planted in pots. I don't see anything else." I commented, "Those are good observations. Now, what do you see that is different about them?" She hesitated, then started, "One has many pretty flowers, lots of arm-like things branching out over the pot. The other one has sharp, pointy things, shaped like round, flat balls stuck together like a snowman." I watched her process her own observations. "I can smell those pretty flowers because it's a safe cactus. You can leave it down and put the second one on the refrigerator." I smiled, "We can do that."

It's amazing the things we can be leery of until the facts and observations are considered. As we gain a wealth of biblical information, it will bring clarity and understanding to our questions about given subjects. We need to search the Scriptures for truths found in the Word to set our minds at ease.

Thank You, LORD, for providing Your Word throughout the centuries in written form for us to read, meditate over, and pray about to discern Your will. I pray we set aside the very best of our day to avail ourselves of this written gift to hide Your words in our hearts and minds.

Psalm 119:11: *I have hidden your word in my heart, that I might not sin against you.*

Deuteronomy 6:6: *These words, which I command you today, shall be on your heart;*

Colossians 3:16: *Let the word of Christ dwell in you richly; in all wisdom teaching and admonishing one another with psalms, hymns, and spiritual songs, singing with grace in your heart to the Lord.*

August 31st

<u>Do I Have To?</u>

As the days of the new school year wear on the children, the rousing becomes a little more difficult with each passing morning. "Good morning, little ones. You have the privilege of going to school again today." Moans and groans were heard as the children tried to shake the sleepiness from their heads. Each child said, "Do I have to? I'm tired and want to sleep in this morning, please." "I'm sorry, but how would we explain this to your teacher and school principal? You know that I cannot lie for you or have that lie on my conscience stand between me and God. Let's say you both get up and get ready for a fabulous day. We will pray for a very special day for each of you, eat a good breakfast, and then head out to school with a positive attitude, knowing Jesus will be with you all day, helping you to think and do your best." They both moved slowly, but with a little more purpose in their steps. Each was very attentive to the session of prayer, then perked up and did all that was asked of them.

Priceless Moments

I continued to pray for them throughout the day. I was excited to pick them up after school to learn about their day. They soon came around the corner of the building. Each spied me and came running. Each one said, "Grandma, Grandma, Grandma, I had a wonderful day." Each proceeded to tell about the events of the day, all glowing from the excitement in their voices. Our granddaughter said, "Thank you for praying for us this morning. Jesus showed up and made my day very special." "Me too, same as her. You were right; Jesus really helped me today, too." chimed in our grandson.

It's so important to learn to pray for guidance to start your day with Jesus, so He is there to help us throughout the rest of the day. We can have the same assistance throughout each day of our lives just by asking.

Thank You, LORD, for being available 24/7/365 for anyone who calls upon You. I pray we meet You in the morning when our day is at its best, clothed in Your full armor, so we are able to face whatever comes our way.

Psalm 25:4-5*: Show me your ways, Yahweh. Teach me your paths. Guide me in your truth, and teach me, for you are the God of my salvation, I wait for you all day long*

Job 6:24*: Teach me, and I will hold my peace. Cause me to understand my error.*

James 1:5*: But if any of you lacks wisdom, let him ask of God, who gives to all liberally and without reproach, and it will be given to him.*

Priceless Moments

Precious Moments

September

*How can a young man
keep his way pure?
By living according
to your word.*

Psalm. 119:9

September 1ST
Have a Boyfriend

Our 4-year-old granddaughter came home from preschool one day and announced, "I have a boyfriend." Not wanting to say anything to hurt her feelings, I replied, "That's nice, honey. What's his name?" Her response kind of took me back a little as she said, "I don't know; I just know I like him. And better yet, he likes me." I cautiously asked her, "How do you know he likes you?" "Oh, Grandma, he gave me this beautiful necklace. All the other girls are jealous." Preschool—really.

Trying to think on my feet and be positive, I told her, "You are one lucky little girl to have such a thoughtful boyfriend. This is what I would call a keeper." She looked puzzled and asked, "What's a keeper?" I explained, "It's when you find a very special person you want to keep around you forever." Her face brightened. She ran over to me, threw her arms around me, and said, "I love you, Grandma. You're a keeper." She touched my soul deeply with her rapid response and expression of love.

I couldn't help but think of God as a keeper. He loves us unconditionally, making us feel special. His arms are always wide open when we run to Him and express our gratitude for the beautiful things He has given us in our lives—like this precious little girl, so ready to declare her love for her new boyfriend and me. In our times of joy and sorrow, may we freely run to God and unashamedly and openly declare our love for Him, sharing what He has done for us. We might, unexpectedly, just touch a needy heart and open their heart to the best "boyfriend" ever, our LORD and Savior, Jesus Christ.

Thank You, LORD, for knowing our names and saying each one of us is a "keeper." I pray Your unconditional love and open arms will provide joy and comfort throughout our days, weeks, and years ahead.

Priceless Moments

Psalm 121:5-8: *Yahweh is your keeper. Yahweh is your shade on your right hand. The sun will not harm you by day, nor the moon by night. Yahweh will keep you from all evil. He will keep your soul. Yahweh will keep your going out and your coming in, from this time forward, and forever more.*

Proverbs 15:3: *Yahweh's eyes are everywhere, keeping watch on the evil and the good.*

Luke 12:4-5: *"I tell you, my friends, don't be afraid of those who kill the body, and after that have no more that they can do. But I will warn you whom you should fear. Fear him who after he has killed, has power to cast into Gehenna. Yes, I tell you, fear him."*

September 2nd

<u>Labor Day</u>

"I know today is a holiday, Grandma, but why do we celebrate it? Do you know who thought of this idea?" "If memory serves me correctly, it was a man named Peter McGuire, a carpenter and labor union leader, around 1882, twelve years before it became a legal holiday when President Grover Cleveland passed a bill in 1894 making the first Monday in September a holiday for workers, also called laborers. This holiday is the result of labor unions and other hardworking people forcing others to recognize both the contributions as well as the poor treatment of workers." "Why would people not treat their workers nice?" "Some people they worked for, called employers, were only interested in making more money, so they pushed the workers without having consideration for the safety and needs of their job, the person, or their families. This holiday gives around ninety percent of Americans a paid day off from work. As a matter of fact, International Workers Day is celebrated in over one hundred sixty countries."

Priceless Moments

"What do people do to celebrate Labor Day?" "With a three-day weekend, often called a long weekend, many people take a short vacation before their children start a new school year. We also fly our American flag along with other patriotic families." "What kinds of things do they do?" "One can go camping, get in the last days at the beach or swimming pool, go to a baseball game, and have a picnic. Others focus on the time to prepare the house, cars, campers, cabins, etcetera for fall, the time when the weather starts turning cooler.

I thought back to the years as we celebrated this holiday. My fondest memories were the church services where our pastors' honored workers from every walk of life, encouraging all to work hard but to rest on the day of worship to enjoy family, friends, and Christian fellowship.

Thank You, LORD, for holidays that give people opportunities to reflect on Your goodness to us. I pray we need Scripture to work to the best of our ability throughout the week, giving our best to You and our boss.

Genesis 2:15: *Yahweh God took the man, and put him into the garden of Eden to cultivate and keep it.*

Exodus 20:9: *You shall labor six days, and do all your work,*

Ecclesiastes 9:10: *Whatever your hand finds to do, do it with your might; for there is no work, nor plan, nor knowledge, nor wisdom, in Sheol, where you are going.*

September 3rd
A Little Bit Of Duck Tape

The grandchildren came over one day for breakfast and to spend the day "keeping me company." Once they got in the house, two of them tried to tell me I had a situation outside and needed to go out immediately, that something was wrong with "your light." Our son came in and said, "One of your solar lights is lying down in the snow; it probably got hit with the shovel." Since breakfast was ready, the light was forgotten, and a hearty breakfast was consumed over a delightful conversation about what "we were going to do today."

After their dad left, they looked out the window to wave goodbye when, once again, they spied the light and became concerned about it again. We donned our coats and hoods and went out to check on the "situation." Realizing the post had broken at the bottom, our grandson said, "Daddy always fixes everything with duck tape. Do you have any?" Knowing what he meant, I said, "Yes, I have some. I'll go get it." I told them it was called duct tape as opposed to duck tape, and they laughed. We wrapped a piece around the post of the light, and it once again stood solid and upright.

I thought of how our "light in the world" can be affected by life's circumstances and events. We can get knocked down, trampled on, and hurt while looking out of sorts. When "Daddy" puts things into perspective for us, we can take a look at it and figure out what to do—take it to the LORD in prayer. He will not use *duck tape* to fix it, but will mend us in ways we would never have thought of before, making us more usable in His kingdom.

Thank You, LORD, for knowing how to mend us because You know our every need before we do. I pray we turn to You before getting some other means of "mending" that are only temporal, but for us to receive the proper care that is eternal.

Psalm 147:3: *He heals the broken in heart, and binds up their wounds.*

Psalm 34:18: *Yahweh is near to those who have a broken heart, and saves those who have a crushed spirit.*

Priceless Moments

John 14:27: *Peace I leave with you. My peace I give to you; not as the world gives, I give to you. Don't let your heart be troubled, neither let it be fearful.*

September 4th

<u>Football Season</u>

Our granddaughters love football season because they get to sit close to their dad and root for his or her favorite team. Daddy and Grandma always root for the same team—the one that's been a favorite for generations. Team clothing, in the form of pajamas for the girls, is worn when watching the game, along with generous helpings of popcorn, cheese and crackers, or a vegetable tray with hummus. After a while, one of the girls slipped over onto my lap and snuggled in, getting really comfortable. At this point, their cheering slows to a halt as their eyelids close in sleep. At halftime, one little fan is sacked by the Sandman and carried off to bed by her favorite quarterback, her dad.

During halftime, the remaining fans take needed breaks, clean up the remaining food, and then regroup for the second half. This time, the remaining little princess is seated between Daddy and Grandma. She leans one way for a little while, then the other way. Again, eyelids get heavy as the second half wears on. By the end of the third quarter, Princess #2 is sacked and is carried off to her "stretcher" upstairs. The remaining quarter is virtually minimized to a dull roar so as not to awaken the girls.

I got to thinking about how we reflect our love for God through football. Are we out there cheering on our favorite, God? Do we dress in clothing that reflects Him as our choice? Do we get weary of serving Him, giving up halfway or three-quarters of the way through life? Or do we make it through to the fourth quarter but get confined by circumstances and become "mum" so as not to arouse the naysayers, you know, those people who dislike or hate

Christians? May we play like Jesus is our quarterback and we are the wide receiver or tight end, running with all our might to catch His pass and carry the ball across the finish line for a touchdown. Only here Jesus caught the pass—the cross—and took us who have accepted Him as our personal Savior with Him across the finish line, which here crosses into heaven.

Thank You, LORD; we do not have to play games with our salvation. I pray that once we accept You as LORD and Savior, may we hold on tight to our gift from You until we receive our reward and are called to join you on the winning team in heaven.

2 Timothy 4:7-8: *I have fought the good fight. I have finished the course. I have kept the faith. From now on, the crown of righteousness is stored up for me, which the Lord, the righteous judge, will give to me on that day; and not to me only, but also to all those who have loved his appearing.*

Philippians 4:9: *The things which you learned, received, heard, and saw in me: do these things, and the God of peace will be with you.*

2 Corinthians 5:17: Therefore if anyone is in Christ, he is a new creation. The old things have passed away. Behold, all things have become new.

September 5th

There's a Monster Under My Bed

On a sleepover, our grandson called out, "Grandma, there's a monster under my bed. Please come quick. I'm really scared." Needless to say, I was out of bed in a flash and by his side. "It's OK, honey; I'm here now." He clung to me and sobbed. I asked, "Did you see a monster or have a bad dream?" "I don't know. It all seemed so real. I knew you would come if I called." I said, "I have

Priceless Moments

an idea. Let's look under the bed together and see if we find anything, OK?" With flashlight in hand, we crawled off the bed onto the floor, lifted up the bed skirt, and searched all under the bed but found nothing. As he was crawling back into bed, he said, "Oh, thank you, Grandma. Now I know it's safe. It must have been a bad dream."

I suggested, "Let's pray and invite Jesus to join us. He wants you to feel comfortable and safe in a house we've dedicated to His service." "OK, let's pray." "Dear Jesus, we want to thank You for being available to hear us when we pray. We know you are watching over all of us because You promised to never leave us. We know you will guard and protect us for the rest of the night as well as the rest of our lives. Thank You." As I covered him up, lovey in hand, and kissed him, I saw he was already fast asleep.

I marveled at the power of prayer to comfort and reassure not only our grandson but people of all ages. Jesus is never too busy to meet us at the point of our need, regardless of how great or small, since all things about us matter to Him.

Thank You, LORD, for Your 24/7 availability. I pray we think to call upon You in our hour of need before we call upon anyone else. When You are our first line of defense, you can have the answer lined up for us before we even ask.

Genesis 26:25*: He built an altar there, and called on Yahweh's name, and pitched his tent there. There Isaac's servants dug a well.*

1 Chronicles 16:8*: Oh give thanks to Yahweh. Call on his name. Make what he has done known among the peoples.*

Romans 10:12-13*: For there is no distinction between Jew and Greek; for the same Lord is Lord of all, and is rich to all who call on him. For, "Whoever will call on the name of the Lord will be saved."*

September 6th

Will You Tuck Me In?

Bedtime is a ritual at our house. We had just finished playing games, so I said, "OK, kiddos, get dressed for bed, brush your teeth, and return to the living room. We will read a story—or two—of your choice before reading a Bible story, saying bedtime prayers, taking one last potty break, and going off to bed." As I took our granddaughter to bed, she said, "Will you tuck me in and cover me with my favorite blanket (from days gone by), give me a big hug and kiss, then pray Jesus over me?" This is repeated from child to child until all are tucked in under the watchful care of Jesus. Occasionally, one will sneak out of bed for another potty stop, then want to be tucked in again with all the *trimmings.*

Our grandson got up again, asking, "Grandma, can you hold me and rock me for a while? I like it when you sing and hum for me. I was having a bad dream and want you to help me feel better so I can go back to bed." "Of course, honey. I'd love to hold you. Come here and bring your lovey." We rocked, sang, and hummed for a while until the little form in my arms went limp. I prayed, "Dear LORD, please watch over this little child of Yours. Help him to forget all about the bad dreams, replacing them with Your peace." I gently tucked him in bed and didn't hear anything from him until the morning.

Ah, the plea of little ones when it's time for bed, giving them the special feeling of being needed. I couldn't help but think of how often we ask God to "tuck us in" during those nights we're away from home, can't sleep, or feel lonely and alone. Somehow, feeling God's comforting arms around us takes away the "loneliness," fears, and reservations, giving us courage and strength to go on.

Thank You, LORD, that You are everywhere to meet the needs of Your people. I pray we reach out to You to get through our difficult times, feeling Your arms of love tucking us in to provide a feeling of safety and security.

Genesis 49:33: *When Jacob finished charging his sons, he gathered up his feet into the bed, breathed his last breath, and was gathered to his people.*

1 Samuel 25:29: *When someone pursues you and attempts to take your life, my lord's life will be tucked safely in the place where the LORD your God protects the living. NIV*

1 Kings 18:46: *Yahweh's hand was on Elijah; and he tucked his cloak into his belt and ran before Ahab to the entrance of Jezreel.*

September 7th
<u>Talk To Me</u>

When the newest member of our family was born, all of our family members came together to meet their new niece or cousin and to see the new parents and their new home. As we were busy getting things ready one day to go on an outing, one granddaughter said, "Grandma, please talk to me." I had gotten so busy with "'things" that I was neglecting this precious little one. I put down what I was doing, scooped her up, and headed for the rocker. She giggled with delight as I made her the center of my attention. She gave me the biggest hug I can ever remember receiving. Then she cupped my face, started kissing me, and hugged me some more.

We talked about her activities back home, her friends, her new toys, and most importantly, what she had been learning in Sunday School, church, and her Wednesday night programs about Jesus. She talked excitedly about each topic, one at a time, until she had exhausted everything she could think of before moving on to the next one. When it came to Jesus, she said she talks with Him "all the time, and I know He listens to me—just like you are listening to me." Time passed so quickly, but I was no longer concerned

Priceless Moments

with the "things" of life getting done. I so enjoyed totally focusing on our granddaughter and her sharing her life with me.

How precious to realize God desires that same kind of undivided attention from us when we sit down to talk with Him. I can imagine Him sitting us on His knee, cupping our faces to get our undivided attention, and showering us with His precious love. Our ACTS (adoration, confession, thanksgiving, and supplication) of praise, confession, and worship should be so much more important than our petitions for God's favor. When we pray so fervently in the first three parts, our needs and requests seem to pale in comparison to our heartfelt worship freely given to our LORD and Savior. The song, *Turn your eyes upon Jesus, look full in His wonderful face, and the things of earth will grow strangely dim in the light of His glory and grace.* fill my lips, heart, and soul.

Thank You, LORD, for these precious little ones reminding us how we need to set the trappings of life aside and totally focus on You. It changes our entire outlook on what "must be done" to what "we should do"—take the opportunity to worship the most important Person in our lives.

Psalm 63:2-3: So I have seen you in the sanctuary, watching your power and your glory. Because your loving kindness is better than life, my lips shall praise you.

Jeremiah 33:3: Call to me, and I will answer you, and will show you great and difficult things, which you don't know.

Romans 10:17: So faith comes by hearing, and hearing by the word of God.

Priceless Moments

September 8th

A New Life

Joy is felt when one of your kids announces, "You're going to be Grandparents again." Oh, the excitement that brings back memories of holding our own infant children and our other precious grandchildren. I've always heard, "A baby is God's opinion that the world should go on." There is nothing like seeing their innocence and feeling that baby-soft skin. Babies smell so sweet—well, most of the time—and seem to fill that aching need to cuddle a little gift from God in your arms.

After much prayer and anticipation, waiting, a baby shower, waiting, and setting up the nursery—did I mention waiting? —the precious little bundle finally arrives. We all try to decide who she looks like, comparing her birth picture with that of Daddy and Mommy, you know, grandparents' stuff. Finally, I got my chance to hold her, making all the long-awaited anticipation dissipate into fulfilled desires of teaching her about her family, her world, but mostly about her Savior.

I found myself rocking her while humming hymns of the faith, telling her about those she probably met in heaven before God sent her to us, and planning our first time together at our house, feeding her, and having sleepovers. She just lay there quietly, sleeping in my arms. She may not have heard me, and I know she certainly didn't understand me, but I knew God heard the desires of my heart to pass along our Christian heritage to the next generation.

Thank You, LORD, for reminders from Your realm of how precious life is and of how from wee tender babes to grow in Your wisdom, stature, and favor with You and man to bear the familial resemblance to our Heavenly Father in thought, word, and deed. I pray we never forget these special gifts You send our way.

***Colossians 1:9-10**: For this cause, we also, since the day we heard this, don't cease praying and making requests for you, that you* *may be filled with the knowledge of his will in all spiritual wisdom and understanding, that you may walk worthily of the Lord, to please him in all respects, bearing fruit in every good work and increasing in the knowledge of God,*

2 Corinthians 5:17: *Therefore if anyone is in Christ, he is a new creation. The old things have passed away. Behold, all things have become new.*

Ephesians 4:24: *and put on the new man, who in the likeness of God has been created in righteousness and holiness of truth.*

September 9th
<u>That's MY Grandma</u>

An interesting conversation occurred at our home today. All the grandchildren were assembled in one place. They were playing and chatting happily until the following statement was made: "She's my grandma." "No, she's my grandma." "No, she's my grandma because I was born first." I had to listen a little to see where this all went, then went in to "chat" with them all. "Hi, guys and gals. How's it going? It sounds like you've been having fun up until the last few minutes. What's up?" A cacophony of answers drifted my way. "OK, it was difficult to understand all your answers since everyone spoke at the same time. I did gather that you are wondering whose Grandma I am, is that right?" A chorus of "Yes" resounded in my ears.

I took a deep breath and said, "OK. I can answer that question for all of you." Each of you has a sibling, right?" Another resounding "Yes." "Your parents were all siblings, and I was their mother. Since you are their children, that makes me a proud grandmother to ALL of you. This makes each one of you my descendant because we are all in the same family line. It is a privilege to have so many loving grandchildren share stories of your parents with you. I wouldn't know those stories if we hadn't raised them over the course of their young lives. Same with you; as your grandmother, I have stories about each of you to share with all of you."

It's interesting how children's minds work. Trying to explain some concepts is difficult, yet their learning curve is not much different than that of most adults. When unchurched people first hear about Christ, they have many questions until they hear it "sorted out" and "arranged" in order for them to understand. Once the "internal light bulb" goes on, the pieces fall into place and understanding is gained.

Thank You, LORD, for Your wisdom and guidance in explaining Your Word. I pray we are always "prayed up" before meetings with seekers so You have their hearts prepared and our mouths filled with the words to show You to them.

Job 32:8*: But there is a spirit in man, and the Spirit of the Almighty gives them understanding.*

Proverbs 28:5*: Evil men don't understand justice; but those who seek Yahweh understand it fully.*

1 Corinthians 2:12*: But we received not the spirit of the world, but the Spirit which is from God, that we might know the things that were freely given to us by God.*

September 10th
<u>Grandparent's Day</u>

"Wow, Grandma, you guys get a holiday where we can celebrate you. But who came up with this idea?" "That is a very interesting question. In 1969, a nine-year-old boy named Russell Capper wrote a letter to President Richard Nixon with the suggestion of dedicating a day for grandparents. A response from his personal Secretary said that usually a Congressional resolution would give him the power to do so. "Why didn't they give credit to the boy since it was his idea?" "Well, two other people, Jacob Reingold (New York in 1961) and Marian McQuade (West Virginia in 1973), people who worked with older people, recognized grandparents at different times. They joined efforts, and in 1978 Congress passed a law establishing Grandparents Day on the first Sunday after Labor Day, nine years after Russell wrote his letter."

"What kinds of things can we do to help you celebrate Grandparents Day?" "My first response is to attend church together, then have dinner together, be it a cookout or a picnic in the backyard. We can do a family activity afterwards, like share more stories that you like so well, go for a walk, drive past previous homes we've lived in, or visit someone who has no family in the area. Reaching out to others at a time when they are all alone on a holiday can make their lives more enjoyable and keep them physically and mentally active as they endeavor to keep up with your little ones. Nothing brings more joy to us than our grandchildren."

I love the bond we have with our grandchildren. It is so important to share stories of ours and their parents lives with them so they feel connected to the past, their family traditions, and their heritage. Also, we have the privilege of making new traditions with them as we watch them grow and become involved in church, school, and extracurricular activities, taking an interest in everything they do. We need to keep intergenerational bonds alive and strong.

Thank You, LORD, for allowing us the privilege of seeing our children's children. I pray we live out our Christian life in front of them to the point where they also desire to follow You.

Proverbs 17:6*: Children's children are the crown of old men; the glory of children are their parents.*

Priceless Moments

Isaiah 46:4*: Even to old age I am he, and even to gray hairs I will carry you. I have made, and I will bear. Yes, I will carry, and will deliver.*

Proverbs 16:31*: Gray hair is a crown of glory. It is attained by a life of righteousness.*

September 11th
<u>Patriot Day</u>

"Grandma, what is Patriot Day, and why do we celebrate it?" "Before your time, back on September 11, 2001, our country was attacked by nineteen terrorists on four airplanes. They used airplanes to attack, or fly into, the Pentagon in Arlington, Virginia, and the Twin Towers at the World Trade Center in Manhattan, New York. Also, a plane headed to Washington, D.C., was brought down by heroic men who wanted to spare more people's lives than their own. In all, almost three thousand people lost their lives on the hijacked planes and on the ground, while thousands more were injured and may suffer long-term health problems from the attack. Over one hundred countries lost citizens to these attacks. As a result of this, President George W. Bush proclaimed September 14–three days later—as a day of remembrance for those who lost their lives."

"But why are we talking about it now?" "The next year, a bill was passed to make September 11, 2002, the first Patriot Day. Each year, the fallen are remembered by flying flags at half-staff or only half way up the flagpole. A moment of silence is observed at 8:46 A.M. (Eastern Time), the time the first plane hit the first tower, the North Tower, while ceremonies are held to remember the victims." "Why don't we get the day off from school like other holidays?" "Good question. Because it is not a federal holiday, schools and most businesses are still open, but they may observe the moment of silence or do an activity for children to learn about the attack."

The most important kind of patriotism is putting God first. Next is an allegiance to our country. Our military people put their lives on hold to go serve our country and keep us safe. As Christians, patriotism should be a way of life, second nature, to follow our official motto, or phrase, engraved on our money: IN GOD WE TRUST.

Thank You, LORD, for countries that celebrate their freedom. I pray it goes way beyond the country to acknowledge the freedom we have in Christ Jesus as our LORD and Savior.

Psalm 33:12: *Blessed is the nation whose God is Yahweh, the people whom he has chosen for his own inheritance.*

1 Timothy 2:1-2: *I exhort therefore, first of all, that petitions, prayers, intercessions, and givings of thanks be made for all men: for kings and all who are in high places, that we may lead a tranquil and quiet life in all godliness and reverence.*

Titus 3:1-2: *Remind them to be in subjection to rulers and to authorities, to be obedient, to be ready for every good work, to speak evil of no one, not to be contentious, to be gentle, showing all humility toward all men.*

September 12th
I Helped Him Up

"Grandma, the saddest thing happened at school yesterday. Some of the kids were not listening to the teacher when she asked us not to run. When the bell rang, they took off running for gym class, knocking over this boy in another class. He started to cry, so I went over to him and helped him up. The other kids kept calling for me to hurry up, but I wanted to be sure he was OK. If he wasn't, I wanted to let our teacher know so she could get him some help." "Oh, I'm so sorry that he was literally run over by a

Priceless Moments

bunch of other kids, but I am so proud of you for staying behind to check on him. Did he seem to be hurt?" "No, but I think he will have a bruise on his knees from hitting them so hard on the cement." "I'm glad to hear he was OK. I'll bet you made Jesus very happy with your good behavior by being a friend to a stranger, now a new friend."

He thought for a moment, then replied, "Yes, I guess I did make a new friend. I don't know his name, but I've seen him before. Next time I see him, I'll have to introduce myself." "Great idea." "You know, all I could think about was how the two guys in the Bible passed up the hurt man, yet a stranger stopped to help him. What was that story called again?" "It was the story of the Good Samaritan." "That's right. I guess I was a Good Samaritan today. It's a good thing I didn't have to give somebody money to take care of him because I didn't have any." "I guess so, but it's a concerned heart that counts."

It's amazing how sensitive some children can be and how reckless others are. Then I realized these individuals grow up to be adults, with most of them continuing on the same path of showing a lack of concern for others.

Thank You, LORD, for parables to point out our behaviors and give us insights into how to change them. I pray we become more sensitive to the needs of others and try to be more considerate of them.

Philippians 2:3-4*: doing nothing through rivalry or through conceit, but in humility, each counting others better than himself; each of you not just looking to his own things, but each of you also to the things of others.*

Romans 15:1–3*: Now we who are strong ought to bear the weaknesses of the weak, and not to please ourselves. Let each one of us please his neighbor for that which is good, to be building him up. For even Christ didn't please himself. But, as it is written, "The reproaches of those who reproached you fell on me."*

Priceless Moments

1 Corinthians 10:24: *Let no one seek his own, but each one his neighbor's good.*

September 13th
Blueberry Muffins

"Do we have time to go to the store? I would like to make muffins for supper tonight." I looked at the clock and said, "If we leave right now, it will work. What kind of muffins do you want to make? Are you wanting it from scratch or a box mix?" As we were getting in the car, she said, "I think I want homemade blueberry muffins. Can we make those in the silicone muffin pans?" I responded, "Buckle up, and yes, silicone pans are a very good idea." She talked excitedly: "Everyone will be surprised and will enjoy the muffins tonight. Can we sample one after they are baked?" "Good idea. You can have one for your afternoon snack." Perfect answer. "Gee, Grandma, I like how you think."

We arrived back home and started the muffins. "Grandma, can I read the recipe and measure everything myself?" I smiled and said, "You've had a lot of practice, so let's give it a try. I will be your sous chef, as needed. Don't worry, I won't let you make a mistake." She breathed a sigh of relief. "Thanks. I really want to try. I want these to taste so good for everyone to enjoy." "Let me tell you something. You are putting the most important ingredient into the muffins." "Oh no, did I miss something? Tell me, and we can add it." "Honey, the most important ingredient is love. You are adding it with the care you are taking to make the muffins." She smiled.

The not-so-secret ingredient for the Christian is the love God put into all of creation. Everything He did was considered good until He made men, saying we were very good. As the pinnacle of His creation, we need to put love into all of our relationships to reflect the love of our Heavenly Father.

Thank You, LORD, for unconditional love. I pray we understand this principle and freely use it in every contact with friends and foes we encounter in our daily lives.

1 John 4:12: *No one has seen God at any time. If we love one another, God remains in us, and his love has been perfected in us.*

Hebrews 13:16: *But don't forget to be doing good and sharing, for with such sacrifices God is well pleased.*

Hebrews 6:10: *For God is not unrighteous, so as to forget your work and the labor of love which you showed toward his name, in that you served the saints, and still do serve them.*

September 14th
Pass It On

There is a man in our church who grows peaches in his own orchards in our home area. Quite frequently, he brings in many boxes of these delightfully refreshing treats to share with our congregation. On one of these occasions, we picked up a box of peaches and brought them home. I had dreams of a fresh peach shortcake and a homemade peach pie or peach cheesecake. But the grandchildren had other ideas. They decided, "We are going to divide these peaches up and give them away to the neighbors." Their giving hearts have grown by always listening to us, always telling them to share with others—the pass it on principle.

I was a little disappointed to think that my tastebuds would not be satisfied, but thrilled that they were thinking of others. So, I got out some grocery bags, and we divided them up to take around the neighborhood. Upon handing them to the different neighbors, the children took turns saying—all on their own accord: "These are from a nice man at our church and the LORD. We wanted to share them with you. We pray you have a great day. Thank you. Goodbye."

This wonderful greeting and spontaneous praise given to the LORD as they were gifting each of the neighbors on the receiving end of this tasteful treat brought pure delight to my soul. This is such a marvelous feeling of unspeakable satisfaction deep down within me. Oh, and, by the way, the LORD graciously left me enough peaches to make that delicious shortcake—enough to be enjoyed by the entire family. Thank you, LORD.

Thank You, LORD, for little people to remind us of the joy of giving, even if it changes our original plans or purpose. I pray that they we always realize that Your ways are always best for everyone.

Isaiah 11:6: *The wolf will live with the lamb, and the leopard will lie down with the young goat, the calf, the young lion, and the fattened calf together; and a little child will lead them.*

Luke 3:10-11: *The multitudes asked him, "What then must we do?" He answered them, "He who has two coats, let him give to him who has none. He who has food, let him do likewise."*

Galatians 6:2: *Bear one another's burdens, and so fulfill the law of Christ.*

September 15th

<u>Little People</u>

"Grandma, why are some people so rude to us just because we are little people? If we had acted the way they did to us, we would have been grounded and sent to our room, spanked, or had our mouth washed out with soap. It's just not fair. We didn't do anything, and they were just plain rude." "I hear you loud and clear. I don't understand why she acted like that either, but we

Priceless Moments

don't know what is going on in her life right now. Maybe she lost her job, she and her husband had a fight, one of her kids was giving her trouble, she got bad news at the doctor's office, a loved one died, or maybe someone else really yelled at her and she was taking it out on you."

They thought the list over for a little bit, then said, "Why didn't you say something to her to stand up for us?" "I thought about it but didn't feel led by the Spirit to engage her at that time." "What do you mean by that?" "Well, the Holy Spirit can tell us what to say back to someone, but her whole body was screaming some type of major pain. Once she finished her tirade, like a kid having a temper tantrum, she stormed off, closing the door to any kind of intervention. I didn't want it to become a confrontation, like I was adding one more bad thing to her day. But I can tell you what we can do." "We know we can pray for her and ask God to take away her pain and help her feel better." "Precisely. Come here and let's pray."

At that moment, my heart was opened to so many possibilities for what that poor soul could have just experienced. Sometimes we need to look beyond the hurt inflicted upon us and give that individual into God's care. He knows her by name and the situation; therefore, He is a better person to interact with this particular person.

Thank You, LORD, for the check in my spirit to not engage her. I pray You meet her at her point of need—as well as others in similar situations—and minister to them as only You can. When they are ready to talk to somebody, I pray we are ready, willing, and able to show Your love to them.

Proverbs 13:20*: One who walks with wise men grows wise, but a companion of fools suffers harm.*

John 3:16*: For God so loved the world, that he gave his one and only Son, that whoever believes in him should not perish, but have eternal life.*

1 Peter 3:9: *not rendering evil for evil, or insult for insult; but instead blessing, knowing that you were called to this, that you may inherit a blessing.*

September 16th
<u>Never "Neverand"</u>

"Oh, I just love the story about Peter Pan and Neverland. Is it possible that somebody could really go there and never grow up?" "Well, the story of Peter Pan is a work of writing called fiction. It's a story that somebody has made up for fun but to also teach a lesson." "I understand fiction, but what kind of lesson are we to learn from the story of Peter Pan?" "The first sentence in the story is, 'All children, except one, grow up. So we know all of us will grow up.'" "What else does the story teach us?" "It tells us not to be afraid of trying new things, like when Wendy, John, and Michael try to fly. Peter Pan even tells the kids to think of the happiest things because it's the same as having wings. He says our dreams are what we need to take flight to be able to accomplish whatever we put our minds to doing. The negative thing is that Peter Pan and later Tinker Bell show us that selfishness is not good, sometimes resulting in others getting hurt."

You could hear the little wheels turning as they were developing their next question(s). "But what would happen if we never grew up?" "Well, there would be many things you would miss out on, like being with your friends as they grow up, driving a car, dating, getting married, having your own family, getting a job, and stuff like that." "Wow, Peter Pan gave up a lot to always be young. I think I'd rather stay with my parents and grandparents here and grow up like God intended me to do. I really don't want to miss out on all the neat things God has in store for my life." "Very well spoken, young man. I don't think I could have said it better myself."

Priceless Moments

It's crazy to think of life being permanently on hold with things never changing. I'm pleased our grandson sees the benefits of doing things God's way so as to not miss out on all the neat things God has in store for each of our lives.

Thank You, LORD, for giving us direction throughout each season of our lives. I pray that when we do seem to get stuck, we make a concerted effort to spend time with You and get our lives back on track.

Jeremiah 29:11: *For I know the thoughts that I think toward you," says Yahweh, "thoughts of peace, and not of evil, to give you hope and a future."*

Romans 8:28: *We know that all things work together for good for those who love God, for those who are called according to his purpose.*

Psalm 33:11: *The counsel of Yahweh stands fast forever, the thoughts of his heart to all generations.*

September 17th
A Little One's Prayer

Our mornings start off with saying the full armor of God, followed by the prayers of each child present, then continue with Bible reading, the Bible app for children, and singing songs. This one morning, "Grandma, can I say the opening armor thing and pray for all of us?" I was impressed she asked, so I said, "Sure. I'd love to hear you sharing God's Word with us." I had written the armor and prayer in a language they could understand. She started, "Today, as we face a new day, we want to put on the full armor of God this morning… She stated the armor verbatim as we had learned it, as well as the prayer we usually end it with. When she finished, she continued, "And, dear LORD, thank You for helping me keep Your Words in my heart so I can share them anytime I want with anyone You want me to share them with. Amen."

As her accuracy soaked into my brain, I said, "Oh, honey, that was absolutely beautiful. God is so proud of you for learning His Word as well as praying that you want to be used by Him whenever and wherever He chooses." "I know, Grandma. But I learned it so I would always know what God wants us to do every morning. I want to be prepared if Satan tries to get me to do things I shouldn't." "You are spot on, honey. Satan is always going after those Christians who are not protected by God's armor. It leaves them weakened and unprepared for Satan's subtle temptations."

I was blown away, speechless, and ever so grateful that the little ones are absorbing such precious truths. Then I wondered how many adults have taken the time to learn the armor, let alone put it on every morning, before Satan has a chance to make an inroad into their lives.

Thank You, LORD, for giving us tender hearts at a young age to learn Your truths. I pray more adults adopt childlike faith and hide Your Word deep within their hearts, so they are prepared for Satan's subtle attacks.

Proverbs 22:6*: Train up a child in the way he should go, and when he is old he will not depart from it.*

John 15:7*: If you remain in me, and my words remain in you, you will ask whatever you desire, and it will be done for you.*

2 Timothy 3:14-15*: But you remain in the things which you have learned and have been assured of, knowing from whom you have learned them. From infancy, you have known the holy Scriptures which are able to make you wise for salvation through faith, which is in Christ Jesus.*

September 18th

My Room

"Grandma, you've got to come and see my room. We changed some things around, and I got new bed sheets, a bedspread, pillow covers, and some cool stuff on the walls that glows in the dark. I am so excited. You've just got to see this." "Awesome. We'd better go right now and take a peek at this creation of yours." "Oh, yes, let's go now. I've waited all morning for you to come, and I can't wait any longer." She grabs my hand and literally runs up the stairs to her bedroom. Before entering the room, she said, "Now close your eyes and don't open them until I tell you, OK?" "Of course, but don't lead me into a wall or anything else, OK." "Oh, Grandma. You know I'd never do that." I laughed, saying, "Just checking…"

I obediently closed my eyes as she took my hand, carefully leading me into her bedroom, pausing and saying, "Wait a minute. Please just stand here and don't open your eyes yet. I need to do something first." I heard a click, then, "Open your eyes." I looked around and saw a unicorn-themed room: unicorn sheets, a bedspread, wall decals of unicorns and stars, and a painted plaster unicorn head on the dresser. The click was turning on the light to charge the decals. "Now let's turn off the light to see if they've been charged enough to glow. She closed the door, turned off the light, and said, "Look, it worked. It was long enough to pick up some charge to glow for you." I said, "Wow, your face is even glowing." "What do you mean? I don't have anything in my face." I smiled at her and said, "Yes, you do; your face is glowing with excitement at your new décor." She just shook her head.

Jesus must react the same way with us when we invite Him into our lives. I have seen people's faces glowing with the new life of freedom from the burden of sin. Yet Jesus will also be delighted that one of His precious creations was lost but has now come home.

Priceless Moments

Thank You, LORD, for giving us the best You have. I pray we invite You into our hearts for a "deep cleaning," then fix up our soul with new life, changing us to glow in front of others so they can see the difference You make in our lives.

2 Corinthians 5:17*: Therefore if anyone is in Christ, he is a new creation. The old things have passed away. Behold, all things have become new.*

2 Peter 3:9*: The Lord is not slow concerning his promise, as some count slowness; but he is patient with us, not wishing that anyone should perish, but that all should come to repentance.*

Deuteronomy 31:6*: Be strong and courageous. Don't be afraid or scared of them; for Yahweh your God himself is who goes with you. He will not fail you nor forsake you.*

September 19th

<u>Booster Seats</u>

"Grandma, what happened to my car seat? There's just a small kind of seat in your car." I had to smile since he's grown up enough to use a booster seat. "Well, young man, you've outgrown the baby car seat, so it's time for a big boy seat called a booster seat. I bought it last night and wanted to surprise you today since Daddy was here to take the other one out of my car and put this one in its place." His face lit up as he said, "So this is no joke, right? I really need a booster seat. Are we going somewhere now so I can try it out?" "As a matter of fact, we are. Another surprise: I am taking you home to spend the night with me. How does that sound?" "Awesome, Grandma. I love staying at your house. Can we have waffles in the morning?" "Of course, we can."

The next morning, when it was time to take him home, he went running out into the garage. I asked, "What are you doing? Can

Priceless Moments

you give me a chance to gather up anything we need to take back to your house?" He replied, "But I can't wait." I asked, "What can't you wait for?" "Don't laugh at me, but I want to be sure that my booster seat is still in the car. I want to be sure you didn't put the big baby car seat back in its place." I was really surprised by his comment. "Oh, honey, I'd never give you something and then turn around and take it away. That would not be a very nice thing to do." As he crawled into the new car seat, he whispered, "Thank you. I love it."

It's marvelous when we change from unsaved to saved, like growing out of the baby seat to the toddler seat. At times, it's amazing to think that God would save someone like me, but then we realize how our lives have changed for the better. Sometimes we keep praying the sinner's prayer to be sure our "seat" in heaven is secured.

Thank You, LORD, for changing our lives when we grow up and realize our need for You. I pray we accept Your forgiveness without having to "keep touching home base" "just to be sure."

Isaiah 41:10: *Don't you be afraid, for I am with you. Don't be dismayed, for I am your God. I will strengthen you. Yes, I will help you. Yes, I will uphold you with the right hand of my righteousness.*
John 1:12: *But as many as received him, to them he gave the right to become God's children, to those who believe in his name*

Hebrews 13:5: *Be free from the love of money, content with such things as you have, for he has said, "I will in no way leave you, neither will I in any way forsake you."*

September 20th
I Lost My Giraffe

Our grandson entered our house crying, mumbling something between the sobs. I got him calmed down enough to understand, "I lost my giraffe… out camping… I couldn't find it. I didn't take it out of the RV. I'm so sad." I gathered him up and headed to the rocker. "I'm so sorry, buddy. That must be really hard to lose your favorite stuffy." "Oh, Grandma, you have to find me another giraffe. I love giraffes, and I don't want to be without one to go to bed. Will you please look for one for me?" "Buddy, I can't make any promise other than that I will look for one when I'm out and about. It may be very difficult to find one this time of year since it isn't a holiday, but I will promise I will look." He jumped up off my lap and gave me the biggest bear hug he could give. All I could think of now was, "The pressure is on."

I searched the internet but didn't find anything I thought he would like—either too big or too small, odd colors, distorted proportions, just not "lovey" material. After they went home, I went. I think I hit every store in town, but no luck. In one of the grocery stores, I finally found a six-foot giraffe—way too big, not lovey material. I thanked God for at least finding a giraffe, giving me hope that there may be one left somewhere. As I walked through the store, I spied a clearance section, so I thought, "Why not?" As I'm digging through the "leftovers," at the very bottom of the pile was one lone giraffe—lovey material. Just the right size and color.

I marveled at God's goodness for having me stop at a grocery store and rummage through the castoffs, only to find a "jewel". It's that, just like us. The world may cast us off, yet Jesus is just waiting for us to come and find Him, wherever we may be. And, yes, he was absolutely thrilled with his new giraffe.

Thank You, LORD, for providing even the obscure things we pray about. I pray we realize no request is too big or too small as long as we are praying within His will for our lives.

Luke 19:10*: For the Son of Man came to seek and to save that which was lost.*

2 John 1:8*: Watch yourselves, that we don't lose the things which we have accomplished, but that we receive a full reward.*

Acts 27:22*: Now I exhort you to cheer up, for there will be no loss of life among you, but only of the ship.*

September 21st
**Bed Time Story**

After supper, the grandchildren came over to give us hugs before they went to bed. "We have to go to bed now, Grandma. Can you tell us a bedtime story before you go home?" I looked up at their parents for a nod of "yes" or "no." Approval was given, so I said, "Sure. Which story would you like to hear?" They discussed several options between themselves, then replied, "Tell us a story about Solomon as a boy." Very interesting and such an unusual choice. "Well, the Bible does not give us any details about Solomon as a young boy, but we can guess what his life would have been like. He grew up in the palace of his father, King David. This time, I would say he would have been privileged to have had a good education and maybe get to travel to some distant lands with his father. He would have learned to ride a horse, and maybe a camel and donkey."

Looks of confusion crossed their faces. Even their parents were listening to see how I'd get through this one. Finally, "OK. Did he have any siblings?" "We know his father had at least eight wives and many concubines. The Bible records at least nineteen named sons in addition to any unnamed sons from his concubines. This would give Solomon three full brothers and fifteen half-brothers, then any unnamed brothers, one half-sister, and possible sisters that were not mentioned." "What do half-brother and half-sister mean?" It means they have one parent the same with the other parent not their parent. In this case, Solomon was everyone's father, and the children had different mothers." "What kinds of games did they play?" "None in particular are mentioned, but they probably played with what was around them: stones, twigs, ropes, drawing different games in the sand, and moving stones as game pieces." "Wow, wouldn't it be interesting to know for sure?" "Yes, it would."

I thought back to our childhood games and activities: climbing trees, hide-and-seek, marbles—all things that some version of could have been played at that time. I can imagine Jesus playing these with his siblings and friends as well. They had board games, different types of ball games, and, I'm sure, fun bedtime stories.

Thank You, LORD, for providing children with a desire to learn more about You—even through bedtime stories. I pray grownups have the same desire to have details answered to provide a better picture of the God we serve.

Matthew 11:28: *Come to me, all you who labor and are heavily burdened, and I will give you rest.*

Proverbs 3:24: *When you lie down, you will not be afraid. Yes, you will lie down, and your sleep will be sweet.*

Psalm 91:1: *He who dwells in the secret place of the Most High will rest in the shadow of the Almighty.*

September 22nd
Autumn or Fall

"Mommy said we changed seasons today. Did you know that, Grandma?" "Yes, I did. I was thinking about some fun things we could talk about today. First, do you have any questions for me?

Priceless Moments

You always ask such great questions." "I have a question. Why is this new season called both autumn and fall?" "Excellent question. Both words are used in England, but the word fall is the word of choice. Autumn is considered a more formal name. What are some fun things to do that this change of season brings?" "I know one, maybe two. I know it's getting darker earlier each night, and the leaves are starting to change colors." "I know one too. The apples are ready to pick, and our tomatoes are ready to eat." "Both of you have excellent answers. Fall is also called the autumn equinox, meaning we have equal hours of day and night. A long time ago, it was called the "harvest" moon because the full moon closest to the autumn equinox was and still is called the harvest moon."

"OK, let's think about fun activities in the fall." "How about hayrides and bobbing for apples?" "Did you know that bobbing for apples was once a British courting game?" "How could that work?" "Well, the man wrote his name on an apple, and the women would bob for them, hoping to get the apple with her man's name on it. If she got it, it was said to mean they were meant to be together. Another interesting fall fact is that when we turn our clocks back one hour in November, the number of deadly heart attacks drops by twenty percent." "Why is that? Should a time change make a difference?" "Yes, it does. The experts say it's because we get an extra hour of sleep. A lack of sleep is one of the greatest stresses on our hearts."

I thought the greatest stressor on our hearts was not knowing Jesus. All the sin and discontentment weighing on our hearts bring emotional problems along with them. Giving our hearts to Jesus leads to a lighter and happier spirit, enabling us to sleep better and thus unburdening the pressure on our hearts. If we start with God in the early seasons of our lives, we can keep stress in on our hearts for the rest of our lives.

Thank You, LORD, for freeing our bodies of the pressure and of a sinful life. I pray we keep our lives unburdened from the "cares" of this world and focus on the "cares" of others as You would desire we do.

Galatians 4:10: *You observe days, months, seasons, and years.*

Genesis 8:22: *While the earth remains, seed time and harvest, and cold and heat, and summer and winter, and day and night will not cease.*

Ecclesiastes 3:1: *For everything there is a season, and a time for every purpose under heaven:*

September 23rd
<u>Can We Pick Apples?</u>

"Grandma, Daddy, Mommy, my brother, and I are going to pick apples today. They said it's the best time of year to pick them. Do you and Papa want to come along? It will be loads of fun getting them fresh from the trees." "Sure. We were talking about going to get some apples, so now would be as good of a time as any. Let us know which orchard, and we'll meet you there." On our way to the orchard, we talked about stopping on the way home to get supplies to make apple pies and dumplings, canning lids for applesauce, and freezer bags to freeze apples for cranberry apples at Thanksgiving.

"Hi, everyone. Did you know, lucky for us, that when the pilgrims came to America, they brought the apple seeds with them?" Our granddaughter added, "We're also fortunate enough to have had a man named Johnny Appleseed plant apple seeds everywhere he went, giving us these delicious treats to eat." "That's right. Kids, what kind of things do you like to do with apples?" "Some of my favorites are making apple pie, applesauce, drinking apple cider, and just eating your yummy cranberry apples." "I also like apple crisp, apple strudel, and just eating apples dipped in caramel or peanut butter." "You both missed some of my favorites—dried apples and apple dumplings. I'm hungry. Let's do this and get home and get started on making these delicious treats." "Yes, let's go. We're right behind you."

All these little round globes of satisfying treats delight my eyes and tummy. But nothing delights my soul as much as knowing God put them here for our good pleasure and nourishment.

Thank You, LORD, for creating such wonderful, healthy foods for us to eat. I pray we acknowledge these are gifts from Your hands—not some fluke of nature caused by the Big Bang Theory, but Your reality.

Psalm 1:3: *He will be like a tree planted by the streams of water, that produces its fruit in its season, whose leaf also does not wither. Whatever he does shall prosper.*

Ezekiel 17:8: *It was planted in a good soil by many waters, that it might produce branches, and that it might bear fruit, that it might be a good vine*

James 5:7: *Be patient therefore, brothers, until the coming of the Lord. Behold, the farmer waits for the precious fruit of the earth, being patient over it, until it receives the early and late rain.*

September 24th

Can We Make an Apple Pie?

"Grandma, did you finish up all of your apples yet? We hope not, because we'd like to help you make an apple pie." "Actually, I did keep some apples out for you to help me make a pie today. I got out the apple peeler, a pie plate, and all the ingredients to make a pie." "What can we do first? We want to help you with every step." "I want you to understand that if there's any fighting over taking turns, the project will be stopped, OK?" "OK." "First, let's make the pie crust so it's ready when we need it. Here is the recipe. I want you to learn how to read it so you can make other good foods to eat. Let's start by measuring out the flour." They took turns reading the recipe, sounding out the words, measuring, and combining ingredients. "OK, done. Can I use the pastry cutter first?" "Sure, then we can switch, but she will be the first one to shake the bowl after the water is added." "That's fine. I understand that." "Now the pie crust is completed. On to the next step."

"You will make the sugar mixture for the pie." Done without a hitch. "Great. Each of you can peel four apples through the peeler and corer." "Next, here is a cutting board to slice the apples." Each child was very careful with the knife, slicing their four apples and placing them in a bowl. "You will take turns mixing the sugar mixture into the apples" "Perfect. It's time to roll out the crust. I will show you how, then you can take turns to finish it so it's large enough to fit in the pie plate." ... "Mission accomplished." "But it's not a perfect circle." "That's fine. Add the apple mixture to the bottom crust, and I'll show you why."... Apples were added, and the top pie crust was rolled out and placed on top of the apples. "You pinch the two crusts together like this. Once it is done, the extra dough will be cut off." When it was done, it was baked and ready for dessert after dinner. It WAS GOOD.

It was amazing how patient they were to take turns, knowing they'd lose out otherwise. Yet, many adults don't care to follow the rules, setting a poor example for children to follow. The perfect example to follow is Jesus.

Thank You, LORD, for Your perfect plan to redeem mankind. I pray we stay with You throughout our lives to get the dessert at the end of life—to live and reign with You in heaven.

Psalm 116:15: Precious in Yahweh's sight is the death of his saints.

Job 1:20-21: Then Job arose, and tore his robe, and shaved his head, and fell down on the ground, and worshiped. He said, "Naked I came out of my mother's womb, and naked will I return there. *Yahweh gave, and Yahweh has taken away. Blessed be Yahweh's name."*

Philippians 3:10-11: *I want to know Christ and the power of His resurrection in the fellowship of sharing in His sufferings, becoming like Him in His death, and so, somehow, to attain the resurrection from the dead. NIV*

September 25th
<u>I Already Found Him</u>

Our sister-brother grandchildren were playing hide-and-seek at their house when we walked in. I heard, "...8-9-10. Ready or not, here I come." She took off searching all of their usual hiding spots, but to no avail. She looked at me, and I just shrugged my shoulders and said, "You need to keep looking. I can't give you any help. This is something you have to do on your own. Besides, I have no idea where he is hiding. Remember, we just walked in." She continued to look in every little nook and cranny she could find. Her frustration was very evident, but she continued looking. In a few minutes, we heard a little giggle coming from the bedroom. Her eyes lit up, and she took off in the direction of the voice she recognized as her brother's.

In a few minutes, they both emerged laughing. She said, "I already found him." He commented, "I was so quiet when she looked right at me one time, but she just didn't seem to see me. I kept quiet, hoping she would leave the room. When she did, I took a very deep breath. I heard her ask you guys where I was. I decided to stay really quiet and see how long it took her to come back again. The more she talked to you and the more frustrated she got, the more I began to laugh to myself. I guess I wasn't as quiet as I thought because she came back in and looked at me." She said, "I know; I looked right at him. I knew something seemed different, but I didn't know what. I need to stay focused on what I am doing." They laughed, walking hand-in-hand to the playroom.

I thought that when we seek Jesus to find Him as our LORD and Savior, it is something we have to do on our own. Other people may be there to give us guidance and pray with and for us. He is right there in front of us, but we have to open the eyes of our hearts to come to the throne of grace and ask Jesus into our hearts.

Thank You, LORD, for our brother in Jesus. I pray we understand we cannot piggyback off of someone else's experience, but we must come to Jesus and make that personal commitment with our own lips and sincere hearts.

Deuteronomy 4:29: *But from there you shall seek Yahweh your God, and you will find him when you search after him with all your heart and with all your soul.*

Jeremiah 29:13: *You shall seek me, and find me, when you search for me with all your heart.*

Acts 17:27: *that they should seek the Lord, if perhaps they might reach out for him and find him, though he is not far from each one of us.*

September 26th
I Have a Brother, Too

All the grandchildren have relatives on both sides of the family. So they are working to master relationships within the family. There are dads, moms, grandparents, uncles, aunts, cousins, brothers, and sisters. The brother-sister combination had an interesting conversation on one visit to our house. Our granddaughter was teasing her brother because she had a brother and he didn't. His thoughts did not turn to stating that he had a sister, and she didn't. Instead, "That's not fair. I want a brother, too. What can I do about this?" he asked, then sat down. She just rolled her eyes at him, but we motioned to her to hold her tongue.

He sat there in deep thought, and we could literally watch the wheels turning in his mind. He had his head down for a while, being quiet for a long time. After what seemed like an eternity, he looked up with a smile on his face, affirming, "I DO HAVE A BROTHER." Of course, the big sister had to try to argue, "You do not." He remained calm and stated, "My big brother is Jesus." This left her totally speechless as she looked to me for a response. Thunderstruck at his answer, I responded, "You are so right. When we accept Jesus as our Savior, that makes God our Heavenly Father, which makes His Son, Jesus, a big brother to all of us, our blood relative."

I remember trying to understand this as a child, which was sometimes a difficult concept. There are many adults unfamiliar with the Word of God who still find this hard to understand. We must go to Him in childlike faith, accepting and believing all He has said, and His Word will not return to Him void (**Isaiah 55:11**).

Thank You, LORD, that You allow such insight and ability to pull theology together, regardless of age. I pray You allow us all to understand more of You every day, regardless of our age.

Hebrews 2:11: *For both he who sanctifies and those who are sanctified are all from one, for which cause he is not ashamed to call them brothers,*

Romans 8:29: *For whom he foreknew, he also predestined to be conformed to the image of his Son, that he might be the firstborn among many brothers.*

Mark 3:34-35: *Looking around at those who sat around him, he said, "Behold, my mother and my brothers! For whoever does the will of God is my brother, my sister, and mother.*

September 27th
Grandma's Closet

It seems like every time the grandchildren come for a sleepover, they like to explore Grandma's closet. Since we have two extra bedrooms, they all claim a bedroom and feel that everything in there belongs to them. Quite often I hear, "Grandma, why is this in my closet? What are you going to do with it? Can we take "such and such" home tonight? So much for trying to keep things a secret until they receive them for birthdays, Christmas, Easter, or just because…

On one particular occasion, I overheard them "whispering" (kids don't know how to whisper very well). "Come here quick. Look what I found in Grandma's closet. She has more stuff in here than in our bedrooms. I've never seen any of this before." I realized I needed to hustle and prevent them from finding the really "good stuff" hidden in the back of the closet. I entered the room and asked, "What are you guys doing?" The response was, "Oh, nothing. Just playing hide and seek." "Ok. Well, my closet is not a safe place to hide. Let's go read a book." Apparently, they had not been there long enough to do too much exploring.

Interesting, I thought of how God must long for us to go exploring in His Word. He would not get angry with us for being "in there," but would encourage us to "explore" often, spending all the time our little hearts would desire to find all the "gems" in His special book—available to everyone who wants to seek and find.

Thank You, LORD, for providing a very special place for us to learn more about You and Your plan for our lives. I pray we enter our "secret closet" to study and pray, allowing You to illuminate Your Word in this dark world.

Matthew 6:6: *But you, when you pray, enter into your inner room, and having shut your door, pray to your Father who is in secret; and your Father who sees in secret will reward you openly.*

Priceless Moments

John 17:1-2: *Jesus said these things, then lifting up his eyes to heaven, he said, "Father, the time has come. Glorify your Son, that your Son may also glorify you; even as you gave him authority over all flesh, so he will give eternal life to all whom you have given him."*

Mark 1:35: *Early in the morning, while it was still dark, he rose up and went out, and departed into a deserted place, and prayed there.*

September 28th
I Have To Do My Chores

There was a tiny knock at the door. I had no idea who it could be, so I went to the door. "Are your grandkids here?" asked a little boy from down the street. "I noticed you were home today and wondered if they were here and wanted to play." I smiled and said, "Yes, they are here today. I will let them talk to you." I called our grandson, and he came running. "Oh, hi. How are you? It's nice to see you again." The little visitor asked, "Would you like to come out and play?" I held my breath, waiting to hear how he would answer. He looked at me, then responded, "That's really kind of you, but I have chores to do. I promised my Grandma I would help her clean up my bedroom, especially since I'm the one who messed it up. Maybe later or another day, OK?"

After the boy left, I remarked, "Wow, I'm really proud of you for keeping your word to me. That means so much more than I can really tell you." He donned a great big smile and said, "Oh, Grandma, I'd do anything for you. I know I've disappointed you before, and I don't want to do it again." My heart was touched by his words. I walked over and picked him up, giving him a great big hug. When he went to draw away after the hug, I said, "Not yet; I'm not done." He reached up and returned the biggest hug he could give and said, "I wasn't done either." We enjoyed a wonderfully satisfying hug, then I said, "Since you were so honest, I will help you finish the job." We walked back into his room to finish cleaning it up. When done, we gave each other a high five.

He reminded me of just how important it is to keep our word to others, but especially to God. We must remember that works do not define faith. Once you accept Christ as Savior, faith leads to works, freely making you want to do a lot of work out of obedience and love for God.

Thank You, LORD, for changing the bent of our hearts after receiving Your forgiveness. I pray we have a desire to do things for others in obedience to Your commands as well as out of the goodness of our hearts.

2 Corinthians 8:21: *Having regard for honorable things, not only in the sight of the Lord, but also in the sight of men.*

Ephesians 4:25: *Therefore putting away falsehood, speak truth each one with his neighbor. For we are members of one another.*

2 Timothy 2:15: *Give diligence to present yourself approved by God, a workman who doesn't need to be ashamed, properly handling the Word of Truth.*

September 29th

The Wrestling Match

The grandchildren came with us after church one Sunday afternoon. As a fun reward for good behavior at Sunday School and church, we took them out for lunch. They talked excitedly about their class and about what we would do at home. First things first, we changed our clothes, then proceeded to play some games. Next thing I knew, I heard, "I've got you, Grandma." Our grandson had attacked me from behind, so I pulled a switch-a-roo on him, pinning him down between the crotch and under the arm.

Priceless Moments

He called, "Help me, Sissy. Grandma's got me good." She was there in a flash, but I figured this would happen, so I caught her legs in a scissor hold and wrapped my free arm around her waist.

We tussled around for a good ten minutes, giggling to the point they were paralyzed in my arms. "Grandma, we give up. Let us go, please." So, I did. Then she says, "Come on, let's get her." Again, I was able to harness their limbs in holds. We had so much fun playing around—until we heard their mother laughing. She had walked into the midst of our frivolity, saying, "You kids have Grandma pinned. Way to go." We immediately looked up and got quiet, explaining, "Actually, Grandma had us pinned." Mommy said, "You go, Grandma."

Their attack would be nothing like Satan's attacks: fun and laugher, whereas Satan wrestles us to steal, kill, and destroy. That thought sobered my delight as I prayed for these precious children to be aware of his evil deeds.

Thank You, LORD, for protecting us from Satan's attacks when we stay close to You. He can try to harm us, but I pray we know to keep up our *full armor of God* daily and be prepared to do battle.

1 Peter 5:8-9: *Be sober and self-controlled. Be watchful. Your adversary, the devil, walks around like a roaring lion, seeking whom he may devour. Withstand him steadfast in your faith, knowing that your brothers who are in the world are undergoing the same sufferings.*

James 4:7, 8: *Be subject therefore to God. Resist the devil, and he will flee from you. Draw near to God, and he will draw near to you. Cleanse your hands, you sinners. Purify your hearts, you double-minded.*

1 Corinthians 10:13: *No temptation has taken you except what is common to man. God is faithful, who will not allow you to be tempted above what you are able, but will with the temptation also make the way of escape, that you may be able to endure it.*

September 30th
Fun Fruits

"Grandma, we're hungry. Is it time for a snack yet?" I laughed and said, "It seems like we just finished eating and you're hungry already. What do you think we should have?" "I don't know. What do you have? Anything would taste good right now. Can we look in the pantry?" as they were already headed in that direction. Squeals of, "Yes, fun fruits. And you have enough for all of us." I stated, "I have an idea. Why don't we go for a walk first, then come back and have fun fruits?" One munchkin chirped, "I have an even better idea. Why don't we each get a pack of fun fruits and eat them on our walk?" You know, it's hard to argue with logic like that. "Why not? It sounds good to me. Should I give you each a pack, or do you want to pick your own?" I already knew the answer, but I had to ask. Almost in unison, "I want to pick my own." So, they did.

On our walk—eating fun fruits, of course—they chatted about the different shapes, colors, and flavors since each new box was opened for the "try them all" approach. The kids swapped with each other to try the delectable treats. "Wow, I really like the 'fruit shapes,' 'movie characters,' 'the pretty colors', and 'these taste just like mine.' comments were hilarious. As far as I was concerned, they were the same thing packaged differently to get people like me to buy them all to keep the kids and grandkids happy. "Grandma, thank you for all these fun fruits. It was fun to exchange with each other while taking a walk with you." Hugs were received from all around, making it worth it to buy or provide them with treats.

I thought about how churches try to repackage God to draw more people to church and/or their programs. But, in reality, all the creative stuff may be taking away from God's simple truth: *you must be born again.* We must humble ourselves and seek His face, and He will heal our land.

Priceless Moments

Thank You, LORD; the straight-forward message of the gospel presented with Your love is what brings people into the kingdom. I pray we remember that the most important part is to plant the seeds of the gospel, and You will bring the increase.

2 Chronicles 7:14: *if my people, who are called by my name, will humble themselves, pray, seek my face, and turn from their wicked ways, then I will hear from heaven, will forgive their sin, and will heal their land.*

John 3:6-7: *That which is born of the flesh is flesh. That which is born of the Spirit is spirit. Don't marvel that I said to you, 'You must be born anew.'*

2 Corinthians 9:6: *Remember this: he who sows sparingly will also reap sparingly. He who sows bountifully will also reap bountifully. Let each man give according as he has determined in his heart, not grudgingly or under compulsion, for God loves a cheerful giver.*

October

He took a little child, and set him in the middle of them. Taking him in his arms, he said to them, "Whoever receives one such little child in my name, receives me, and whoever receives me, doesn't receive me, but him who sent me."

Mark. 9:36-37

Priceless Moments

October 1ˢᵗ
Story Time

One of our favorite activities with the grandchildren is to create expanded "off-the-cuff" versions of Bible stories they've learned. David and Goliath is an all-time favorite. In their version, Goliath is very scary, making funny faces and hand gestures designed to scare anyone observing the story-in-progress. When Goliath walks, he shakes the entire earth, rips up trees with his bare hands, makes his voice so loud it echoes throughout the valley (to the point one has to cover their ears), and even causes rockslides around them.

Next, poor little David is scared but says, "I realize I serve a great big God, One greater than the mean Goliath." They kneel down and pray, "Dear God, you know that I know you can do anything. Don't let that big mouth make You sound bad." They jump up, singing *My God Is So Big*, while "running" to the stream, grabbing five small stones, adding, "These are for Goliath's brothers, if they would dare try to challenge God." They "run" back to the battle, yelling, "I come after you in the name of the LORD," and put a "stone" in the "sling," twirling it around for "hours" before hurling it at Goliath. Of course, it's a perfect hit every time. They "run over" and look at Goliath's head, reminding the listeners, "Remember he face-planted, not landing on the back of his head. Thank You, God, for victory." and cut off Goliath's head, adding, "And I'm carrying it all the way back to Jerusalem." Of course, this excellent storytelling, complete with drama, is completed with a bow and another "Thank You" to God.

I love how unashamed they are in proclaiming "how great is our God," not caring who sees or hears them, but letting it all hang out for the LORD. They tell the story like it is—with embellishments—to anyone who will listen. May we have that same child-like attitude and faith to declare the Word of God across hill and dale: our homes, jobs, restaurant prayers, vacations, anywhere we encounter people, letting them know our God reigns and that He is bigger than any "Goliath" we encounter in our lives. The most important lesson I learned was to thank God at all times, something not in the original story but something their little hearts felt was important to do.

Thank You, LORD, for little ones who are willing to break through our grown-up exteriors to realize You are bigger than any of our problems and to be in an attitude of gratitude. As we practice saying thanks, may it get easier for us to do and enable us to realize more things for which we need to be thankful.

Psalm 9:1-2*: I will give thanks to Yahweh with my whole heart. I will tell of all your marvelous works. I will be glad and rejoice in you. I will sing praise to your name, O Most High.*

Colossians 4:2*: Continue steadfastly in prayer, watching in it with thanksgiving*

2 Corinthians 9:11*: You will be made rich in every way so that you can be generous on every occasion, and through us your generosity will result in thanksgiving to God. NIV*

October 2nd

What's My Surprise?

"I told you if you guys gave me good behavior while we were in the store, I would give you a surprise. Do you remember that?" "Yes, we do, but we didn't want to ask. Now, since you brought it up, what is our surprise?" I walked over to them and said, "Group hug. How's that?" No, it has to be more than a group hug. Really, what is it?" I said, "OK," and gave them a single hug each. "How's that? Your very own hug." "Grandma, we know you better than that. What do you have for us?" "OK, OK, I'll give you a couple of choices. Do you want a fruit snack or a picnic lunch? Either way, we're going to the park. How does this sound?"

Priceless Moments

"Awesome, but why don't we have a picnic lunch with fruit snacks at the park?" I replied, "I think you read my mind."

It was a beautiful day as we sat down to eat our lunch. I said, "I have another surprise for you. Are you ready? Close your eyes." Familiar voices said, "Hi guys. Can we join you for lunch?" They opened their eyes to see their cousins. "We came to eat lunch and play with you. Grandma invited us and said she packed a lunch for all of us." "Yes, that's correct. Your moms and I want to see you eat a good lunch so you have the strength to play with each other." "How long do we get to stay here?" they asked. "Well, we decided we could stay as long as you all play well together or it's supper time, whichever comes first. So, go have a good time."

I imagined Jesus playing with His brothers, sisters, cousins, and neighbors, then thinking about how our family and friends were growing up. Although their lives would all have been very different from ours, families and friends still act the same way together, enjoying the fun and the company, just like these precious grandchildren.

Thank You, LORD, for Your plan for family and friends. I pray we understand the value You place on life and enjoy it to the max.

Psalm 133:1: *See how good and how pleasant it is for brothers to live together in unity!*

Proverbs 17:6: *Children's children are the crown of old men; the glory of children are their parents.*

Colossians 3:13: *Bear with each other and forgive whatever grievances you may have against one another. Forgive as the LORD forgave you. And over all these virtues put on love, which binds them all together in perfect unity. NIV*

October 3rd

I Carry My Bible

"Grandma, I am so excited you and Papa gave me a Bible for Easter. Every Sunday when I go to church, I carry my Bible. I am learning to look up Scriptures when we talk about them—in my own Bible." "Honey, that is wonderful news. We know that having your own Bible is important so you can look up verses, read certain stories, or pick verses to memorize any time you want to do so." "True, but I feel bad because a lot of my friends can't do that since they don't own a Bible of their own." "I'm sorry to hear that since having your own Bible is a wonderful gift for people of all ages since you can hold God's Word in the palm of your hand."

He went and brought his Bible into the room and said, "We read from the Bible for our devotions and as bedtime stories. Grandma, do you think we could pray for my friends that God would provide them a Bible, too?" "I think that is a wonderful idea. We can certainly pray for them. We can even put feet to our prayers and talk to your Sunday School teacher to see if there is a way to present Bibles to those who currently don't own a Bible." "Oh, I love that idea. How soon can we talk to her?"

I remember when I received my first Bible. It meant the world to me. It has grown even more precious and important over the years as I continue to study and now share it with our beautiful grandchildren. I want them to understand the feeling of holding, reading, studying, and sharing God's precious Word to feed their own souls and to feel the need to share God's Word with every soul in this world.

Thank You, LORD, for inspiring over forty authors to write the sixty-six books of the Bible under the direction of the Holy Spirit. I pray we understand that You did it right the first time, not needing any additions or revisions to always make it accurate; rather, it is always accurate as written to give us clear direction on history and prophecy as You have planned. Now we know what to look for in our future—both on earth and in heaven.

Psalm 119:18: *Open my eyes, that I may see wondrous things out of your law*

Luke 24:45: *Then he opened their minds, that they might understand the Scriptures.*

Nehemiah 8:12: *All the people went their way to eat, to drink, to send portions, and to celebrate, because they had understood the words that were declared to them.*

October 4th

The Bobblehead

When driving down the road, the kids noticed something moving on the dash of the car behind us, saying, "Grandma, what is that thing moving all around in the front part of those people's car behind us?" Between trying to watch the road and looking in the rear-view mirror, I saw this image of a man connected by a spring to the rest of his body. "Nice spot," I said. "That's called a bobblehead. These wiggle around when given a light touch or by the movement of the car. Years ago, they were made from a breakable material called bisque porcelain, then papier-mâché, or ceramic. Baseball teams had one made for each team or a few select players. Music groups, like the Beatles, and baseball teams and select players became desirable items to collect. A few baseball teams gave away bobbleheads to attract fans to games. Post Cereals put them in boxes of cereal."

"They had times of great popularity and other times of little interest. To increase sales, bobbleheads of political figures, well-known people, and movie characters were created, once again increasing sales. Some people will line the front dash of their car with many of these collectible figures. Due to their rise in popularity, the National Bobblehead Hall of Fame was opened in

2016. The *Guinness Book of World Records* of 2016 set the record for the world's largest bobblehead at 15' 4".

It's amazing how fads come and go, with creators working to develop the next best thing. Bobbleheads of Jesus have gone through several phases, with the most recent being more respectful and realistic than previous ones. Yet, our Jesus never changes; He's the same yesterday, today, and forever.

Thank You, LORD, you're not some action figure whose head bobbles to and fro with movement, but a stalwart figure ever-present in our lives. I pray we don't get caught up in *Jesus movement* fads but keep our heads about us and look up to Your steadfast guidance daily.

Exodus 15:13: You, in your loving kindness, have led the people that you have redeemed. You have guided them in your strength to your holy habitation.

Job 10:12: You have granted me life and loving kindness. Your visitation has preserved my spirit.

Psalm 63:3: Because your loving kindness is better than life, my lips shall praise you.

October 5th

It's Spam Again

For a long period of time, it seemed every time my phone rang, it was spam. It always came on the same ring tone, so the grandchildren soon started saying, "Grandma, it's spam again." If I were not close to the phone, they would grab it and turn off the ringer. As our baby granddaughter grew, she became very aware of the ring tone, dancing in my arms as she enjoyed the music. Over time, as the older kids turned off the ringer, she began to get fussy, which was totally unlike her. As this was occurring day

Priceless Moments

after day, we started to realize just how much she was enjoying the music. "Hey, Grandma, I have a great idea. Let's let the music play all the way through one time, and the next time shut it off to see what she does." "Great idea. Let's try it."

About an hour later, the phone rang again—spam. As suggested, we let it ring. The baby was delighted, clapping her hands and smiling. Then, a couple of minutes passed when it rang again, so they shut off the ringer. The baby got really fussy and started chattering to her cousin. Of course, they laughed. "Grandma, she is upset with me for shutting off the music and is letting me know." Well, the theory immediately got tested again as the phone rang—spam. Again, as planned, we let it ring. Needless to say, she got really excited, laughing and clapping her hands. So, now, when spam comes calling, we just let it ring—and all eyes watch the baby.

It's amazing how something so simple in one sense and annoying in another can bring such joy and annoyance in the same situation. How God must view us like that. We may find pleasure in doing something not pleasing to God and feel drudgery in doing something we know we should for the kingdom. Yet, God will still not be pleased with our motive. We should endeavor to do things out of the goodness of our hearts.

Thank You, LORD, for opportunities to reflect upon our motives and actions. I pray we think things through before we react to situations so our actions can be a good reflection on us and pleasing to You.

Proverbs 16:2: *All the ways of a man are clean in his own eyes; but Yahweh weighs the motives.*

1 Corinthians 4:5: *Therefore judge nothing before the time, until the Lord comes, who will both bring to light the hidden things of darkness, and reveal the counsels of the hearts. Then each man will get his praise from God*

Priceless Moments

James 4:3*: You ask, and don't receive, because you ask with wrong motives, so that you may spend it on your pleasures.*

October 6th
The Circus

"Have you ever been to a circus, Grandma? Some kids at school said they went to one last week. Do you know where the circus was held? What happens there?" "Each circus is slightly different, with a different theme they want to share with the audience. The first circus to start in England had jugglers, a rope dancer, acrobats, and a fiddle player. Soon, the circus came to America, adding animal acts like horses, wild animals, and clowns. Eventually, the idea of selling food and souvenirs made going to the circus even more fun." "What does a circus place look like?" "Actually, it is a large round tent area called an arena. There are seats all around the inside of the tent to watch the show. They take the tent down and travel from place to place so people in many different areas can enjoy the fun."

A long pause, then the question, "Have you ever been to a circus?" "I've been to several different circuses. On my job, I used to take clients to see a small circus at our worksite. In the evening, we would take your dad to see the same circus, only much bigger, in our town. We also saw several different bigger circuses while on vacation." "Were they all the same, or were they different? Do you think we can go to the circus sometime? What was your favorite part about the show, Grandma?" "I enjoyed all of it, but the highlight was seeing the joy on the children's faces as they watched the entertainment. At different times, we got to know a few of the workers. They traveled with their families, working, eating, and playing together every day. Their children complete schoolwork during the day and learn good work ethics at night. I'm not sure when a circus will be close to us, but we can watch for flyers around town and for information in the newspaper."

Priceless Moments

I thought of how many times we go to church wanting to be entertained, but church is not for entertainment. Our focus is to worship God through fellowship, singing, prayer, having the truth of the Word opened to us, and communion.

Thank You, LORD, for Your faithfulness and truth. I pray we attend a church that preaches God's Word straight from the Bible and where the Holy Spirit still joins us in corporate worship.

Acts 10:44: While Peter was still speaking these words, the Holy Spirit fell on all those who heard the word.

1 Corinthians 6:19: Or don't you know that your body is a temple of the Holy Spirit who is in you, whom you have from God? You are not your own,

John 4:24: God is spirit, and those who worship him must worship in spirit and truth.

October 7th
Watch Your Attitude

On occasion, I find myself repeating the words, "Watch your attitude, young lady or young man," whichever is appropriate for the given day. I heard those words, once again, escaping from my mouth: "Watch your attitude, young lady." To my surprise, not giving more grief, she stopped, asking, "What is an attitude, anyway?" Rather surprised, I responded, "Attitude is a manner of acting, feeling, or thinking that shows your disposition, opinion, and how you will respond to and approach things, then communicate that to others. Attitude shows up in the way you talk, your behavior, your body posture, and whether you work with or against something or someone. It is more important than facts or anything else because it really stands out. People will judge you based on the attitude you show or portray. Your attitude can make a good or bad impression on others."

I could see the wheels turning in her little head as she mulled over what she had just heard. "Tell me more," she said. "It's OK to think differently from someone else. Tell them how you feel or what you think in a calm, cool manner. A bad attitude may seem cool, but a good attitude will rule. You need to focus and work on believing in yourself to develop this positive attitude. Even if you don't believe it much at first, the more you practice it, the more you will look positively at yourself. It's a win-win for everyone. We are in charge of our attitudes. Attitude can make or break you; it's everything, so pick a good, positive one."

Our attitude toward God is so important. It is reflected in the way we treat and react to others. I thought about a saying of Charles Swindoll: "I am convinced that life is ten percent what happens to me and ninety percent how I react to it. And so it is with us. We are in charge of our attitudes."

Thank You, LORD, for reminding us how important our attitude really is—at home, at church, at work, at play, but especially with You. I pray we keep our attitude in check to reflect more of You.

Romans 15:5: *Now the God of perseverance and of encouragement grant you to be of the same mind with one another according to Christ Jesus, that with one accord you may with one mouth glorify the God and Father of our Lord Jesus Christ.*

1 Peter 4:1: *Therefore, since Christ suffered for us in the flesh, arm yourselves also with the same mind; for he who has suffered in the flesh has ceased from sin,*

Ephesians 4:23: *and that you be renewed in the spirit of your mind*

Priceless Moments

October 8th

What is Wisdom and Knowledge?

"Hey, Grandma, we heard the words wisdom and knowledge in our Bible reading. What are they?" "I think to better understand them, let's look at what each word means separately. For more help, I'm going to give you another word, too. The word knowledge deals with facts. Understanding is the ability to restate what you've heard to let others know you've grasped its meaning. Wisdom is the ability to take what you've learned and know what to do with it after determining the facts and circumstances of the situation." "OK, I get that, so how do I use them?"

"Good question. You must learn to use all three together by collecting the facts, and then make sure you understand what those facts are telling you. Wisdom will help you decide which way to go once you understand the situation. But, for a Christian, there is a vital part of this that needs to be added to the decision." "What is that, prayer?" "Exactly. Papa and I never make a decision without praying about it first and discussing what options are to be considered. God has never failed to give us the right direction to follow because we have always sought His will before going ahead with our plans."

I thought of how at any time we would have made a different choice, but God's leading changed the direction of our path. Afterwards, when looking back, we could see that "Father knows best," indeed. I would not like to see how things would have turned out if we had proceeded in our own "wisdom."

Thank You, LORD, for being faithful to lead, guide, and protect us by first taking our needs and cares to You. I pray our first thoughts are to ask You what we should do in our life's decisions, so we are honoring You in all that we do.

Proverbs 1:7*: The fear of Yahweh is the beginning of knowledge; but the foolish despise wisdom and instruction.*

Priceless Moments

Proverbs 2:6: *For Yahweh gives wisdom. Out of his mouth comes knowledge and understanding.*

Isaiah 11:2: *Yahweh's Spirit will rest on him: the spirit of wisdom and understanding, the spirit of counsel and might, the spirit of knowledge and of the fear of Yahweh.*

October 9th
The Birthday Cake

Our grandson enjoys baking, so he asked, "Can we bake something today for your birthday?" I asked, "What do you have in mind?" He replied, "I don't know; I would just like to bake something. What would you like?" I thought for a minute, then said, "I'm really hungry for a peanut butter cake. How does that sound to you?" His face lit up, and he said, "Oh, Grandma, that sounds so good. We haven't had one for a long time. Let's do it." My little helper was right there, pulling ingredients for our creation. He washed his hands, helped measure, stirred with a whisk, and poured the batter into the pan. I took over and popped the cake in the oven. He said, "Can I have two peanut butter chips, please and thank you, for being a good helper?" "Well, you've done such a fine job so far, I don't see why not," I said, handing him three peanut butter chips.

We decided to make the icing while the cake baked, so it could set up some while the cake cooled. Again, he measured out the ingredients while I melted the butter. Everything was combined, once again, with the icing until it was ready for the refrigerator. He asked, "Can you turn on the oven light so I can watch the cake bake?" "Sure," I responded, "if I can do dishes while you keep an eye on the cake." He just smiled.

I smiled, realizing he knew it was my birthday and wanted to make me something. How much more our Heavenly Father smiles at us and wants to do nice things for us as well. His love is so great that He will lavish it upon us every time He feels we deserve it.

Thank You, LORD, for special days when we make an effort to do nice things for others. I pray we realize that every day is an opportunity to share Your goodness with everyone we meet, making them feel important too.

Psalm 118:24: *This is the day that Yahweh has made. We will rejoice and be glad in it!*

Psalm 71:6: *I have relied on you from the womb. You are he who took me out of my mother's womb. I will always praise you.*

Ephesians 2:10: *For we are his workmanship, created in Christ Jesus for good works, which God prepared before that we would walk in them.*

October 10th
Television

"Grandma, can we watch something on TV today? I know some shows are really good for our minds and others are not, so you can help us decide what would be good to watch. Maybe we could watch something that you like to watch." I responded, "It's possible we could do something like that as long as we watch what is good for our minds, like an educational show or one of the old-time shows with clean language and fun things to watch." "Can you give us some ideas of what those might be?" "Let's start here: do you want to watch a game show, cartoons, westerns, Disney, or comedy?" "Let's watch a funny comedy. And if we can't find something on television, we can watch a DVD."

"While we're flipping through channels, I'll tell you a little bit about the beginnings of television. Did you know the first TV came in black-and-white and only had a few hours of programming throughout each day, usually in the morning when the kids were at school? You could hardly see because the picture was snowy-looking until you had to spread a thing called rabbit ears to try and bring in the picture more clearly. The shows where the good guys always won, families always resolved their problems, fathers always knew best, and people believed in God. A promise made was a promise kept; people never swore or broke their vows. Unfortunately, those kinds of things no longer hold true on television or in our world." "Man, Grandma, you could have watched anything you wanted, right?"

I thought about how the show *Father Knows Best* is like our Heavenly Father. No matter the situation, God is there. God always knows what is best for us and will accomplish that for us when we live for Him.

Thank You, LORD, for a Heavenly Father Who is interested in our lives and takes care of us 24/7/365 when we put our trust in You. I pray we stay tuned to Your channel of communication to see the news regarding our heavenly future as it unfolds before our very eyes.

Matthew 24:33: *Even so you also, when you see all these things, know that he is near, even at the doors.*

Luke 12:56: *You hypocrites! You know how to interpret the appearance of the earth and the sky, but how is it that you don't interpret this time.*

2 Timothy 3:1: *But know this: that in the last days, grievous times will come.*

October 11th
<u>The Magic Pen</u>

Another granddaughter found a special pen she thought I would like. After she gave it to me, I remarked, "The pen I've been using just ran out of ink, so I need one. Thank you so much, honey." giving her a big hug and a kiss. She said, "You're welcome. You can write us some fun stories to read. But Grandma, after you use it for a while, can I have it back? I really like it, and they didn't have another one for me to get one for myself." Ah, history is repeating itself. I guess there's a first time for everything since this is the second time I've been asked moments after receiving something—a pen—if I could give it back. I looked at her and said, "I'll consider giving it back to you." Excitedly, she said, "Oh, thank you, Grandma; you're the best."

Fast forward to Christmas. She came over one day and asked, "Grandma, did you use the pen I gave you? Are you ready to give it back now?" Frankly, I hadn't forgotten about this conversation in October, but I was surprised she remembered. I had used the pen several times but hadn't used it in a while. I said, "Thank you for your patience concerning the pen. Indeed, it is very nice, but I have a question for you. I gave you a special doll for Christmas, so can I have it back?" She gave me the funniest look, asking, "Why do you want something back that you gave me?" As soon as it came out of her mouth, she understood why I asked such a question. "Oh, Grandma, I'm so sorry. Will you forgive me?" "Absolutely. But I have a special "just because" gift for you because I love you." I handed her a small, wrapped package. She gave me the funniest look, shook the package, then ripped it open. Inside was the pen she had given me. A breathless "Thank you" escaped her lips, followed by a big hug. I said, "For future reference, don't give something away you want for yourself. That way, you avoid hurting someone else's feelings." She had a look of understanding, shaking her head in agreement.

Priceless Moments

LORD, how many times have we given You something or promised You something, only to change our minds later? Scripturally, we are not to promise something, but let our "yes" be "yes" and our "no" be "no."

Thank You, LORD, for never asking to take back our salvation. I pray we realize what a precious gift You have given us, forever treasuring something we could never pay for and appreciating Your sacrifice on our behalf.

John 4:10: Jesus answered her, "If you knew the gift of God, and who it is who says to you, 'Give me a drink,' you would have asked him, and he would have given you living water."

2 Corinthians 9:15: Now thanks be to God for his unspeakable gift!

Ephesians 2:8, 9: for by grace you have been saved through faith, and that not of yourselves; it is the gift of God, not of works, that no one would boas

October 12th
<u>The Quilt</u>

We have several quilts on a rack in our home. The children love to run their hands over them. On this day, a burning question was asked: "Where did you get all these quilts? They are really nice. I've never seen anything like these before." "Thank you. They are from important people in our lives. One is from my parents, one from Papa's aunt that her grandmother had made, and one Papa bought for us for our twenty-fifth wedding anniversary." "Why would Papa buy you a quilt?" "Because quilts remind us of memories, dreams, and any personal experiences that you may have gone through in your life that are represented by each square

Priceless Moments

used. The one he bought contained many pieces similar to ones that reminded us of both of our childhoods."

She thought for a minute, then asked, "How can quilts remind you of your childhood?" "Traditionally, quilts were made from scrap pieces of clothing. As a child outgrew their clothes, they were repurposed, or used again, by cutting out the good pieces and sewing them together for use later as bed coverings. Sometimes America has been referred to as a quilt because of the many different people and cultures that have come here looking for a better way of life. Once here, they become a part of a "quilt" by connecting us with a common bond as we work together to make this a better country."

Our lives are much like a quilt. God takes pieces from our lives and places them all together to make a beautiful covering. As we look back on each scrap, we are reminded of good times and bad times. The amazing "ah-ha" moment comes when we realize the opposite is true of what we may have thought. There are a few bad memories woven in among the mostly happy memories of our lives. So, if life gives you scraps, make a quilt.

Once I read a quote that said: *In your life, the people become like a patchwork quilt. Some leave with you a piece that is bigger than you wanted, and others smaller than you thought you needed.* Also, *quilts are like friends—a great source of comfort.*

Thank You, LORD, for showing us visuals to understand Your perfect plan for each of us. I pray that although we may not have put it together this way, you have indeed made a much better end product than we could have done on our own.

Proverbs 10:12*: Hatred stirs up strife, but love covers all wrongs.*

2 Corinthians 1:3-4*: Blessed be the God and Father of our Lord Jesus Christ, the Father of mercies and God of all comfort; who comforts us in all our affliction, that we may be able to comfort those who are in any affliction, through the comfort with which we ourselves are comforted by God.*

Priceless Moments

John 16:7*: Nevertheless I tell you the truth: It is to your advantage that I go away, for if I don't go away, the Counselor won't come to you. But if I go, I will send him to you.*

October 13th
<u>Open That Bible</u>

A new friend of ours was visiting church this morning. After service, we were walking to the parking lot together when our grandchildren came running up to say hi. She said, "Oh, man. I really don't know what to do right now. I have so many decisions to make that I almost feel overwhelmed. What should I do?" Our grandson overheard this comment from our friend, so he responded, "Open that Bible in your hand. God has so many cool answers in there for you to read. I know Grandma and Papa look for answers in there all the time. And it's also important that you pray about your decisions. God also gives you answers that way, too." And he was off to catch up with his parents.

I almost froze in place, not knowing how she would respond to his abrupt yet spot-on answer. I could see her inhale deeply, responding, "Wow. That was a lot coming from such a little person." To give her a moment to digest his information, I responded, "Yes, it is. We've been teaching them from infancy about the goodness of God and His ability to take care of all our needs, but we must take it to Him in prayer, read His Word, and be open to His leading." A smile started to illuminate her face as understanding was taking place. "I know what I'm doing this afternoon," she said. "I'm going to go home and search the Scriptures and pray. I wish someone would have taught me this when I was his age." I responded, "And I'll be praying with and for you, too."

Oh, for the boldness of a child. They are so forthright and honest about everything, telling it like it is. No pretense here. The plain, "in your face truth" is what people need more now than platitudes to counter the twisting, deceiving work of Satan.

Thank You, LORD, for the ability to ask You to prepare people's hearts to hear and receive Your truth. I pray we go to You and ask for Your guidance on our mouths to prepare hearts, then ask for You to give us the boldness to proclaim Your truth to everyone since You will have prepared their hearts to hear Your truth.

Psalm 119:105: *Your word is a lamp to my feet, and a light for my path.*

1 Peter 3:15: *But sanctify the Lord God in your hearts. Always be ready to give an answer to everyone who asks you a reason concerning the hope that is in you, with humility and fear.*

Luke 12:47: *That servant, who knew his lord's will, and didn't prepare, nor do what he wanted, will be beaten with many stripes,*

October 14th

Columbus Day

"Guess what, Grandma? We talked about Columbus Day in school today. Did you know he is given credit for discovering America?" "Very good. The holiday is a national holiday here to celebrate him sailing across the Atlantic Ocean and landing in the Bahamas, close to America. The official date was October 12, 1492."
"You're right. Our teacher taught us a little rhyme that says, 'In 1492, Columbus sailed the ocean blue.' We also learned he brought three ships with ninety men: the Niña, La Pinta, and the Santa Maria. He was an Italian, like my other Grandma, sailing Spanish ships cross the Atlantic to find a new all-water trading route from Europe to Asia. Instead, he found us." He made me smile.

Priceless Moments

I had to ask, "Do you know where he got the idea to sail West?" "No. Where and why did he?" "From reading his Bible. He figured if God created the world in six days with a day of rest, it would be six parts land and one part water. He knew how far it was to cross the land to Asia—the six parts. Then he figured out how far it would be to sail in the opposite direction on an all-water route. He thought the earth was about 2,400 miles around. So, if he sailed one hundred miles per day, he could reach Asia in thirty days. But, like you said, he didn't find an all-water route; he found us."

Ah, the importance of being found, especially if it's by our LORD and Savior. Sometimes we may try to sail away from God—like Jonah—or just turn our backs on Him, hoping He'll forget us. If we, like Columbus, would study our Bibles, we would know that God sees us all the time. He knows where we're at and what we're doing, thinking, and saying. Fortunately, He is always ready to forgive us and accept us into His family.

Thank You, LORD, for Your extended grace that is long-suffering and patiently waiting for us to return to You. I pray we seek You while You may be found, before the end of the world, before it's too late…

2 Chronicles 7:14: *if my people, who are called by my name, will humble themselves, pray, seek my face, and turn from their wicked ways, then I will hear from heaven, will forgive their sin, and will heal their land*

Isaiah 55:6: *Seek Yahweh while he may be found. Call on him while he is near.*

Proverbs 18:10: *Yahweh's name is a strong tower: the righteous run to him, and are safe.*

Priceless Moments

October 15th
<u>Empty Arms</u>

I had just received word that my mother had passed away. I was feeling so much pain that it felt like my heart was breaking apart. Our grandson sensed my grief and came running over to me, threw his arms around me, and said, "I'm so sorry, Grandma. I will miss her, too. But it will be OK because Jesus will be with us, and He will take good care of her for us because we know she is in heaven right now, helping Him make room for the rest of us to join her someday." "Sweetheart, you are so right. God knows we will have grief during our time on this earth. He's given us each other so we don't have to go through this alone, as well as words of comfort from Scripture, family, friends, neighbors, coworkers, and fellow Christians. How much more will our LORD be with us to comfort and hold our hand throughout those early days, months, years, and beyond?" "Wow, Grandma, that's really awesome. Jesus said He would never leave us, and I believe Him."

His tenderness and attempts to comfort me truly touched my heart. I pulled him close and asked, "Do you know what else makes me feel better?" He gave me a funny look, and then the answer dawned on him. "Grandma, we should make some tea and tell fun stories about Great-Grandma. I can go ask Dad, Mom, and my sister to join us. It's always a lot more fun to laugh than cry. Maybe we could even make some popcorn to have with our tea. What do you think?" "I think Jesus sent you down to us so you can help all of us feel better." He just smiled, squeezed me tight, and said, "I have an idea. You make the tea, and I'll go get the others. I'll be right back," and off he went. Mister organizer—so I started the tea.

I realized that when we are hurting, we can crawl up in our Heavenly Daddy's lap and sob as long as needed. He is not judgmental, nor does He rush us off His lap. He is willing to take as much time for us as is needed until we are ready to get down and continue living. Only His love can help fill the hole in our aching hearts.

Thank You, LORD, for Your availability, day or night, when news arrives that breaks our hearts. I pray we turn to You to help us through these rough times, knowing You will never leave us nor forsake us.

Psalm 34:18: *Yahweh is near to those who have a broken heart, and saves those who have a crushed spirit.*

1 Thessalonians 4:13: *But we don't want you to be ignorant, brothers, concerning those who have fallen asleep, so that you don't grieve like the rest, who have no hope.*

2 Corinthians 1:3-5: *Blessed be the God and Father of our Lord Jesus Christ, the Father of mercies and God of all comfort; who comforts us in all our affliction, that we may be able to comfort those who are in any affliction, through the comfort with which we ourselves are comforted by God. For as the sufferings of Christ abound to us, even so our comfort also abounds through Christ.*

October 16th

Painting Rocks

Recently, I learned how to paint rocks, an art project I really enjoyed. We were given the opportunity to do as many as we desired, so I made a ladybug for each grandchild. When I gave them each one, they were thrilled. I was asked, "Can you teach us to do that? It looks like fun." Since I wanted to do more, I said, "Sure, but I don't have any supplies here. If we go to Hobby Lobby, we can get paints, brushes, and paint trays. We need to look for rocks in our xeriscape and your driveway." En route to the store, the kids talked excitedly about different designs they wanted to make, like ladybugs, birds, trees, turtles, and unicorns.

Priceless Moments

At the store, the kids selected the desired colors of paint while I gathered the other supplies. "Grandma, can we stop at our house and each pick five stones? We didn't find many bigger stones in your yard, and we want to paint them today." I realized I needed stones as well. "Sure. We can swing by there on the way back to our house." A quick stop yielded fifteen nicely shaped rocks for whatever designs they wanted to paint. Back at the house, newspaper was placed on the table, paints and brushes were taken out, and the fun began. Much to their delight, each progressive rock painted showed an improvement in quality." "How long will it take for these to dry? How soon can we spray them? Can we take them home tonight?" Questions were answered; rocks were completed, finished, and taken home. The kids were so excited to show their parents and start a rock garden.

I pondered how God puts us through a series of improvements to arrive at the end product He desires before He takes us home. It's the interim time between the "improvements" and "going home" when God can paint us as many times as needed to design our lives for His glory.

Thank You, LORD, for seeing each one of us as a special project to design, paint, and rework to bring honor and glory to Your name. I pray that each stroke of Your brush brings us closer to the ultimate picture You desire us to be.

Isaiah 64:8: *But now, Yahweh, you are our Father. We are the clay and you our potter. We all are the work of your hand.*

Ephesians 1:13: *In him you also, having heard the word of the truth, the Good News of your salvation—in whom, having also believed, you were sealed with the promised Holy Spirit,*

Ecclesiastes 3:11: *He has made everything beautiful in its time. He has also set eternity in their hearts, yet so that man can't find out the work that God has done from the beginning even to the end.*

Priceless Moments

October 17th
Bone Broth

"Grandma, what are you drinking? It looks like colored water." "Actually, I'm drinking bone broth. It's very good for your muscles, bones, digestion, kidneys, blood, weight loss—you name it, it's good for it." "Why is it good for you?" "There are many good vitamins and minerals, things called amino acids and essential fatty acids, and other things that are very healthy for the body. So much so that in the 12th century, the Egyptians prescribed it as a medicine remedy for colds and flu to heal their people. In Jewish culture, they actually referred to bone soup as "Jewish penicillin" because it helped keep people's feet and legs from swelling." "What else can you use it for besides drinking it?" "I use it to cook vegetables, make mashed potatoes, gravy, pasta, and things like that."

"What do you use to make bone broth?" "That's a very good question. I'm ready to make some now. Would you like to help me?" "Sure, what can we do?" "I'll have you get the chicken bones already cleaned from the refrigerator, please and thank you. I'll fill the crockpot with some water. Then we'll add those ingredients—a bay leaf, garlic, salt, and pepper—cover, and cook for 24 hours." "Why do you cook it for so long?" "The longer it's cooked, the more nutritious and delicious it is because it helps the marrow in the bones break down, releasing all the healthy stuff in them. When it's done, I'll pour it through a strainer to remove any bones. After that, I can drink it plain or add chicken, carrots, or other seasonings, whatever I like, to make delicious soup. As a matter of fact, I'm going to use this for chicken soup tomorrow. It will be a perfect meal for a cold, snowy day."

I was reminded of how easy and beneficial making and using homemade bone broth is for our body, just like accepting Jesus as our Savior is healthy for our soul. The longer we serve Him, the sweeter He grows, yielding more benefit to our body and soul.

Priceless Moments

Thank You, LORD, for curious minds that help us see You in everything. I pray we can keep a child-like curiosity about the need to know that reveals so many hidden things about Your creation. Hiding the "gift of life" in animal bones for us to find keeps us guessing about what other miracles You've hidden for us to find.

Luke 8:17*: For nothing is hidden that will not be revealed; nor anything secret that will not be known and come to light.*

Daniel 2:22*: He reveals the deep and secret things. He knows what is in the darkness, and the light dwells with him.*

Amos 3:7*: Surely the Lord Yahweh will do nothing, unless he reveals his secret to his servants the prophets.*

October 18th
<u>You Dog-Gone Grandma</u>

Our grandson arrived with a runny nose. Frequently, he would touch his nose, then dab it with a Kleenex. Each time, I asked him to please wash his hands. One time, he said, "No, I don't want to." I said, "I need you to do hand washing to stop germs from getting on everything and passing it on to others to get sick." He stomped off, washed his hands, then came back out, yelling, "You dog-gone Grandma. I didn't want to wash my hands, and you made me. I'll never play with your toys again. I'll never read your books again. I'll never come to your house again. I'll not eat any of your birthday cake." Thunderstruck by his outburst, I decided to yell back, saying, "I really don't care if you choose to not return here, but you will not yell at me when I was only trying to protect you and everyone around you."

He froze in place, eyes huge, and yelled, "Don't yell at me. You make me mad." I calmly said to him, "I apologize for yelling at you, but I wanted you to understand and feel how much it hurts to be treated like that." His little head dropped. "I'm sorry, Grandma." I scooped him up and headed for the rocker. I said, "Can you tell me why your heart and tongue spewed those words?" Head still down, he said, "Satan made me have bad behavior." We talked about how his hand washing could keep all of us healthy, and he finally agreed.

How many times have we had a temper tantrum when we felt like God was forcing our hand to do something, only to unload on Him after completing the task? Once we have vented, remorse and embarrassment settle upon us, and we apologize, opening our ears to listen and our hearts to understand His will for us.

Thank You, LORD, for Your broad shoulders to endure our unacceptable behavior, your loving heart to extend forgiveness once we understand Your leading in our lives, and your open arms of acceptance. I pray we have broad enough shoulders to accept Your rebuke and get our hearts right with the Giver of life.

Proverbs 8:17: *I love those who love me. Those who seek me diligently will find me.*

Jeremiah 29:13: *You shall seek me, and find me, when you search for me with all your heart.*

Matthew 6:33: *But seek first God's Kingdom and his righteousness; and all these things will be given to you as well.*

October 19th

Help, My Tooth Is Loose

"Oh, Grandma, come here quick. My front tooth is loose, and I'm scared. Can you help me?" "I walked over to see what she was talking about, only to find her with her hand covering her mouth. She looked panic-stricken, so I quietly said, "Let me take a look. I promise not to touch anything, but maybe your lip if I need to lift it up to look in your mouth." She slowly lowered her hand and let me look. She said, "See, this front tooth is wiggling." She proceeded to wiggle it for me and then began to cry. I told her, "That's a sign you're growing up. It's one of your baby teeth, and everybody has to lose all twenty of their baby teeth to make room for their adult teeth." "But why is it loose?" "There could be a couple different reasons. One is that maybe you bumped it and knocked it loose, and another is that maybe your new adult front tooth is coming in and it's pushing the baby tooth out."

After a few minutes of thought, she responded, "Then everything is OK?" "As far as I can tell, everything is fine. It is probably just a little scary to find your first loose tooth, but it is just the way God programmed our bodies to give us bigger teeth to eat better things more easily. We have a tradition of putting a lost tooth under our pillow so the tooth fairy can take the tooth and leave you a little money in its place. Not a bad deal, right? She takes what you can no longer use and gives you something you can use." With this in mind, she relaxed and was able to enjoy the rest of her day.

It's amazing how a loose tooth can upset the apple cart, yet when they learn of a reward afterwards, it's OK. We're like that with God. When we talk about death, many people are afraid of the unknown. As Christians, our future is assured. When our last breath is taken on earth, our next breath will be taken in heaven.

Thank You, LORD, for the assurances of our heavenly home. I pray we can reach more people so they can move from the fear of death to rejoicing in the fact of an eternal heavenly home.

Deuteronomy 31:8: *Yahweh himself is who goes before you. He will be with you. He will not fail you nor forsake you. Don't be afraid. Don't be discouraged.*

Psalm 34:17: *The righteous cry, and Yahweh hears, and delivers them out of all their troubles.*

Priceless Moments

Isaiah 41:10: *Don't you be afraid, for I am with you. Don't be dismayed, for I am your God. I will strengthen you. Yes, I will help you. Yes, I will uphold you with the right hand of my righteousness.*

October 20th
That Man Smiled At Me

Our one granddaughter and I were out to lunch on a date. She sat down and said, "Grandma, do you see that man over there? He smiled at me. Should I smile back or should I just ignore him?" I looked over to see who she was talking about, only to see an elderly gentleman by himself. "Since you are with me, I don't see any harm in you smiling back at him. He may be lonely and is just trying to be friendly." She smiled back at him and ultimately waved. By the end of our meal, we noticed the gentleman walking towards us. He stated, "Thank you for making my day. Your young lady reminded me of my daughter when she was young. She and my wife are both gone, so these days I'm all alone. All I have are my memories. Just know that you made an old man very happy today."

He started to walk away, then returned. "Again, thank you. My name is Paul. If you see me again, I would be delighted if you would say hello," then walked away before we had time to respond. We talked about how hard it is to lose your loved ones and to be all alone. "Grandma, as long as I'm with an adult, is it OK if I say 'hi' to people?" "That should be fine. When you are sad and lonely, I'm sure you enjoy others trying to cheer you up, as well." We asked for our bill only to learn that the gentleman had paid our bill plus tip, telling the waitress how much he appreciated the kindness of a little girl to wave at him and say hi.

Priceless Moments

I thought of how we never know if we're entertaining angels or not. To me, the gentleman was paying a kindness forward in appreciation for a kindness he received. We should do the same.

Thank You, LORD, for making us social beings. I pray that regardless of our lot in life, we can share smiles—free and fully returnable—and kind words, being a witness to Your love shining through us. We must be cheerful receivers as well as cheerful givers.

Galatians 5:13: *For you, brothers, were called for freedom. Only don't use your freedom for gain to the flesh, but through love be servants to one another. For the whole law is fulfilled in one word, in this: "You shall love your neighbor as yourself."*

Galatians 6:9: *Let's not be weary in doing good, for we will reap in due season, if we don't give up.*

Proverbs 12:25: *Anxiety in a man's heart weighs it down, but a kind word makes it glad.*

October 21st
My Dad's Like Noah

"Grandma, did you know my dad's like Noah?" "No, I didn't. Why do you say that?" "He works all the time. He worked for one-hundred years to build our metal building behind the house. You know, just like Noah, who took one hundred years to build the ark." "Wow. That's really interesting. But I don't think it took your dad that long to build the building; maybe more like three to four months. It may have seemed like longer to you since you were waiting for it to get done." "That could be true, but it seemed like a long time. I know it took him all summer." "Correct. He had some problems with the cement job and the materials they sent him, so he had to figure out how to make it work."

Priceless Moments

A quick jerk of the head produced this question: "Well, then, why didn't he just have them come and take it back? Wouldn't that have been easier?" That's a good point, but he wanted the cement and the building to be strong so they could hold up against the winds whipping through here at times." "Did Noah encounter problems like that too when he built the ark?" "That's an interesting question. I never thought about it before, but I'll bet he did encounter some difficulties here and there. He would have had to go to the LORD to get answers so he could proceed to make the ark sturdy to save his family, all of the animals on board, and all of their supplies."

Many unthought-of questions can arise when talking with children, leaving us stumped. But we can never ask the LORD a question that would stump Him. As the Architect of the world, He definitely has all the answers.

Thank You, LORD, for children to keep us on our toes and our minds active. I pray we realize no question is too hard or project too big that we are called to do because You are always available to lend a hand or send someone our way who can be Your hands and feet.

1 Corinthians 12:27: *Now you are the body of Christ, and members individually.*

Romans 10:15: *And how will they preach unless they are sent? As it is written: "How beautiful are the feet of those who preach the Good News of peace, who bring glad tidings of good things!"*

Ephesians 2:10: *For we are his workmanship, created in Christ Jesus for good works, which God prepared before that we would walk in them.*

Priceless Moments

October 22nd
<u>Color Changing Spoons</u>

One of the kids favorite activities is making smoothies when they are here. Today we had just gotten back from a walk on a beautiful, warm October day when I heard, "Grandma, can we make smoothies this afternoon? It is hot out today, and smoothies would taste really good to cool us down." They knew where everything was, so each one gathered a few items while I got out the blender. "Can I put in the stuff I got out?" followed by, "Me too?" "Sure, you can each take turns adding your 'stuff' because that will make it taste extra good. OK, all you want in the smoothie is in the blender?" A chorus of "Yes" rang throughout the kitchen. One plugged in the blender, and another hit the start button. When it was well blended, another hit the stop button, which let the last one unplug the blender. "I'll pour out the smoothies while you get yourselves a spoon."

The kids were digging deep in the silverware drawer when they found some unusual spoons buried in the back. "Grandma, can we use these? They look really different." I smiled and said, "Of course you can. I think you'll really like them." Each one took their shake to the back patio and sat down. Within seconds, you would have thought they'd struck gold. "Hey, look, Grandma. Our spoons are changing colors just like the trees do in the fall. These are really awesome. Where did you get them?" "Actually, they belonged to your parents when they were young. I'd forgotten all about them, so I'm really happy you found them and can enjoy them as well." "Somehow the smoothies taste even better when using a special color-changing spoon." I had to agree.

It's amazing how something so simple can bring so much pleasure. Fortunately, God's plan of salvation is simple to understand and easy to accept. He wants to delight mankind with their own color-changing experience—bringing them from the darkness into the light.

Thank You, LORD, for creating a plan of salvation so simple that even a child can come to You. I pray we can put aside our haughtiness and humble ourselves like children to see the delight You want to bring into our lives.

Romans 12:2*: Don't be conformed to this world, but be transformed by the renewing of your mind, so that you may prove what is the good, well-pleasing, and perfect will of God.*

2 Corinthians 5:17*: Therefore if anyone is in Christ, he is a new creation. The old things have passed away. Behold, all things have become new.*

Psalm 51:10-12*: Create in me a clean heart, O God. Renew a right spirit within me. Don't throw me from your presence, and don't take your Holy Spirit from me. Restore to me the joy of your salvation. Uphold me with a willing spirit.*

October 23rd
Don't Yell At Me

One afternoon, while working on dinner, I heard a commotion in the living room. I walked in to hear our little man yelling at his sister, saying, "Don't yell at me." He began to sob, running to me after he became aware of my presence in the room. I quietly asked, "What are you guys doing in here?" He said, "I had a toy, and she took it from me. I asked her to give it back, but she yelled at me, saying she wanted it too. So I yelled back at her." I looked at her and asked, "Is what he said true?" She rolled her eyes and stated, "Yes, but I wanted the toy. I haven't played with it all day." I asked, "What is the rule at our house about seats and toys?" In unison, I heard, "Move your feet, lose your seat." "That is correct, and it will never change."

Priceless Moments

Some pondering was noted. "OK, Grandma, I know. I need to apologize to my brother." "Looking at him, she haughtily said, "I'm sorry." I stopped and said, "What. If the shoe were on the other foot, would you accept a begrudgingly given apology?" "Well, no. He needs to treat me with respect." "Very interesting. If you want respect, you need to show or give it to others, and then you will be worthy of receiving respect in return." She hung her head and began to cry. Through her sobs, I heard, "I'm sorry, little brother. Will you forgive me?" He responded with a hug and a "Yes," then freely gave her the toy, saying, "All you had to do was ask."

I realize that in order to hear a soft-spoken person, we have to be listening, but we will turn off our ears to a harsh, loud person. We also need to have the right heart attitude in order to be able to respond to others appropriately. With time, prayer, and patience, we become ready to tell God we are sorry and repent of our sin.

Thank You, LORD, for not yelling at us—even when we deserve it. I pray we are listening for Your still small voice giving correction, direction, comfort, or even asking questions since Your goal is to bring us into reconciliation with You.

Job 38:4: Where were you when I laid the foundations of the earth? Declare, if you have understanding.

Jonah 4:9: God said to Jonah, "Is it right for you to be angry about the vine?" He said, "I am right to be angry, even to death."

Proverbs 14:29: He who is slow to anger has great understanding, but he who has a quick temper displays folly.

Priceless Moments

October 24th
RUN!

"Tag, you're it. Run!" I see little bodies scattering everywhere, only to realize they've included me in the game—and I'm it. "Ok, everyone, be on your guard. I'm it, and I'm coming to get you." I took a moment to assess where they all were, then made a mad dash towards the cluster to my right. Knowing it's no fun to tag someone right away, I made several passes but missed them all. Wild laughter filled the air as I dodged them. "Grandma, you can't get us," she taunted me. "Can't you run any faster?" After several rounds of missing kids, I decided it was time. I grabbed one in each arm, yelling, "Tag, you're both it!" I put them down and took off. Next thing I know, they're all chasing me, saying, "Get her." Now we're playing dodge 'em.

About ten minutes later, the peewee track team of exhausted kids called it quits, asking, "Can we stop now? Is it time to eat yet? We're starving. What's for lunch?" Man, I felt good—my energy outlasted the kids. "Sure, let's stop and go have some lunch." I listed several options, and each wanted something different. "Ok, everyone pitch in here, and we can make a buffet of food for lunch." "Yes. I get to do the wraps." "I get to do the veggies and hummus." "I'll get the silverware and plates." "We'll get drinks." I told them, "Awesome. All is ready. Who had a good time this morning?" "Me's" were heard everywhere. "Thank you, Grandma, for the fun, and thank You, LORD, for the fun, food, and a special Grandma who likes to have fun with us. Amen."

I felt very humbled for the blessings of grandchildren who can appreciate me, as well as for thanking our LORD for all the good things in our lives.

Thank You, LORD, for fun, food, family, fellowship, and a generational faith. I pray we continue to set the example of Your love in all things, encouraging everyone we encounter to see You reflected in our lives.

Ecclesiastes 8:15*: Then I commended mirth, because a man has no better thing under the sun than to eat, to drink, and to be joyful: for that will accompany him in his labor all the days of his life which God has given him under the sun.*

Colossians 3:17*: Whatever you do, in word or in deed, do all in the name of the Lord Jesus, giving thanks to God the Father, through him.*

Ecclesiastes 11:9a*: Rejoice, young man, in your youth, and let your heart cheer you in the days of your youth,*

October 25th
Is There Really a God?

"Grandma, a boy in my class says there's no God. I know there's a God because you told me there was, and I believe you because I know you don't lie. I know he's wrong, but how can we explain it to him?" "Wow, what an amazing experience for this child. "OK, first I will ask you a few questions and see if you can answer them. Maybe this will help you answer your friend. Can you see the wind? Can you see your heart, your lungs, or your brain? There are so many things that we cannot see, called invisible, but we know they are there." "How do we know they are there?" Help me, LORD, I prayed. "How do you think the trees sway, or do you feel a breeze in your face? That is because the results of the invisible wind are how we know there is wind. As for your heart, lungs, and brain, called internal organs, you know they are working because you can feel your heart beating in your chest, the lungs working when you breathe, and your mind because you can think and ask questions."

While he thought for a minute, I added, "Do you always see the animals in the water, yet hear a splash? Do you not see the birds flying overhead but hear them squawking? Or do you see a lion at the zoo but hear his roar? God is out there in the spiritual world, but we can't see Him down here in our earthly or physical world. Yet we see the results of the things He does for us here. The sun, moon, and stars come and go every day; He places a rainbow in the sky after it rains; and He has healed some people you know who were sick. His touch is upon us, and our physical world is all around us. We have to be willing to look, see, and understand or accept His work for us." His eyes lit up, and he stated, "I understand. Because we don't see things with our eyes, we can still feel them at work outside and inside us. God is the same. He works outside our world, so we learn to accept His help. I know exactly what I'll tell my friend."

A child shall lead them: He asked questions, got answers he understood, and then was willing to go tell another how he knows there is a God. How many times do we not ask questions to have the answers, for ourselves or others, but deny the existence of some of God's Word? Worse yet, do we question the existence of God altogether?

Thank You, LORD, for making Yourself known to those seeking You. I pray we are always seeking Your face and growing in Your grace.

1 Chronicles 16:11: Seek Yahweh and his strength. Seek his face forever more.

Jeremiah 29:13: You shall seek me, and find me, when you search for me with all your heart.

Matthew 6:33: But seek first God's Kingdom and his righteousness; and all these things will be given to you as well.

Priceless Moments

October 26th
<u>Can We Pray?</u>

Before our grandson was going to school, he asked, "Grandma, can we pray this morning? I want to have God walk with me, so I say the right things to my friend about how I know there is a God. I prayed last night, but I want us to pray again." I whispered my own prayer for the right words and responded, "Of course, honey, we can pray. 'Dear LORD, we come to You this morning, seeking wisdom and the right words for him to say to his friend who said there is no God. Keep him calm, clear-minded, and on target with his goal of speaking Your truth. Also, we pray You prepare this friend's heart to receive the examples to show You exist and help him be ready to accept You into his heart. If either boy has more questions to prove Your existence, I pray You give them the courage and desire to ask them so they both know You are alive and well, taking care of us, Your children."

All day, not sure when this vital talk was going to take place, I found myself continually lifting up both boys for God to provide a successful, clearly spoken conversation. As the end of the school day arrived, I anxiously awaited "pick-up" time, ready to hear the flip side of their chat. He came running, talking as he approached, "Oh, Grandma, I talked to my friend, and now he believes in God. When I told him about the heart, he put his hand there. I think that's when God spoke to him. He said he never thought about the unseen things we shared, but he knows about some stuff. I told him I learned a lot of these things from talking to you and going to church. He is going to ask his mom if he can go too." I said, "God and I are so proud of you for sharing your faith. He may lead his whole family to Jesus because you were faithful to answer his statement with truth about God."

Oh, for the faith and lack of inhibitions of a child. The lessons he learned about witnessing are for us all: have your answers ready, be prayed up for yourself and the person or people you are going

Priceless Moments

to talk with, go boldly in the confidence only God can give, and give Him praise for the seeds planted for Him to yield the increase.

Thank You, LORD, for little ones to keep us seeking answers and guidance from You. I pray we never shy away from spreading Your truth. You may have given us the opportunity to start a ripple effect for You.

Matthew 25:21: *"His lord said to him, 'Well done, good and faithful servant. You have been faithful over a few things, I will set you over many things. Enter into the joy of your lord.'*

1 Corinthians 4:2: *Here, moreover, it is required of stewards that they be found faithful.*

Hebrews 13:21: *make you complete in every good work to do his will, working in you that which is well pleasing in his sight, through Jesus Christ, to whom be the glory forever and ever. Amen*

October 27th
Shine Your Light

"In Sunday School today, we learned the song, *This Little Light of Mine*. We stomped our feet, clapped, and wiggled around while we sang. Do you know the song?" "Yes, as a matter of fact, I learned it when I was about your age. I loved singing those songs to Jesus because I knew how much He appreciated the praises of His people. **Psalm 98:4** and **100:1** tell us to *Shout for joy to the LORD, all the earth.* Some other versions say to make a joyful noise. Your new song has an important meaning. Do you know what it is?" "Well, we learned not to hide it under a bushel, but to let it shine so the whole world can see it, and not to let Satan blow it out, but let it shine till Jesus comes." "Excellent job. That's called a surface meaning."

Priceless Moments

"Let's take it one step further. Do you understand the deeper meaning of the song?" "Just what are the words that I told you? Does it have another meaning?" "Yes, it does. As Christians, we are to let our light—Who is Jesus—shine through us by helping others and being an example for our families, friends, neighbors, and strangers. Our reactions, the way we act, the language we use, and the places we go are what others will view as what Christians are. We may be the only type of Jesus they will ever see. For you, other children will see how well you listen to your teachers and parents, how you treat your sister, and how you manage your behavior." "You mean they're going to be watching me just like Jesus does? Wow. I'd better really watch what I say and do. Thanks, Grandma."

I love it when something you say seems to register. This must be how God feels when He speaks to us repeatedly, only for it to be like water off a duck's back. But when we get it, I'm sure there will be rejoicing in heaven just like parents and grandparents rejoice on earth.

Thank You, LORD, for those individuals who have been patient with us, endeavoring to stick with us until we have our ah-ha moment. I pray for the seeker and provider to maintain their endurance to see it through until both can let their light shine for You. We must remember that the word *sing* appears over four hundred times in Scripture, with at least fifty of them being given as a command to sing.

Psalm 98:1: *Sing to Yahweh a new song, for he has done marvelous things! His right hand and his holy arm have worked salvation for him.*

Ephesians 5:19-20: *speaking to one another in psalms, hymns, and spiritual songs; singing and making melody in your heart to the Lord; giving thanks always concerning all things in the name of our Lord Jesus Christ, to God, even the Father;*

Priceless Moments

Psalm 104:33: *I will sing to Yahweh as long as I live. I will sing praise to my God while I have any being.*

October 28th
I Love Music

"Grandma, are we going to sing some of our usual songs today or do you have some new ones to teach us?" "Either one is possible, so which one do you prefer?" "Could we mix them, like a usual one and a new one? I think that would be fun." "Awesome idea. I really like that. You choose the familiar one, and I'll teach you a new one. You choose first, then I'll pick a totally different song." "I want to do *My God is so Big* first. So, what do you want to teach us?" "Let me see… I think I'll do *I Am A C-H-R-I-S-T-I-A-N* and *The Family of God* or *Father Abraham*, all fun songs to learn." "I have a great idea. Let's start with one of your songs, then sing my song, and finish with your other song. Isn't that a great idea?"

"Absolutely. I think you have a winner there." We sang through *I Am a C-H-R-I-S-T-I-A-N* several times, then our granddaughter piped up, "Hey, you just taught us to spell a couple new words." "That's correct. It's five new words to be exact: Christian, Christ, heart, live, and eternally." "Wow, some of those are big words. The song sure makes it easier to remember how to spell them. After we do *My God is so Big*, can we come back and sing this one again so we don't forget how to spell those big words?"

I thought of what a vital part music has played in my life. Listening to wholesome music creates wholesome thoughts, which produce wholesome interactions with others. Scripture is filled with songs they sang to give thanks and praise to God. Our lives are so much easier, so we have so much more for which to give thanks and praise. It doesn't matter the quality of your voice; rather, it matters the quality of your worship.

Thank You, LORD, for inspiring men and women to write such heart-felt words and music. I pray we take the time to listen to the style of music that feeds our soul and whose rhythm enables us to bury God's Word deep in our hearts and minds.

Exodus 15:1: Then Moses and the children of Israel sang this song to Yahweh, and said, "I will sing to Yahweh, for he has triumphed gloriously. He has thrown the horse and his rider into the sea!
Psalm 95:1: Oh come, let's sing to Yahweh. Let's shout aloud to the rock of our salvation!
Ephesians 5:19: speaking to one another in psalms, hymns, and spiritual songs; singing and making melody in your heart to the Lord; giving thanks always concerning all things in the name of our Lord Jesus Christ, to God, even the Father;

October 29th
The Water Wheel

"Grandma, did you see in that book the cool picture of water falling off of some kind of a wheel? Is that something they made up, or do people really use something like that?" "Those things are actually called watermills. That one is called a horizontal type and has water flowing over the wheel paddles to help it turn, changing the energy from the water into mechanical energy used to make material goods like grinding grains, sawing lumber, and making paper. The vertical wheel uses gears to make it move; it is used on ships and in factories where there is high water." "Are they still used today?" "Not many are since they are big and heavy, making them turn slowly and have difficulty making energy. When water wheels are built well and carefully placed, they could be able to make enough electric power to power a small farm, or at least the house."

Priceless Moments

"Why were these wheels made?" "Throughout history, men have always been looking for ways to make their lives easier. In this case, not only did it help man, but it also helped their animals to not have to do all the grinding of the grain." "Were there any problems with the wheels?" "Besides their size, one thing that made them difficult to use was the need for water to turn the paddles or gears. Some advantages were that they were cheap to operate, easy to repair, and lasted a long time. We used to take your dad to see a water wheel in a beautiful country setting. It was used to make electricity for their house."

I thought of how the wheel component was dependent on water to make it move. We are reliant on God for His breath of life to get us moving. Like the water, as long as God grants us breath, we can continue to move, hopefully doing the Father's will—as we were designed to do.

Thank You, LORD, for all of Your promises to sustain us through the ups and downs of life. I pray we, like the water wheel paddles, are powered by the Holy Spirit, creating energy to use for witnessing and sharing the strength of the LORD with everyone we meet.

Deuteronomy 20:4: *For Yahweh your God is he who goes with you, to fight for you against your enemies, to save you.*

2 Corinthians 12:9-10: *He has said to me, "My grace is sufficient for you, for my power is made perfect in weakness." Most gladly therefore I will rather glory in my weaknesses, that the power of Christ may rest on me. Therefore I take pleasure in weaknesses, in injuries, in necessities, in persecutions, and in distresses, for Christ's sake. For when I am weak, then am I strong.*

2 Thessalonians 3:3: *But the Lord is faithful, who will establish you and guard you from the evil one.*

Priceless Moments

October 30th
Let's Make Cookies

"Hey, Grandma. Tomorrow is Halloween. Do you think we can make some kind of Halloween cookie today? I just like to bake with you." "Sure. What kind of cookies do you have in mind?" "I'd like to make sugar cookies that we can cut out in the shape of pumpkins. Do you think we could put some orange food coloring in the dough to help them look more like pumpkins?" "Great idea. I happen to have some orange food coloring. And, if I look in the cupboard, I'm sure I can find a pumpkin cookie cutter." I did a little rooting around, and I found two different-sized cookie cutters. "Look what I found. We can make different sizes, just like real pumpkins." "Awesome. Can we get started now?" "Sure, I'd like that."

We got out the recipe and all the necessary ingredients, measuring them out and combining them in the mixer until the desired texture of dough was achieved. Let's put the dough in the refrigerator to chill for an hour." "What can we do while we're waiting?" "Never fear; there is always plenty to do. We need to clean up the mess we've made so far, get out the cookie sheets and cooling racks, and clear off the counter so we have space to work." "OK, the dough's ready." We rolled out and cut out pumpkins galore. Now the baking, cooling, and icing were complete. "Grandma, can we have a cookie now?" "After all this hard work, we need to be the taste-testers to be sure they are safe to share with others." "Grandma, I like the way you think." Tasty....

Fortunately, God doesn't look at us with a cookie-cutter approach. He sees each one of us as unique and special in His sight. Our differences make life so much more enjoyable, just as He planned it.

Thank You, LORD, that Your treatment of mankind is individualized, meeting each one of us at our point of need. I pray we are willing to be cut and shaped by Your Master hand, allowing You to choose which path is best for our lives.

Psalm 37:23-24*: A man's steps are established by Yahweh. He delights in his way. Though he stumble, he shall not fall, for Yahweh holds him up with his hand*

Proverbs 16:9*: A man's heart plans his course, but Yahweh directs his steps.*

Isaiah 48:17*: Yahweh, your Redeemer, the Holy One of Israel says: "I am Yahweh your God, who teaches you to profit, who leads you by the way that you should go."*

October 31ˢᵗ
Halloween

"Grandma, I've heard people say Halloween is a bad holiday. What do you think?" "Halloween can be traced back to a time period called the Middle Ages, when sacrifices were made to gods during the Celtic festival of Samhain. People dressed up in disguises to look evil to escape being attacked. On November 1, All Saints Day, the poor people would go to the homes of rich people and pray, and the rich people would give them food and drinks. Yet, those symbols of death and demons brought the dark side to Halloween. As Christians, we need to encourage others to understand the pitfalls of dabbling in satanic worship, showing them the lighter side of life with Jesus as our Savior."

She was quiet for quite a while, thinking about the two sides of Halloween. "Then should we participate in the holiday?" "My answer is that each person has to decide that for themselves." "What could we do to still be a part of the fun side?" "Churches that still preach God's Word are doing harvest parties, using them as an outreach to the community. After attending the party, many families started coming to church when they felt the open arms of

Priceless Moments

God's people. People are longing for something to fill the empty spots in their hearts that can only be filled by Jesus."

I thought of how each one of us has been created with a built-in need for Jesus in our lives. When we refuse to entertain anything about Jesus, we will always have a longing for something that can never be filled, no matter what we try. It's like putting a square peg in a round hole. It won't work until you put a round peg in a round hole and accept Jesus to fill the hole with His Name on it to become whole.

Thank You, LORD, for creating us with a built-in need for Your presence in our lives. I pray we realize that no matter what we try, nothing can ever fill the spot created just for You, except You.

1 Corinthians 10:21: *You can't both drink the cup of the Lord and the cup of demons. You can't both partake of the table of the Lord and of the table of demons.*

Ephesians 5:11: *Have no fellowship with the unfruitful deeds of darkness, but rather even reprove them.*

1 Peter 5:8: *Be sober and self-controlled. Be watchful. Your adversary, the devil, walks around like a roaring lion, seeking whom he may devour.*

November

*Behold, children are a heritage of Yahweh.
The fruit of the womb is his reward.
As arrows in the hand of a mighty man,
so are the children of youth.
Happy is the man who has his quiver full of them.*

Psalm. 127:3-4

Priceless Moments

November 1ˢᵀ

Feeding Time

I was feeding a bottle to our four-month-old granddaughter when I was struck by her relaxed and totally trusting demeanor as she lay in my arms, greedily sucking away on her bottle. Her little porcelain face with those deep blue pools of eyes was fixed on me, as if she were searching me, looking for a window into my soul to find out who I really was to her.

As she slowed down near the end of the bottle, her eyes became transfixed upward toward the ceiling. Many times, she would share a picture of her smiling from underneath the bottle, then return to her favorite pastime of eating some more. When she finished her bottle, she broke out in her newly discovered Mariah Carey "voice," singing at the top of her lungs with hands lifted up toward the ceiling.

I was struck by the innocence and full dependence she demonstrated upon her caregiver to meet her every need, then her unashamed and uninhibited ability to say thanks with uplifted hands for all God and her earthly family have done for her.

God gave me the inspiration to realize how we need to follow her lead to be so relaxed and trusting in Him as we lay relaxed in His arms. We need to feed upon His Word daily, taking in as much as we can and pausing to smile at His goodness throughout our devotion. When finished, we, too, need to lift our heads, hearts, and hands upward and sing praises to our Heavenly Father. He doesn't care if we are off-key or get some of the words wrong; He just cares that we are giving our undivided devotion to our Maker, Sustainer, ever-present Provider, and Friend. Start today in humble submission and reliance upon God the Father, looking up to Him for guidance and protection throughout our day.

Thank You, LORD, for Your goodness to us and that Your "hotline" is always open 24/7/365 when we call upon You in praise or petition. I pray we appreciate and thank You for the little ones you have placed in our lives to help us see You differently and more intimately.

Psalm 121:3-4: *He will not allow your foot to be moved. He who keeps you will not slumber. Behold, he who keeps Israel will neither slumber nor sleep.*

Proverbs 28:26: *One who trusts in himself is a fool; but one who walks in wisdom is kept safe.*

Philippians 4:19: *My God will supply every need of yours according to his riches in glory in Christ Jesus.*

November 2nd

The Raisin Factory

Two of our granddaughters go to a daycare called The Raisin Factory. The parents are always asking the younger granddaughter, "Did you bring home any raisins today?" Her response was, "No, I didn't make any raisins. I don't think I've ever made any raisins." Then they ask, "What did you do there all day?" She has a blank look on her face and is shaking her head, trying to think of what to say. After some thought, she said, "Now that I think about it, none of the other kids made any raisins there, either." Her dad asked, "Then why are we sending you there? I thought you were going to make some raisins so Grandma can make us cinnamon rolls."

She thought for a minute, looking around as if to find the appropriate answer written somewhere in the sky, on the walls, or hidden behind something in the recesses of her mind. It was difficult not to laugh out loud as she was being very serious and trying to find the correct answer. Finally, she responded, "Maybe you could go and buy some at the store on your way to work or when you're coming home from work and bring them with you

Priceless Moments

when you come back home. Or, maybe Grandma could bring some with her when she comes because I don't think making raisins is what we're supposed to do there." Her thought process was excellent, so her response was right on the mark.

It's surprising how we can expect one thing when something else is in play. We need to reevaluate our motives for our actions. Once we understand what we want, we need to pray for God's leading to determine if it's His direction for our lives.

Thank You, LORD, for being available 24/7/365 to hear our petition(s). I pray we stay humble and open to hear and follow Your leading, doing the things we are supposed to do for the kingdom.

Proverbs 16:2: *All the ways of a man are clean in his own eyes; but Yahweh weighs the motives.*

Proverbs 21:2: *Every way of a man is right in his own eyes, but Yahweh weighs the hearts.*

1 Corinthians 4:5: *Therefore judge nothing before the time, until the Lord comes, who will both bring to light the hidden things of darkness, and reveal the counsels of the hearts. Then each man will get his praise from God.*

November 3rd
The BOMBSHELL Masterpiece

Caring for little ones is such a delightful time in our lives, but into every delightful time, a bombshell will come, usually on a daily basis. You know, when your little darling is sitting there all sweet and cute, but then your nose goes, "Oh no." Yes, my friends, the bombshell has dropped, and our precious little bundle needs a diaper change, with the used diaper bundled to encapsulate the little gift.

Priceless Moments

So, I scooped up our granddaughter from her little chair. Her little pink elephant blanket was not pink anymore, nor was her peach-colored outfit peach-colored anymore. We headed to the changing table and proceeded to extract this precious bundle from her masterpiece. Initially, she was not happy with the whole process—until she felt the mess being cleaned off her bottom, the soiled clothes removed, and receiving a head-to-toe wet-wipe bath, all the while talking gently and sweetly to her. She began to smile and laugh, getting into the frivolity of it all and ignoring her bottom half.

Soon, she was chatting and singing while being redressed and ready to play again, acting as if nothing had ever happened. But her stained clothes told a different story and still needed to be scrubbed and made clean again.

Oh, how God must see us like this sometimes. We are wallowing in our filth of sin, sometimes oblivious to how bad it has gotten until it is pointed out to us. At that point, we are not very happy, realizing we need to be scrubbed clean of our mess from head to toe. God is there, patiently waiting to help us through the thick of it, then pointing out the areas that need a deeper cleansing. Once the process is complete, we put on our robes of righteousness. As with babies, we will need to recommit to cleansing on a daily basis. But God's love will always be with us to keep cleaning us up along our earthly journey.

Thank You, LORD, for Your continued presence in our lives, guiding each step we take and leading us in paths of righteousness, removing our filth and making us clean and whole in Your presence.

Psalm 51:7: *Purify me with hyssop, and I will be clean. Wash me, and I will be whiter than snow.*

Ephesians 5:26-27: *To make her holy, cleansing her by the washing with water through the Word, and to present her to*

Priceless Moments

Himself as a radiant church, without stain or wrinkle or any other blemish, but holy and blameless. NIV

John 15:3: *You are already pruned clean because of the word which I have spoken to you.*

November 4th

<u>Photo Albums</u>

I had made photo albums of our children throughout their childhood and marriage, keeping them within arm's reach for easy viewing by anyone who was interested in perusing them. The grandchildren had noticed them, asking, "Grandma, do you have any pictures of our dads? If so, can we look at them?" I smiled at their interest. "You bet I do. Let's get down a few albums, and you can take a look through them. If you have any questions, feel free to ask me, and I'll see if I can answer them."

They looked at and talked about all the pictures, laughing over some of the really silly ones as well as the serious ones. A series of questions were sent my way. "Grandma, can you please come over here?" "Can you tell us what they are doing here?" "What are you doing here?" "Why are they doing that?" "Who is who in this picture?" "Did they really jump off those cliffs?" They were each full of questions, asking them nonstop throughout their perusal of the albums. We went through each picture and answered the questions about many of the things they had wondered about their parents as they were growing up.

Looking at our memories in print, I had to smile at how God has blessed our lives over the years. The pictures showed that He has provided ways for us to see His goodness in print in our lives and in others' lives.

Thank You, LORD, for demonstrating Your goodness over and over, even when we don't deserve it. I pray for Your presence daily to keep us aware of and in tune with You. May Your word pictures in the Bible and Your continual goodness to us be engraved on our hearts now and through eternity.

Luke 2:19: *But Mary kept all these sayings, pondering them in her heart.*

1 Peter 1:12: *To them it was revealed, that they served not themselves, but you, in these things, which now have been announced to you through those who preached the Good News to you by the Holy Spirit sent out from heaven; which things angels desire to look into.*

Ephesians 2:12-13: *that you were at that time separate from Christ, alienated from the commonwealth of Israel, and strangers from the covenants of the promise, having no hope and without God in the world. But now in Christ Jesus you who once were far off are made near in the blood of Christ.*

November 5th

Election Day

"Hi guys. Did you know today is a special day in our country?" "No, what is it?" "It's called Election Day." "What is Election Day, and why do we celebrate it?" "Actually, Election Day is not a holiday but rather a special day set aside for good citizens to go and vote for the people we feel most closely represent the biblical values we believe, because whoever gets more votes than the other person will be working for or against us." "What kinds of things do you base your decision on as to who you choose?" "First I review what they have to say, check their previous voting record, like what they did or did not vote for, check to see how this information aligns with biblical principles, and then I pray about it before I vote."

Priceless Moments

She thought for a moment, then asked, "Why do you always pray about everything?" "Because I may have missed something in my review of the candidates that God will show me during prayer time." "What's a candidate?" "They are the people running for office." "Oh, that makes sense. So, you're saying that they may say all the right things to people, but if God says no, you listen to God." "Exactly. The problem comes down to the fact that most people today just do what looks right to them, not bothering to pray. Once you cast your vote, you're stuck with whoever wins. Then our obligation is to earnestly pray for them, just like we were commanded in **1 Timothy 2**.

Many times, we are disheartened when our candidate does not win the position we had desired for them. But something much more important is at stake here. Regardless of party lines, we need to be voting based on biblical principles. If we don't vote as well as *vote the Bible*, we have negated our Christian obligation.

Thank You, LORD, that You place those in leadership to either help us or cause us to turn back to You. I pray, whether or not we agree with our elected officials, that we pray for them as You have so commanded.

***1 Timothy 2:1-3**: I exhort therefore, first of all, that petitions, prayers, intercessions, and givings of thanks be made for all men: for kings and all who are in high places, that we may lead a tranquil and quiet life in all godliness and reverence. For this is good and acceptable in the sight of God our Savior*

***Romans 13:1**: Let every soul be in subjection to the higher authorities, for there is no authority except from God, and those who exist are ordained by God.*

***Titus 3:1-2**: Remind them to be in subjection to rulers and to authorities, to be obedient, to be ready for every good work, to speak evil of no one, not to be contentious, to be gentle, showing all humility toward all men.*

November 6th
Rubber Band Necklace

Our granddaughter came to visit, all excited, saying, "Grandma, I made something for you. It's in my coat pocket. Once I get my shoes off, I'll show it to you." After a few minutes, as she was pulling something out of her pocket, she said, "Please come and sit down with me." Curious as to what she had in her hand and her need to show me so quickly, I walked over to the couch with her and sat down. With a big smile on her face, she said, "Close your eyes and hold out your hands. Once I give it to you, I want you to guess what it is before you open your eyes."

Obediently, I closed my eyes, held out my hands, and waited for my surprise. She placed something in my hand. I told her, "It's small, soft, smooth, rubbery, and long, but in one piece, like a circle. I don't think I can eat it, and I certainly can't wear it like a dress." To myself, I had guessed what it was but didn't want to disappoint her, so I said, "Gee, honey, I really don't know." In my mind's eye, I could visualize her rolling her eyes and shaking her head when I heard her say, "Oh Grandma. You can wear it around your neck." I responded, "You made me a necklace." I opened my eyes and saw a pastel, loom-made rubber band necklace. "Oh, honey, it's beautiful. And you made this for me. I love it. Thank you." She was delighted as I smothered her with hugs and kisses.

I thought of how this child was so delighted to make something for me out of the goodness of her heart. How much more our Heavenly Father, who created this world with all of its delights just to have fellowship with mankind, is delighted when we freely bring ourselves and others into fellowship with Him.

Thank You, LORD, for these young children reinforcing to us how important and appreciated it is to show and express gratitude. You must feel so excited to give something beautiful to us, and I pray we get all excited and say thank You for this world, our life, our spouse, our children and grandchildren. Thank You.

1 Corinthians 1:4*: I always thank my God concerning you, for the grace of God which was given you in Christ Jesus;*

Psalm 7:17*: I will give thanks to Yahweh according to his righteousness, and will sing praise to the name of Yahweh Most High.*

James 1:17*: Every good gift and every perfect gift is from above, coming down from the Father of lights, with whom can be no variation, nor turning shadow.*

November 7th

The Rubber Band Necklace Demise

Several hours after receiving the beautiful gift of the loom-made rubber band necklace, our grandson saw it lying on the coffee table and began playing with it. He was cautioned, "Please be careful with it, as it was a gift to me from your sister." With that no sooner said, the necklace was flying across the couch with little, tiny rubber bands flying behind it from being overstretched. He said, "It's OK, Grandma; she knows how to fix it because she made it." I responded, "Although that may be true, that is not the point. You were asked to be careful with it so no repairs would need to be made."

Our granddaughter yelled at him, and immediately a flood of tears flowed down his precious cheeks, and he screamed at his sister, "I'm sorry." Knowing that was unacceptable behavior, I worked to calm him down, then asked him to give her an appropriate, heartfelt apology, which he did. We talked about valuing things over people. Usually things can be fixed, but relationships can be much harder to mend. We need to learn to think before we react to protect those close to us, so our behavior does not get out of control, too.

Priceless Moments

How often do we find ourselves giving that knee-jerk reaction towards God, then yelling at Him for what happened? I thought of how He gave us two ears and one mouth so we could listen twice before we spoke once. It takes eight to ten good experiences or acts of kindness to undo one unkind experience or word spoken in haste. Thankfully, God has a big, forgiving heart and readily forgives when we ask for forgiveness—the first time. Our biggest problem at this point is forgiving ourselves. Take that, too, to the LORD in prayer.

Thank You, LORD, for understanding us, knowing how to deal with us in our challenging times, and leading us back to a position of wholeness with You. I pray we appreciate Your great love and return it to You, as well as spread Your love to others.

1 Peter 5:10: *But may the God of all grace, who called you to his eternal glory by Christ Jesus, after you have suffered a little while, perfect, establish, strengthen, and settle you.*

Ephesians 4:32: *And be kind to one another, tender hearted, forgiving each other, just as God also in Christ forgave you.*

Matthew 6:14: *For if you forgive men their trespasses, your heavenly Father will also forgive you. But if you don't forgive men their trespasses, neither will your Father forgive your trespasses.*

November 8th

My Fleecy Jacket

"Did you know, Grandma, that one of my favorite pieces of clothing is my fleecy jacket?" "No, I didn't. Tell me why it's your favorite." "I just love putting it on and feeling its softness. I don't have it on very long until I feel it warming me up and helping me relax in the cold. Sometimes I feel cold in my other jacket because the wind seems to blow right through it. Do you know what else I

Priceless Moments

really like?" "No, please tell me." "I love, love, love the fleecy pajamas you got me for Christmas last year. I wear them sometimes when I come home just to warm me up and to feel so comfortable in them." "Wow, it sounds like you really like the fleece materials. I have a fleece jacket that I enjoy wearing for the same reasons you just said."

"Grandma, do you know what I saw in a magazine the other day?" "No, I don't. Can you share it with me?" "Sure. You know that I like unicorns, right? Well, there was a fleece top with a unicorn on it. I was going to ask Mom if she could get it for me for my birthday. She always asks me if I have any ideas—so now I do." "That sounds like a wonderful idea. I'm sure you would enjoy having something you like so well, but you'd better be careful." "Why would you tell me to be careful?" "Simply because you may end up with a new favorite piece of clothing." "Oh, Grandma, you're so silly, but you may be right."

Ah, childlike faith and trust in having all that you like surrounding you. God wants to surround us, as well, with the things in life that will draw us closer to Him. We may not always agree with His choices, but I guarantee they are always the best for us.

Thank You, LORD, for Your thoughtful and considerate care of us to meet our needs—not always our wants. I pray we look beyond ourselves to Your perfect will and accept the gifts You have provided for us.

Psalm 91:4: *He will cover you with his feathers. Under his wings you will take refuge. His faithfulness is your shield and rampart.*

Psalm 46:1: *God is our refuge and strength, a very present help in trouble.*

Proverbs 30:5: *Every word of God is flawless. He is a shield to those who take refuge in him.*

Priceless Moments

November 9th

Cheese, Crackers and Soup

"It's cold out today, Grandma. Can we have soup with cheese and crackers? That just sounds so good; it makes my mouth water." "You're right, that does sound really good. I think I have one more jar of homemade vegetable beef soup, and a cold day like today is the perfect time to use it. One of you can get the spoons and napkins, while the other gets the crackers and drinks. I will get the soup, cheese, and bowls." Each one got their items and brought them over to the counter. I proceeded to heat the soup and slice the cheese while they set the table and took the crackers out of the box.

When everything was ready, we sat down to eat. Our grandson said the blessing, ending with, "You can't have one without the other. Thank You, Jesus. Amen." That totally caught me off guard, so I asked, 'Where did you hear that?" "Oh, it was on some commercial, and I thought it sounded really neat. It just seemed to fit right here with what we're having." I couldn't argue with that, so I let it go, and we enjoyed the foods all together.

I thought of how many religions take Jesus out of the equation—that He's not God's Son. The little ditty fits so perfectly because we cannot have God the Father, God the Son, and God the Holy Spirit separated into any other combination but the Trinity.

Thank You, LORD, for fostering harmony among all men. I pray we recognize the pot-stirrings of the devil endeavoring to create disunity among Your members. When we feel the evil presence, may we rebuke Satan and bring it to You immediately to avoid dissension among Your people and those seeking to find You.

Romans 8:28: *We know that all things work together for good for those who love God, for those who are called according to his purpose.*

Priceless Moments

1 Peter 3:8: *Finally, all of you be like-minded, compassionate, loving as brothers, tenderhearted, courteous, not rendering evil for evil, or insult for insult; but instead blessing, knowing that you were called to this, that you may inherit a blessing.*

1 Corinthians 1:10: *Now I beg you, brothers, through the name of our Lord, Jesus Christ, that you all speak the same thing, and that there be no divisions among you, but that you be perfected together in the same mind and in the same judgment.*

November 10th

Sparkles

When our granddaughters get together, dress-up becomes a very important part of their play. They enjoy bringing out all the things that sparkle, shine, and shimmer, from their array of glitter on shoes to sequins on shirts and dresses. Their eyes dance as much as they do when stepping into make-believe. They cajole our grandson into being their escort to the ball, the dance, or on some other adventure—as long as they require the glitz of the wardrobe. "Hey kids, time for supper." Little did I know I played right into their hands. Each girl came dressed to the nines while their escort wore tuxedo-style pajamas to escort his "ladies in waiting" to the table. What a procession, indeed.

After seating all of his "ladies," he seated himself and announced, "Ladies and gentlemen, members of the court, we have arrived for the feast." I had to stifle a chuckle and a comment, which would have been, "Sire, we are so honored to have the presence of you and your harem in our humble abode," but it would have been lost on them anyway. The blessing was said, and plates were filled. Somewhere between the seating of the "royals" and the filling of the plates, our princesses turned into pumpkins. Nevertheless, they had a good time with the glitz and sparkle of make-believe.

I can't remember a time when they didn't dress up and pretend as long as they could. This reflection turned into the realization that we cannot pretend with our LORD. We must be as real as who we were created to be, going beyond our natural selves to being transformed into the forgiven children of God to bear His image.

Thank You, LORD, that we can be real with You, bearing our souls in problematic times and in praise. I pray we never lose sight of reality because it allows us to realize we can be anyone You want us to be.

Zechariah 9:16*: "The LORD your God will save them on that day as the flock of His people. They will sparkle in His land like jewels in a crown. NIV*

Ezekiel 1:27*: I saw as it were glowing metal, as the appearance of fire within it all around, from the appearance of his waist and upward; and from the appearance of his waist and downward I saw as it were the appearance of fire, and there was brightness around him.*

Luke 9:29*: As he was praying, the appearance of his face was altered, and his clothing became white and dazzling.*

November 11th

Veteran's Day

"Can you tell us about Veterans Day? When did it start, and how is it celebrated? We know Papa is a veteran, and we should honor him today." "I think it's very special for you to want to honor Papa. Before this, it was called Armistice and Remembrance Day, created on November 11, 1919, at the end of World War 1, to remember the surviving and deceased soldiers. To have a federal holiday for celebrating only military veterans—those who have retired or passed away—President Dwight D. Eisenhower renamed

Priceless Moments

November 11 as Veterans Day in 1954. Although some of the other holidays have dates that change from year to year, Veterans Day remains a set date of November 11."

"What does Papa like to do on Veterans Day?" "He likes to go out and eat and go shopping. When we go out anywhere, Papa likes to wear a military hat or shirt. People always stop him and say, 'Thank you for your service.' It's so nice to hear people's appreciation for somebody who was willing to give up time out of their lives to go protect our country." "You know, Grandma, we should go in and tell Papa, 'Thank you for your service.'"

I never really thought about it like this before, but our veterans have followed the example of Jesus by laying their lives on the line to give us freedom. Many of them never come home after giving it their all. Others live every day on the battlefield of their minds. Thankfully, Jesus came to serve, giving His all so we could take the battlefield of our minds and give them to Him for peace and true freedom. May we show our appreciation to Jesus.

Thank You, LORD, for Your willingness to give all so we can have spiritual freedom. I pray we thank You daily for Your service to mankind, reaching out to the lost with the good news of all You've done for us.

John 15:12-13: *This is my commandment, that you love one another, even as I have loved you. Greater love has no one than this, that someone lay down his life for his friends.*

2 Thessalonians 1:3-4: *We are bound to always give thanks to God for you, brothers, even as it is appropriate, because your faith grows exceedingly, and the love of each and every one of you toward one another abounds, so that we ourselves boast about you in the assemblies of God for your perseverance and faith in all your persecutions and in the afflictions which you endure.*

Isaiah 38:16-17: *Lord, men live by these things; and my spirit finds life in all of them: you restore me, and cause me to live. Behold, for peace I had great anguish, but you have in love for my soul delivered it from the pit of corruption; for you have cast all my sins behind your back.*

November 12th
<u>Papa's Hat</u>

"Hey, Grandma. Papa went outside without his favorite hat. Can I put it on for a while?" I looked around to see him carrying my husband's U.S. Navy hat. "I think it would be fine—and I bet it will look great on you." His excitement was palpable as he donned Papa's favorite hat, grinning from ear to ear. He headed off to the closest mirror to take a look. "Oh, honey. You are a miniature version of Papa. Not only do you act like him, you look like him, too, especially in that lid." "Grandma, it's not a lid, it's a hat." "My, my, little one, let's talk about this. Where do you put a lid?" "On top of a jar." "OK, then, where did you put this hat when it left your hand?" He gave me the funniest look, then said, "On my head." The look of confusion seemed to be clearing. "I get it. It's a lid because I put it on my head, just like putting a lid on a jar. That's really funny."

"Can you tell me again why Papa has this hat?" "Papa served in the U.S. Navy. He wasn't sure what to do after graduation from high school, so he and a couple friends went and enlisted to serve our country. After four years of service, he was honorably discharged, returned home, and went to college. That's when I met him. Shortly after, he bought me a U.S. Navy hat to wear." "Where is your hat?" "We wore them so much that it was no longer nice to wear them anymore, so Papa gave those hats to our boys to wear, and he bought another one."

Having something new and using it until it is worn out is descriptive of how our Bibles should be. We need to take it with us wherever we go, not being ashamed of the gospel. Rather, we should use and share God's Word with everyone we meet. Like the hat, they will know we are Christians by the "wear" our Bibles should show.

Thank You, LORD, for Your Word at our fingertips, written on our hearts and foreheads, protected by our helmet of salvation. May we display our allegiance to You in thought, word, and deed. I pray our Bibles are more than a coffee table ornament; they are a true weapon in our hands.

Ephesians 6:17: *And take the helmet of salvation, and the sword of the Spirit, which is the word of God.*

Hebrews 4:12: *For the word of God is living and active, and sharper than any two-edged sword, piercing even to the dividing of soul and spirit, of both joints and marrow, and is able to discern the thoughts and intentions of the heart.*

Proverbs 30:5: *Every word of God is flawless. He is a shield to those who take refuge in him.*

November 13th
I Like My Teacher

Our granddaughter came home from school one day and announced, "I like my teacher. She is really nice. She likes to treat us well and do nice things for us. She even told us some stories about Jesus." I smiled and said, "That's wonderful, honey. I'm thrilled you have a Christian teacher who can teach you about Jesus. We never seem to learn enough, so every little bit you can get along the way with your regular studies is wonderful." "Did you know she made us special treats to celebrate her birthday? They were really yummy. The entire class said they would each like to have another one, but there weren't enough to go around. She said, 'If we can do all of our work and everyone has good behavior, maybe I'll bring some more in just because I love you all so much.' Wouldn't it be really nice of her, Grandma?"

As I sat and listened to her talk, I thought about how a yummy this special treat would taste. I commented, "Yes, that sounds really special, and I'm really happy for you and your class. For some teachers, it's not just a job. It's about helping children reach their potential and having fun while doing it. When a teacher spends time and energy preparing lessons and comes in with a cheerful attitude and helping hands, they provide the needed encouragement to teach you responsibility and respect for yourself and others." "Wow, do you know her? It sounds like you just described her."

I thought about her teacher and how her love for the children describes Jesus. She spends countless hours at home preparing and giving of herself to provide opportunities for the children to be the best they can be. Jesus left heaven, spent a predetermined number of years on earth teaching and preparing His disciples, and left a legacy for all of us to follow.

Thank You, LORD, for Your dedication to us to train some, who also gave up all for You, to go out and make more disciples, causing a ripple effect that has changed the world. I pray we can continue this ripple effect by leading others to You and teaching and training them to the best of our ability.

Mark 16:15: He said to them, "Go into all the world, and preach the Good News to the whole creation." "

John 1:45: Philip found Nathanael, and said to him, "We have found him, of whom Moses in the law, and the prophets, wrote: Jesus of Nazareth, the son of Joseph

Acts 1:8: But you will receive power when the Holy Spirit has come upon you. You will be witnesses to me in Jerusalem, in all Judea and Samaria, and to the uttermost parts of the earth.

November 14th
The Wrapped Present

"Grandma, I have a question. Why is there a wrapped present outside? It is really pretty. Aren't you worried someone will take it?" "Not really. We've made friends with the neighbors, and we all look out for each other. Several people have cameras outside that also cover our house. If something were to disappear, they could check their cameras to find out who took it and when it disappeared." "Do you think it could possibly blow away?" "No, it's just an empty box with a rock in it." "Wow, I never would have guessed that. It looks too nice to just be empty."

"Honey, when you said 'empty,' I thought of how the tomb was a 'big box' wrapped with the Roman imperial seal from Pilate to keep people out until it was time to be opened. It, too, was empty except for 'the place' where He was laid and his burial cloths. The Roman guard, consisting of sixteen men, was not able to keep Him confined within a sealed grave. He was not there as He 'was crucified' (past tense), conquered death, and rose again, no longer confined by material barriers. No seal, guard, or heavy stone can contain our LORD."

I thought that this goes one step further: the disciples were not able to steal Jesus' body because He was already up and about His Father's business. This present God and Jesus had planned so long ago had come to fruition, providing a way for all of us to conquer death when we acknowledge and accept Jesus as LORD and Savior. This confession of faith assures us of eternal life in heaven for eternity, freeing us of the "sealed tomb of death" Satan had planned for us.

Thank You, LORD, for the present of Jesus, no longer wrapped in grave clothes in a sealed tomb. I pray we invite You to live in our hearts so we can spend eternity with You, taking as many other people with us as we can.

Priceless Moments

Isaiah 53:9: *They made his grave with the wicked, and with a rich man in his death, although he had done no violence, nor was any deceit in his mouth.*

Colossians 2:12: *having been buried with him in baptism, in which you were also raised with him through faith in the working of God, who raised him from the dead.*

1 Corinthians 15:14: *If Christ has not been raised, then our preaching is in vain, and your faith also is in vain.*

November 15th
Emptying the Dishwasher

Emptying the dishwasher can be a chore or loads of fun. I opt for the latter. After our Thursday night family dinners, the dishwasher is always full, so I run it. When the kids come on Friday, we'll make the chore a challenge. "OK, it's time to empty the dishwasher. The reward for a job well done is a pack of yogurt-covered fun fruits. Are you ready?" "Yes, ma'am. Let's go." "All hands on deck, to the dishes, and earn treats." They emptied the dishwasher while I put away the glass items and things in the upper cupboards. They put away everything else. "We're done. That was fun because we know what's coming next."

As I headed towards the pantry, I said, "Yes, another job well done and greatly appreciated. Here they are. Do you want blueberry, strawberry, or peach?" holding up the offerings. One took blueberry, one took strawberry, so I took the peach. As we sat down to enjoy the "fruits" of our labor, I said, "There is an Amish saying that many hands make light work." "What does that mean?" "Good question. When they work together as one unit for the common good, like ants carrying something or digging out their home, nobody has to do all the work alone; therefore, a lot more work gets done and done more quickly and efficiently."

Priceless Moments

It's amazing how we tend to want to do everything ourselves so we can control exactly how it's done to suit the "picture in our mind." It will take us two to three times longer and may not be done as well if we have help. One of the few times we have to do it ourselves is when accepting Jesus into our lives. It's a personal decision.

Thank You, LORD, for giving us Jesus and Christian friends. I pray we know when to work and when to work as part of a team, being humble enough not to try to run the show but to truly be equal with our team members.

Ecclesiastes 4:9-12: *Two are better than one, because they have a good reward for their labor. For if they fall, the one will lift up his fellow; but woe to him who is alone when he falls, and doesn't have another to lift him up. Again, if two lie together, then they have warmth; but how can one keep warm alone? If a man prevails against one who is alone, two shall withstand him; and a threefold cord is not quickly broken.*

Psalm 133:1: *See how good and how pleasant it is for brothers to live together in unity!*

1 Corinthians 3:9: *For we are God's fellow workers. You are God's farming, God's building.*

November 16th

My Favorite Movie

"Grandma, what are we going to do tonight? Mom said I could spend the night with you if you would like." "I don't have any particular plans, so what would you like to do?" "Well, can I—I mean, can we watch my favorite movie? I've been really good today and have helped you do a lot of things since I got here." "Wow, you presented a good case for getting to watch part of a

Priceless Moments

movie. If it's OK with you, we can start it before bedtime, and then after going to bed without any problems, you can watch the rest of it tomorrow." "Sounds fair to me. Can I watch *The Prince of Egypt*? I like to watch how he changes from a troublemaker to a man who followed God completely."

I was surprised by his response about the movie. After getting the movie ready, I asked, "Someday, how will people look at you from today compared to when you're grown up?" "Man, Grandma, that's a tough question. I hope to still be living with Jesus in my heart when I'm grown up. I know He's the only way to heaven, and I want to go there to see all of the rest of our family." Again, I was blown away by his answer. "Buddy, I pray you stay committed to Jesus all your life, too. I see you growing daily and becoming more like Jesus every day."

I remember making a commitment to Jesus when I was five years old. Being supported by my parents, grandparents, and others to help me learn and grow in my faith, I've never looked back.

Thank You, LORD, for tender hearts at a young age. I pray we all stay committed to You, regardless of the season in our lives in which we came to You, growing in faith and discipleship with each passing day and year.

***1 Kings 8:61**: Let your heart therefore be perfect with Yahweh our God, to walk in his statutes, and to keep his commandments, as it is today.*

***2 Timothy 1:12**: For this cause I also suffer these things. Yet I am not ashamed, for I know him whom I have believed, and I am persuaded that he is able to guard that which I have committed to him against that day.*

***Acts 2:42**: They continued steadfastly in the apostles' teaching and fellowship, in the breaking of bread, and prayer.*

Priceless Moments

November 17th
<u>Monkey In the Middle</u>

"Guess what, Grandma, we learned to play a new game today. It's called *Monkey in the Middle.* Have you ever played it before?" "As a matter of fact, my brothers and I used to play this game. I know it's a lot of fun, and I can see why you would enjoy it. Do you want to see if the other kids want to play as well? Do you know that the more the merrier is true here? We used to play with up to five players." "We learned to play it with three people." "The same rules apply to any number of players. One person, the monkey, stands in the middle of a circle, trying to catch the ball, be it thrown or kicked from one person to another in the outer circle."

He went running to ask the other kids if they wanted to play. They all came running to the backyard, ready to play. We quickly reviewed the rules of the game to make sure everyone was on the same page. One asked, "Can I be the first monkey in the middle?" I said, "Sure," because usually no one volunteers for the job. She was really good at catching the ball, showing her skills from playing shortstop. We played most of the afternoon, resulting in everyone having a turn in the middle. I bowed out of the position since my height was putting them at a disadvantage, to which they agreed.

Playing the game brought back wonderful memories of my childhood. The neighborhood kids got together to play, just like the grandchildren did today. I thought of how Jesus probably played some type of game with his siblings, friends, and disciples. Learning to get along together is a wonderful lesson for all ages.

Thank You, LORD, for fun times together with other people. I pray we enjoy the company of Christian friends for their clean living, wholesome speech, and mannerisms, all things that identify us as part of the family of God. With righteous living, we can set godly examples for our non-Christian friends.

John 13:34-35: *A new commandment I give to you, that you love one another. Just as I have loved you, you also love one another. By this everyone will know that you are my disciples, if you have love for one another.*

Matthew 7:16, 17: *By their fruits you will know them. Do you gather grapes from thorns or figs from thistles? Even so, every good tree produces good fruit, but the corrupt tree produces evil fruit.*

Acts 11:26: *When he had found him, he brought him to Antioch. For a whole year they were gathered together with the assembly, and taught many people. The disciples were first called Christians in Antioch*

November 18th

The Matching Snowmen

In our guest bathroom, we keep a matching set of snowmen, one filled with hand soap and the other with lotion. They became an instant hit with the grandchildren as well as our guests. "Grandma, do you use the new snowmen in the bathroom? I love the scent of the soap and lotion you put in them." "Not really because I have some other things back in our bathroom, but I'm happy you are enjoying them." "Well, thank you for thinking of us. I'm sure all of us appreciate the fun way we get to take care of our hands. Have you thought about getting snowman towels or a snowman night light to match? I think they would be a lot of fun for us, too."

OK, now they're helping me decorate. "Do you know what? Maybe we could sit down and look for some things to match. Would you like to help me? You have such good ideas, I'm sure you could pick out some fun stuff to match." "Oh, Grandma, I'd love to help you do that. Can we do it right now?" "Sure." We sat down and looked through some catalogs and then some websites but couldn't find anything to match close enough to look like they went together. "Hey, I've got an idea. You know that store where we found the snowflake tablecloth last time? Maybe we could look there to see what they have." "That's an excellent idea since that's the place we bought the matching snowmen. Why don't we go out for lunch and check it out?" … They had what we wanted.

My mind raced back to other matching sets we've had, then on to something completely different. It was God the Father, God the Son, and God the Holy Spirit. They go together so perfectly yet are distinct personages within the Trinity. When I learn more about them, I go back to the Bible for clarification. For other needs, I go back to the Bible for direction. And when I wonder what I'm doing in life, I go back to the Bible for purpose. When I go back to the same place—the Bible—it always has the answers I need.

Thank You, LORD, for thinking of us all the time and making provisions available as needed. I pray we tap into this free and always-available gift from You.

Amos 3:7: *Surely the Lord Yahweh will do nothing, unless he reveals his secret to his servants the prophets.*

Isaiah 30:21: *and when you turn to the right hand, and when you turn to the left, your ears will hear a voice behind you, saying, "This is the way. Walk in it.*

Ephesians 2:8-10: *for by grace you have been saved through faith, and that not of yourselves; it is the gift of God, not of works, that no one would boast. For we are his workmanship, created in Christ Jesus for good works, which God prepared before that we would walk in them.*

Priceless Moments

November 19th

Chai Tea

One of our favorite types of tea is chai tea lattes. It doesn't matter if it's spicy or not, hot or cold, or used in a shake. We also have recipes for chai latte cookies and cakes. We really enjoy the break from "regular" recipes and branching out into something different. The grandchildren are always ready to try any recipe involving chai. "Grandma, can we have some chai tea today? I'd like something different from regular tea, and your chai tea is always the best." "Well, thank you, kind one. Certainly, we can have chai. I haven't had any in a while, so it would really hit the spot."

We got busy getting things ready to make chai when I heard, "Can we make some cookies to go with it?" "That would be nice. What kind of cookies do you want to make?" "Can we make some chai cookies? What makes chai taste so good anyway?" "It is loaded with a variety of spices like cinnamon, clove, ginger, cardamom, pepper, and nutmeg. The combination of spices used can change the flavor." "Can we make our own combination of spices for our tea? That sounds like it would be a lot of fun." "Sure, I'm game."

Baking is so much fun because you can always vary a recipe for a new twist on an old favorite. One "recipe" I never want to change is God's "recipe" for salvation. It has been tested and tried, and it has stood the test of time as the perfect remedy for sin.

Although chai has the ability to detoxify and cleanse the body as well as satisfy the taste buds, there is someone who does an even better job—Jesus. Jesus cleanses every nook and cranny of our soul without having to work at it for months at a time, like it would take to cleanse the body with a certain drink or special diet.

Thank You, LORD, for cleansing and detoxifying us from our sin. I pray we turn to You for a complete job that's done the instant we give our lives to You.

Psalm 51:7*: Purify me with hyssop, and I will be clean. Wash me, and I will be whiter than snow.*

John 15:3*: You are already pruned clean because of the word which I have spoken to you.*

2 Peter 1:9*: For he who lacks these things is blind, seeing only what is near, having forgotten the cleansing from his old sins.*

November 20th
<u>Oh, No! Not Rules Again</u>

"But, Grandma, why do we have to follow all these rules: make your bed, wash your hands, brush your teeth—do they ever end?" I replied, "I know following rules can be difficult and boring at times, but we have them for a reason." "What kind of reason makes rules a good thing." Wow, where do I start? There are so many responses to this loaded question. So, "Do you know why we have stop lights and STOP signs?" Our granddaughter responded, "To prevent accidents." "Exactly," I said. "Why do we put gas in our vehicles?" "Really—so they keep running and don't run out of gas." Then I asked, "Why do we eat three meals a day and sometimes snacks?" She laughed, "As you always say, to have fuel in our bodily tank."

Most importantly, "Why did God give the Israelites the Ten Commandments? Then, when Jesus came, why did He tell people to love God with all their heart, soul, and mind, then to love their neighbor as themselves?" She thought a little, then said, "So we had rules to live by to keep us from sinning." No sooner were the words out of her mouth than you could see the proverbial "light go on" in her mind. "I get it. Rules protect us down here, so we have a better life." Exactly.

I thought about how there are six hundred and thirteen rules in the Old Testament, but only ten are Commandments. Man has imposed so many of his own rules; no wonder people are having difficulty trying to obey them all.

Thank You, LORD, for the new covenant, where You promise to forgive our sin and restore us to You when we turn our hearts to You. I pray, when we follow Your two rules: *Love God with all your heart, soul, and mind, and love your neighbor as yourself*, we are assured of eternal life in heaven for a happy ever after.

Hebrews 8:10b: *I will put my laws into their mind, I will also write them on their heart. I will be their God, and they will be my people.*

Galatians 2:16: *yet knowing that a man is not justified by the works of the law but through faith in Jesus Christ, even we believed in Christ Jesus, that we might be justified by faith in Christ, and not by the works of the law, because no flesh will be justified by the works of the law.*

John 1:16-17: *From his fullness we all received grace upon grace. For the law was given through Moses. Grace and truth were realized through Jesus Christ*

November 21ˢᵗ

<u>The Fruitcake</u>

"I have a question for you, Grandma. Have you ever eaten something with nuts and hard fruit in a dry cake before? I don't remember what they called it, but I certainly didn't like it. I felt bad, but after taking a bite of it, I spit it out and threw out the rest." "I'm not exactly sure what you're talking about, but by chance, is it fruitcake?" "Yeah, that's it. I knew it had a funny name." "Oh, yes, I've had fruitcake. Fruitcake was always a part of our holidays. There are so many different kinds of fruitcake: some really good, some really bad, and others just tolerable or OK.

Priceless Moments

When I was in high school, our band sold a brand from Texas that was the best I'd ever eaten. It was always moist, full of soft candied fruit and nuts, and had a wonderful texture and flavor. She said, "Now that sounds like something I'd like to try."

I had to smile, as I could almost taste that fruitcake from years ago. "Grandma, what are you thinking about?" "I was just remembering the good taste our fruitcake left in my mouth—always satisfying, never disappointing." "Have you had fruitcake since you were a kid?" "Yes, I keep trying different types to find one close to my favorite one, but I've not had any luck so far." "Have you ever tried to make one?" "No, I haven't, but I have two that claim to be moist, and the pictures show lots of fruits and nuts." "Do you think we could try it the next time we bake?" "Why not. I'll get all the ingredients and be ready."

I thought about how God is full of all kinds of goodness, satisfying our souls. We are only disappointed when our wants are not His best for us, sometimes giving Him grief until we allow ourselves to realize His way is always best. It is up to us to pick up His Word, open it, and partake of all He has to share with us throughout His love letter to mankind. **Psalm 34:8** says, *"Oh, taste and see that the LORD is good."*

Thank You, LORD, for Your steadfast, unchanging nature—Someone we know we can count on every minute of every day and beyond. I pray people can look beyond the din of the world to listen for Your still, small voice offering guidance throughout each day of our lives.

1 Chronicles 16:34: Oh give thanks to Yahweh, for he is good, for his loving kindness endures forever.

Psalm 27:13: I am still confident of this: I will see the goodness of Yahweh in the land of the living.

Nahum 1:7: Yahweh is good, a stronghold in the day of trouble; and he knows those who take refuge in him.

Priceless Moments

November 22ⁿᵈ

The Broken Snowflake

We have been teaching our grandchildren how to cut out paper snowflakes. "First, let's get a sheet of paper and a pair of scissors for each person. Now, let's fold the paper like we learned last time. The folds don't have to be perfect, but they are the beginning of cutting out snowflakes. When we start to cut, we need to be sure to leave some of the folded sides or edges intact so that when you open it up, it doesn't fall apart. If you want, you can draw some lines, circles, triangles, or some random shapes first, and then we can look at them to be sure not to cut too much of the edges that hold the snowflake together. Are you ready?" Each child picked up a pencil to sketch out their design. We checked each one, and they all looked good.

"The next step is to pick up those scissors and start cutting, being careful to follow your lines. We will also be cutting out a snowflake to show you we can practice what we preach." Everyone began cutting, some having difficulty making the scissors cooperate with their mind's eye on paper. When we were done, everyone opened up their snowflake. "For your first snowflake, those look pretty good. Put your name on your snowflake so we know who made each one." As they were printing, one little girl began to cry. "The pencil slipped off the paper and broke my snowflake." Her heart was broken, too. "Guess what? I think a little bit of tape will make it good as new." We put tape on it, then cut the extra tape to fold through the holes, looking like new. She smiled again.

It's amazing how the right kind of "first aid" can mend a "limb" and a broken heart. The best results are when you bring your broken life before the feet of Jesus and surrender it all to the Great Physician. You may bear the physical scars of your past life forever, but, more importantly, your heart is healed for eternity.

Thank You, LORD, for total forgiveness and mending our broken lives. I pray that no matter how far we have strayed from You or the number of scars we have picked up along the way, you can make us new creatures through Your love and forgiveness. When we come humbly, seeking Your face, you will heal, meeting our needs.

Psalm 34:18: *Yahweh is near to those who have a broken heart, and saves those who have a crushed spirit.*

Malachi 4:2: *But to you who fear my name shall the sun of righteousness arise with healing in its wings. You will go out, and leap like calves of the stall.*

John 14:27: *Peace I leave with you. My peace I give to you; not as the world gives, I give to you. Don't let your heart be troubled, neither let it be fearful.*

November 23rd
<u>Turtlenecks</u>

"Grandma, I really like to wear these collars that come up around my neck in the cold weather." "That's great, honey. They are called turtlenecks." "Why are they called that?" "They were created to protect the knights' necks from getting sore when turning their heads quickly in battle because the heavy, uncomfortable chainmail rubbed or chafed their necks. As regular clothing, they were first worn in the 1800s by working-class people, like those in the Navy, fishermen, and others who worked outside, to keep them warm and protected from the cold weather. When polo players started wearing them while playing, they got the original name of polo neck. In the cold weather, it is the most practical and popular clothing item." "Did girls ever wear them?" "Not until around 1890 did it become connected with upper-class women as beautiful and independent. About thirty years later, the turtleneck was worn by most people."

Priceless Moments

"What happened to how people felt about turtlenecks as more people got to wear them?" "History says turtlenecks initially were symbols of strength, then rebellion, and now style and modesty. They are considered a fashion statement, or showing others the type of person you are." "That's cool. I guess my fashion statement is telling others I'm cold and I like to stay warm. Does that sound good to you?" I thought of how to respond while holding back the giggles. I finally said, "Everybody has the right to make their own fashion statement."

It amazes me how much others read into a choice of clothing. Sometimes they're right; other times they're way off. But the most important type of statement we can make is that we are living for Jesus in thought, word, deed, clothing, places we go, and lifestyle. Others are watching our every move to see how we are different from the rest of them. I liked this quote: *The greatest prison people live in is the fear of what other people think.*

Thank You, LORD; the only opinion of us that really matters is Yours. I pray we can rise above the verbal abuse and hateful glances of nonbelievers who are trying to make us give up our faith. We need to show them so much love and acceptance in spite of themselves that they see You in us and want more of You.

Proverbs 29:25: *The fear of man proves to be a snare, but whoever puts his trust in Yahweh is kept safe.*

Romans 14:13: *Therefore let's not judge one another any more, but judge this rather, that no man put a stumbling block in his brother's way, or an occasion for falling.*

2 Corinthians 5:13: *For if we are beside ourselves, it is for God. Or if we are of sober mind, it is for you.*

Priceless Moments

November 24th

Snowball Battle

Ah, recent snowfalls have made today's activity possible. When the grandchildren arrive, I hope they feel like playing in the snow. Here they are now. "Hi, Grandma. Have you noticed how much snow is on the ground? Can we stay out and play in the snow?" "I think that sounds like a fun idea. I think I'll join you. What are some fun things you'd like to do today?" "Can we have a snowball battle?" "Absolutely. I was hoping you would say that. Let me get my coat, boots, scarf, and gloves, and I'll be right with you." "OK. We'll wait right here for you. But don't take too long because we can hear the snowballs calling."

"I'm ready. Is everyone here ready to go have some fun?" The rafters quaked at their resounding "Yes." "OK, then, what are we waiting for? Be out with you *youngens*." Squeals of laughter echoed as they charged out the door." "Can we build a fort so we can take sides in the battle?" "Stellar idea. I have a couple of boxes the same size in the garage that we can use to make the blocks." With boxes in hand, they built walls to divide the fort into two sides. "OK, let's make snowballs so the next phase of fun can begin." Snowballs were made, and one of the kids yelled, "Fire." Both sides were winners.

Playing in the snow brings out the kid in everyone. It's a great release to satisfy the inner kid in all of us. But there is still a better way to satisfy our inner child. When we come like children to the LORD, we have no pretense but are honest and open with Him, surrendering everything to Him for eternity.

Thank You, LORD, for accepting us as we are at any stage of our lives. I pray we totally surrender to You before it's too late.

John 11:25*: Jesus said to her, "I am the resurrection and the life. He who believes in me will still live, even if he dies."*

Romans 1:16: *For I am not ashamed of the Good News of Christ, because it is the power of God for salvation for everyone who believes, for the Jew first, and also for the Greek. "For I am not ashamed of the gospel, for it is the power of God for salvation to everyone who believes, to the Jew first and also to the Greek."*

1 John 5:10: *He who believes in the Son of God has the testimony in himself. He who doesn't believe God has made him a liar, because he has not believed in the testimony that God has given concerning his Son.*

November 25th
My B-I-B-L-E

"Grandma, we learned a new song at children's church today. Have you ever heard the song *The B-I-B-L-E, Yes, that's the Book for me, I stand alone on the Word of God, The B-I-B-L-E*." "Yes, I learned it when I was about your age. My favorite part was yelling the word Bible at the end." "We didn't do that. Can you show me how it's done?" "Absolutely!" We sang the song clear through and ended with shouting "Bible" together. "Wow, Grandma, I really like ending it like that. It makes the word Bible really stand out in my mind. When we sing it at children's church again, I will tell our teacher about this and hope he will let us all do it together. Can we do it again? The more I sing it, the more I will remember the words—and I like shouting 'Bible,' too."

We sang the song together several times before he asked, "Do you know any other songs that have spelling words in them?" I thought that was a unique way to look at the words in the song as spelling words. I responded, "Yes, I do. If you remember, we learned to spell the words Christian, heart, and a few other words in some other songs that we learned before." "Oh, you're right. I forgot about those. Do you think we can sing them again so I can get all those spelling words right?" "Of course, we can. Those are probably some of the best words you can ever learn to spell."

Music has a unique way of helping us remember words and phrases that otherwise would be lost to us on recall. I was impressed that enthusiastically shouting a single word seemed to cement the special word *Bible* so it could be ingrained in the hearts and minds of every child who participated. May we, like children, become so involved in learning God's songs of praise that we ingrain them forever in our hearts and minds, learning the special spiritual message related to each one.

Thank You, LORD, for inspiring people to write music that really speaks to the heart. I pray we follow the words of the psalm, *Thy Word have I hid in my heart that I might not sin against Thee.*

Isaiah 55:11: *so is my word that goes out of my mouth: it will not return to me void, but it will accomplish that which I please, and it will prosper in the thing I sent it to do.*

Hebrews 4:12: *For the word of God is living and active, and sharper than any two-edged sword, piercing even to the dividing of soul and spirit, of both joints and marrow, and is able to discern the thoughts and intentions of the heart.*

Psalm 119:11: *Thy word have I hid in mine heart, that I might not sin against thee. KJV*

November 26th

Indians

"Grandma, did you know that Thanksgiving is coming real soon? In school, we've been learning about the American Indians. They were here before the pilgrims came to America. Isn't that interesting?" "Yes, it is." Did you know they can also be called Native Americans? I remember reading that there are five hundred seventy-four federally recognized Indian nations in our country, plus hundreds of tribal sovereign nations." "Cool. I didn't know there were that many Indians." "I know of one Indian you can name now. She is in a movie you have watched." "I know, I know. It was Pocahontas, and her father was Powhatan. She fell in love with John Smith." "You are absolutely correct." "Other famous Indians are Cornplanter, Black Hawk, Crazy Horse, Lone Wolf, and Sitting Bull, to name a few."

He thought for a little while, then asked, "Why did they have such unusual names? I've never heard those before." "Most of their names came from nature, their culture, or had deep spiritual meanings, like the early people in the Bible." "What kind of homes did the Indians live in back then? I remember seeing teepees in the movie." "Yes, and they also lived in long houses, row houses, pueblos, or anything that could provide them shelter."

I remember that the Native Americans were a healthy, robust lot until the white man brought them war and disease. They offered friendship, and later we repaid them by forcing them to live on reservations, no longer free men in their country. Just like people treated Jesus. He offered teaching that was *out of this world*, healing, peace, love, and hope. In return, He endured suffering and tribulation, resulting in His crucifixion. But Jesus wasn't confined to men's tactics. He rose from the dead—Hallelujah!

Thank You, LORD, that You are not confined to time and space. I pray we are more like You when we approach the unsaved. May we radiate Your love to the point where they are compelled to come and see and to seek and find.

John 13:34-35: *A new commandment I give to you, that you love one another. Just as I have loved you, you also love one another. By this everyone will know that you are my disciples, if you have love for one another.*

Matthew 25:37-40: *"Then the righteous will answer him, saying, 'Lord, when did we see you hungry and feed you, or thirsty and give you a drink? When did we see you as a stranger and take you in, or naked and clothe you? When did we see you sick or in prison and come to you? The King will answer them, 'Most certainly I tell you, because you did it to one of the least of these my brothers, you did it to me.'*

John 14:6: *Jesus said to him, "I am the way, the truth, and the life. No one comes to the Father, except through me."*

November 27th

<u>Pilgrims</u>

"OK, Grandma. We need to talk about the Pilgrims today since they went with the Indians." "So true, my dear. What all do you know about the Pilgrims?" "I learned they came over on a ship called the Mayflower, but I don't know why." "They left England for Holland, where they had religious freedom. They worked to make textiles by weaving, spinning, and making materials, while others worked as carpenters, teachers, pipe makers, hat makers, and even soldiers. Although the Dutch tolerated their religious freedom, they were corrupting the morals of their children. The wool market fell apart as war with Spain became a possibility. Since their children were being drawn into non-Christian society, drawing them away from the church and their English heritage, they decided to leave. Even though they wanted their children to remain English citizens, they couldn't go back, so they had no choice but to cross the Atlantic Ocean to America."

"How did they know to come here?" "Good question. They knew English businessmen had been paying for people to come and settle here over a period of years. This would give them an opportunity to still have religious freedom and find good jobs while still keeping their English heritage. They also saw this as a mission field to bring Christ to the Indian people." "Wow, that sounds awesome. God had to be leading them here to share His Word with these new people." "You know, I believe you're right."

I thought about how the Pilgrims were between a rock and a hard place in their lives, making tough decisions for their faith and family. In retrospect, he was right; God was pushing them into a new mission field where their gentle nature and desire to serve were brought together by coming to America.

Thank You, LORD, for teaching children to look beyond the stress and strains of daily life and see opportunities as given by You. I pray we learn to do the same, looking for opportunities to share and reach others for the gospel.

Hebrews 11:15, 16*: If indeed they had been thinking of that country from which they went out, they would have had enough time to return. But now they desire a better country, that is, a heavenly one. Therefore God is not ashamed of them, to be called their God, for he has prepared a city for them.*

Isaiah 50:7*: For the Lord Yahweh will help me. Therefore I have not been confounded. Therefore I have set my face like a flint, and I know that I won't be disappointed.*

Joel 2:26*: You will have plenty to eat, and be satisfied, and will praise the name of Yahweh, your God, who has dealt wondrously with you; and my people will never again be disappointed.*

November 28th

<u>Thanksgiving</u>

"We've talked about the American Indians and the Pilgrims, so how did we get to know the Indians?" "The Pilgrims left on the Mayflower with one hundred and two passengers—men, women, and children. In 1620, after sixty-six days on the ship, they finally landed at Plymouth Rock with their supplies and livestock. They

Priceless Moments

were aware of tough times ahead with the Indians due to the actions of others here before them." "People, like Governor Radcliffe in the movie, were mistreating and taking advantage of the Indians. So, the Pilgrims knew to be careful and not take sides. They prepared for winter but were unprepared for the extreme winters. Many of them died. Chief Massasoit tried to make peace and help the 'white man' settle and survive, teaching them to hunt, fish, and plant crops." "Sounds like God sent them a friend to help them out." "Yes, you're right."

"The Pilgrims had survived the testing and trials of a hard and devastating first year. After a plentiful harvest, they wanted to show their gratitude and thankfulness to God and the Chief for their kindness in showing them how to live in this new place. The Chief and ninety of his men were invited to celebrate with the Pilgrims, sharing in their harvest as a way of thanking their new friends. Four women and two teenage girls prepared a meal for everyone."

This first Thanksgiving was truly an example of friendship and unity among different ethnic backgrounds, setting the perfect example for us to follow as we strive for peace in our world today. Anything is possible when we put our lives in His hands, trusting Him to bring the harvest—not only of food but also hungry souls.

Thank You, LORD, for making friendships in unlikely places and harsh circumstances. I pray we bring all of our needs to You, as You can use anyone anywhere to meet our needs as You deem fit.

Psalm 95:2: *Let's come before his presence with thanksgiving. Let's extol him with songs!*

1 Thessalonians 5:16-18: *Always rejoice. Pray without ceasing. In everything give thanks, for this is the will of God in Christ Jesus toward you.*

Psalm 103:1-4: *Praise Yahweh, my soul! All that is within me, praise his holy name! Praise Yahweh, my soul,*
    and don't forget all his benefits, who forgives all your sins, who

heals all your diseases, who redeems your life from destruction, who crowns you with loving kindness and tender mercies,

November 29th
<u>Yay, It's Snowing</u>

"Oh, look, it's snowing. I just love to see the snow falling from the sky. Don't you, Grandma?" "Yes, I do. I love to watch the snowflakes flutter and swirl around before gently falling to the ground. I find it relaxing to sit inside by the fireplace and watch God paint a white blanket on the ground. I like to see the snow without any footprints except for the animals and birds. Their footprints are really fun to look at." "What are snowflakes made from?" "Actually, snowflakes are really soft, light frozen crystals of water. We can have wet snow, which is good for making snowballs, or dry snow, which is more like powder. A fresh coating of snow quiets the noise outside and reflects all the lights, particularly the winter snowfalls that reflect the mesmerizing Christmas lights."

An excited voice came back: "Can we go outside and play in the snow now? I like to try to catch snowflakes on my tongue. When I get one, they feel so funny on my tongue, but they don't last long. So, I keep trying to see how many I can catch." "That sounds like a great idea. While we're out there, what else can we do?" "If we get enough snow, we can build a snowman and dress him up. We could make snow angels; that's always fun. Or we could build a snow fort, but we'd need a lot of snow for that. Maybe you guys and my parents could take us up in the mountains where there's lots of snow and we can ski and go sled riding." "You are just full of terrific ideas. Let's go see what they're doing now." "You rock. Let's go."

Priceless Moments

God's creation delights most hearts—at least for the first snowfall. I hear people grumble and complain about the snow, but if one would just sit back and see the beauty of the snowflakes racing, dancing, or gently floating to the ground to join up with hundreds, thousands, or millions of fellow crystals, we could see God's handiwork bringing us a precious moment—or hours of precious moments.

Thank You, LORD, for the variety of beauty You created for us to enjoy. I pray we look beyond the mundane to the majesty of creation, knowing things can change at any moment. Just like with Your coming return, may we not get too "comfortable" and miss the grand finale.

Psalm 147:16: *He gives snow like wool, and scatters frost like ashes.*

Proverbs 25:13: *As the cold of snow in the time of harvest, so is a faithful messenger to those who send him; for he refreshes the soul of his masters.*

Matthew 28:3: *His appearance was like lightning, and his clothing white as snow.*

November 30th
Look At That Star

We were out shopping one day when the kids saw a brilliant red, white, and blue snowflake. "Oh, Grandma, look at that star. Isn't it beautiful. It would look so awesome on your front door. Can we go over and look at it? Can you get it?" I looked in the direction he was pointing and saw this beautiful star in the aisle across from us. "That's odd," I commented. "This star should have been sold during the summer." I picked it up and saw a clearance tag on it—and so did the kids. "Oh, Grandma, it's on sale, and it's your favorite colors. You have to get it now. God was saving it just for you." He is so persuasive, and I really liked his logic. "But, honey, we just celebrated Thanksgiving and should be decorating for Christmas." "But Grandma, when you want to find something this beautiful next summer, even on sale, there may not be any more."

He really made me think because he was right. Next summer, if they have these stars, they will be full price and will sell out often; then, of course, the shelves will be bare when I get there. "OK, little man, you've convinced me." An immediate clenched fist flew up in the air. As he was pulling his clenched fist on his bent elbow down to his waist, he said, "Yes. Now, can we hang it when we get back home—pretty please?" And, yes, it hangs proudly on our front door. Who says you can't be patriotic—and show it—all year round—even at Christmas.

Something about the colors red, white, and blue stirs my heart—and now the grandkids. We've talked about the meaning of each of those colors for patriotism, always bringing them back to represent God in some way.

Thank You, LORD, for the ability to see You in everything—as we should. I pray we become more sensitive to looking for You in all that we see and do. It would certainly make the world a better place.

Psalm 144:15: *Happy are the people who are in such a situation. Happy are the people whose God is Yahweh.*

Philippians 3:20: *For our citizenship is in heaven, from where we also wait for a Savior, the Lord Jesus Christ,*

Hebrews 11:13-16: *These all died in faith, not having received the promises, but having seen them and embraced them from afar, and having confessed that they were strangers and pilgrims on the earth. For those who say such things make it clear that they are seeking a country of their own. If indeed they had been thinking of that country from which they went out, they would have had enough time to return. But now they desire a better country, that*

Priceless Moments

is, a heavenly one. Therefore God is not ashamed of them, to be called their God, for he has prepared a city for them.

December

...that he would grant you, according to the riches of his glory, that you may be strengthened with power through his Spirit in the inner person, that Christ may dwell in your hearts through faith, to the end that you, being rooted and grounded in love, may be strengthened to comprehend with all the saints what is the width and length and height and depth, and to know Christ's love which surpasses knowledge, that you may be filled with all the fullness of God.

Ephesians 3:16-19

Priceless Moments

December 1ˢᵀ
It's Coming, It's Coming

Our granddaughter burst into our house one day with excitement oozing out of every pore in her body. She exclaimed, "It's Coming! It's Coming!" I just had to ask, "What's coming, honey?" A look of shock crossed her face as she continued, "Oh, Grandma, really. ITS CHRISTMAS. It will be here in twenty-four more sleeps." I asked, "But what are you so excited about?" At that moment, her little brother burst through the door, saying, "Grandma, in twenty-four more sleeps, it will be Christmas."

I was reminding myself—priorities, priorities. I hugged them both and said, "Good morning, dear ones. Yes, you're both right. In twenty-four more sleeps, it will be Christmas Day. I am excited, too. Do you know why we celebrate Christmas?" Our granddaughter said, "Well, for two reasons. We celebrate because Santa Claus brings us presents under the Christmas tree and fills our stockings with goodies." Her palpable excitement was overflowing, as evidenced by her jumping up and down as she spoke rapidly, adding, "There really was a man named St. Nicholas who gave gifts to the poor." Her little brother chimed in, "And Jesus is the main reason for the season. He was God's best Christmas present to the world." BINGO. This was music to my ears.

His spot-on answer let my mind drift off to the very first Christmas, when God's precious Son came as a wee babe to save us from our sins. Born in a stable, laid in an animal's feeding trough, rejected by those who were looking for His arrival, yet honored by foreigners. I pray we always honor Him.

Thank You, LORD, that we are fortunate to live in a day and age when our children have been taught the true meaning of Christmas and can describe Your gift so awesomely. I pray we strive to keep them—and ourselves—on "the mark" to someday stay with You permanently in Your home in heaven.

Priceless Moments

John 1:11: *He came to his own, and those who were his own didn't receive him*

1 Timothy 1:15: *The saying is faithful and worthy of all acceptance, that Christ Jesus came into the world to save sinners, of whom I am chief.*

Isaiah 7:14: *Therefore the Lord himself will give you a sign. Behold, the virgin will conceive, and bear a son, and shall call his name Immanuel.*

December 2nd
What Are WE Doing For Christmas?

Oh, what a loaded question… It's the we part… What do the grandkids want me to do now? Christmas is coming, and they are ready to do all kinds of crafts, read Christmas stories, bake cookies, shop for surprise presents for their parents, and make a gingerbread house. They even offered to help set up and decorate the Christmas tree, complete with the train set, for some of the options given. I said, "Well, you're good kids, and you listen well most of the time, so I guess we can start on your list and see how far we get." The shrieks and peals of laughter warmed my heart to see them so happy.

"Which one should we do first?" I asked, adding, "You know we will probably have to go shopping since I don't keep a gingerbread man in my cupboard. The last time I did that, he knocked everything over trying to get out." Between the giggles, I heard, "Oh, Grandma, you're so funny. No one can keep a real gingerbread man in their cupboard." I couldn't help myself. I walked over to the cupboard and pulled out a box of gingerbread mix that, you guessed it, just happened to have a picture of a gingerbread man on the front. Their little mouths dropped open, and then they started to laugh again. Their favorite phrase is "gotcha" – AND I got to say it to them. "Gotcha."

I thought about all the times God has helped man do things, often surprising us because our faith is too small for our request. Does He ever feel like saying, "Gotcha." but always in a good way. I remember talking to the little ones about how big our God is and their singing the song *My God Is So Big* in response. May we always remember every day of the year that NOTHING is impossible for our God.

Thank You, LORD, for not being a picture of a gingerbread man, but a real, live, interested, loving God, which You will once again remind us of as we celebrate the birth of Your Son. Hallelujah, our God reigns. I pray we never lose the joy and wonder of Your special gift for this Christmas season.

Psalm 147:5*: Great is our Lord, and mighty in power. His understanding is infinite.*

Zephaniah 3:17*: Yahweh, your God, is among you, a mighty one who will save. He will rejoice over you with joy. He will calm you in his love. He will rejoice over you with singing.*

Ephesians 6:10*: Finally, be strong in the Lord, and in the strength of his might.*

December 3rd

Picture With Santa Claus

For children, Christmas time evokes thoughts of presents, stockings, decorations, and, of course, pictures with Santa. Once the grandchildren see the big chair and decorations set up at the mall, they start asking, "When do we get to go see Santa and sit on his knee? Will we get our picture taken with him?" I thought a moment, then responded, "This is something I will have to talk about with your parents to see what their plans are for a visit and pictures." Dodged that one.

So I asked, "Have you thought about what you would like for Christmas this year?" Both children started talking at once, with noted excitement and anticipation filling their voices. I caught Lego's, trucks, dolls, coloring books, markers, and a car. I said, "Wait a minute, what was that last thing you just said?" Again, they must have known which item I was questioning, as they both repeated, "A car." I inquired, "But neither one of you is old enough to drive. Why would you want a car at such a young age?" Heads shook and eyes rolled as I was told, "Grandma, a matchbox car. You know, one that is sporty-looking." How do they know what *sporty looking* even means?

I couldn't help but think of how aware they are, taking in the language of the adults around them and then being able to spit it back out appropriately. Oh, how it behooves us to think before we speak to young minds since they are absorbing what we say.

Thank You, LORD, for controlling my brain and my mouth so I only spit back out the words of praise through my lips and not things that would hurt someone else, teach the grandchildren something other than good things about You, or hinder my walk with You. I pray we all adopt this mode of thinking and responding to others, but mostly to You.

Hebrews 13:15: *Through him, then, let's offer up a sacrifice of praise to God continually, that is, the fruit of lips which proclaim allegiance to his name.*

Psalm 71:23: *My lips shall shout for joy! My soul, which you have redeemed, sings praises to you.*

1 Corinthians 14:15: *What is it then? I will pray with the spirit, and I will pray with the understanding also. I will sing with the spirit, and I will sing with the understanding also.*

Priceless Moments

December 4th

The Christmas Program—Part 1

Our granddaughters participated in a Christmas program at their church. The program theme was *It All Happened In the Country* Our older granddaughter was very involved and focused on her participation. Her *bundle of energy* sister was also very involved, but in a very entertaining way. Her constant movement on stage showed she was very comfortable in her role, executing it perfectly when needed. As each scene changed, so did her antics. She was very respectful of the theme, just adding her own extra version to the staging. The program took on a whole new meaning to see all the youngsters adding their own personalities to what happens in the country.

The program was very well done, and I'm sure each of the children involved will always remember their part, as well as the overall theme of being open with their faith and readily sharing it with others while living it out in front of them. In the closing scene of the program, the new people in their lives saw something wonderful and accepted Jesus into their hearts.

I was very impressed that the different behaviors exhibited on stage reflect a nice cross-section of the people we encounter in our everyday lives. I thought about how these individuals, from small children to teens to adults, unashamedly oozed Christ throughout the presentation. We may live in different areas and reflect different ways of living, but we can still live for Jesus, regardless of our race, gender, political affiliation, socioeconomic status, or occupation. Jesus was born to die for ALL of us.

Thank You, LORD, for the Christian heritage being passed on to the next generation of those who will be our future leaders. I pray we become so invested in our children, our friends, and our neighbors that we can start another Jesus Revolution to celebrate all You have done for us with the bundle of energy and enthusiasm of children.

Luke 19:10: *For the Son of Man came to seek and to save that which was lost.*

Philippians 2:13: *That energy is God's energy, an energy deep within you, God Himself willing and working at what will give Him the most pleasure. NIV*

John 16:33: *I have told you these things, that in me you may have peace. In the world you have trouble; but cheer up! I have overcome the world.*

December 5th
<u>The Christmas Program—Part 2</u>

Our grandson participated in a Christmas program with his Christian preschool class. He was going through the house singing Christmas carols from the day he started to learn them. As the program date drew closer, he was surer of the words and more confident in his ability to be a part of the program. He said, "I really like the songs we're singing, but I don't want to be up in front of a bunch of people I don't know." (Just like his dad.) I reassured him he would be fine, saying, "Hey, big guy, you've put the time and energy into learning carols about Jesus, so He will be there to help you do your best." For the encouragement, I received a big hug.

The night of the program, we met his parents at the school. When he walked out on the stage with his class, I saw a handsome young man dressed in a vest and tie trying to look out through the audience to find us. When he spied us, his face lit up. That was the last time we saw that smile. He sang but was not really invested in the program. He was looking around, swinging back and forth, seldom doing the motions accompanying the songs. Eventually, his class was done, and he hurried off the stage. When we met up with him, he said he was ready for the ice cream his dad had promised him. So, off we go to receive a sweet treat for his effort to participate.

His participation level reminded me of how many Christians treat their faith. They show up for church on Sunday but don't really get tuned in to the singing, sermon, or fellowship time. They can talk the talk, but they don't really walk the walk.

Thank You, LORD, for being truly long-suffering and putting others in our way to help re-light our fire for You. I pray You will help us to get deep into Your Word, prayer, and witnessing to be Christians, to make You proud of Your children, and to be effective missionaries wherever we are planted.

Psalm 18:28: *For you will light my lamp, Yahweh. My God will light up my darkness.*

Matthew 5:16: *Even so, let your light shine before men, that they may see your good works and glorify your Father who is in heaven.*

Micah 7:8: *Don't rejoice against me, my enemy. When I fall, I will arise. When I sit in darkness, Yahweh will be a light to me.*

December 6th

Hanukkah

"Grandma, what is Hanukkah?" I said, "Hanukkah means dedication." "Why do we celebrate it?" "Antiochus, ruler of Israel and a Greek Hellenistic king, banned the Jews from practicing their faith and demanded they convert to a Hellenistic way of life. "What is a *help-nick* way of life?" "Good question. These people blended different parts of Persian, Indian, and Egyptian cultures with their own way of life in Greece. The Maccabees, a clan of Jewish freedom fighters who refused to accept Greek culture, believed in their right to religious freedom. They successfully rebelled against and recaptured the Temple in 165 B.C. There, they found only enough oil to keep the Temple lantern burning for one day to read the Torah, yet the lantern stayed lit for eight days."

"Since Hanukkah is also known as the Festival of Lights, representing joy, now the Jews light eight candles on menorahs to symbolize these historic days, recite a prayer, and praise God for the miracle. Since it occurs during the winter, the candle-lighting creates a warm, cozy ritual, encouraging people to stay home with family and friends to eat and drink together, share stories, and play games. The celebration is often accompanied with gift-giving and decorating their homes."

The review of the holiday got me thinking about the Jewish people celebrating God's goodness to them. So many times, we overlook or fall away from celebrating a faithful God, yet the Jews never fail to celebrate their holidays. They remain faithful to the celebrations, but most don't accept Jesus as their personal Savior.

Thank You, LORD, for taking care of Your chosen people and including us in Your provisions. I pray we realize you have commanded us to pray for the Jewish nation so they, too, may find You as their Savior.

Psalm 122:6, 7: *Pray for the peace of Jerusalem. Those who love you will prosper. Peace be within your walls, and prosperity within your palaces.*

Jeremiah 3:17: *At that time they will call Jerusalem 'Yahweh's Throne;' and all the nations will be gathered to it, to Yahweh's name, to Jerusalem. They will no longer walk after the stubbornness of their evil heart.*

Hebrews 12:2: *looking to Jesus, the author and perfecter of faith, who for the joy that was set before him endured the cross, despising its shame, and has sat down at the right hand of the throne of God.*

Priceless Moments

December 7th

Pearl Harbor

"Grandma, did Papa serve in Pearl Harbor? I think you told Mommy that when I was doing a lesson on veterans. Can you tell me more about it?" I was impressed that she remembered. I said, "Yes, honey, he was stationed there after boot camp and was assigned there until his last six months in the U.S. Navy." She asked, "What happened at Pearl Harbor?"

"Prior to December 7, 1941, many countries had been fighting a battle called World War II. The United States had remained neutral while helping Great Britain in its fight against the German Nazis. When the Japanese decided to make their one-hour, fifteen-minute surprise attack on the naval base at Pearl Harbor, they destroyed or damaged nineteen Navy ships, including eight battleships, killing eighty-eight civilians and two thousand four hundred three military personnel, of whom half were on the USS Arizona. Fortunately, our three aircraft carriers were out on maneuvers. As Americans, our hearts and minds returned to God, asking for His divine intervention to help rebuild and prepare for war. We did so within six months. We recovered from our losses and joined the war, ultimately defeating the Japanese navy.

Upon reflection, my heart is saddened that mankind only seems to return to God and unite as a people during a time of crisis, then slowly falls away once the crisis has passed. I am heartened that there are children out there who still want to hear the truth, not a rewritten American history where important facts are changed or deleted.

Thank You, LORD, for Your protection every day, in wartime and peace, when men will call upon the name of the LORD. I pray that if all men were truly reaching out to You, their behaviors would change, and Satan would not have so much influence in our world.

Priceless Moments

2 Chronicles 7:14: *if my people, who are called by my name, will humble themselves, pray, seek my face, and turn from their wicked ways, then I will hear from heaven, will forgive their sin, and will heal their land.*

Jeremiah 30:17: *For I will restore health to you, and I will heal you of your wounds," says Yahweh; "because they have called you an outcast, saying, 'It is Zion, whom no man seeks after.'"*

Exodus 23:25: *You shall serve Yahweh your God, and he will bless your bread and your water, and I will take sickness away from among you.*

December 8th

<u>What Is Chrismas?</u>

Our grandson is just full of questions this time of year. Little minds are trying to absorb so much information about Jesus' birth. After celebrating Christmas at preschool and talking about Santa Claus, questions were a dime a dozen. "Grandma, what is Christmas really about?" I found myself sending up a quick silent prayer for wisdom and guidance to answer this hungry heart.

I began, "It's all about the birth of Jesus coming to bring hope, joy, and love. The word Christmas means Christian Mass, or a special ceremony to celebrate Jesus. It's at this time that we remember Jesus' birth, which leads to His death on the cross and, most importantly, His resurrection from the dead on Easter Sunday. This is to commemorate the time of the Eucharist, or communion, we take each Sunday at church. This means it is a day to remember the birth of Jesus, the Son of God, because without His birth there would be no death and resurrection."

"When did Christmas start?" he asked. "It was in A.D. 336 that Jesus's birth, or Christmas, was celebrated on December 25th, during the time of a Roman Emperor named Constantine." He

Priceless Moments

interrupts, "Since they didn't celebrate His birthday for a long time, why did he pick that date? Was Jesus really born on December 25th?" Deep questions. "No one knows the true date of Jesus' birth except God Himself. But the true date isn't nearly as important as the fact that Jesus willingly left heaven and came to earth to be born as a little baby. He chose to do this so He could grow up, totally understand all we will experience as we grow up, and ultimately die on the cross for each one of us. Let me find some other things to share with you over the next several days."

Thank You, LORD, for curious little hearts that make our big hearts take a second look at this special holiday You have given us. I pray we always remember, God, that You gave the very first and very best present ever.

Luke 2:10-11: *The angel said to them, "Don't be afraid, for behold, I bring you good news of great joy which will be to all the people. For there is born to you today, in David's city, a Savior, who is Christ the Lord.*

1 Timothy 1:15-17: *The saying is faithful and worthy of all acceptance, that Christ Jesus came into the world to save sinners, of whom I am chief. However, for this cause I obtained mercy, that in me first, Jesus Christ might display all his patience for an example of those who were going to believe in him for eternal life. Now to the King eternal, immortal, invisible, to God who alone is wise, be honor and glory forever and ever. Amen.*

Acts 5:31: *God exalted him with his right hand to be a Prince and a Savior, to give repentance to Israel, and remission of sins.*

Priceless Moments

December 9th

The Christmas Traditions —Part 1

As soon as I saw our *champion question asker* walk into the house, I knew he would be asking for more information. "Hi, Grandma, what did you find out? I have been waiting all day to learn something more about Christmas because I can share it with my friends at school and church." His excitement was catchy, making me feel like I had started something he was really interested in, so I had to be really thorough in my answers because he is a lot like an elephant—he seldom forgets.

"As promised, I have more to share with you. Christmas is celebrated around the world with various traditions, or cultural themes, from different countries. Here, we celebrate anything from attending Christmas Eve and Christmas Day church services to enjoying children's programs and adult Christmas cantatas. Churches and homes have manger scene displays that can be either inflatable, wooden cutouts, plastic materials, or even live scenes with real people and real animals creating the manger scene. Many people decorate their homes inside and out with trees, lights, bells, wreaths, candles, luminaries, candy canes, and stars and enjoy gift-giving. Although most of the traditions had their start in pagan celebrations, each item has a significant or meaningful reason for its use by Christians at Christmas. We can talk about several of these each day throughout the week."

Thank You, LORD, for Christians having the tenacity to take on pagan holidays and items and turn them into something special that warms our hearts as well as giving us something very special to share with our grandchildren. I pray these extra things we will talk about in the coming days will be treasured by them throughout their years ahead, so I ask for Your wisdom in sharing from our Christian point of view.

Priceless Moments

Psalm 118:24: *This is the day that Yahweh has made. We will rejoice and be glad in it!*

Deuteronomy 6:6-7: *These words, which I command you today, shall be on your heart; and you shall teach them diligently to your children, and shall talk of them when you sit in your house, and when you walk by the way, and when you lie down, and when you rise up.*

2 Thessalonians 2:15: *So then, brothers, stand firm and hold the traditions which you were taught by us, whether by word or by letter.*

December 10th

<u>The Christmas Tree—Part 2</u>

"Hi, Grandma. I'm ready for more cool stuff. First, why do we have a Christmas tree? I think it's so neat to watch the lights twinkle and to look at them reflecting off the different things we put on the tree, like pictures of us and ornaments that we made. What does all of this mean?"

Interesting question. Again, a quick prayer for wisdom proceeded answering him. "The Christmas tree represents the birth and resurrection of Jesus. It's triangular, or a three-sided shape, representing the Trinity—God the Father, God the Son, and God the Holy Spirit. The creation of these thorn-like branches was eventually used as the crown of thorns thrust upon Jesus' head on His way to the cross. Thus, the crown of thorns came to be represented by the Christmas wreath, the circle of unending true love, like that of God's love for us."

"Trees have long been held as important to the Christian faith, like the first trees in the Garden of Eden; the burning bush speaking to Moses; the root or branch of Jesse, King David's father; the cross or tree upon which Jesus was crucified; and John's reference in the

Priceless Moments

last book of the Bible (**Revelation 22:2** referring back to **Ezekiel 47:12**) about the tree of life yielding fruit each month and its leaves being used for healing the nations."

"Some historians say the pine or palm tree was one of three woods used for the cross, along with cypress and cedar." He asked, "Why were three different woods used on the cross?" Again, a good question, I thought. "The three different types represent the Trinity. There are different stories recorded about different woods used for making a cross, dating back as far as the time of Adam, Seth, Moses, King David, and King Solomon. Of course, we must keep in mind that there are no Bible verses to say this is true."

Thank You, LORD, for putting questions in little tender hearts to keep us adults from becoming too sure of ourselves, rather than constantly looking up to You for guidance. I pray we come to You in childlike faith, hanging on every word that comes out of Your mouth.

Isaiah 44:14: He cuts down cedars for himself, and takes the cypress and the oak, and strengthens for himself one among the trees of the forest. He plants a cypress tree, and the rain nourishes it.

Jeremiah 1:11-12: Moreover, Yahweh's word came to me, saying, "Jeremiah, what do you see?" I said, "I see a branch of an almond tree." Then Yahweh said to me, "You have seen well; for I watch over my word to perform it."

Psalm 52:8: But as for me, I am like a green olive tree in God's house. I trust in God's loving kindness forever and ever.

Priceless Moments

December 11th
<u>The Christmas Lights, Candles & Luminaries—Part 3</u>

"What we do know is that anything can be used for good or bad, depending on the way someone chooses to use it. The Christians started using the Christmas tree as a way to distract or take away from people worshiping false gods. By choosing December 25 as Jesus' birthday, the attention was taken away from false worship of the sun to worshiping the true Son, Jesus."

He asked, "What about the lights, ornaments, and other stuff on the tree?" "Originally, people placed candles on their trees and lit them. As the trees dried out, they became a fire hazard. When electric lights were invented, they replaced candles. The lights represent the light of Jesus in our lives, lighting the darkness for all to see. Unfortunately, some people take those lights and turn them off and back on again, depending upon the circumstances or situation they are experiencing at the time, instead of letting their light shine all the time for Jesus, like the strands of lights do on the Christmas tree. Luminaries, candles, or battery-operated tea lights are placed in bags to light the walkway. Jesus is considered our luminary, lighting our path to Him.

Another form of light are the advent candles used as part of the Christmas wreath, the circle of life, to bring hope throughout the dark time of winter. There were four candles used: three were purple, representing prayer, penance, and preparation. The fourth candle is rose- or white-colored, indicating a time of rejoicing. Together, these indicate Jesus is the "light of the world."

At this point, I got to thinking about how You have little ones ask thought-provoking questions, so we realize how You have taken the different forms of light and shown man how to glorify You.

Thank You, LORD, for being that shining light in our lives we never want to put out. I pray we want to let our light shine so bright for all the world to see; thus, the saved and unsaved will know we belong to You.

Matthew 5:16: *Even so, let your light shine before men, that they may see your good works and glorify your Father who is in heaven.*

Numbers 6:24-26: *'Yahweh bless you, and keep you. Yahweh make his face to shine on you, and be gracious to you. Yahweh lift up his face toward you, and give you peace.'*

John 8:12: *Again, therefore, Jesus spoke to them, saying, "I am the light of the world. He who follows me will not walk in the darkness, but will have the light of life."*

December 12th

The Christmas Ornaments & Candy Canes—Part4

"What are we going to talk about today, Grandma? Is there still more to share?" Oh, how I enjoy the openness of little ones. I answered, "Yes, my little man, there is more to share. The ornaments were originally made of real apples, cranberries, and nuts, which represent our spiritual qualities, like the fruits of the Spirit: love, joy, peace, patience, kindness, goodness, faithfulness, gentleness, and self-control. As each one of us is different and unique, we are like ornaments as we show the beauty in our lives as we reflect God's love through the light of His Son. As the ornaments are placed on the tree each year, they never seem to be put back in the same place, always giving it a different look as the lights reflect off the ornaments from a different perspective each year.

Priceless Moments

"Do you like candy canes? I'm sure you do. Well, back in 1670, a choirmaster changed the shape of the original straight white sugar stick, curving it so it was shaped like the shepherd's crook of his staff, or the letter 'J' for Jesus, representing the Good Shepherd. The colors red, white, and green appear in many different places, but basically, they represent the same thing. The color red represents Jesus's blood shed on the cross. The white color is for His purity, like living a good, clean life and doing only what is good. The green represents the newness of life, the everlasting life of Jesus after His resurrection from the dead." Like any good grandmother, I pulled out a candy cane to reward his interest. He was DELIGHTED....

Reflecting on today's conversation, I couldn't help but think, again, how You have designed our hearts and minds to perceive the good in things when we desire to find them through You.

Thank You, LORD, for the excitement created in our grandson's and my hearts at seeing You throughout these Christmas traditions. When Christmas is gone again for another year, I pray we will be able to see more of You in our everyday lives.

Acts 4:12: *There is salvation in no one else, for there is no other name under heaven that is given among men, by which we must be saved!*

John 1: 12-13: *But as many as received him, to them he gave the right to become God's children, to those who believe in his name: who were born not of blood, nor of the will of the flesh, nor of the will of man, but of God.*

Romans 1:16: *For I am not ashamed of the Good News of Christ, because it is the power of God for salvation for everyone who believes, for the Jew first, and also for the Greek.*

Priceless Moments

December 13th

The Christmas Bells, Tree Topper & Gift Giving—Part 5

"Hi, Grandma. This is exciting. What do you have for me today? Any treats with this one?" Ah, he is always so forthcoming with his thoughts. "We'll see, buddy, what all we learn first, OK." He smiled and nodded his head—what a good boy. "Now, we can talk about more Christmas traditions. The bells are used to ring out joy and happiness as well as to alert people when it is time to start church services. Thus, bells could be heard over long distances, sometimes from five to ten miles, depending on weather, the size of the bell, and the way the bell was rung. Because bells were very important to the communities, they would buy the biggest and loudest bells they could afford. Therefore, whether announcing church services, special events, or moments of need, the big bells would ensure people all around the area would know what was needed."

"The tree topper is usually in the shape of a star or an angel. Some of the tree toppers light up, some don't. The angel represents their announcement of Jesus' birth to the shepherds and singing praises to God; the star represents the guiding light by bringing the wisemen from afar as well as others to Jesus."

"As for gift giving, we receive gifts because the Wise Men brought valuable gifts of gold, frankincense, and myrrh to Jesus, but God gave the ultimate gift of Jesus at Christmas to prepare for the ultimate gift ever—His death on the cross and resurrection to save all who are willing to give their lives to Him. The neat thing about this is that the Wise Men traveled a long way to get to Jesus, even when His own Jewish people rejected Him. But we can ask Jesus into our hearts wherever we are and whenever we are ready. The most valuable gifts we can give Jesus are our hearts, love, devotion, time, and leading others to Him.

Priceless Moments

Thank You, LORD, for the new song in our hearts that keeps playing over and over, filling up the soul with joy overflowing and unfathomable peace in the midst of our troubled world. I pray this joy overflows into others every day for the rest of our lives.

Romans 15:13: *Now may the God of hope fill you with all joy and peace in believing, that you may abound in hope, in the power of the Holy Spirit.*

Philippians 4:4–7: *Rejoice in the Lord always! Again I will say, "Rejoice!" Let your gentleness be known to all men. The Lord is at hand. In nothing be anxious, but in everything, by prayer and petition with thanksgiving, let your requests be made known to God. And the peace of God, which surpasses all understanding, will guard your hearts and your thoughts in Christ Jesus.*

James 1:2-3: *Count it all joy, my brothers, when you fall into various temptations, knowing that the testing of your faith produces endurance.*

December 14th
The Christmas Star & Christmas Carols—Part 6

"Hi, Grandma. Can we talk about the star today?" "Sure, honey. The Christmas star is one of the most popular symbols of Christmas. It is associated with the appearance of the bright new star, which appeared in the sky to announce the birth of Jesus to the shepherds and, also, to lead the Wisemen to find the young child Jesus.

"I've heard you singing Christmas carols for the past several weeks. Do you want to talk about them next?" He got excited and said, "I'd love to do that. Can we sing some songs after our lesson

Priceless Moments

today?" He was hooked. "Of course we can. Singing Christmas carols, which are songs or hymns, brings a heartwarming feeling of joy and peace to the season's chill. The Christmas carols celebrate the birth of Christ, the nativity story, as a way of telling His story in such a way to help us remember the events surrounding Jesus's birth more easily. They also spread joy to the hearer, helping to spread light in the midst of the darkness of the late fall and early winter seasons. The fun thing about Christmas carols is we can sing them any time of the year."

This renewed my passion for singing Christmas carols, so we sang the ones he chose—just like he requested. Then I introduced him to a few new ones he hadn't heard before. It was so rewarding to hear him sing the praises of our LORD and Savior. Songs found in Scripture: **Luke 1:46-55** (Mary's song), **Luke 1:67-79** (Zechariah's song), and **Luke 2:1-14** (angel's song) are the inspiration for Scripture-based Christmas carols.

Thank You, LORD, for inspiring men to write songs of inspiration about Your birth, songs to warm our hearts and keep the news of Your birth fresh in our minds. I pray we think of You when gazing up at the stars and when singing Your praises.

Psalm 59:16: But I will sing of your strength. Yes, I will sing aloud of your loving kindness in the morning. For you have been my high tower, a refuge in the day of my distress.

Acts 16:25: But about midnight Paul and Silas were praying and singing hymns to God, and the prisoners were listening to them.

Colossians 3:16: Let the word of Christ dwell in you richly; in all wisdom teaching and admonishing one another with psalms, hymns, and spiritual songs, singing with grace in your heart to the Lord.

Priceless Moments

December 15th

<u>The Holly, Ivy, Wreaths, Poinsettias & Dove—Part 7</u>

"Here we are again to talk about our last few traditions. The holly is made up of glossy green ivy and red berries. They are mostly woven into Christmas wreaths of twigs or green branches of pine. Again, the color red on the berries represents the blood of Jesus, while the glossy green ivy represents His new life at the resurrection. The evergreen tree itself can also be representative of eternal life. The tree and its berries are often used in wreaths, made in a circular shape to represent eternal life. Holly and ivy can also be used in making garland and in small pieces placed on cards to help celebrate Christmas. Holly is frequently associated with courage, defense, and foresight. A gift of holly wishes the receiver good luck, good cheer, and peace."

"Poinsettia flowers and leaves, which bloom around Christmas, represent the Star of Bethlehem, often called the "Flower of the Holy Night." The red-colored leaves represent the blood of Jesus, which He willingly shed for mankind. White-colored leaves represent the purity of Christ. They are found at most places you will visit during the Christmas season, particularly churches and homes. Doves, a symbol of peace, are often used to represent the simpler gifts given to Jesus by the shepherds: fruits, honey, and doves. When compared to the more valuable gifts of the Wise Men of gold, frankincense, and myrrh, all are equal in God's sight when you give the best you can.

I couldn't help but think He is not concerned about the dollar value of our gifts but about our giving freely from the heart to truly benefit others. What a precious lesson to teach our young grandchildren: the most valuable gift we can give is our devotion and love.

Thank You, LORD, for such a wide variety of items representing You and how we can honor You by the way we choose to decorate and celebrate Your birthday. I pray we are discerning about the trappings of life that surround us, filtering out those that lead us away from You, and focusing on those that remind us daily of Your sacrifice because of Your great love for us.

Philippians 4:4-5: *Rejoice in the Lord always! Again I will say, "Rejoice!" Let your gentleness be known to all men. The Lord is at hand.*

Psalm 9:2: *I will be glad and rejoice in you. I will sing praise to your name, O Most High*

1 John 3:16: *By this we know love, because he laid down his life for us. And we ought to lay down our lives for the brothers.*

December 16th
Can We Go See Chrismas Lights?

One of the pleasures our family enjoys is driving through the various neighborhoods and looking at all the beautiful decorations and enticing Christmas lights, some complete with timed music for the displays. Our granddaughter asked, "Can we go look at all the beautiful Christmas lights? I just love looking at all the different designs and watching the lights dance to the music." I responded, "What a splendid idea. Since we sometimes have to wait in line for our turn to drive through each area, let's take a little snack to help the wait time pass more quickly." Well, that idea was a hit.

Coats, shoes, and snacks were grabbed without wasting a minute. Everyone headed out the door and loaded up in the van, ready for an enjoyable evening of "oohs" and "aahs" throughout the drive. Our son took the wheel, and off we went on a tour of various neighborhoods, some of which had decoration themes throughout the entire neighborhood and others where each family did as they desired, but, when viewed in succession, they were all delightful.

Priceless Moments

Each person had their favorites, but they were very happy to have seen them all.

When we were driving home, I thought about how each country celebrates Christmas differently. Within each of those countries, people individualize the celebration to meet their family's needs; sometimes an HOA can dictate how outdoor decorations will be done. In any case, this also represents our beliefs about Jesus' birth. Our Christian community opts for nativity scenes and Christmas carols for music, sometimes passing out hot chocolate and/or popcorn, letting the world around us observe our witness for our LORD—loving and caring.

Thank You, LORD, for Your birth and for allowing us to celebrate You whenever possible. I pray You help us to always remember that Your birth was necessary in order to get to the most crucial part—Your death and resurrection.

Romans 15:13: Now may the God of hope fill you with all joy and peace in believing, that you may abound in hope, in the power of the Holy Spirit. "Now may the God of hope fill you with all joy and peace in believing, that you may abound in hope by the power of the Holy Spirit."

Psalm 4:8: In peace I will both lay myself down and sleep, for you, Yahweh alone, make me live in safety.

1 Peter 3:10-11: He who would love life and see good days, let him keep his tongue from evil and his lips from speaking deceit. Let him turn away from evil and do good. Let him seek peace and pursue it.

Priceless Moments

December 17th

Singing Carol

"Hey, Grandma, why do people always talk about the singing Carol this time of year? Is she a really good singer? Have you ever heard her sing?" "Whoa," I said, "who are you talking about? I don't remember meeting anyone or hearing about a singer named Carol." I figured it must be someone they really enjoyed who did a program at their school.

Seeing the wheels turning in my head, they asked, "Don't you know her?" I honestly had to reply, "No." Their next comment really floored me. "Grandma, you know Carol. We sing her all the time at church and at school." Ah-ha. They are talking about singing Christmas carols. Oh, what a difference an 's' makes. This started an afternoon of singing all the Christmas carols they knew. What fun to hear their concept of some of the words within the songs.

The little ones heard what they thought was one thing, but in reality, one little 's' changed the meaning they were trying to impart. How often do we do the same thing and misinterpret something so simple that it changes its true meaning? I started thinking about how we often misunderstand some important information when reading our Bibles or not fully listening to sermons. God has a very specific message for us, yet Satan will do his best to twist our hearing or misconception of His message. Satan is always trying to get us to sing a different tune—his tune.

Thank You, LORD, for Your clear, concise message in Your Word. When we call upon the Holy Spirit to guide our interpretation, we don't forget an 's' or to dot every 'i' or cross every 't'. I pray we always keep our hearts and minds in tune with you, taking EVERYTHING to You in prayer.

***Proverbs 12:22**: Lying lips are an abomination to Yahweh, but those who do the truth are his delight.*

Priceless Moments

***1 Peter 5:7**: casting all your worries on him, because he cares for you.*

***Romans 12:17-19**: Repay no one evil for evil. Respect what is honorable in the sight of all men. If it is possible, as much as it is up to you, be at peace with all men. Don't seek revenge yourselves, beloved, but give place to God's wrath. For it is written, "Vengeance belongs to me; I will repay, says the Lord."*

December 18th
Gingerbread House

I surprised our four-year-old grandson with the fixings to make his own gingerbread house. His excitement was overwhelming and catching. We started by laying out the basic framework for the house and then gluing it together with icing. Once the construction part was done, the glue needed time to dry. Not willing to wait for the process to happen, he was talked into deciding how to decorate the house. He said, "I have a great idea," then talked for several hours about plans for the decorating. Finally, he said, "You can be my glue girl." I decided to let him take the reins and see what he would design. After two hours, he couldn't wait any longer.

He started putting windows and gumdrops on the sides of the house. The front received two windows and a door, with gumdrops above each window and a gumdrop and hard candy wreath above the door. Striped candy canes were broken to line the roof. Gingerbread Kit Kat bars became cornerstones for the house. Next, he started in the middle of the roof, adding icing to hold gumdrops, little balls of candy, and more gumdrops. At the eaves, icing held lightbulb-shaped gumdrops. Their name was very appropriate since they kept sliding and dropping off the roof. He persevered until they stayed on. He was so happy and proud of himself when the house itself was done, but in no way was he done yet. He added a peppermint bark front porch, complete with a

Priceless Moments

lamppost sporting—you guessed it—a lightbulb gumdrop, to complete his creation. His accomplishment became dessert that night.

God has a plan for each of our lives. Our bodies are knit together in our mother's womb; they are our basic framework. We are His masterpiece under construction. We wonder why the puzzle pieces of our lives do not always seem to fit. Give Him time. We have to be patient to follow His leading as He works to perfect us, filling in the pieces until we understand His design for our lives. Don't forget to follow the path to His light on the lamppost. It is those extra-little embellishments that will leave a pleasant taste in your mouth.

Thank You, LORD, for little children keeping us humble to let them take the lead, just like we need to be humble and let You take the lead. I pray we keep the child-like wonder of what You can do in our lives.

Ephesians 2:8-10: for by grace you have been saved through faith, and that not of yourselves; it is the gift of God, not of works, that no one would boast. For we are his workmanship, created in Christ Jesus for good works, which God prepared before that we would walk in them.

Proverbs 16:9: A man's heart plans his course, but Yahweh directs his steps.

John 14:26: But the Counselor, the Holy Spirit, whom the Father will send in my name, will teach you all things, and will remind you of all that I said to you.

Priceless Moments

December 19th
The Christmas Wreath

Have you ever made a wreath out of fresh pine, holly, ivy, pine cones, ribbon, and bows? Me, neither. I enjoy smelling the fragrance and seeing the beauty created by masterful hands. I took the grandchildren to a craft show that featured many different types of offerings, of which the wreaths were their favorites. "The first thing I want you to understand is that there is no touching of the things at the show. The vendors, or the people who make these things, have spent many hours creating them just so you can look at them in hopes you will buy something. I heard, "Oh, Grandma, look at this. Oh, look at this one. Did you see all the neat stuff on this one? Can you smell the wonderful scent coming from this one? This one is my favorite." In spite of their excitement, they were careful not to touch them. On and on the enthusiastic comments flowed—until we saw one particular wreath…

"Oh, wow, do you see this? Grandma, you have to come and take it in. It is my all-time favorite from any of the others we have seen—ever." That makes it very special, so I made my way over to take it in. Upon viewing the wreath, I had to agree with the admiration it had earned from the little ones. It had a base of fresh pine, ribbon interwoven among the greenery, pine cones, berries, small snowballs, and a mini manger scene suspended in the center. The entire wreath was lightly sprayed with fake snow. It was absolutely gorgeous.

The variety of objects in the wreath were tastefully chosen to coordinate and were meticulously placed to make a stunning presentation of God's creation—all in one place. The creator described this particular wreath as an inspiration from God. Needless to say, we could not let this one get away— "We'll take it."

Thank You, LORD, for blessing Your creations with beautiful designs so they can create something to bless us. I pray we learn to

Priceless Moments

appreciate all You send our way, being discerning enough to accept all things, good and bad, from Your hand.

Psalm 19:1: *The heavens declare the glory of God. The expanse shows his handiwork.*

Isaiah 42:5-6a: *God Yahweh, he who created the heavens and stretched them out, he who spread out the earth and that which comes out of it, he who gives breath to its people and spirit to those who walk in it, says: "I, Yahweh, have called you in righteousness. I will hold your hand."*

John 1:3: *All things were made through him. Without him, nothing was made that has been made.*

December 20th

Winter

It's December 20th, the winter solstice, so I must look out the window and hope for snow. Yes. I'm greeted with a rewarding sight. Ah, nothing delights the eye more than the presentation of an undisturbed, freshly fallen quilt of snow. The snow crystals sparkle in the sunlight, the trees are laden with a new coat, and the sense of stillness that hangs in the air is so invigorating. It is so restorative to drink in this scene provided by our God in heaven—until the grandchildren arrive. Coats on, gloves donned, hats secured, and boots ready for stomping meet my tranquil scene—and it is forever lost, at least for now. We play, throw snowballs, run around, and build a snowman when I hear those familiar words, "I'm cold. I want to go in. Can we have some hot chocolate—with marshmallows?" Who could refuse such a sweet request?

Winter gear is removed and hung out to dry as a warming treat is made and enjoyed. "Grandma, as a kid, did you like to play in the

Priceless Moments

snow?" "Of course. My brothers and I made snow ramps for sled riding, snow forts for our snowball fights, and whatever else we could think of doing. Actually, I'm just a big kid who enjoys you. As a matter of fact, I had so much fun that I'd like to do this again tomorrow. What do you think?" A deafening "Yes" resounded throughout the kitchen.

Flashbacks of fond memories from days of yore, along with making new ones with these precious little gifts from God, show His love for us as His faithfulness continues throughout all generations. I pray each different gift from God is appreciated and enjoyed by all, never getting too old or sophisticated to enjoy such beauty.

Thank You, LORD, for Your storehouses of snow that create so much beauty that is pleasing to the eye and fun to play in for kids of all ages. I pray we adults keep our child-like enthusiasm for life, which these little ones so enjoy.

Psalm 147:16: *He gives snow like wool, and scatters frost like ashes.*

Isaiah 55:10, 11: *For as the rain comes down and the snow from the sky, and doesn't return there, but waters the earth, and makes it grow and bud, and gives seed to the sower and bread to the eater; so is my word that goes out of my mouth: it will not return to me void, but it will accomplish that which I please, and it will prosper in the thing I sent it to do.*

Matthew 28:3: *His appearance was like lightning, and his clothing white as snow.*

Priceless Moments

December 21st

Making Snow Angels

Making snow angels in the freshly fallen snow, unmarred by animal tracks or human means, is a great winter activity. On one of these snowfalls, the grandchildren asked, "Can we go out and play in the snow? Can we, please?" I am a softy when I hear those courtesy words, so I responded, "Sure. Everyone go to the bathroom so we can stay out longer, then get your winter duds on and we will head outside. I had just put on a crockpot of homemade chicken noodle soup that we can have later to warm us back up."

Excitement was very catching as everyone—including me—did as asked and were ready to head out the door. I asked, "Please stand on the sidewalk and line up so we can make snow angels first. Then I can take a picture of my little angels all in a row. After that, have at it." Very compliant children marched out, lined up, and spaced out on the sidewalk, waiting for the signal to "Drop and spread your tiny wings—but don't fly away. On your mark, get set, go." The little angels dropped their backs into the snow and spread their wings. Pictures and videos were taken to create lasting memories of this moment.

I thought of how much fun they had—the smiles, the giggles, just plain down-home fun. God must be delighted to see us setting aside the troubles and pressures of life and enjoying family and His creation, just as He intended it to be.

Thank You, LORD, for Your goodness in giving us families to love and make memories with whenever time and circumstances allow. I pray we stay close to You as a family and enjoy all the good pleasures You have planned for our lives.

1 Timothy 4:4: For every creature of God is good, and nothing is to be rejected, if it is received with thanksgiving.

Priceless Moments

Psalm 104:24: *Yahweh, how many are your works! In wisdom, you have made them all. The earth is full of your riches.*

Job 12: 7-10: *But ask the animals, now, and they will teach you; the birds of the sky, and they will tell you. Or speak to the earth, and it will teach you. The fish of the sea will declare to you. Who doesn't know that in all these, Yahweh's hand has done this, in whose hand is the life of every living thing, and the breath of all mankind?*

December 22nd
My Favorite Spot For Christmas

The grandchildren all seem to have one favorite spot in our house— the electric fireplace. It is used as a reward for good behavior. They grab blankets and cuddle up near them to play games, tell stories, or watch a movie. The warmth is so relaxing that behavior is seldom an issue. Tonight is no exception. The kids were spending the night, so we made some plans for after dinner. "Grandma, can we sit in front of the fireplace and watch a movie tonight?" I thought a minute and said, "It's been a long time since we watched a movie, so why not? The excitement was palpable. I prayed nothing would happen to cause them to lose their desired privilege.

"First we need to clean up the kitchen, get ready for bed, and make popcorn before movie time." "OKs" echoed all around. Dishes were done, we all got dressed for bed, teeth were brushed, popcorn was popped, and blankets were claimed for a movie by the fireplace. As the movie wore on, the living room was getting a little toasty, so I turned off the heat selection and let the look off the fire continue in the logs. They looked at me throughout this process, then at the fireplace. Seeing that the logs were still "lit," their focus returned to the movie.

Priceless Moments

I wondered how often our focus gets shifted from the warmth of God's love onto something else when Satan does his cunning twisting of reality. He will twist things just enough for us to assume all is well when, in reality, we start pushing God aside—all part of Satan's plan.

Thank You, LORD, for helping us keep our focus on You when we cry out to You, asking for guidance and direction in our daily lives and in our special challenges. I pray we are vigilant in checking in with You daily—at a minimum—to be sure Satan is not silently "switching a switch" on us to lead us in the wrong direction.

***Hebrews 12:2**: looking to Jesus, the author and perfecter of faith, who for the joy that was set before him endured the cross, despising its shame, and has sat down at the right hand of the throne of God.*

***Psalm 141:8**: For my eyes are on you, Yahweh, the Lord. In you, I take refuge. Don't leave my soul destitute.*

***1 Peter 3:12**: For the eyes of the Lord are on the righteous, and his ears open to their prayer; but the face of the Lord is against those who do evil.*

December 23rd
<u>The People Who Don't Have Anything</u>

Somewhere along the way, our grandson got the idea that the people next door didn't have anything to eat. One morning, when we had finished breakfast, he asked, "Can we take some of our left-overs to the neighbors so they can have something to eat?" I said, "Sure. I bet they would appreciate that." This has led to a

Priceless Moments

parade of breakfasts and dinners across the yard. For example: breakfast before, blueberry French toast casserole, chicken delight—complete with baked potatoes and fried carrots. Desserts like apple pie, peaches, apples, cookies, and Rice Krispie treats round out the offerings. They have been very gracious in accepting the gift from the children, always saying, "Thank you so much for thinking of us. We truly appreciate it."

One day, they stopped me when we were outside and asked to whom they should attribute the gifting of all the goodies. I explained, "Somehow our grandson has gotten the idea that you need things, as he calls you "the people who don't have anything." He feels he has to see that you have food. If you would prefer, I can tell him you do not wish to have any more deliveries." They were very kind and said, "No, it's fine. We understand. Besides, we are the beneficiaries of his generosity. By all means, keep it coming. We enjoy it—and seeing him."

I was touched to realize a child's generosity was meeting the needs of some terrific neighbors by bringing them joy as well as meeting his need to share. I realize it is important to give, but we also need to be gracious receivers since we cannot have givers without receivers.

Thank You, LORD, for speaking to a child's heart and showing adults that both sides of the giving and receiving process are necessary for effective stewardship of our time, talents, and finances. I pray we view these gifts from You as part of Your giving to us, the receivers, so we can become the givers in reaching out to others.

Proverbs 12:25*: Anxiety in a man's heart weighs it down, but a kind word makes it glad.*

Luke 6:31*: As you would like people to do to you, do exactly so to them.*

Galatians 5:13-14*: For you, brothers, were called for freedom. Only don't use your freedom for gain to the flesh, but through love* *be servants to one another. For the whole law is fulfilled in one word, in this: "You shall love your neighbor as yourself."*

December 24th
<u>Jesus' Birthday Cake</u>

Every year since our children were little, we baked a birthday cake for Jesus. Now, with the grandchildren, we are continuing this time-honored family tradition. Now, Christmas is tomorrow, so I was prepared to make the cake and present it tomorrow. But, as we were talking about the food for tomorrow, I heard a gasp from one of the grandchildren, followed by, "Oh, no, I haven't heard anyone talk about our birthday cake for Jesus. We can't forget that, or Christmas will be ruined."

I couldn't help myself and said, "Oh, no, what shall we do? What kind of cake shall we bake?" Again, a gasp was heard, with the following response: "There can only be one type of cake for Jesus." True to my form, I baited her and asked, "What kind is that?" An exasperated reply of, "You know, an angel food cake. with cloud icing (whipped cream icing) and strawberries. Grandma, you know, we have it every year." Not being able to contain myself or keep her going any longer, I responded, "That's right. You know what? I think I have all the ingredients at home and can make one tonight." The adult children could hardly contain themselves over this exchange.

I realized just how important family traditions are to the little ones in our lives. Every year, they have something to count on and share with the extended family unit and any others who join us to celebrate Christ's birth.

Thank You, LORD, for carrying on the family tradition of celebrating Your birth. But, more importantly, of passing on the family tradition of giving our hearts and lives to You and sharing You with others this Christmas season as well as every other day of the year. I pray we stay tenderhearted about the importance of these traditions, particularly when it comes to passing on our Christian faith.

2 Corinthians 5:20: *We are therefore ambassadors on behalf of Christ, as though God were entreating by us: we beg you on behalf of Christ, be reconciled to God.*

Psalm 127:3-5a: *Behold, children are a heritage of Yahweh. The fruit of the womb is his reward. As arrows in the hand of a mighty man, so are the children of youth. Happy is the man who has his quiver full of them.*

Psalm 118:24: *This is the day that Yahweh has made. We will rejoice and be glad in it!*

December 25th

Bubble Bread

One of our favorite tasty family traditions is to make bubble bread for Christmas morning—and birthdays. This is how it all started. Our kids had bubble bread for their birthdays, and we felt we should do the same for Jesus. The delectable combination of little balls of carbs wrapped in butter, sugar, cinnamon, and nuts is certainly a crowd pleaser. Upon arriving at the grandchildren's home, the greeting was not "Merry Christmas," "hi," or "look what I got," but "We had bubble bread for Jesus' birthday—and we ate it all." My hopes were dashed…

One of our little angels said, "I'm sorry, Papa and Grandma, that we didn't save you any bubble bread. It was just so good that I started out with five pieces, then took a couple more, and a few more, just like everyone else. Before we knew it, the whole thing was gone. It wasn't until after it was all gone that we each realized we hadn't saved any for you guys. Next time we will have to make two of them."

My dreams turned to the mouth-watering treat that had eluded me this year. I thought about how God is ever faithful, always there for the asking. He is certainly a crowd-pleaser in most Christian circles, but not in most of the secular world. How I long for others to see Jesus as a sweet yearning in our souls and to develop that deep, satisfying joy He leaves in our hearts.

Thank You, LORD, for opportunities to celebrate Your birth and family traditions to remind us of Your sweet, satisfying love. I pray we cherish these moments together in sweet communion with each other to remember the most important birth to ever take place on this earth. It is truly wonderful that we never "get finished" enjoying Your goodness to us throughout the year.

Psalm 37:4: *Also delight yourself in Yahweh, and he will give you the desires of your heart.*

1 Corinthians 11:2: *Now I praise you, brothers, that you remember me in all things, and hold firm the traditions, even as I delivered them to you.*

Jeremiah 31:3: *Yahweh appeared of old to me, saying, "Yes, I have loved you with an everlasting love. Therefore I have drawn you with loving kindness.*

December 26th

<u>Thank You For the Presents</u>

Wide-eyed little wonders bring so much delight to the Christmas celebration. Weeks—maybe even months—of anticipation have culminated into this one special day as they race down the steps—or out the hallway—to find out what was left for them under the Christmas tree. They frantically searched each package, looking

Priceless Moments

for names. When they found one with their name on it, they picked it up and shook it, trying to guess what might be inside. After all, they did make a list and give it to Santa. Yet, the coolest gifts of all are from the parents—and are appropriately labeled.

As the wrapping paper is torn off and discarded, little eyes and hands work to behold the gift. It's either sheer delight—as with Legos, cars and trucks, or dolls—or whatever—as with clothes, socks, underwear, or shoes. As they work through their cache, they are thanking the givers for their contributions to their joy—or dismay. Someday, they will understand that when there is a need for clothes, socks, underwear, or shoes, now is as good a time as any other to *present* them.

My reaction was, sometimes we are like that with God. He gives us the joys of our hearts, be it a special someone in our lives, a new baby, or a cool vacation, as well as the needs of our existence, be it a new job, a raise, or a new clunker of a car that runs because we can't afford anything better—BUT IT RUNS. I hope we realize God didn't promise us a rose garden without taking the thorns as part of the package deal. Yet He gave us the coolest gift ever: His One and Only Son Jesus, a gift that will never stop giving and can never be topped.

Thank You, LORD, for You are the present of Your presence in our lives. You are the greatest gift we could ever receive. I pray we open our hearts and minds to receive You as our LORD and Savior, then return daily for a "refresher" to keep our cup full to overflowing.

Ecclesiastes 6:9: *Being satisfied with what you have is better than always wanting more. That doesn't have any meaning either, it's like chasing the wind. NIV*

Ecclesiastes 8:15: *Then I commended mirth, because a man has no better thing under the sun than to eat, to drink, and to be joyful: for that will accompany him in his labor all the days of his life which God has given him under the sun.*

Priceless Moments

***Nehemiah 8:10**: Then he said to them, "Go your way. Eat the fat, drink the sweet, and send portions to him for whom nothing is prepared, for today is holy to our Lord. Don't be grieved, for the joy of Yahweh is your strength."*

December 27th
When Jesus Was a Boy Like Me

Our grandson was in one of his questioning moods. "Grandma, when Jesus was a little boy like me, what was He like? Did He listen to His parents and grandparents? Did He like helping His Dad make things? Did He fight with His brothers and sisters? Did He run and play with His friends? What kind of clothes did He wear? Did He go swimming, play sports, or throw a frisbee?" "Whoa, let's stop a minute," I said. "I don't know if I can remember all those questions, let alone have an answer for each one."

I took a deep breath, quickly prayed for wisdom, and then answered, "We don't know much about Jesus as a young boy, but we can imagine what He was like from what we know about Jewish culture at that time. Being the Son of God, I am fairly sure He did a good job of listening to His earthly parents and grandparents and helping His stepfather Joseph in the carpentry shop. I would imagine He and His friends played with pebbles, stones, and ropes. One time I read that they may have played Chinese checkers and chess by drawing the game board in sand or loose dirt. I read that sports in Jesus' day were foot racing, archery, javelin throwing, discus throwing—heavier yet similar to a frisbee—high-jumping, and rolling dice. They probably went swimming since they lived near water. I am sure Jesus and His siblings got along well. Jesus would have worn sandals, a basic tunic slightly below the knees, a mantle, or a large shawl for cool days and to sleep in for warmth. Since He was not born into or raised in a wealthy home, He was clean but did not dress in fancy or colorful clothes.

I thought of how different Jesus' life would have been from ours. Even the poorest in America are considered wealthy by some other countries standards. Yet Jesus had a wealth of knowledge and love to share with everyone He met, if they were willing to listen to His wisdom.

Thank You, LORD, for insights into Your life. You left the splendor of heaven to become like one of us, even personally experiencing childhood to understand our little ones hearts. I pray we can impart the snippets we know about Your life to our grandchildren, so they strive to grow in wisdom, stature, and favor with You.

Luke 2:40: *The child was growing, and was becoming strong in spirit, being filled with wisdom, and the grace of God was upon him.*

Luke 2:52: *And Jesus increased in wisdom and stature, and in favor with God and men.*

Hebrews 4:15: *For we don't have a high priest who can't be touched with the feeling of our infirmities, but one who has been in all points tempted like we are, yet without sin.*

December 28th
<u>My Glow In the Dark Dinosaur Sleeping Bag</u>

"I received a very special gift from you, and I love it. I just need to charge it." At first, I thought I was tracking what he was saying, but we didn't give him anything that needed to be charged. I must have had a perplexed look on my face because he asked, "But it

Priceless Moments

doesn't glow. Why?" I must have still had a blank look on my face because he asked, "Grandma, what's wrong?" I thought hard about what was in those packages that had been wrapped months ago. Finally, it dawned on me: a glow-in-the-dark dinosaur sleeping bag. I responded, "Well, it's been wrapped up away from the sunlight, so it will need to be charged again by the sun to glow." "OK then, I can hardly wait to charge it up. Do you want to come with me while I take my new glow-in-the-dark sleeping bag over to the sun to charge?"

We continued to talk and play for a while, then he asked, "Can we take the sleeping bag into my closet to watch it glow?" We gathered up the sleeping bag and headed to his bedroom closet. All the while, I was hoping it had enough time to "charge." As we were entering the closet, the soft fleece sleeping bag with eleven different dinosaurs, footprints, and eggs began to glow and became even brighter as he slid the door closed. We sat in there a while, enjoying the different shapes of light, until they began to fade. I explained, "Well, I guess we will have to do this again after the bag has had a chance to get more of a charge."

As we walked back downstairs, the thought hit me that we glow for Jesus, too. But does our glow begin to fade after a while? If so, we need to spend more time with Him to recharge our spiritual batteries so we can be a lighthouse in the darkness for our LORD.

Thank You, LORD, for simple things to remind us of You and our need to stay close to the Source of our spiritual power. I pray we read, study, and share Your Word with everyone we meet so we glow for You.

John 8:12*: Again, therefore, Jesus spoke to them, saying, "I am the light of the world. He who follows me will not walk in the darkness, but will have the light of life."*

Ecclesiastes 8:1*: Who is like the wise man? And who knows the interpretation of a thing? A man's wisdom makes his face shine, and the hardness of his face is changed.*

Priceless Moments

Acts 6:15: *All who sat in the council, fastening their eyes on him, saw his face like it was the face of an angel.*

December 29th
My Light-Up Shoes

Our granddaughter was opening a present very carefully because, when she shook it, it hit hard against what she thought was a box, not giving her any clue as to its content(s). The paper was ripped off, and she commented, "It's a box, but what's inside?" The lid had been taped on, so she had to pull really hard to get it to open—all part of the plan. As the lid was forcibly removed, something started glowing in the box. Excitement peeked as she saw the light-up shoes. "Oh, Grandma, these are just what I've always wanted." Score.

She jumped up and ran over to me, almost knocking us both over, and said, "Thank you, thank you, thank you. You are the best." Well, that just made my day. I told her, "You are most welcome, sweetheart. We're so glad you like them." "I like them, but it's more than that; I love them." Then I received another series of hugs and kisses. By this time, we were both lying on the floor laughing, just enjoying the revelry of it all. Once she was done thanking me profusely, she tried on the shoes—a perfect fit. She proceeded to dance around the room, stomping her feet so she could enjoy the lights in her shoes.

It's amazing how something as simple as the right pair of new shoes can delight a young heart. May we not require the outlandish things but rather find delight in the simple things of life given to us by the Greatest Gift Giver of all time.

Thank You, LORD, that what we require is Your forgiveness, mercy, and love. All the other things are like icing on a cake. I pray we are discerning enough to realize the difference between needs and wants, not being concerned with the frivolous but rather what You have deemed right for us.

Proverbs 23:26: *My son, give me your heart; and let your eyes keep in my ways.*

Jeremiah 15:16: *Your words were found, and I ate them. Your words were to me a joy and the rejoicing of my heart, for I am called by your name, Yahweh, God of Armies.*

Isaiah 61:10: *I will greatly rejoice in Yahweh! My soul will be joyful in my God, for he has clothed me with the garments of salvation. He has covered me with the robe of righteousness, as a bridegroom decks himself with a garland and as a bride adorns herself with her jewels.*

December 30th
New Years Restitutions

Our grandson heard Papa and I talking about and trying to decide if we were going to make any New Year's resolutions this coming year. As we talked, his curiosity peaked, and he just had to ask, "What are New Year's Restitutions?" I explained, "The word is resolutions. This is when a person decides to do something to better themselves and then works toward it as a goal for the year. For example, if I decide to lose ten pounds, I will go to the gym to work out and take longer, more challenging walks to burn off the weight I want to lose.

He sat very puzzled for a while, then said, "But I thought restitutions were when you made something right with someone else." Realizing he had still misunderstood the word; I explained the difference between his word choice and mine. Restitution is giving back or restoring something that was lost or stolen by its owner. Resolution is making a strong choice to do or not do

Priceless Moments

something to change a behavior or way of doing something." You could see the wheels turning in his mind, and then he finally said, "I get it. I need to decide to give my heart to Jesus and then not take things from other people or break their toys." Bingo. For his age, he understood and even combined the two concepts.

This got me thinking… It is so nice to know that once we decide to accept Jesus as our Savior, it is just a matter of asking Him into our hearts to be the King of our lives. We don't have to do any works to earn salvation because He freely saves all those who humble themselves, like children, and our sins are buried in the sea of His forgetfulness. When forgiven, we desire to do works, for "faith apart from works is dead" (**James 2:26**). But we are actually making restitution—giving back to God what He or we lost when Adam and Eve sinned. So, making a resolution to accept Christ leads to restitution for all we have done wrong to God and others.

Thank You, LORD, that we are not saved by our good works but by Your grace through faith in You. Thank You for accepting us into Your kingdom when we accept You into our hearts. I pray that one of our goals for the new year is to learn more about You.

Ephesians 2:8-9: for by grace you have been saved through faith, and that not of yourselves; it is the gift of God, not of works, that no one would boast. For we are his workmanship, created in Christ Jesus for good works, which God prepared before that we would walk in them.

Isaiah 43:18-19: Don't remember the former things, and don't consider the things of old. Behold, I will do a new thing. It springs out now. Don't you know it? I will even make a way in the wilderness, and rivers in the desert.

Lamentations 3:22-23: It is because of Yahweh's loving kindnesses that we are not consumed, because his compassion doesn't fail. They are new every morning. Great is your faithfulness. "Yahweh is my portion," says my soul. "Therefore I will hope in him."

Priceless Moments

December 31ˢᵗ

Happy New Year's Eve

On the last day of the year, when we were getting ready to go home, I told our grandson I would see him next year. He sat there for the longest time, kind of cocking his head to the side as if really thinking about something. He finally said, "Grandma, did I make you mad?" Unsure of where he got that idea, I reassured him I was fine but was just ready to go home. He asked, "But why are you going away for so long?" At that point, I realized the cause of his consternation. I explained, "Today is the end of this current year, and tomorrow would be the start of a brand-new year. The reason you are home from school this week is for a Christmas vacation to celebrate Jesus' birthday. And, at the end of this year, one week later, or seven sleeps away, we would celebrate the new year." I could sense we weren't quite there yet. So, calendar in hand, we looked at how the pages were all used up on the old calendar, ending with Saturday. We looked at a calendar for the upcoming year, and how it started on a Sunday. Then the light of understanding went on, and he said, "I'll see you next year."

I thought of how many times God will try to guide us in something, yet we do not seem to have a clue as to the purpose or reason for our mission. So, God will find another way to get His message across. Being still a little dense and slow to understand, He will employ another method to get our attention for comprehension of His desire in our lives. This may be through a vivid dream, coincidental circumstances, or another person—a friend, acquaintance, or stranger. God knows what it will take, but we have to be open to His will.

Thank You, LORD, for Your patience with us to keep explaining and showing us Your will for our lives. I pray the veil obscuring comprehension is removed so we can move into compliance with Your will. Thank you for Your patience throughout this learning situation.

Priceless Moments

2 Corinthians 3:15-16: *But to this day, when Moses is read, a veil lies on their heart. But whenever someone turns to the Lord, the veil is taken away.*

2 Corinthians 4:3-4: *Even if our Good News is veiled, it is veiled in those who are dying, in whom the god of this world has blinded the minds of the unbelieving, that the light of the Good News of the glory of Christ, who is the image of God, should not dawn on them.*

Luke 24:45: *Then he opened their minds, that they might understand the Scriptures.*

Have a Happy New Year blessed by our wonderful LORD and Savior. May the upcoming year be your best year yet!

Epilogue

The grandchildren continue to display more in-depth curiosity about the Holy Scriptures, so I'm listening and answering their questions. Our goal as grandparents, parents, or interested adult spiritual leaders should be to *"Train up a child in the way he should go; Even when he is old he will not depart from it."* (**Proverbs 22:6**). The world (Satan) is subtly and other times not so subtly vying for their very souls every moment of their young lives. The key decision on whom to serve will mostly be determined during this tender age. May God give each one of us the strength, patience, and words to explain who Jesus is to them and how they can accept Him as their LORD and Savior today!

About the Author

Darlene Welsh now lives in Grand Junction, Colorado. Following her retirement in Pennsylvania, she and her husband traveled by car, bus, train, ship, airplane, and RV throughout the United States, Canada, Mexico, and the Caribbean. These various opportunities enabled her to see the differences as well as the similarities between all people groups they encountered. Her husband was a great source of encouragement to record their experiences and later share them with others.

Now the time has come for her to share different types of experiences about the joy of her life, the precious God-given grandchildren, as she is encouraged to do so by our LORD.

LOOK FOR THESE GREAT BOOKS FROM BROKEN YOKE PUBLISHING

Exclusive North American distributor of
The World English Bible

Rocky Mountain Medley Novella Collection
Uranium Downs by Jessica Bertrand
Interruption by Robin Densmore Fuson
The Orchard's Secret *by Templa Melnick*
Price of Grace by Debra Shelton

Books by Templa Melnick
Season of Forgiveness
Season of Redemption *(coming soon)*

Books by Jessica Bertrand
Dinosaurs, Assassins, and Monarchs
Purloined in Paris (coming soon)

Books by Chris Melnick
The Messianic Passover Celebration – Leader's Manual
The Messianic Passover Celebration – Participant Handbook
Civil War Poems of Enoch Fearey

Made in United States
Troutdale, OR
03/29/2024

18808741R00319